Copyright © 2019 National Fire Protection Association®. All Rights Reserved.

NFPA® 25

Standard for the

Inspection, Testing, and Maintenance of Water-Based Fire Protection Systems

2020 Edition

This edition of NFPA 25, *Standard for the Inspection, Testing, and Maintenance of Water-Based Fire Protection Systems,* was prepared by the Technical Committee on Inspection, Testing, and Maintenance of Water-Based Systems and acted on by NFPA at its Association Technical Meeting held June 17–20, 2019, in San Antonio, TX. It was issued by the Standards Council on August 5, 2019, with an effective date of August 25, 2019, and supersedes all previous editions.

This edition of NFPA 25 was approved as an American National Standard on August 25, 2019.

Origin and Development of NFPA 25

The first edition of NFPA 25, published in 1992, was a collection of inspection, testing, and maintenance provisions that helped ensure the successful operation of water-based fire protection systems. NFPA 25 was developed as an extension of existing documents such as NFPA 13A, *Recommended Practice for the Inspection, Testing, and Maintenance of Sprinkler Systems,* and NFPA 14A, *Recommended Practice for the Inspection, Testing, and Maintenance of Standpipe and Hose Systems,* both of which successfully assisted authorities having jurisdiction and property owners with routine inspections of sprinkler systems and standpipes. These documents have since been withdrawn from the NFPA standards system. NFPA 25 became the main document governing sprinkler systems as well as related systems, including underground piping, fire pumps, storage tanks, water spray systems, and foam-water sprinkler systems.

This document provides instruction on how to conduct inspection, testing, and maintenance activities. It also stipulates how often such activities are required to be completed. Requirements are provided for impairment procedures, notification processes, and system restoration. This type of information, where incorporated into a building maintenance program, enhances the demonstrated favorable experience of all water-based fire protection systems.

The 1995 edition incorporated several improvements that reflected the initial experience with the standard. A new chapter was added that addressed obstructions in pipe as well as appropriate corrective actions.

The 1998 edition refined testing requirements and frequencies and provided additional guidance for preplanned impairment programs. The document scope was expanded to include marine systems.

The 2002 edition continued to refine testing frequencies for waterflow devices and evaluation of the annual fire pump test data. This edition also included additional information regarding evaluation and test methods for microbiologically influenced corrosion (MIC).

In the 2008 edition, a section permitting performance-based testing was added, providing guidance on alternative means for determining testing frequencies based on system/component failure rates. Component replacement testing tables were introduced in this edition to provide guidance for the appropriate tests to be performed following replacement of system components. Inspection, testing, and maintenance requirements for water mist systems were extracted from NFPA 750, *Standard on Water Mist Fire Protection Systems,* and were inserted into a new chapter. This action consolidated inspection, testing, and maintenance requirements for all water-based fire protection systems into one document.

The 2011 edition further updated testing frequencies based on a growing database of inspection, testing, and maintenance records. In two new annexes, information was provided for classification of needed repairs and hazard evaluation. The 2011 edition also added new definitions differentiating the levels of deficiency for determining the priority of repair.

The 2014 edition of NFPA 25 had many significant changes with many specific to the chapter on fire pumps. The operating test requirements were rewritten to consider a baseline weekly test for all pumps, with a series of exceptions that would allow for a modified testing frequency. New language was added to address confirmation of pressure recordings and a new fuel quality test for diesel-driven pumps.

Definitions were added for the various frequencies of inspection, testing, and maintenance tasks to create a "window" for completion of the tasks. The concept of internal inspection was modified to an internal assessment concept, in which a performance-based assessment frequency is explicitly addressed. The scope of the Technical Committee on Inspection, Testing, and Water-Based Systems was updated to address water mist systems specifically. The water mist system was modified such that the extract tags from NFPA 750 were removed because the material in the relevant chapter is now in the jurisdiction of NFPA 25.

A new chapter was added to address NFPA 13D, *Standard for the Installation of Sprinkler Systems in One- and Two-Family Dwellings and Manufactured Homes*, systems that are installed outside of one- and two-family homes. The requirements for inspecting antifreeze systems were updated to include the latest information from the Fire Protection Research Foundation testing on standard spray sprinklers. The table providing examples of classifications for deficiencies and impairments was relocated from Annex E to Annex A and attached to the definition of *deficiency*.

For the 2017 edition, new fire pump terms were defined to align with NFPA 20, *Standard for the Installation of Stationary Pumps for Fire Protection*. Criteria were added to Chapter 4 on automated inspections and testing. Residential sprinkler replacement requirements were added to address sprinklers that are no longer available. New requirements were added regarding missing escutcheons or, if listed, escutcheons that are no longer available. ITM tables were updated throughout the chapters, and new no-flow test requirements for fire pumps were added. Chapter 13 added new requirements for the inspection, testing, and maintenance of waterflow alarm devices; separated and added new requirements for the inspection, testing, and maintenance of preaction and deluge valves; and added criteria for air compressors. As of this edition, it contains all the general pressure gauge criteria. Additionally, two new annexes were added: one on connectivity and data collection and another on color-coded tagging programs.

In the 2020 edition, the term *electrically operated sprinklers*, which is a new technology, has been defined, and inspection, testing, and maintenance requirements have been added. Requirements addressing recalled sprinklers has been added to Chapter 4, and a section on dry hydrants has been added to Chapter 7. Dry sprinkler test requirements have been modified from 10 years to 15 years, and additional clarifications to the automated testing requirements for waterflow alarm devices have been made. Chapter 8 clarifies, for safety reasons, that energized pump controllers should not be opened and introduces the concept of an isolating switch in a separate compartment as part of the pump controller. Fire pump annual flow test and evaluation requirements of the test have been revised. Several new requirements have been added to Chapter 12 regarding water mist systems.

Technical Committee on Inspection, Testing, and Maintenance of Water-Based Systems

William E. Koffel, *Chair*
Koffel Associates, Inc., MD [SE]

Niels Henrik Abrahamsen, Vid Fire-Kill, Denmark [M]
Rep. International Water Mist Association

Gary S. Andress, Liberty Mutual Insurance Company, MA [I]

Kerry M. Bell, UL LLC, IL [RT]

Michael J. Bosma, The Viking Corporation, MI [M]
Rep. National Fire Sprinkler Association

Bruce H. Clarke, American International Group, Inc. (AIG), SC [I]

David A. Dagenais, Partners/Wentworth-Douglass Hospital, NH [U]
Rep. NFPA Health Care Section

Matthew G. Drysdale, The DuPont Company, Inc., DE [U]
Rep. NFPA Industrial Fire Protection Section

Timothy S. Fox, Viking Fire Protection, Canada [IM]
Rep. Canadian Automatic Sprinkler Association

David W. Frable, U.S. General Services Administration, IL [U]

Christina F. Francis, The Procter & Gamble Company, AL [M]

David B. Fuller, FM Approvals, RI [I]

Greg Garber, Pittsburg Tank & Tower Inc., VA [M]

Donald Hopkins, Jr., JENSEN HUGHES, MD [SE]

Mark Hopkins, National Fire Sprinkler Association, MD [IM]
Rep. National Fire Sprinkler Association

Larry Keeping, PLC Fire Safety Solutions, Canada [SE]

Charles W. Ketner, National Automatic Sprinkler Fitters LU 669, MD [L]
Rep. United Assn. of Journeymen & Apprentices of the Plumbing & Pipe Fitting Industry

John Lake, City of Gainesville, FL [E]

Peter A. Larrimer, U.S. Department of Veterans Affairs, PA [U]

Russell B. Leavitt, Telgian Corporation, AZ [U]
Rep. The Home Depot

Kenneth W. Linder, Swiss Re, CT [I]

Brock Mitchell, Extended Stay Hotels, NC [U]

John D. Munno, Arthur J. Gallagher Risk Management Services, Inc., OK [U]
Rep. Edison Electric Institute

Top Myers, Myers Risk Services, Inc., FL [SE]

Scott Newman, Walgreens, IL [U]

Clayton Norred, Jr., Norred Fire Systems, LLC, LA [IM]
Rep. National Association of Fire Equipment Distributors

Erik G. Olsen, Chubb Limited, NJ [I]

Richard M. Ray, Cybor Fire Protection Company, IL [IM]
Rep. Illinois Fire Prevention Association

John F. Saidi, USDOE Stanford Site Office, CA [U]

Gregory R. Stein, Tank Industry Consultants, IN [SE]

Darrell W. Underwood, Underwood Fire Equipment, Inc., MI [IM]

Terry L. Victor, Johnson Controls, MD [M]

John Whitney, Clarke Fire Protection Products, Inc., OH [M]

Jason R. Williams, American Fire Sprinkler Association (AFSA), TX [IM]
Rep. American Fire Sprinkler Association

Alternates

Erik H. Anderson, Koffel Associates, Inc., MD [SE]
(Alt. to William E. Koffel)

Gabriel Arroyo, American International Group, Inc (AIG), TX [I]
(Alt. to Bruce H. Clarke)

David R. Baron, Global Fire Protection Company, IL [IM]
(Alt. to Richard M. Ray)

Tracey D. Bellamy, Telgian Corporation, GA [U]
(Alt. to Russell B. Leavitt)

Patrick Jon Brown, Tank Industry Consultants, IN [SE]
(Alt. to Gregory R. Stein)

Howard G. Clay, VSC Fire & Security, Inc., VA [IM]
(Alt. to Jason R. Williams)

Aaron Terrance Dickens, Delta Fire Systems, UT [IM]
(Alt. to Clayton Norred, Jr.)

John DiGirolomo, St. Barnabas Hospital, NY [U]
(Alt. to David A. Dagenais)

John A. Donner, Dominion Energy, VA [U]
(Alt. to John D. Munno)

Russell P. Fleming, Northeast Fire Suppression Associates, LLC, NH [SE]
(Alt. to Larry Keeping)

Brandon W. Frakes, AXA XL/Global Asset Protection Services, LLC, NC [I]
(Alt. to Kenneth W. Linder)

Jeff Hebenstreit, UL LLC, IL [RT]
(Alt. to Kerry M. Bell)

Stephen M. Jaskolka, The DuPont Company, Inc., DE [U]
(Alt. to Matthew G. Drysdale)

Wilton Marburger, Risk Suppression Partners, PA [SE]
(Alt. to Top Myers)

Gayle Pennel, JENSEN HUGHES, IL [SE]
(Alt. to Donald Hopkins, Jr.)

Damon T. Pietraz, Underwood Fire Equipment, Inc., MI [IM]
(Alt. to Darrell W. Underwood)

Charles David Raborn, Cape Coral Fire Department, FL [E]
(Alt. to John Lake)

Todd M. Roeder, U.S. General Services Administration, IN [U]
(Alt. to David W. Frable)

Jason W. Ryckman, Canadian Automatic Sprinkler Association, Canada [IM]
(Alt. to Timothy S. Fox)

Timothy Dwain Schmidle, Liberty Mutual Group Prop, OH [I]
(Alt. to Gary S. Andress)

Michael J. Spaziani, FM Global, MA [I]
(Alt. to David B. Fuller)

George W. Stanley, Wiginton Fire Protection Engineering, Inc., FL [IM]
(Alt. to Mark Hopkins)

Jeffrey James Vanrhyn, Local 669 JATC, NV [L]
(Alt. to Charles W. Ketner)

Cary Webber, Reliable Automatic Sprinkler, SC [M]
(Alt. to Michael J. Bosma)

John T. Whitney, III, Clarke Fire Protection Products, Inc., OH [M]
(Alt. to John Whitney)

Roger S. Wilkins, Johnson Controls, RI [M]
(Alt. to Terry L. Victor)

Nonvoting

Cecil Bilbo, Jr., Academy of Fire Sprinkler Technology, Inc., IL [SE]

Robert G. Caputo, Fire & Life Safety America, AZ [IM]
    Rep. TC on Sprinkler System Installation Criteria

Chad Duffy, NFPA Staff Liaison

Rohit Khanna, U.S. Consumer Product Safety Commission, MD [C]
    Rep. U.S. Consumer Product Safety Commission

Thomas F. Norton, Norel Service Company, Inc., MA [IM]

This list represents the membership at the time the Committee was balloted on the final text of this edition. Since that time, changes in the membership may have occurred. A key to classifications is found at the back of the document.

NOTE: Membership on a committee shall not in and of itself constitute an endorsement of the Association or any document developed by the committee on which the member serves.

Committee Scope: This Committee shall have primary responsibility for documents on inspection, testing, and maintenance of systems utilizing water as a method of extinguishment. These include sprinkler systems (excluding sprinkler systems installed in one-and two-family dwellings and manufactured homes), standpipe and hose systems, fire service piping and appurtenances, fire pumps, water storage tanks, fixed water spray systems, water mist systems, foam-water systems, valves, and allied equipment. This Committee shall also develop procedures for the conduct and reporting of routine system impairments.

Contents

NFPA 25

Standard for the

Inspection, Testing, and Maintenance of Water-Based Fire Protection Systems

2020 Edition

IMPORTANT NOTE: This NFPA document is made available for use subject to important notices and legal disclaimers. These notices and disclaimers appear in all publications containing this document and may be found under the heading "Important Notices and Disclaimers Concerning NFPA Standards." They can also be viewed at www.nfpa.org/disclaimers or obtained on request from NFPA.

UPDATES, ALERTS, AND FUTURE EDITIONS: New editions of NFPA codes, standards, recommended practices, and guides (i.e., NFPA Standards) are released on scheduled revision cycles. This edition may be superseded by a later one, or it may be amended outside of its scheduled revision cycle through the issuance of Tentative Interim Amendments (TIAs). An official NFPA Standard at any point in time consists of the current edition of the document, together with all TIAs and Errata in effect. To verify that this document is the current edition or to determine if it has been amended by TIAs or Errata, please consult the National Fire Codes® Subscription Service or the "List of NFPA Codes & Standards" at www.nfpa.org/docinfo. In addition to TIAs and Errata, the document information pages also include the option to sign up for alerts for individual documents and to be involved in the development of the next edition.

NOTICE: An asterisk (*) following the number or letter designating a paragraph indicates that explanatory material on the paragraph can be found in Annex A.

A reference in brackets [ ] following a section or paragraph indicates material that has been extracted from another NFPA document. Extracted text may be edited for consistency and style and may include the revision of internal paragraph references and other references as appropriate. Requests for interpretations or revisions of extracted text shall be sent to the technical committee responsible for the source document.

Information on referenced and extracted publications can be found in Chapter 2 and Annex H.

Chapter 1 Administration

1.1 Scope. This document establishes the minimum requirements for the periodic inspection, testing, and maintenance of water-based fire protection systems and the actions to undertake when changes in occupancy, use, process, materials, hazard, or water supply that potentially impact the performance of the water-based system are planned or identified.

Δ **1.1.1 Coordination with *NFPA 72* Testing Requirements.**

1.1.1.1 The inspection, testing, and maintenance required by this standard and *NFPA 72* shall be coordinated so that the system operates as intended.

1.1.1.2* All inspections, testing, and maintenance required by *NFPA 72* shall conform to *NFPA 72*, and all inspections, testing, and maintenance required by this standard shall conform to this standard.

N **1.1.1.3** This standard does not address all of the inspection, testing, and maintenance of the electrical components of the automatic fire detection equipment used to activate preaction and deluge systems that are addressed by *NFPA 72*.

1.1.2 Types of Systems.

1.1.2.1 The types of systems addressed by this standard include, but are not limited to, sprinkler, standpipe and hose, fixed water spray, private fire hydrants, water mist, and foam water.

1.1.2.2 Water supplies that are part of these systems, such as private fire service mains and appurtenances, fire pumps and water storage tanks, and valves that control system flow, are also included in this standard.

1.1.3* This standard addresses the operating condition of fire protection systems as well as impairment handling and reporting and applies to fire protection systems that have been properly installed in accordance with generally accepted practice.

1.1.3.1* This standard does not require the inspector to verify the adequacy of the design of the system.

1.1.4* Corrective action needed to ensure that a system operates in a satisfactory manner shall be in accordance with this standard unless this standard specifically refers to an appropriate installation standard.

1.1.5 Unless required by Chapter 16, this standard shall not apply to sprinkler systems designed, installed, and maintained in accordance with NFPA 13D.

1.2* Purpose.

1.2.1 The purpose of this document is to provide requirements that ensure a reasonable degree of protection for life and property from fire through minimum inspection, testing, and maintenance methods for water-based fire protection systems.

1.2.2 In those cases where it is determined that an existing situation involves a distinct hazard to life or property, the authority having jurisdiction shall be permitted to require inspection, testing, and maintenance methods in excess of those required by the standard.

1.3* Application.

1.3.1 It is not the intent of this standard to limit or restrict the use of other inspection, testing, or maintenance programs that provide an equivalent level of system integrity and performance to that detailed in this standard.

1.3.2 The authority having jurisdiction shall be consulted and approval obtained for such alternative programs.

1.4* Units. Metric units of measurement in this standard are in accordance with the modernized metric system known as the International System of Units (SI).

1.4.1 If a value for measurement as given in this standard is followed by an equivalent value in other units, the first stated shall be regarded as the requirement. A given equivalent value shall be considered to be approximate.

1.4.2 SI units have been converted by multiplying the quantity by the conversion factor and then rounding the result to the appropriate number of significant digits. Where nominal or trade sizes exist, the nominal dimension has been recognized in each unit.

Chapter 2 Referenced Publications

2.1 General. The documents or portions thereof listed in this chapter are referenced within this standard and shall be considered part of the requirements of this document.

Δ 2.2 NFPA Publications. National Fire Protection Association, 1 Batterymarch Park, Quincy, MA 02169-7471.

NFPA 11, *Standard for Low-, Medium-, and High-Expansion Foam,* 2016 edition.

NFPA 13, *Standard for the Installation of Sprinkler Systems,* 2019 edition.

NFPA 13D, *Standard for the Installation of Sprinkler Systems in One- and Two-Family Dwellings and Manufactured Homes,* 2019 edition.

NFPA 14, *Standard for the Installation of Standpipe and Hose Systems,* 2019 edition.

NFPA 15, *Standard for Water Spray Fixed Systems for Fire Protection,* 2017 edition.

NFPA 16, *Standard for the Installation of Foam-Water Sprinkler and Foam-Water Spray Systems,* 2019 edition.

NFPA 20, *Standard for the Installation of Stationary Pumps for Fire Protection,* 2019 edition.

NFPA 22, *Standard for Water Tanks for Private Fire Protection,* 2018 edition.

NFPA 24, *Standard for the Installation of Private Fire Service Mains and Their Appurtenances,* 2019 edition.

NFPA 70E®, *Standard for Electrical Safety in the Workplace®,* 2018 edition.

NFPA 72®, *National Fire Alarm and Signaling Code®,* 2019 edition.

NFPA 101®, *Life Safety Code®,* 2018 edition.

NFPA 110, *Standard for Emergency and Standby Power Systems,* 2019 edition.

NFPA 307, *Standard for the Construction and Fire Protection of Marine Terminals, Piers, and Wharves,* 2016 edition.

NFPA 409, *Standard on Aircraft Hangars,* 2016 edition.

NFPA 750, *Standard on Water Mist Fire Protection Systems,* 2019 edition.

NFPA 1962, *Standard for the Care, Use, Inspection, Service Testing, and Replacement of Fire Hose, Couplings, Nozzles, and Fire Hose Appliances,* 2018 edition.

2.3 Other Publications.

2.3.1 ASTM Publications. ASTM International, 100 Barr Harbor Drive, P.O. Box C700, West Conshohocken, PA 19428-2959.

ASTM D975, *Standard Specification for Diesel Fuel Oils,* 2015.

ASTM D3359, *Standard Test Methods for Rating Adhesion by Tape Test,* 2017.

ASTM D6751, *Standard Specification for Biodiesel Fuel Blend Stock (B100) for Middle Distillate Fuels,* 2015ce1.

ASTM D7462, *Standard Test Method for Oxidation Stability of Biodiesel (B100) and Blends of Biodiesel with Middle Distillate Petroleum Fuel (Accelerated Method),* 2011.

N 2.3.2 CGA Publications. Compressed Gas Association, 14501 George Carter Way, Suite 103, Chantilly, VA 20151.

CGA C-6, *Standard for Visual Inspection of Steel Compressed Gas Cylinders,* 2013.

2.3.3 HI Publications. Hydraulic Institute, 6 Campus Drive, First Floor North, Parsippany, NJ 07054-4405.

HI 3.6, *Rotary Pump Tests,* 2016.

2.3.4 Other Publications.

Merriam-Webster's Collegiate Dictionary, 11th edition, Merriam-Webster, Inc., Springfield, MA, 2003.

Δ 2.4 References for Extracts in Mandatory Sections.

NFPA 11, *Standard for Low-, Medium-, and High-Expansion Foam,* 2016 edition.

NFPA 13, *Standard for the Installation of Sprinkler Systems,* 2019 edition.

NFPA 14, *Standard for the Installation of Standpipe and Hose Systems,* 2019 edition.

NFPA 15, *Standard for Water Spray Fixed Systems for Fire Protection,* 2017 edition.

NFPA 16, *Standard for the Installation of Foam-Water Sprinkler and Foam-Water Spray Systems,* 2019 edition.

NFPA 20, *Standard for the Installation of Stationary Pumps for Fire Protection,* 2019 edition.

NFPA 24, *Standard for the Installation of Private Fire Service Mains and Their Appurtenances,* 2019 edition.

NFPA 72®, *National Fire Alarm and Signaling Code®,* 2019 edition.

NFPA 96, *Standard for Ventilation Control and Fire Protection of Commercial Cooking Operations,* 2017 edition.

NFPA 110, *Standard for Emergency and Standby Power Systems,* 2019 edition.

NFPA 750, *Standard on Water Mist Fire Protection Systems,* 2019 edition.

NFPA 820, *Standard for Fire Protection in Wastewater Treatment and Collection Facilities,* 2020 edition.

NFPA 1141, *Standard for Fire Protection Infrastructure for Land Development in Wildland, Rural, and Suburban Areas,* 2017 edition.

NFPA 1142, *Standard on Water Supplies for Suburban and Rural Fire Fighting,* 2017 edition.

NFPA 1911, *Standard for the Inspection, Maintenance, Testing, and Retirement of In-Service Emergency Vehicles,* 2017 edition.

Chapter 3 Definitions

3.1 General. The definitions contained in this chapter shall apply to the terms used in this standard. Where terms are not defined in this chapter or within another chapter, they shall be defined using their ordinarily accepted meanings within the context in which they are used. *Merriam-Webster's Collegiate Dictionary,* 11th edition, shall be the source for the ordinarily accepted meaning.

3.2 NFPA Official Definitions.

3.2.1* Approved. Acceptable to the authority having jurisdiction.

3.2.2* Authority Having Jurisdiction (AHJ). An organization, office, or individual responsible for enforcing the requirements of a code or standard, or for approving equipment, materials, an installation, or a procedure.

3.2.3* Listed. Equipment, materials, or services included in a list published by an organization that is acceptable to the authority having jurisdiction and concerned with evaluation of products or services, that maintains periodic inspection of production of listed equipment or materials or periodic evaluation of services, and whose listing states that either the equipment, material, or service meets appropriate designated standards or has been tested and found suitable for a specified purpose.

3.2.4 Shall. Indicates a mandatory requirement.

3.2.5 Should. Indicates a recommendation or that which is advised but not required.

3.2.6 Standard. An NFPA Standard, the main text of which contains only mandatory provisions using the word "shall" to indicate requirements and that is in a form generally suitable for mandatory reference by another standard or code or for adoption into law. Nonmandatory provisions are not to be considered a part of the requirements of a standard and shall be located in an appendix, annex, footnote, informational note, or other means as permitted in the NFPA Manuals of Style. When used in a generic sense, such as in the phrase "standards development process" or "standards development activities," the term "standards" includes all NFPA Standards, including Codes, Standards, Recommended Practices, and Guides.

3.3 General Definitions.

3.3.1 Adjust. To maintain or regulate, within prescribed limits, by setting the operating characteristics to specified parameters. [**1911,** 2017]

3.3.2* Alarm Receiving Facility. The place where alarm or supervisory signals are received.

N **3.3.3 Automated Inspection and Testing.** The performance of inspections and tests at a distant location from the system or component being inspected or tested through the use of electronic devices or equipment installed for the purpose.

3.3.4* Automatic Detection Equipment. Equipment that automatically detects heat, flame, products of combustion, flammable gases, or other conditions likely to produce fire or explosion and cause other automatic actuation of alarm and protection equipment.

3.3.5* Automatic Operation. Operation without human intervention.

3.3.6 Automatic Transfer Switch (ATS). Self-acting equipment for transferring the connected load from one power source to another power source. [**110,** 2019]

3.3.7 Clean. To remove dirt, scale, and debris.

3.3.8* Deficiency. For the purposes of inspection, testing, and maintenance of water-based fire protection systems, a condition that will or has the potential to adversely impact the performance of a system or portion thereof but does not rise to the level of an impairment.

> **3.3.8.1** *Critical Deficiency.* A deficiency that, if not corrected, can have a material effect on the ability of the fire protection system or unit to function as intended in a fire event.

> **3.3.8.2** *Noncritical Deficiency.* A deficiency that does not have a material effect on the ability of the fire protection system or unit to function in a fire event, but correction is needed to meet the requirements of this standard or for the proper inspection, testing, and maintenance of the system or unit.

3.3.9 Discharge Device. A device designed to discharge water or foam-water solution in a predetermined, fixed, or adjustable pattern. Examples include, but are not limited to, sprinklers, spray nozzles, and hose nozzles. [**16,** 2019]

3.3.10 Double Check Valve Assembly (DCVA). This assembly consists of two internally loaded check valves, either spring-loaded or internally weighted, installed as a unit between two tightly closing resilient-seated shutoff valves as an assembly, and fittings with properly located resilient-seated test cocks.

3.3.11 Drain.

> **3.3.11.1** *Main Drain.* The primary drain connection located on the system riser.

> **3.3.11.2*** *Sectional Drain.* A drain located beyond a sectional control valve that drains only a portion of the system.

3.3.12 Fire Department Connection. A connection through which the fire department can pump supplemental water into the sprinkler system, standpipe, or other system furnishing water for fire extinguishment to supplement existing water supplies.

3.3.13* Fire Hydrant. A valved connection on a water supply system having one or more outlets and that is used to supply hose and fire department pumpers with water. [**1141,** 2017]

> **3.3.13.1*** *Dry Barrel Hydrant (Frostproof Hydrant).* A type of hydrant with the main control valve below the frost line between the footpiece and the barrel.

> *N* **3.3.13.2** *Dry Hydrant.* An arrangement of pipe permanently connected to a water source other than a piped, pressurized water supply system that provides a ready means of water supply for fire-fighting purposes and that utilizes the drafting (suction) capability of a fire department pump. [**1142,** 2017]

> **3.3.13.3*** *Monitor Nozzle Hydrant.* A hydrant equipped with a monitor nozzle capable of delivering more than 250 gpm (946 L/min).

> **3.3.13.4*** *Wall Hydrant.* A hydrant mounted on the outside of a wall of a building, fed from interior piping, and equipped with control valves located inside the building that normally are key-operated from the building's exterior.

> **3.3.13.5*** *Wet Barrel Hydrant.* A type of hydrant that is intended for use where there is no danger of freezing weather and where each outlet is provided with a valve and an outlet. [**24,** 2019]

3.3.14* Foam Concentrate. A concentrated liquid foaming agent as received from the manufacturer. [**11,** 2016]

3.3.15 [Foam] Discharge Device. A device designed to discharge water or foam-water solution in a predetermined, fixed, or adjustable pattern. Examples include, but are not limited to, sprinklers, spray nozzles, and hose nozzles. [**16,** 2019]

3.3.16 Hose Connection. The outlet of a hose valve installed on a standpipe system for connection of fire hose. [**14,** 2019]

3.3.17* Hose House. An enclosure located over or adjacent to a hydrant or other water supply designed to contain the necessary hose nozzles, hose wrenches, gaskets, and spanners to be used in fire fighting in conjunction with and to provide aid to the local fire department.

3.3.18 Hose Nozzle. A device intended for discharging water for manual suppression or extinguishment of a fire.

3.3.19 Hose Station. A combination of a hose rack or reel, hose nozzle, hose, and hose connection. [14, 2019]

3.3.20 Hose Storage Devices.

3.3.20.1* *Conventional Pin Rack.* A hose rack where the hose is folded vertically and attached over the pins.

3.3.20.2* *Horizontal Rack.* A hose rack where the hose is connected to the valve, then stack-folded horizontally to the top of the rack.

3.3.20.3* *Hose Reel.* A circular device used to store hose.

3.3.20.4* *Semiautomatic Hose Rack Assembly.* The same as a "conventional" pin rack or hose reel except that, after the valve is opened, a retaining device holds the hose and water until the last few feet are removed.

3.3.21 Hydrostatic Test. A test of a closed piping system and its attached appurtenances consisting of subjecting the piping to an increased internal pressure for a specified duration to verify system integrity and system leakage rates. [24, 2019]

3.3.22* **Impairment.** A condition where a fire protection system or unit or portion thereof is out of order, and the condition can result in the fire protection system or unit not functioning in a fire event.

3.3.22.1* *Emergency Impairment.* A condition where a water-based fire protection system or portion thereof is out of order due to an unplanned occurrence, or the impairment is found while performing inspection testing or maintenance activities.

3.3.22.2 *Preplanned Impairment.* A condition where a water-based fire protection system or a portion thereof is out of service due to work planned in advance, such as revisions to the water supply or sprinkler system piping.

3.3.23 Inspect. See 3.3.24, Inspection.

3.3.24 Inspection. A visual examination of a system or portion thereof to verify that it appears to be in operating condition and is free of physical damage. [820, 2020]

3.3.25* **Inspection, Testing, and Maintenance Service.** A service program provided by a qualified contractor or qualified property owner's representative in which all components unique to the property's systems are inspected and tested at the required times and necessary maintenance is provided.

N **3.3.26*** **Lowest Permissible Suction Pressure.** The lowest suction pressure permitted by this standard and the authority having jurisdiction. [20, 2019]

3.3.27* **Maintenance.** In water-based fire protection systems, work performed to keep equipment operable.

3.3.28 Manual Operation. Operation of a system or its components through human action.

3.3.29 Nozzle.

3.3.29.1* *Monitor Nozzle.* A permanently mounted device specifically designed with a high flow rate to provide a far-reaching stream for locations where large amounts of water need to be available without the delay of laying hose lines.

3.3.29.2* *Water Spray Nozzle.* An open or automatic water discharge device that, when discharging water under pressure, will distribute the water in a specific, directional pattern.

3.3.30 Orifice Plate Proportioning. This system utilizes an orifice plate(s) through which passes a specific amount of foam concentrate at a specific pressure drop across the orifice plate(s).

3.3.31 Performance-Based Program. Methods and frequencies that have been demonstrated to deliver equivalent or superior levels of performance through quantitative performance-based analysis.

3.3.32* **Pressure-Regulating Device.** A device designed for the purpose of reducing, regulating, controlling, or restricting water pressure. [14, 2019]

3.3.33 Pressure-Restricting Device. A valve or device designed for the purpose of reducing the downstream water pressure under flowing (residual) conditions only. [14, 2019]

3.3.34* **Pressure Vacuum Vent.** A venting device mounted on atmospheric foam concentrate storage vessels to allow for concentrate expansion and contraction and for tank breathing during concentrate discharge or filling.

3.3.35* **Proportioner.**

3.3.35.1* *Bladder Tank Proportioner.* A system that is similar to a standard pressure proportioner, except the foam concentrate is contained inside a diaphragm bag that is contained inside a pressure vessel.

3.3.35.2* *In-Line Balanced Pressure Proportioner.* A system that is similar to a standard balanced pressure system, except the pumped concentrate pressure is maintained at a fixed preset value.

3.3.35.3* *Line Proportioner.* A system that uses a venturi pickup-type device where water passing through the unit creates a vacuum, thereby allowing foam concentrate to be picked up from an atmospheric storage container.

3.3.35.4* *Standard Balanced Pressure Proportioner.* A system that utilizes a foam concentrate pump where foam concentrate is drawn from an atmospheric storage tank, is pressurized by the pump, and passes back through a diaphragm balancing valve to the storage tank.

3.3.35.5* *Standard Pressure Proportioner.* A system that uses a pressure vessel containing foam concentrate where water is supplied to the proportioner, which directs an amount of the supply downward onto the contained concentrate, thereby pressurizing the tank.

3.3.36 Qualified. A competent and capable person who has met the requirements and training for a given field acceptable to the AHJ. [96, 2017]

3.3.37 Rebuild. To restore working condition by replacement or repair of worn or damaged parts.

Shaded text = Revisions.   **Δ** = Text deletions and figure/table revisions.   • = Section deletions.   *N* = New material.

3.3.38 Reduced-Pressure Principle Backflow Prevention Assembly (RPBA). Two independently acting check valves together with a hydraulically operating, mechanically independent pressure differential relief valve located between the check valves, along with two resilient-seated shutoff valves, all as an assembly, and equipped with properly located test cocks.

3.3.39 Remove. To physically take away or eliminate.

3.3.40 Repair. Restore to sound working condition or to fix damage.

3.3.41 Replace. To remove a component and install a new or equivalent component.

3.3.42 Sprinkler.

3.3.42.1 *Installation Orientation.* The following sprinklers are defined according to orientation.

3.3.42.1.1 *Concealed Sprinkler.* A recessed sprinkler with cover plate. [**13,** 2019]

3.3.42.1.2 *Flush Sprinkler.* A sprinkler in which all or part of the body, including the shank thread, is mounted above the lower plane of the ceiling. [**13,** 2019]

3.3.42.1.3 *Pendent Sprinkler.* A sprinkler designed to be installed in such a way that the water stream is directed downward against the deflector. [**13,** 2019]

3.3.42.1.4 *Recessed Sprinkler.* A sprinkler in which all or part of the body, other than the shank thread, is mounted within a recessed housing. [**13,** 2019]

3.3.42.1.5 *Sidewall Sprinkler.* A sprinkler having special deflectors that are designed to discharge most of the water away from the nearby wall in a pattern resembling one-quarter of a sphere, with a small portion of the discharge directed at the wall behind the sprinkler. [**13,** 2019]

3.3.42.1.6 *Upright Sprinkler.* A sprinkler designed to be installed in such a way that the water spray is directed upwards against the deflector. [**13,** 2019]

3.3.42.2* *Control Mode Specific Application (CMSA) Sprinkler.* A type of spray sprinkler that is capable of producing characteristic large water droplets and that is listed for its capability to provide fire control of specific high-challenge fire hazards. [**13,** 2019]

3.3.42.3 *Corrosion-Resistant Sprinkler.* A sprinkler fabricated with corrosion-resistant material, or with special coatings or platings, to be used in an atmosphere that would normally corrode sprinklers. [**13,** 2019]

3.3.42.4 *Dry Sprinkler.* A sprinkler secured in an extension nipple that has a seal at the inlet end to prevent water from entering the nipple until the sprinkler operates. [**13,** 2019]

3.3.42.5 *Early Suppression Fast-Response (ESFR) Sprinkler.* A type of fast-response sprinkler that has a thermal element with an RTI of 50 (meters-seconds)$^{1/2}$ or less and is listed for its capability to provide fire suppression of specific high-challenge fire hazards. [**13,** 2019]

N **3.3.42.6 *Electrically Operated Sprinklers.*** A sprinkler that is equipped with an integral means of activation using electricity.

3.3.42.7 *Extended Coverage Sprinkler.* A type of spray sprinkler with maximum coverage areas as specified in Sections 11.2 and 11.3 of NFPA 13. [**13,** 2019]

3.3.42.8 *Nozzle.* A device for use in applications requiring special water discharge patterns, directional spray, or other unusual discharge characteristics. [**13,** 2019]

3.3.42.9 *Old-Style/Conventional Sprinkler.* A sprinkler that directs from 40 percent to 60 percent of the total water initially in a downward direction and that is designed to be installed with the deflector either upright or pendent. [**13,** 2019]

3.3.42.10 *Open Sprinkler.* A sprinkler that does not have actuators or heat-responsive elements. [**13,** 2019]

3.3.42.11 *Ornamental/Decorative Sprinkler.* A sprinkler that has been painted or plated by the manufacturer. [**13,** 2019]

3.3.42.12 *Quick-Response Early Suppression (QRES) Sprinkler.* A type of quick-response sprinkler that has a thermal element with an RTI of 50 (meters-seconds)$^{1/2}$ or less and is listed for its capability to provide fire suppression of specific fire hazards. [**13,** 2019]

3.3.42.13 *Quick-Response Extended Coverage Sprinkler.* A type of quick-response sprinkler that has a thermal element with an RTI of 50 (meters-seconds)$^{1/2}$ or less and complies with the extended protection areas defined in Chapter 8 of NFPA 13. [**13,** 2019]

3.3.42.14 *Quick-Response (QR) Sprinkler.* A type of spray sprinkler that has a thermal element with an RTI of 50 (meters-seconds)$^{1/2}$ or less and is listed as a quick-response sprinkler for its intended use. [**13,** 2019]

△ **3.3.42.15 *Residential Sprinkler.*** A type of fast-response sprinkler having a thermal element with an RTI of 50 (meters-seconds)$^{1/2}$ or less that has been specifically investigated for its ability to enhance survivability in the room of fire origin and that is listed for use in the protection of dwelling units. [**13,** 2019]

3.3.42.16 *Special Sprinkler.* A sprinkler that has been tested and listed as prescribed in Section 15.2 of NFPA 13. [**13,** 2019]

3.3.42.17 *Spray Sprinkler.* A type of sprinkler listed for its capability to provide fire control for a wide range of fire hazards. [**13,** 2019]

3.3.42.18 *Standard Spray Sprinkler.* A spray sprinkler with maximum coverage areas as specified in Sections 10.2 and 10.3 of NFPA 13. [**13,** 2019]

3.3.43* Standpipe System. An arrangement of piping, valves, hose connections, and associated equipment installed in a building or structure, with the hose connections located in such a manner that water can be discharged in streams or spray patterns through attached hose and nozzles, for the purpose of extinguishing a fire, thereby protecting a building or structure and its contents in addition to protecting the occupants. [**14,** 2019]

3.3.43.1 *Automatic Standpipe System.* A standpipe system that is attached to a water supply capable of supplying the system demand and that requires no action other than opening a hose valve to provide water at hose connections.

3.3.43.2 Dry Standpipe. A standpipe system designed to have piping contain water only when the system is being utilized.

3.3.43.3 Manual Standpipe. Standpipe system that relies exclusively on the fire department connection to supply the system demand.

3.3.43.4 Semiautomatic Dry Standpipe System. A standpipe system permanently attached to a water supply that is capable of supplying the system demand at all times arranged through the use of a device such as a deluge valve and that requires activation of a remote control device to provide water at hose connections. [14, 2019]

3.3.43.5 Wet Standpipe System. A standpipe system having piping containing water at all times. [14, 2019]

3.3.44 Standpipe System Classes.

3.3.44.1 Class I System. A system that provides 2½ in. (65 mm) hose connections to supply water for use by fire departments. [14, 2019]

3.3.44.2 Class II System. A system that provides 1½ in. (40 mm) hose stations to supply water for use primarily by trained personnel or by the fire department during initial response. [14, 2019]

3.3.44.3 Class III System. A system that provides 1½ in. (40 mm) hose stations to supply water for use by trained personnel and 2½ in. (65 mm) hose connections to supply a larger volume of water for use by fire departments. [14, 2019]

3.3.45* Strainer. A device capable of removing from the water all solids of sufficient size that are obstructing water spray nozzles.

3.3.46 Supervision. In water-based fire protection systems, a means of monitoring system status and indicating abnormal conditions.

3.3.47 Test. The operation of a device to verify that it is functioning correctly, or the measurement of a system characteristic to determine if it meets requirements.

3.3.48* Testing. A procedure used to determine the operational status of a component or system by conducting periodic physical checks, such as waterflow tests, fire pump tests, alarm tests, and trip tests of dry pipe, deluge, or preaction valves.

3.3.49 Valve Status Test. Flowing water to verify that valves for a portion of the system are not closed.

3.3.50* Valve Status Test Connection. A point in the system where water is discharged for purposes of performing a valve status test.

3.3.51* Water Spray. Water in a form having a predetermined pattern, particle size, velocity, and density discharge from specially designed nozzles or devices. [15, 2017]

3.3.52 Water Supply. A source of water that provides the flows [gal/min (L/min)] and pressures [psi (bar)] required by the water-based fire protection system.

3.3.53 Waterflow Alarm Device. An attachment to a water-based fire protection system that detects and signals a predetermined waterflow.

3.4 Deluge Foam-Water Sprinkler and Foam-Water Spray Systems Definitions.

3.4.1 Foam-Water Spray System. A foam-water sprinkler system designed to use nozzles rather than sprinklers. [16, 2019]

3.4.2 Foam-Water Sprinkler System. A piping network employing automatic sprinklers, nozzles or other discharge devices, connected to a source of foam concentrate and to a water supply. [16, 2019]

3.5 Valve Definitions.

3.5.1* Control Valve. A valve controlling flow to water-based fire protection systems.

3.5.2* Deluge Valve. A water supply control valve intended to be operated by actuation of an automatic detection system that is installed in the same area as the discharge devices.

3.5.3 Hose Valve. The valve to an individual hose connection with an outlet for attaching a fire hose. [14, 2019]

3.5.4 Pressure Control Valve. A pilot-operated pressure-reducing valve designed for the purpose of reducing the downstream water pressure to a specific value under both flowing (residual) and nonflowing (static) conditions. [14, 2019]

3.5.5 Pressure-Reducing Valve. A valve designed for the purpose of reducing the downstream water pressure under both flowing (residual) and nonflowing (static) conditions. [14, 2019]

3.5.5.1* Master Pressure-Reducing Valve. A pressure-reducing valve installed to regulate pressures in an entire fire protection system and/or standpipe system zone.

3.5.6 [Pressure] Relief Valve. A device that allows the diversion of liquid to limit excess pressure in a system. [20, 2019]

3.5.6.1 Circulation Relief Valve. A valve used to cool a pump by discharging a small quantity of water. This valve is separate from and independent of the main relief valve. [20, 2019]

3.6 Water-Based Fire Protection System Definitions.

3.6.1 Combined Standpipe and Sprinkler System. A system where the water piping services both 2½ in. (65 mm) outlets for fire department use and outlets for automatic sprinklers.

3.6.2 Fire Pump Definitions.

3.6.2.1 Churn. See 3.6.2.4, No Flow (Churn, Shutoff)

3.6.2.2 Discharge Pressure. See 3.6.2.6.1.

3.6.2.2.1 Net Pressure (Differential Pressure). See 3.6.2.6.2.

3.6.2.3 Fire Pump. A pump that is a provider of liquid flow and pressure dedicated to fire protection. [20, 2019]

3.6.2.4* No Flow (Churn, Shutoff). The condition of zero flow when the fire pump is running but the only water passing through the pump is a small flow that is discharged through the pump circulation relief valve or supplies the cooling for a diesel engine driver. [20, 2019]

Δ **3.6.2.5* Peak Load.** As pertains to annual testing in this standard, the maximum power required to drive the pump at any flow rate up to 150 percent of rated capacity (flow).

3.6.2.6 *Pressure.*

3.6.2.6.1 *Discharge Pressure.* The total pressure available at the fire pump discharge flange. [**20**, 2019]

3.6.2.6.2* *Net Pressure (Differential Pressure).* For vertical turbine fire pumps, the total pressure at the fire pump discharge flange plus the total suction lift. For other fire pumps, the total pressure at the fire pump discharge flange minus the total pressure at the fire pump suction flange. [**20**, 2019]

3.6.2.6.3 *Rated Pressure.* The net pressure (differential pressure) at rated flow and rated speed as marked on the manufacturer's nameplate. [**20**, 2019]

3.6.2.6.4 *Suction Pressure.* The total pressure available at the fire pump suction flange. [**20**, 2019]

3.6.2.7 *Rated Flow.* The capacity of the pump at rated speed and rated pressure as marked on the manufacturer's nameplate. [**20**, 2019]

3.6.2.8 *Rated Pressure.* See 3.6.2.6.3.

3.6.2.9 *Shutoff (No Flow, Churn).* See 3.6.2.4, No Flow.

3.6.2.10 *Suction Pressure.* See 3.6.2.6.4.

3.6.2.11 *Unadjusted Field Test Curve.* A fire pump discharge curve including churn, 100 percent rate flow, and maximum flow up to 150 percent of rated flow, based on discharge gauge readings without speed or velocity pressure adjustments.

N **3.6.2.12** *Variable Speed Pump.* A fire pump with variable speed pressure limiting control or self-regulating variable speed fire pump unit. [**20**, 2019]

3.6.3* **Private Fire Service Main.** A private fire service main, as used in this standard, is that pipe and its appurtenances on private property that is between a source of water and the base of the system riser for water-based fire protection systems; between a source of water and inlets to foam-making systems; between a source of water and the base elbow of private hydrants or monitor nozzles; and used as fire pump suction and discharge piping, beginning at the inlet side of the check valve on a gravity or pressure tank. [**24**, 2019]

Δ **3.6.4*** **Sprinkler System.** A system, commonly activated by heat from a fire and discharges water over the fire area, that consists of an integrated network of piping designed in accordance with fire protection engineering standards that includes a water supply source, a water control valve, a waterflow alarm, and a drain. The portion of the sprinkler system above ground is a network of specifically sized or hydraulically designed piping installed in a building, structure, or area, generally overhead, and to which sprinklers are attached in a systematic pattern. [**13**, 2019]

3.6.4.1 *Antifreeze Sprinkler System.* A wet pipe system using automatic sprinklers that contains a liquid solution to prevent freezing of the system, intended to discharge the solution upon sprinkler operation, followed immediately by water from a water supply. [**13**, 2019]

3.6.4.1.1 *Premixed Antifreeze Solution.* A mixture of an antifreeze material with water that is prepared and factory-mixed by the manufacturer with a quality control procedure in place that ensures that the antifreeze solution remains homogeneous and that the concentration is as specified. [**13**, 2019]

3.6.4.2 *Deluge Sprinkler System.* A sprinkler system employing open sprinklers or nozzles that are attached to a piping system that is connected to a water supply through a valve that is opened by the operation of a detection system installed in the same areas as the sprinklers or the nozzles. When this valve opens, water flows into the piping system and discharges from all sprinklers or nozzles attached thereto. [**13**, 2019]

3.6.4.3 *Dry Pipe Sprinkler System.* A sprinkler system employing automatic sprinklers that are attached to a piping system containing air or nitrogen under pressure, the release of which (as from the opening of a sprinkler) permits the water pressure to open a valve known as a dry pipe valve, and the water then flows into the piping system and out the opened sprinklers. [**13**, 2019]

3.6.4.4 *Marine System.* A sprinkler system installed on a ship, boat, or other floating structure that takes its supply from the water on which the vessel floats.

3.6.4.5 *Preaction Sprinkler System.* A sprinkler system employing automatic sprinklers that are attached to a piping system that contains air that might or might not be under pressure, with a supplemental detection system installed in the same areas as the sprinklers. [**13**, 2019]

3.6.4.6* *Wet Pipe Sprinkler System.* A sprinkler system employing automatic sprinklers attached to a piping system containing water and connected to a water supply so that water discharges immediately from sprinklers opened by heat from a fire. [**13**, 2019]

3.6.5 **Water Mist System.** A distribution system connected to a water supply or water and atomizing media supplies that is equipped with one or more nozzles capable of delivering water mist intended to control, suppress, or extinguish fires and that has been demonstrated to meet the performance requirements of its listing and [the applicable] standard. [**750**, 2019]

3.6.6* **Water Spray System.** An automatic or manually actuated fixed pipe system connected to a water supply and equipped with water spray nozzles designed to provide a specific water discharge and distribution over the protected surfaces or area. [**15**, 2017]

3.6.6.1 *Ultra High-Speed Water Spray System.* A type of automatic water spray system where water spray is rapidly applied to protect specific hazards where deflagrations are anticipated. [**15**, 2017]

3.6.7 **Water Tank.** A tank supplying water for water-based fire protection systems.

3.7 **Inspection, Testing, and Maintenance (ITM) Task Frequencies.**

3.7.1* **Frequency.** Minimum and maximum time between events.

3.7.1.1 *Daily Frequency.* Occurring every day.

3.7.1.2 *Weekly Frequency.* Occurring once per calendar week.

3.7.1.3 *Monthly Frequency.* Occurring once per calendar month.

3.7.1.4 *Quarterly Frequency.* Occurring four times per year with a minimum of 2 months and a maximum of 4 months.

3.7.1.5 *Semiannual Frequency.* Occurring twice per year with a minimum of 4 months and a maximum of 8 months.

3.7.1.6 *Annual Frequency.* Occurring once per year with a minimum of 9 months and a maximum of 15 months.

3.7.1.7 *Three Years Frequency.* Occurring once every 36 months with a minimum of 30 months and a maximum of 40 months.

3.7.1.8 *Five Years Frequency.* Occurring once every 60 months with a minimum of 54 months and a maximum of 66 months.

Chapter 4   General Requirements

4.1 Responsibility of Property Owner or Designated Representative.

4.1.1* Responsibility for Inspection, Testing, Maintenance, and Impairment. The property owner or designated representative shall be responsible for properly maintaining a water-based fire protection system.

4.1.1.1 Inspection, testing, maintenance, and impairment procedures shall be implemented in accordance with those established in this document and in accordance with the manufacturer's instructions.

4.1.1.2 Inspection, testing, and maintenance shall be performed by qualified personnel.

4.1.1.2.1* The owner shall coordinate with the entity conducting the inspection, testing, and maintenance activities to minimize any water damage caused by the discharge of water.

4.1.1.3* Where the property owner or designated representative is not the occupant, the property owner or designated representative shall be permitted to delegate the authority for inspecting, testing, maintenance, and the managing of impairments of the fire protection system to a designated representative.

4.1.1.4 Where a designated representative has received the authority for inspecting, testing, maintenance, and the managing of impairments, the designated representative shall comply with the requirements identified for the property owner or designated representative throughout this standard.

4.1.2* Freeze Protection. The property owner or designated representative shall ensure that water-filled piping is maintained at a minimum temperature of 40°F (4°C) unless an approved antifreeze solution is utilized.

4.1.2.1* All areas of the building containing water-filled piping that does not have another means of freeze protection shall be maintained at a minimum temperature of 40°F (4°C).

N **4.1.2.2*** The requirements of 4.1.2 shall not apply where water-filled piping is located in unconditioned building spaces or areas outside the building envelope and are not subject to freezing.

4.1.2.3 Aboveground water-filled pipes that pass through open areas, cold rooms, passageways, or other areas exposed to temperatures below 40°F (4°C), protected against freezing by insulating coverings, frostproof casings, listed heat tracing systems, or other reliable means, shall be maintained at temperatures between 40°F (4°C) and 120°F (48.9°C).

4.1.2.4 Where other approved means of freeze protection for water-filled piping as described in 4.1.2.3 are utilized, they shall be inspected, tested, and maintained in accordance with this standard.

N **4.1.2.5** Valve enclosures for preaction valves, deluge valves, and dry pipe valves subject to freezing shall be inspected daily during cold weather to verify a minimum temperature of 40°F (4°C).

N **4.1.2.5.1** Valve enclosures equipped with low-temperature alarms shall be allowed to be inspected weekly.

N **4.1.2.5.2** Low-temperature alarms, if installed in valve enclosures, shall be inspected annually at the beginning of the heating season to verify that they are free of physical damage.

4.1.3* Accessibility. The property owner or designated representative shall provide ready accessibility to components of water-based fire protection systems that require inspection, testing, and maintenance.

4.1.4 Notification of System Shutdown or Testing. The property owner or designated representative shall notify the authority having jurisdiction, the fire department, if required, and the alarm-receiving facility before testing or shutting down a system or its supply.

4.1.4.1 The notification of system shutdown or test shall include the purpose for the shutdown or test, the system or component involved, the estimated time of shutdown or test, and the expected duration of the shutdown or test.

4.1.4.2 The authority having jurisdiction, the fire department, and the alarm-receiving facility shall be notified when the system, supply, or component is returned to service or when the test is complete.

4.1.5* Corrections and Repairs.

4.1.5.1* The property owner or designated representative shall correct or repair deficiencies or impairments.

N **4.1.5.1.1*** Upon discovery of any component and equipment under recall or replacement programs by the owner's maintenance personnel, designated representative, or contractor, the owner shall be notified in writing.

N **4.1.5.1.2*** The property owner or designated representative shall correct, remedy, repair, or replace components and equipment under recall or replacement program.

4.1.5.2 Corrections and repairs shall be performed by qualified maintenance personnel or a qualified contractor.

4.1.6* Changes in Occupancy, Use, Process, or Materials. The property owner or designated representative shall not make changes in the occupancy, the use or process, or the materials used or stored in the building without evaluation of the fire protection system(s) for its capability to protect the new occupancy, use, or materials.

4.1.6.1 The evaluation required by 4.1.6 shall not be considered part of the normal inspection, testing, and maintenance required by this standard.

4.1.6.2* The evaluation shall consider factors that include, but are not limited to, the following:

(1) Occupancy changes such as converting office or production space into warehousing
(2) Process or material changes such as metal stamping to molded plastics
(3) Building revisions such as relocated walls, added mezzanines, and ceilings added below sprinklers
(4) Removal of heating systems in spaces with piping subject to freezing
(5) Changes to the storage method, arrangement, height or commodities
(6) Changes in water supplies

4.1.7* Addressing Changes in Hazard.

4.1.7.1 Where changes in the occupancy, hazard, water supply, storage commodity, storage arrangement, building modification, or other condition that affects the installation criteria of the system are identified, the property owner or designated representative shall promptly take steps to evaluate the adequacy of the installed system in order to protect the building or hazard in question.

4.1.7.2 Where the evaluation reveals that the installed system is inadequate to protect the building or hazard in question, the property owner or designated representative shall make the required corrections.

4.1.7.3 Corrections shall be approved.

4.1.8 Valve Location. The location of shutoff valves shall be identified at the system riser or other approved locations.

4.1.9* Information Sign.

4.1.9.1 A permanently marked metal or rigid plastic information sign shall be placed at the system control riser supplying an antifreeze loop, dry system, preaction system, or auxiliary system control valve.

4.1.9.2 Each sign shall be secured with a corrosion-resistant wire, chain, or other approved means and shall indicate at least the following information:

(1) Location of the area served by the system
(2) Location of auxiliary drains and low-point drains for dry pipe and preaction systems
(3) Presence and location of antifreeze or other auxiliary systems
(4) Presence and location(s) of heat tape

4.1.10 Antifreeze Information Sign. An antifreeze information sign shall be placed on the antifreeze system main valve, which indicates the manufacture type and brand of the antifreeze solution, the concentration by volume of the antifreeze solution used, and the volume of the antifreeze solution used in the system.

4.1.11 Impairments.

4.1.11.1 Where an impairment to a water-based fire protection system occurs or is identified during inspection, testing, or maintenance activities, the procedures outlined in Chapter 15 shall be followed, including the attachment of a tag to the impaired system.

4.1.11.2 Where a water-based fire protection system is returned to service following an impairment, the system shall be verified to be working properly by means of an appropriate inspection or test as described in the table "Summary of Component Replacement [Action] Requirements" in the applicable chapters of this document.

4.2 Manufacturer's Corrective Action. Manufacturers shall be permitted to make modifications to their own listed product in the field with listed devices that restore the original performance as intended by the listing, where acceptable to the authority having jurisdiction.

4.3 Records.

Δ 4.3.1* Records shall be made for all inspections, tests, and maintenance of the system and its components.

N 4.3.1.1 Records shall be maintained by the property owner.

4.3.1.2* Records shall be permitted to be stored and accessed electronically.

4.3.2 Records shall indicate the following:

(1) The procedure/activity performed (e.g., inspection, test, or maintenance)
(2) The organization that performed the activity
(3) The required frequency of the activity
(4) The results and date of the activity
(5) The name and contact information of the qualified contractor or owner, including lead person for activity

4.3.3* Records shall be made available to the authority having jurisdiction upon request.

4.3.4 As-built system installation drawings, hydraulic calculations, original acceptance test records, and device manufacturer's data sheets shall be retained for the life of the system.

4.3.5 Subsequent records shall be retained for a period of 1 year after the next inspection, test, or maintenance of that type required by the standard.

4.4 Water Supply Status. During inspection, testing, and maintenance, water supplies, including fire pumps, shall remain in service unless under constant attendance by qualified personnel or unless impairment procedures in Chapter 15 are followed.

4.5* Inspection. System components shall be inspected at intervals specified in the appropriate chapters.

4.6 Testing.

4.6.1 All components and systems shall be tested to verify that they function as intended.

4.6.1.1 When automated testing in accordance with 4.6.6 is being utilized, the testing shall be observed at a minimum frequency of once every 3 years.

4.6.1.2 Where the automated testing cannot be visually observed, the testing shall be conducted manually at a minimum frequency of once every 3 years.

4.6.2 The frequency of tests shall be in accordance with this standard.

4.6.3 Fire protection system components shall be restored to full operational condition following testing, including reinstallation of plugs and caps for auxiliary drains and test valves.

4.6.4* Test results shall be compared with those of the original acceptance test (if available) and with the most recent test results.

4.6.5* When a component or subsystem is adjusted, repaired, reconditioned, or replaced, it shall be tested in accordance with the original acceptance test required for that subsystem or the requirements where specified by the standard.

4.6.6* Automated Inspection and Testing.

4.6.6.1 Automated inspection and testing procedures performed in accordance with the requirements in this standard shall be permitted to be used.

4.6.6.2* Automated inspection equipment that meets the intent of a required visual inspection shall be permitted to replace the visual inspection.

4.6.6.3 Automated testing equipment shall produce the same action required by this standard to test a device.

4.6.6.4 The testing shall discharge water where required in this standard.

Δ **4.6.6.4.1** Automated testing equipment that does not discharge water for a test shall be permitted except as required in 4.6.6.4.2.

4.6.6.4.2* The discharge shall be visually observed at a minimum frequency of once every 3 years.

4.6.6.5 Where required in this standard, personnel shall observe the testing and intervene in the testing procedures when necessary to prevent injury or property damage.

4.6.6.6 Automated test devices and equipment shall be listed for the purpose of the test being conducted.

N **4.6.6.7*** Devices and equipment utilized to perform automated inspection and testing procedures that are not subjected to system pressure or are not integral to the operation of the system during a fire event shall not be required to be listed.

4.6.6.8 Failure of the testing equipment shall not impair the operation of the system unless indicated by a supervisory signal in accordance with *NFPA 72*.

4.6.6.9 Failure of a component or system to pass an automated test shall result in an audible supervisory signal.

4.6.6.10 Failure of automated inspection and testing equipment shall result in a trouble signal in accordance with *NFPA 72*.

4.6.6.11 Failure of a component or system that impairs the system shall require that impairment procedures be followed.

4.6.6.12 The testing frequencies of this standard shall be maintained regardless of the functionality of the automated testing equipment.

4.6.6.13 A record of all inspections and testing shall be maintained in accordance with 4.3.2.

4.7* Performance-Based Compliance Programs. Components and systems shall be permitted to be inspected, tested, and maintained under an approved performance-based program.

4.7.1* Performance-based programs shall have clearly identifiable goals and clearly define how the program meets those goals.

4.7.2 Compliance with an approved performance-based program shall be deemed as compliance with this standard.

4.7.3 The goals and goal achievement obtained with the approved performance-based program shall be reviewed a minimum of every 3 years and inspection, testing, and maintenance frequencies adjusted to reflect current conditions and the historical record.

4.7.4 The historical record shall be available for review by the authority having jurisdiction.

4.8 Maintenance. Maintenance shall be performed to keep the system equipment operable.

4.9 Safety.

4.9.1 General. Inspection, testing, and maintenance activities shall be conducted in accordance with applicable safety regulations.

4.9.2 Confined Spaces. Legally required precautions shall be taken prior to entering confined spaces such as tanks, valve pits, or trenches.

4.9.3 Fall Protection. Legally required equipment shall be worn or used to prevent injury from falls to personnel.

4.9.4 Hazards. Precautions shall be taken to address any hazards, such as protection against drowning where working on the top of a filled embankment or a supported, rubberized fabric tank, or over open water or other liquids.

4.9.5* Hazardous Materials.

4.9.5.1 Legally required equipment shall be used where working in an environment with hazardous materials present.

4.9.5.2 The property owner or designated representative shall advise anyone performing inspection, testing, and maintenance on any system under the scope of this document, with regard to hazardous materials stored on the premises.

4.9.6* Electrical Safety.

4.9.6.1 Legally required precautions shall be taken when testing or maintaining electric controllers for motor-driven fire pumps.

Δ **4.9.6.2*** At a minimum, the provisions of NFPA *70E* or an approved equivalent shall be applied.

Chapter 5   Sprinkler Systems

5.1 General.

5.1.1 Minimum Requirements.

5.1.1.1 This chapter shall provide the minimum requirements for the routine inspection, testing, and maintenance of sprinkler systems.

5.1.1.2 Table 5.1.1.2 shall be used to determine the minimum required frequencies for inspection, testing, and maintenance.

5.1.2 Common Components and Valves. Common components and valves shall be inspected, tested, and maintained in accordance with Chapter 13.

5.1.3 Obstruction Investigations. The procedures outlined in Chapter 14 shall be followed where there is a need to conduct an obstruction investigation.

Δ **Table 5.1.1.2 Summary of Sprinkler System Inspection, Testing, and Maintenance**

Item	Frequency	Reference
Inspection		
Assessment of the internal piping condition		Chapter 14
Control valves		Chapter 13
Fire department connections		Chapter 13
Gauges (wet and deluge systems)		Chapter 13
Gauges (dry and preaction systems)		Chapter 13
Hanger/braces/supports	Annually	5.2.3
Heat tracing	Per manufacturer's requirements	5.2.6
Hydraulic design information sign	Annually	5.2.5
Information signs	Annually	5.2.7, 5.2.8, 5.2.9
Pipe and fittings	Annually	5.2.2
Sprinklers	Annually	5.2.1
Sprinklers (spare)	Annually	5.2.1.4
Supervisory signal devices (except valve supervisory switches)		5.2.4, Chapter 13
System valves		Chapter 13
Valve supervisory signal devices		5.2.4, Chapter 13
Waterflow alarm devices	Quarterly	5.2.4
Test		
Antifreeze solution	Annually	5.3.4
Control valves		Chapter 13
Gauges		Chapter 13
Main drain		Chapter 13
Sprinklers	At 50 years and every 10 years thereafter	5.3.1.1.1, 5.3.1.1.1.1, 5.3.1.1.1.2
Sprinklers	At 75 years and every 5 years thereafter	5.3.1.1.1.5
Sprinklers (dry)	15 years and every 10 years thereafter	5.3.1.1.1.6
Sprinklers (extra-high or greater temperature solder type)	5 years	5.3.1.1.1.4
Sprinklers (fast-response)	At 20 years and every 10 years thereafter	5.3.1.1.1.3
Sprinklers (harsh environments)	5 years	5.3.1.1.2
Supervisory signal devices (except valve supervisory switches)		Chapter 13
System valves		Chapter 13
Valve supervisory signal devices		Chapter 13
Waterflow alarm devices (mechanical)	Quarterly	5.3.3.1
Waterflow alarm devices (vane and pressure switch type)	Semiannually	5.3.3.2
Maintenance		
Low-point drains (dry pipe and preaction systems)		Chapter 13
Sprinklers and automatic spray nozzles protecting commercial cooking equipment and ventilation systems	Annually	5.4.1.7
Replacement of sprinklers	Removed for any reason	5.4.1.1
Valves (all types)		Chapter 13
Investigation		
Obstruction		Chapter 14

Shaded text = Revisions.　Δ = Text deletions and figure/table revisions.　• = Section deletions.　*N* = New material.

5.1.4 Impairments. The procedures outlined in Chapter 15 shall be followed where an impairment to protection occurs.

5.1.5 Hose Connections. Hose connections shall be inspected, tested, and maintained in accordance with Chapters 6 and 13.

5.2* Inspection.

5.2.1 Sprinklers.

5.2.1.1* Sprinklers shall be inspected from the floor level annually.

5.2.1.1.1* Any sprinkler that shows signs of any of the following shall be replaced:

(1) Leakage
(2) Corrosion detrimental to sprinkler performance
(3) Physical damage
(4) Loss of fluid in the glass bulb heat-responsive element
(5) Loading detrimental to sprinkler performance
(6) Paint other than that applied by the sprinkler manufacturer

5.2.1.1.2 Any sprinkler that has been installed in the incorrect orientation shall be corrected by repositioning the branchline, drop, or sprig, or shall be replaced.

5.2.1.1.3* Sprinklers installed in concealed spaces such as above suspended ceilings shall not require inspection.

5.2.1.1.4 Sprinklers installed in areas that are inaccessible for safety considerations due to process operations shall be inspected during each scheduled shutdown.

5.2.1.1.5 Escutcheons and coverplates for recessed, flush, and concealed sprinklers shall be replaced with their listed escutcheon or coverplate if found missing during the inspection.

5.2.1.1.5.1 Where the listed escutcheon or coverplate from a listed assembly is missing and is no longer commercially available, the sprinkler shall be replaced.

5.2.1.1.6 Escutcheons for pendent sprinklers that are not recessed, flush, or concealed shall not be required to be replaced if found missing during the inspection.

5.2.1.2* The minimum clearance to storage as described in 5.2.1.2.1 through 5.2.1.2.6 shall be maintained below all sprinkler deflectors.

5.2.1.2.1* Unless greater distances are required by 5.2.1.2.2, 5.2.1.2.3, or 5.2.1.2.4, or lesser distances are permitted by 5.2.1.2.6, clearance between the deflector and the top of storage shall be 18 in. (457 mm) or greater.

5.2.1.2.2 Where standards other than NFPA 13 specify greater clearance to storage minimums, they shall be followed.

5.2.1.2.3* Clearance between the deflector and the top of storage shall be 36 in. (914 mm) or greater for special sprinklers.

5.2.1.2.4 Clearance from the top of storage to sprinkler deflectors shall be 36 in. (914 mm) or greater where rubber tires are stored.

5.2.1.2.5 In-rack sprinklers shall not be required to meet the obstruction criteria and clearance from storage requirements.

5.2.1.2.6* Clearance between the deflector and the top of storage shall be permitted to be less than 18 in. (457 mm) where shown to be permitted by the installation standard.

5.2.1.3* Storage closer to the sprinkler deflector than permitted by the clearance rules of the installation standard described in 5.2.1.2.1 through 5.2.1.2.4 shall be corrected.

5.2.1.4 The supply of spare sprinklers shall be inspected annually for the following:

(1) The correct number and type of sprinklers as required by 5.4.1.5
(2) A sprinkler wrench for each type of sprinkler as required by 5.4.1.5.5
(3) The list of spare sprinklers as required by 5.4.1.5.6

5.2.2* Pipe and Fittings. Sprinkler pipe and fittings shall be inspected annually from the floor level.

5.2.2.1* Pipe and fittings shall be free of mechanical damage, leakage, and corrosion.

5.2.2.2 Sprinkler piping shall not be subjected to external loads by materials either resting on the pipe or hung from the pipe.

5.2.2.3* Pipe and fittings installed in concealed spaces such as above suspended ceilings shall not require inspection.

5.2.2.4 Pipe and fittings installed in areas that are inaccessible for safety considerations due to process operations shall be inspected during each scheduled shutdown.

5.2.3* Hangers, Braces, and Supports. Sprinkler pipe hangers, braces, and supports shall be inspected annually from the floor level.

5.2.3.1 Hangers, braces, and supports shall not be damaged, loose, or unattached.

5.2.3.2 Hangers, braces, and supports that are damaged, loose, or unattached shall be replaced or refastened.

5.2.3.3* Hangers, braces, and supports installed in concealed spaces such as above suspended ceilings shall not require inspection.

5.2.3.4 Hangers, braces, and supports installed in areas that are inaccessible for safety considerations due to process operations shall be inspected during each scheduled shutdown.

5.2.4 Waterflow Alarm and Supervisory Signal Initiating Device. Waterflow alarm and supervisory signal initiating devices shall be inspected quarterly to verify that they are free of physical damage.

5.2.5* Hydraulic Design Information Sign. The hydraulic design information sign shall be inspected annually to verify that it is provided, attached securely to the sprinkler riser, and is legible.

5.2.5.1 A hydraulic design information sign that is missing or illegible shall be replaced.

5.2.5.2 A pipe schedule system shall have a hydraulic design information sign that reads "Pipe Schedule System."

5.2.6 Heat Tracing. Heat tracing shall be inspected and maintained in accordance with manufacturer's requirements.

Shaded text = Revisions.   Δ = Text deletions and figure/table revisions.   • = Section deletions.   *N* = New material.

5.2.7 Information Sign. The information sign required by 4.1.9 shall be inspected annually to verify that it is provided, securely attached, and legible.

5.2.8* General Information Sign. The general information sign required by NFPA 13 shall be inspected annually to verify that it is provided, securely attached, and legible.

5.2.9 Antifreeze Information Sign. The antifreeze information sign required by 4.1.10 shall be inspected annually to verify that it is present, securely attached, and legible.

5.3 Testing.

5.3.1* Sprinklers.

5.3.1.1* Where required by this section, sample sprinklers shall be submitted to a recognized testing laboratory acceptable to the authority having jurisdiction for field service testing.

5.3.1.1.1 Where sprinklers have been installed for 50 years, they shall be replaced or representative samples from one or more sample areas shall be tested.

5.3.1.1.1.1 Test procedures shall be repeated at 10-year intervals.

5.3.1.1.1.2 Sprinklers manufactured prior to 1920 shall be replaced.

5.3.1.1.1.3* Sprinklers manufactured using fast-response elements that have been installed for 20 years shall be replaced or representative samples shall be tested and then retested at 10-year intervals.

5.3.1.1.1.4* Representative samples of solder-type sprinklers with a temperature classification of extra high [325°F (163°C)] or greater that are exposed to semicontinuous to continuous maximum allowable ambient temperature conditions shall be tested at 5-year intervals.

5.3.1.1.1.5 Where sprinklers have been installed for 75 years, they shall be replaced or representative samples from one or more sample areas shall be submitted to a recognized testing laboratory acceptable to the authority having jurisdiction for field service testing and repeated at 5-year intervals.

5.3.1.1.1.6* Dry sprinklers that have been installed for 15 years shall be replaced or representative samples shall be tested and then retested at 10-year intervals.

5.3.1.1.2* Sprinklers exposed to harsh environments, including corrosive atmospheres, shall be one of the following:

(1) Replaced
(2) Tested via representative sprinkler samples on a 5-year basis

N 5.3.1.1.3 Listed corrosion-resistant sprinklers installed in harsh environments shall be permitted to be tested on a 10-year basis.

5.3.1.1.4 Where historical data indicate, longer intervals between testing shall be permitted.

5.3.1.2* A representative sample of sprinklers for testing per 5.3.1.1 shall consist of a minimum of not less than four sprinklers or 1 percent of the number of sprinklers per individual sprinkler sample, whichever is greater.

5.3.1.3 Where one sprinkler within a representative sample fails to meet the test requirement, all sprinklers within the area represented by that sample shall be replaced.

5.3.1.3.1 Manufacturers shall be permitted to make modifications to their own sprinklers in the field with listed devices that restore the original performance as intended by the listing, where acceptable to the authority having jurisdiction.

N 5.3.2 Electrically Operated Sprinklers.

N 5.3.2.1 Electrically operated sprinklers shall be tested in accordance with the manufacturer's requirements.

N 5.3.2.2 The testing of the electronic actuation and supervision shall be in accordance with the manufacturer's requirements and *NFPA 72* or the local fire alarm code.

5.3.3 Waterflow Alarm Devices.

5.3.3.1 Mechanical waterflow alarm devices including, but not limited to, water motor gongs, shall be tested quarterly.

5.3.3.2* Vane-type and pressure switch–type waterflow alarm devices shall be tested semiannually.

5.3.3.3 Testing of pressure switch–type waterflow alarm devices on wet pipe systems shall be accomplished by opening the inspector's test connection.

5.3.3.3.1 Where freezing weather conditions or other circumstances prohibit use of the inspector's test connection, the bypass connection shall be permitted to be used.

5.3.3.4 Except as permitted in 5.3.3.4.1, testing of vane-type waterflow alarm devices on wet pipe systems shall be accomplished by a flow of water equivalent to the flow out of the smallest single k-factor sprinkler (or smaller) past the flow switch.

N 5.3.3.4.1 A vane-type waterflow alarm device listed with an integral automated test feature that is capable of verifying the presence of water at the location of the water flow alarm device and function of the water flow device and alarm shall be permitted to be used.

5.3.3.4.2 Vane-type waterflow alarm devices tested semiannually using circulated water or as described in 5.3.3.4.1 shall be tested by opening the inspector's test connection at a minimum frequency of once every 3 years.

5.3.3.5 Fire pumps shall not be taken out of service during testing unless constantly attended by qualified personnel or all impairment procedures contained in Chapter 15 are followed.

5.3.4* Antifreeze Systems. Annually, before the onset of freezing weather, the antifreeze solution shall be tested using the following procedure:

(1) Using the antifreeze information sign required by 4.1.10, installation records, maintenance records, information from the owner, chemical tests, or other reliable sources of information, the type of antifreeze in the system shall be determined and (a) or (b) implemented if necessary:

  (a) If the antifreeze is found to be a type that is no longer permitted, the system shall be drained completely and the antifreeze replaced with an acceptable solution.

Shaded text = Revisions.   Δ = Text deletions and figure/table revisions.   • = Section deletions.   N = New material.

2020 Edition

(b) If the type of antifreeze cannot be reliably determined, the system shall be drained completely and the antifreeze replaced with an acceptable solution in accordance with 5.3.4.4.

(2) If the antifreeze is not replaced in accordance with 5.3.4(1)(a) and 5.3.4(1)(b), test samples shall be taken at the top of each system and at the bottom of each system as follows:

(a) If the most remote portion of the system is not near the top or the bottom of the system, an additional sample shall be taken at the most remote portion.

(b) If the connection to the water supply piping is not near the top or the bottom of the system, an additional sample shall be taken at the connection to the water supply.

(3) The specific gravity of each solution shall be checked using a hydrometer with a suitable scale or a refractometer having a scale calibrated for the antifreeze solution.

(4) If any of the samples exhibits a concentration in excess of what is permitted by 5.3.4.4, the system shall be emptied and refilled with a new acceptable solution.

(5) If a concentration greater than what is currently permitted by 5.3.4.4 was necessary to keep the fluid from freezing, alternative methods for preventing the pipe from freezing shall be employed.

5.3.4.1 The antifreeze solution shall be tested at its most remote portion and where it interfaces with the wet pipe system.

5.3.4.2 Where antifreeze systems have a capacity larger than 150 gal (568 L), tests at one additional point for every 100 gal (379 L) shall be made.

5.3.4.2.1 If the results indicate an incorrect freeze point at any point in the system, the system shall be drained and refilled with new premixed antifreeze.

5.3.4.2.2 For premixed solutions, the manufacturer's instructions shall be permitted to be used with regard to the number of test points and the refill procedure.

5.3.4.3 The use of antifreeze solutions shall be in conformity with state and local health regulations.

5.3.4.3.1* Listed CPVC sprinkler pipe and fittings shall be protected from freezing with glycerine only.

5.3.4.3.1.1 The use of diethylene, ethylene, or propylene glycols shall be specifically prohibited.

5.3.4.4 Except as permitted by 5.3.4.4.1 and 5.3.4.4.3, all antifreeze systems shall utilize listed antifreeze solutions.

5.3.4.4.1* For systems installed prior to September 30, 2012, listed antifreeze solutions shall not be required until September 30, 2022, where one of the following conditions is met:

(1)* The concentration of the antifreeze solution shall be limited to 30 percent propylene glycol by volume or 38 percent glycerine by volume.

(2)* Antifreeze systems with concentrations in excess of 30 percent but not more than 40 percent propylene glycol by volume and 38 percent but not more than 50 percent glycerine by volume shall be permitted based upon an approved deterministic risk assessment prepared by a qualified person approved by the authority having jurisdiction.

5.3.4.4.2 Newly introduced solutions shall be factory premixed antifreeze solutions (chemically pure or United States Pharmacopeia 96.5 percent).

5.3.4.4.3 Premixed antifreeze solutions of propylene glycol exceeding 30 percent concentration by volume shall be permitted for use with ESFR sprinklers where the ESFR sprinklers are listed for such use in a specific application.

5.4 Maintenance.

5.4.1 Sprinklers.

5.4.1.1 Where a sprinkler has been removed for any reason, it shall not be reinstalled.

5.4.1.2* Replacement sprinklers shall have the proper characteristics for the application intended, which include the following:

(1) Style
(2) Orifice size and K-factor
(3) Temperature rating
(4) Coating, if any
(5) Deflector type (e.g., upright, pendent, sidewall)
(6) Design requirements

5.4.1.2.1* Spray sprinklers shall be permitted to replace old-style sprinklers.

5.4.1.2.2* Where replacing residential sprinklers manufactured prior to 2003 that are no longer available from the manufacturer and are installed using a design density less than 0.05 gpm/ft^2 (204 mm/min), a residential sprinkler with an equivalent K-factor (± 5 percent) shall be permitted to be used provided the currently listed coverage area for the replacement sprinkler is not exceeded.

5.4.1.2.3 Replacement sprinklers for piers and wharves shall comply with NFPA 307.

5.4.1.3 Only new, listed sprinklers shall be used to replace existing sprinklers.

5.4.1.4* Special and quick-response sprinklers as defined by NFPA 13 shall be replaced with sprinklers of the same orifice, size, temperature range and thermal response characteristics, and K-factor.

5.4.1.5* A supply of at least six spare sprinklers shall be maintained on the premises so that any sprinklers that have operated or been damaged in any way can be promptly replaced.

5.4.1.5.1 The sprinklers shall correspond to the types and temperature ratings of the sprinklers in the property.

5.4.1.5.2 The stock of spare sprinklers shall be kept in a cabinet located where the temperature to which they are subjected will at no time exceed the maximum ceiling temperatures specified in Table 5.4.1.5.2 for each of the sprinklers within the cabinet.

5.4.1.5.3 Where dry sprinklers of different lengths are installed, spare dry sprinklers shall not be required, provided that a means of returning the system to service is furnished.

N **Table 5.4.1.5.2 Temperature Ratings, Classifications, and Color Codings**

Maximum Ceiling Temperature		Temperature Rating		Temperature Classification	Color Code	Glass Bulb Colors
°F	°C	°F	°C			
100	38	135–170	57–77	Ordinary	Uncolored or black	Orange or red
150	66	175–225	79–107	Intermediate	White	Yellow or green
225	107	250–300	121–149	High	Blue	Blue
300	149	325–375	163–191	Extra high	Red	Purple
375	191	400–475	204–246	Very extra high	Green	Black
475	246	500–575	260–302	Ultra high	Orange	Black
625	329	650	343	Ultra high	Orange	Black

[13:Table 7.2.4.1]

5.4.1.5.4 The stock of spare sprinklers shall include all types and ratings installed and shall be as follows:

(1) For protected facilities having under 300 sprinklers — no fewer than 6 sprinklers
(2) For protected facilities having 300 to 1000 sprinklers — no fewer than 12 sprinklers
(3) For protected facilities having over 1000 sprinklers — no fewer than 24 sprinklers

5.4.1.5.5* One sprinkler wrench as specified by the sprinkler manufacturer shall be provided in the cabinet for each type of sprinkler installed to be used for the removal and installation of sprinklers in the system.

5.4.1.5.6 A list of the sprinklers installed in the property shall be posted in the sprinkler cabinet.

5.4.1.5.6.1* The list shall include the following:

(1) Sprinkler identification number (SIN) if equipped; or the manufacturer, model, orifice, deflector type, thermal sensitivity, and pressure rating
(2) General description
(3) Quantity of each type to be contained in the cabinet
(4) Issue or revision date of the list

5.4.1.6* Sprinklers shall not be altered in any respect or have any type of ornamentation, paint, or coatings applied after shipment from the place of manufacture.

5.4.1.7 Sprinklers and automatic spray nozzles used for protecting commercial-type cooking equipment and ventilating systems shall be replaced annually.

5.4.1.7.1 Where automatic bulb-type sprinklers or spray nozzles are used and annual examination shows no buildup of grease or other material on the sprinklers or spray nozzles, such sprinklers and spray nozzles shall not be required to be replaced.

N **5.4.1.8** Electrically operated sprinklers shall be maintained in accordance with the manufacturer's requirements.

5.4.1.9 Protective Coverings.

5.4.1.9.1* Sprinklers protecting spray areas and mixing rooms in resin application areas installed with protective coverings shall continue to be protected against overspray residue so that they will operate in the event of fire.

5.4.1.9.2 Sprinklers installed as described in 5.4.1.9.1 shall be protected using cellophane bags having a thickness of 0.003 in. (0.076 mm) or less or thin paper bags.

5.4.1.9.3 Coverings shall be replaced periodically so that heavy deposits of residue do not accumulate.

5.4.2* Dry Pipe Systems. Dry pipe systems shall be kept dry at all times.

5.4.2.1 During nonfreezing weather, a dry pipe system shall be permitted to be left wet if the only other option is to remove the system from service while waiting for parts or during repair activities.

5.4.2.2 Refrigerated spaces or other areas within the building interior where temperatures are maintained at or below 40°F (4°C) shall not be permitted to be left wet.

5.4.2.3 Air driers shall be maintained in accordance with the manufacturer's instructions.

5.4.2.4 Compressors used in conjunction with dry pipe sprinkler systems shall be inspected, tested, and maintained in accordance with Chapter 13 and the manufacturer's instructions.

5.4.3* Marine Systems. Sprinkler systems that are normally maintained using fresh water as a source shall be drained and refilled, then drained and refilled again with fresh water following the introduction of raw water into the system.

5.5 Component Action Requirements.

5.5.1 Whenever a component in a sprinkler system is adjusted, repaired, reconditioned, or replaced, the actions required in Table 5.5.1 shall be performed.

5.5.2 Where the original installation standard is different from the cited standard, the use of the appropriate installing standard shall be permitted.

5.5.3 These actions shall not require a design review, which is outside the scope of this standard.

Shaded text = Revisions.   Δ = Text deletions and figure/table revisions.   • = Section deletions.   N = New material.

2020 Edition

△ **Table 5.5.1 Summary of Component Action Requirements**

Component	Adjust	Repair/ Recondition	Replace	Required Action
Water Delivery Components				
Antifreeze solution	X		X	Inspect freezing point of solution Inspect for leaks at system working pressure
Fire department connections	X	X	X	See Chapter 13
Pipe and fittings affecting not more than 20 sprinklers	X	X	X	Inspect for leaks at system working pressure
Pipe and fittings affecting more than 20 sprinklers	X	X	X	Hydrostatic test in conformance with NFPA 13
Sprinklers, regardless of number	X		X	Inspect for leaks at system working pressure
Alarm and Supervisory Components				
Detection system (for deluge or preaction system)	X	X	X	Operational test for conformance with NFPA 13 and/or *NFPA 72*
High– and low– air pressure switch	X	X	X	Operational test of high and low settings
Pressure switch–type waterflow	X	X	X	Operational test using the inspector's test connection or alarm bypass test valve
Valve supervisory signal initiating device	X	X	X	Test for conformance with NFPA 13 and/or *NFPA 72*
Vane-type waterflow	X	X	X	Operational test using inspector's test connection
Water motor gong	X	X	X	Operational test using inspector's test connection
Testing and Maintenance Components				
Air compressor	X	X	X	Operational test for conformance with NFPA 13
Automatic air maintenance device	X	X	X	Operational test for conformance with NFPA 13
Auxiliary drains	X	X	X	Inspect for leaks at system working pressure; main drain test
Gauges	X		X	Verify at 0 bar (0 psi) and system working pressure
Inspector's test connection	X	X	X	Inspect for leaks at system working pressure; main drain test
Main drain	X	X	X	Main drain test
Structural Components				
Hanger/seismic bracing	X	X	X	Inspect for conformance with NFPA 13
Pipe stands	X	X	X	Inspect for conformance with NFPA 13
Informational Components				
Antifreeze information sign	X	X	X	Inspect for conformance with this standard
General information sign	X	X	X	Inspect for conformance with this standard
Hydraulic design information sign	X	X	X	Inspect for conformance with NFPA 13 and this standard
Identification sign	X	X	X	Inspect for conformance with NFPA 13 and this standard
Information sign	X	X	X	Inspect for conformance with this standard

Chapter 6   Standpipe and Hose Systems

6.1 General.

6.1.1 Minimum Requirements.

6.1.1.1 This chapter shall provide the minimum requirements for the routine inspection, testing, and maintenance of standpipe and hose systems.

6.1.1.2 Table 6.1.1.2 shall be used to determine the minimum required frequencies for inspection, testing, and maintenance.

6.1.2 Inspection, testing, and maintenance activities required by this chapter shall be followed to determine that components are free of corrosion, foreign material, physical damage, tampering, or other conditions that adversely affect system operation.

6.1.3 Common components and valves shall be inspected, tested, and maintained in accordance with Chapter 13.

6.1.4 The procedures outlined in Chapter 14 shall be followed where there is a need to conduct an obstruction investigation.

6.1.5 Where the inspection, testing, and maintenance of standpipe and hose systems results or involves a system that is out of service, the impairment procedures outlined in Chapter 15 shall be followed.

6.1.6 Where approved by the authority having jurisdiction, existing hose shall be permitted to be removed and shall not be recorded as a deficiency.

△ **Table 6.1.1.2 Summary of Standpipe and Hose Systems Inspection, Testing, and Maintenance**

Item	Frequency	Reference
Inspection		
Cabinet	Annually	6.2.8
Control valves		Chapter 13
Gauges		Chapter 13
Hose	Annually	6.2.5
Hose connection	Annually	6.2.3
Hose nozzle	Annually and after each use	6.2.6
Hose storage device	Annually	6.2.7
Hydraulic design information sign	Annually	6.2.2
Hose valves		Chapter 13
Piping	Annually	6.2.4
Pressure-regulating devices		Chapter 13
Supervisory devices (except valve supervisory devices)		Chapter 13
Valve supervisory devices		Chapter 13
Test		
Control valves		Chapter 13
System valves		Chapter 13
Flow test	5 years	6.3.1
Hose		NFPA 1962
Hose connection pressure regulating devices		Chapter 13
Hose valves		Chapter 13
Hydrostatic test	5 years	6.3.2
Main drain test		Chapter 13
Pressure control valve		Chapter 13
Pressure-reducing valve		Chapter 13
Supervisory signal devices (except valve supervisory switches)		Chapter 13
Valve status test		Chapter 13
Valve supervisory devices		Chapter 13
Waterflow alarm devices		Chapter 13
Maintenance		
Hose valves		Chapter 13
Pressure gauges		Chapter 13
Valves (all types)	Annually/as needed	Chapter 13

6.2 Inspection.

6.2.1 Components. Components of standpipe and hose systems shall be visually inspected annually or as specified in Table 6.1.1.2.

6.2.2* Hydraulic Design Information Sign. The hydraulic design information sign for standpipe systems shall be inspected annually to verify that it is provided, attached securely, and legible.

6.2.2.1 A hydraulic design information sign that is missing or illegible shall be replaced.

6.2.2.2 A standpipe system that was not sized by hydraulic design shall have a hydraulic design information sign that reads "Pipe Schedule System."

6.2.3 Hose Connections.

6.2.3.1 Hose connections shall be inspected annually for the following conditions:

(1) Valve cap(s) missing or damaged
(2) Fire hose connection damaged
(3) Valve handles missing or damaged
(4) Cap gaskets missing or deteriorated
(5) Valve leaking
(6) Visible and physical obstructions to hose connections
(7) Pressure restricting device missing
(8) Manual, semiautomatic, or dry standpipe valve does not operate smoothly
(9) Valve threads damaged

6.2.3.2 Where any deficiency is noted, the appropriate corrective action shall be taken.

6.2.4 Piping.

6.2.4.1 Piping shall be inspected annually for the following conditions:

(1) Damaged piping
(2) Damaged control valves

Shaded text = Revisions.   △ = Text deletions and figure/table revisions.   • = Section deletions.   *N* = New material.

2020 Edition

(3) Missing or damaged pipe support device (i.e., missing or damaged hanger or seismic brace)
(4) Damaged supervisory signal initiating device

6.2.4.2 Where any deficiency is noted, the appropriate corrective action shall be taken.

6.2.5 Hose.

6.2.5.1 Hose shall be inspected annually for the following conditions as required by NFPA 1962:

(1) Mildew, cuts, abrasions, and deterioration
(2) Couplings hose threads damaged
(3) Gaskets missing or deteriorated
(4) Incompatible threads on coupling
(5) Hose not connected to hose rack nipple or valve
(6) Hose test outdated

6.2.5.2 Where any deficiency is noted, the appropriate corrective action shall be taken.

6.2.6 Hose Nozzle.

6.2.6.1 Hose nozzles shall be inspected annually for the following conditions:

(1) Hose nozzle missing
(2) Gasket missing or deteriorated
(3) Obstructions
(4) Does not operate smoothly

6.2.6.2 Where any deficiency is noted, the appropriate corrective action shall be taken.

6.2.7 Hose Storage Device.

6.2.7.1 Hose storage devices shall be inspected annually for the following conditions:

(1) Difficult to operate
(2) Damaged
(3) Visible or physical obstruction
(4) Hose improperly racked or rolled
(5) Nozzle clip not in place and nozzle not correctly contained
(6) Hose rack enclosed in cabinet not swinging out at least 90 degrees

6.2.7.2 Where any deficiency is noted, the appropriate corrective action shall be taken.

6.2.8 Cabinet.

6.2.8.1 Cabinets shall be inspected annually for the following conditions:

(1) Overall for corroded or damaged parts
(2) Difficult to open
(3) Cabinet door not opening fully
(4) Door glazing cracked or broken
(5) Lock on break glass–type cabinet not functioning properly
(6) Glass break device missing or not attached
(7) Not properly identified as containing fire equipment
(8) Visible or physical obstructions
(9) All valves, hose, nozzles, fire extinguishers, and so forth, easily accessible

6.2.8.2 Where any deficiency is noted, the appropriate corrective action shall be taken.

6.3 Testing. Where water damage is a possibility, an air test shall be conducted on the system at 25 psi (1.7 bar) prior to introducing water to the system.

6.3.1 Flow Tests.

6.3.1.1* A flow test shall be conducted every 5 years on all automatic standpipe systems to verify that the required flow and pressure are available at the hydraulically most remote hose valve outlet(s) while flowing the standpipe system demand.

6.3.1.1.1 Where a flow test of the hydraulically most remote outlet(s) is not practical, the authority having jurisdiction shall be consulted for the appropriate location for the test.

6.3.1.1.2 Pressure gauges maintained in accordance with 8.3.3.5.2 shall be provided for the test.

6.3.1.2* Class I and Class III standpipe system demand shall include 500 gpm (1892 L/min) for the most remote standpipe and 250 gpm (946 L/min) for each additional standpipe until the total system demand is simultaneously flowing.

6.3.1.2.1* The 250 gpm (946 L/min) required from each additional Class I and Class III standpipe shall be allowed to be flowed from the most convenient hose valve on that standpipe.

6.3.1.2.2* Where the 250 gpm (946 L/min) cannot be flowed from each additional Class I and Class III standpipe, the authority having jurisdiction shall determine where the additional flow can be taken.

6.3.1.3 Class II standpipe system demand shall include 100 gpm (379 L/min) for the most remote standpipe connection.

6.3.1.4 The standpipe system demand shall be based on the design criteria in effect at the time of the installation.

6.3.1.4.1 Where the standpipe system demand cannot be determined, the authority having jurisdiction shall determine the standpipe system demand.

6.3.1.4.2 The actual test method(s) and performance criteria shall be discussed in advance with the authority having jurisdiction.

6.3.1.5 Standpipes, sprinkler connections to standpipes, or hose stations equipped with pressure-reducing valves or pressure-regulating valves shall have these valves inspected, tested, and maintained in accordance with the requirements of Chapter 13.

6.3.1.6 A main drain test shall be performed on all standpipe systems with automatic water supplies in accordance with the requirements of Chapter 13.

6.3.1.6.1 The test shall be performed at the low point drain for each standpipe or the main drain test connection where the supply main enters the building (when provided).

6.3.1.6.2 Pressure gauges maintained in accordance with Chapter 13 shall be provided for the test.

6.3.2 Hydrostatic Tests.

6.3.2.1* Hydrostatic tests of not less than 200 psi (13.8 bar) pressure for 2 hours, or at 50 psi (3.4 bar) in excess of the maximum pressure, where maximum pressure is in excess of 150 psi (10.3 bar), shall be conducted every 5 years on manual standpipe systems and semiautomatic dry standpipe systems, including piping in the fire department connection.

6.3.2.1.1 Manual wet standpipes that are part of a combined sprinkler/standpipe system shall not be required to be tested in accordance with 6.3.2.1.

6.3.2.2 The hydrostatic test pressure shall be measured at the low elevation point of the individual system or zone being tested.

6.3.2.2.1 The inside standpipe piping shall show no leakage.

6.3.3 Waterflow Alarm and Supervisory Alarm Devices.

6.3.3.1 Where provided, waterflow alarm and supervisory alarm devices shall be tested in accordance with 13.2.4 and 13.3.3.5.

6.3.3.2 Where freezing conditions necessitate a delay in testing, tests shall be performed as soon as weather allows.

6.4 Maintenance.

Δ **6.4.1** Maintenance and repairs shall be in accordance with 6.1.3 and Table 6.1.1.2.

6.4.2 Equipment that does not pass the inspection or testing requirements shall be repaired and tested again or replaced.

6.5 Component Action Requirements.

6.5.1 Whenever components in standpipe and hose systems are adjusted, repaired, reconditioned, or replaced, the actions required in Table 6.5.1 shall be performed.

6.5.2 Where the original installation standard is different from the cited standard, the use of the appropriate installing standard shall be permitted.

6.5.3 These actions shall not require a design review, which is outside the scope of this standard.

Δ **Table 6.5.1 Summary of Component Action Requirements**

Component	Adjust	Repair	Replace	Required Action
Water Delivery Components				
Backflow prevention device	X	X	X	See Chapter 13
Control valves	X	X	X	See Chapter 13
Fire department connections	X	X	X	See Chapter 13
Fire hose			X	No action required
Fire hose		X		Perform hydrostatic test in accordance with NFPA 1962
Hose valve	X	X	X	See Chapter 13
Hose valve pressure-regulating devices	X	X	X	See Chapter 13
Piping	X	X	X	Hydrostatic test in conformance with NFPA 14
System pressure-regulating devices	X	X	X	See Chapter 13
Alarm and Supervisory Components				
Pressure switch–type waterflow	X	X	X	Operational test using inspector's test connection
Valve supervisory device	X	X	X	Operational test for receipt of alarms and verification of conformance with NFPA 14 and/or *NFPA 72*
Vane-type waterflow	X	X	X	Operational test using inspector's test connection
Water motor gong	X	X	X	Operational test using inspector's test connection
Status-Indicating Components				
Gauges	X		X	Verify at 0 psi (0 bar) and system working pressure
System Housing and Protection Components				
Cabinet	X	X	X	Verify conformance with NFPA 14
Hose storage rack	X	X	X	Verify conformance with NFPA 14
Testing and Maintenance Components				
Auxiliary drains	X	X	X	Inspect for leaks at system working pressure
Drain riser	X	X	X	Inspect for leaks while flowing from connection above the repair
Main drain	X	X	X	Inspect for leaks and residual pressure during main drain test
Structural Components				
Hanger/seismic bracing	X	X	X	Verify conformance with NFPA 14
Pipe stands	X	X	X	Verify conformance with NFPA 14
Informational Components				
Hydraulic design information sign	X	X	X	Verify conformance with NFPA 14
Identification signs	X	X	X	Verify conformance with NFPA 14

Shaded text = Revisions.   Δ = Text deletions and figure/table revisions.   • = Section deletions.   *N* = New material.   2020 Edition

Chapter 7 Private Fire Service Mains

7.1 General.

7.1.1 Minimum Requirements.

7.1.1.1 This chapter shall provide the minimum requirements for the routine inspection, testing, and maintenance of private fire service mains and their appurtenances.

7.1.1.2 Table 7.1.1.2 shall be used to determine the minimum required frequencies for inspection, testing, and maintenance.

7.1.2 Common Components and Valves. Common components and valves shall be inspected, tested, and maintained in accordance with Chapter 13.

7.1.3 Obstruction Investigations. The procedures outlined in Chapter 14 shall be followed where there is a need to conduct an obstruction investigation.

7.1.4 Fire Hose. Fire hose shall be maintained in accordance with NFPA 1962.

7.1.5 Impairments. The procedures outlined in Chapter 15 shall be followed wherever such an impairment to protection occurs.

7.2 Inspection and Corrective Action.

7.2.1 General. Private fire service mains and their appurtenances shall be inspected at the intervals specified in Table 7.1.1.2.

7.2.2* Procedures. All procedures shall be carried out in accordance with the manufacturer's instructions, where applicable.

7.2.2.1 Exposed Piping.

7.2.2.1.1 Exposed piping shall be inspected annually.

7.2.2.1.2 Piping shall be inspected for the following conditions:

(1) Leaks
(2) Physical damage
(3) Corrosion
(4) Restraint methods

7.2.2.1.2.1 Where any deficiency is noted, the appropriate corrective action shall be taken.

7.2.2.1.3 Piping installed in areas that are inaccessible for safety considerations due to process operations shall be inspected during each scheduled shutdown.

Δ Table 7.1.1.2 Summary of Private Fire Service Main Inspection, Testing, and Maintenance

Item	Frequency	Reference
Inspection		
Backflow preventer		Chapter 13
Check valve		Chapter 13
Control valve		Chapter 13
Fire department connection		Chapter 13
Hose houses	Quarterly	7.2.2.8
Hydrants (dry barrel and wall)	Annually and after each operation	7.2.2.4
Hydrants (wet barrel)	Annually and after each operation	7.2.2.5
Mainline strainers	Annually and after each significant flow	7.2.2.3
Monitor nozzles	Semiannually	7.2.2.7
Pipe and fittings (exposed)	Annually	7.2.2.1
Valve supervisory devices		Chapter 13
Test		
Backflow preventer		Chapter 13
Control valve		Chapter 13
Hydrants	Flow, annually	7.3.2
Monitor nozzles	Flow, annually (range and operation)	7.3.3
Piping (exposed and underground) (flow test)	5 years	7.3.1
Valve status test		Chapter 13
Valve supervisory devices		Chapter 13
Maintenance		
Backflow preventer		Chapter 13
Check valve		Chapter 13
Control valve		Chapter 13
Hydrants	Annually	7.4.2
Mainline strainers	Annually and after each operation	7.2.2.3
Monitor nozzles	Annually	7.4.3

Shaded text = Revisions. **Δ** = Text deletions and figure/table revisions. • = Section deletions. *N* = New material.

7.2.2.2* Underground Piping.

7.2.2.3* Mainline Strainers.

7.2.2.3.1 Mainline strainers shall be inspected and cleaned after each system flow exceeding that of a nominal 2 in. (50 mm) orifice.

7.2.2.3.2 Mainline strainers shall be removed and inspected annually for plugging, fouling, and damaged and corroded parts.

7.2.2.4 Dry Barrel and Wall Hydrants. Dry barrel and wall hydrants shall be inspected annually and after each operation for the following conditions:

(1) Inaccessibility
(2) Presence of water or ice in barrel, which could indicate a faulty drain, a leaky hydrant valve, or high groundwater table)
(3) Improper drainage from barrel
(4) Leaks in outlets or at top of hydrant
(5) Cracks in hydrant barrel
(6) Tightness of outlet caps
(7) Worn outlet threads
(8) Worn hydrant operating nut
(9) Availability of operating wrench
(10) Corrosion detrimental to hydrant integrity

7.2.2.4.1 Where any deficiency is noted, the appropriate corrective action shall be taken.

7.2.2.5 Wet Barrel Hydrants. Wet barrel hydrants shall be inspected annually and after each operation for the following conditions:

(1) Inaccessibility
(2) Leaks in outlets or at top of hydrant
(3) Cracks in hydrant barrel
(4) Tightness of outlet caps
(5) Worn outlet threads
(6) Worn hydrant operating nut
(7) Availability of operating wrench
(8) Corrosion detrimental to hydrant integrity

7.2.2.5.1 Where any deficiency is noted, the appropriate corrective action shall be taken.

N 7.2.2.6* Dry Hydrants. Dry hydrants shall be inspected at least quarterly and maintained as necessary to keep them in good operating condition. [**1142,** 2017]

N 7.2.2.6.1 Thorough surveys shall be conducted, to reveal any deterioration in the water supply situation in ponds, streams, or cisterns. [**1142,** 2017]

N 7.2.2.6.2 Vegetation shall be cleared for a minimum 3 ft (0.9 m) radius from around hydrants. [**1142,** 2017]

N 7.2.2.6.3 The reflective material marking the hydrant and signage shall be inspected at least annually to verify that it is being maintained in accordance with 8.4.7 of NFPA 1142. [**1142,** 2017]

N 7.2.2.6.4 Hydrant risers shall be protected from ultraviolet (UV) degradation by painting or other measures. [**1142,** 2017]

N 7.2.2.6.5* The hydrants shall be flow tested at least annually with an approved pump to ensure that the minimum design flow is maintained. [**1142,** 2017]

7.2.2.7 Monitor Nozzles. Monitor nozzles shall be inspected semiannually for the following conditions:

(1) Leakage
(2) Physical damage
(3) Corrosion

7.2.2.7.1 Where any deficiency is noted, the appropriate corrective action shall be taken.

7.2.2.8 Hose Houses. Hose houses shall be inspected quarterly for the following conditions:

(1) Inaccessibility
(2) Physical damage
(3) Missing equipment

7.2.2.8.1 Where any deficiency is noted, the appropriate corrective action shall be taken.

7.3 Testing.

7.3.1* Underground and Exposed Piping Flow Tests. Underground and exposed piping shall be flow tested at minimum 5-year intervals.

7.3.1.1 Any flow test results that indicate deterioration of available waterflow and pressure shall be investigated to the complete satisfaction of the authority having jurisdiction to ensure that the required flow and pressure are available for fire protection.

7.3.1.2 Where underground piping supplies individual fire sprinkler, standpipe, water spray, or foam-water sprinkler systems and there are no means to conduct full flow tests, tests generating the maximum available flows shall be permitted.

7.3.2 Hydrants. Hydrants shall be tested annually to ensure proper functioning.

7.3.2.1 Each hydrant shall be opened fully and water flowed until all foreign material has cleared.

7.3.2.2 Flow shall be maintained for not less than 1 minute.

7.3.2.3 After operation, dry barrel and wall hydrants shall be observed for proper drainage from the barrel.

7.3.2.4 Full drainage shall take no longer than 60 minutes.

7.3.2.5 Where soil conditions or other factors are such that the hydrant barrel does not drain within 60 minutes, or where the groundwater level is above that of the hydrant drain, the hydrant drain shall be plugged and the water in the barrel shall be pumped out.

7.3.2.6 Dry barrel hydrants that are located in areas subject to freezing weather and that have plugged drains shall be identified clearly as needing pumping after operation.

7.3.3 Monitor Nozzles.

7.3.3.1 Monitor nozzles that are mounted on hydrants shall be tested as specified in 7.3.2.

7.3.3.2 All monitor nozzles shall be oscillated and moved throughout their full range annually to ensure proper operability.

Shaded text = Revisions.   Δ = Text deletions and figure/table revisions.   • = Section deletions.   N = New material.

2020 Edition

7.4 Maintenance.

7.4.1 General. All equipment shall be maintained in proper working condition, consistent with the manufacturer's recommendations.

7.4.2 Hydrants.

7.4.2.1 Hydrants shall be lubricated annually to ensure that all stems, caps, plugs, and threads are in proper operating condition.

7.4.2.2* Hydrants shall be kept free of snow, ice, or other materials and protected against mechanical damage so that free access is ensured.

7.4.3 Monitor Nozzles. Monitor nozzles shall be lubricated annually to ensure proper operating condition.

7.5 Component Action Requirements.

7.5.1 Whenever a component in a private fire service system is adjusted, repaired, reconditioned, or replaced, the action required in Table 7.5.1 shall be performed.

7.5.2 Where the original installation standard is different from the cited standard, the use of the appropriate installing standard shall be permitted.

7.5.3* Where a main drain is not provided, other equivalent means of flow testing shall be permitted.

7.5.4 The actions of 7.5.1 shall not require a design review, which is outside the scope of this standard.

Δ **Table 7.5.1 Summary of Component Action Requirements**

Component	Adjust	Repair/ Recondition	Replace	Test Criteria
Water Delivery Components				
Pipe and fittings (exposed and underground)	X	X	X	Hydrostatic test in conformance with NFPA 24 Flush in conformance with NFPA 24 or NFPA 20, as appropriate
Hydrants	X	X	X	Hydrostatic test in conformance with NFPA 24 Waterflow in conformance with NFPA 24 Inspect for proper drainage
Monitor nozzles	X	X	X	Flow test to confirm required coverage
Mainline strainers	X	X	X	Flow test downstream of strainer
Fire department connection	X	X	X	See Chapter 13
Alarm and Supervisory Components				
Valve supervisory device	X	X	X	Operational test for conformance with NFPA 24 and/or *NFPA 72*
System-Indicating Components				
Gauges			X	Verify at 0 psi (0 bar) and system working pressure
System Housing and Protection Components				
Hose houses	X	X	X	Verify integrity of hose house and hose house components
Hose		X		Repair and test hose in accordance with NFPA 1962
Hose			X	No action required
Structural Components				
Thrust blocks	X	X	X	Test at system working pressure
Tie rods	X	X	X	Test at system working pressure
Retainer glands	X	X	X	Test at system working pressure
Informational Components				
Identification signs	X	X	X	Verify conformance with NFPA 24

Shaded text = Revisions.   Δ = Text deletions and figure/table revisions.   • = Section deletions.   *N* = New material.

Chapter 8 Fire Pumps

8.1* General.

8.1.1 Minimum Requirements.

8.1.1.1 This chapter shall provide the minimum requirements for the routine inspection, testing, and maintenance of fire pump assemblies.

8.1.1.2* The minimum frequency of inspection, testing, and maintenance shall be in accordance with the manufacturer's recommendations and Table 8.1.1.2.

8.1.1.2.1* Shaft movement or end play shall be inspected annually with the pump operating.

Δ **8.1.1.2.2 Electrical Connections.**

N **8.1.1.2.2.1*** Electrical connections shall be inspected annually and repaired as necessary to the extent that such work can be completed without opening an energized electric-motor-driven fire pump controller.

N **8.1.1.2.2.2*** The isolating switch in the fire pump controller that is located in a separate compartment from the other controller components shall be permitted to be used to meet the requirement of 8.1.1.2.2.1.

8.1.1.2.3 Pump and motor bearings and couplings shall be greased annually or as required.

Δ **8.1.1.2.4 Printed Circuit Boards.**

N **8.1.1.2.4.1** Printed circuit boards (PCBs) shall be inspected annually for corrosion to the extent that such work can be completed without opening an energized electric-motor-driven fire pump controller. *(See A.8.1.1.2.2.2.)*

N **8.1.1.2.4.2** The isolating switch in the fire pump controller that is located in a separate compartment from the other controller components shall be permitted to be used to meet the requirement of 8.1.1.2.4.1. *(See A.8.1.1.2.2.1.)*

Δ **8.1.1.2.5 Cable and Wire Insulation.**

N **8.1.1.2.5.1** Cable and/or wire insulation shall be inspected annually for cracking to the extent that such work can be completed without opening an energized electric-motor-driven fire pump controller. *(See A.8.1.1.2.2.2.)*

N **8.1.1.2.5.2** The isolating switch in the fire pump controller that is located in a separate compartment from the other controller components shall be permitted to be used to meet the requirement of 8.1.1.2.5.1. *(See A.8.1.1.2.2.1.)*

Δ **8.1.1.2.6 Plumbing.**

N **8.1.1.2.6.1** Plumbing parts, both inside and outside of electrical panels, shall be inspected annually for any leaks to the extent that such work can be completed without opening an energized electric-motor-driven fire pump controller. *(See A.8.1.1.2.2.2.)*

N **8.1.1.2.6.2** The isolating switch in the fire pump controller that is located in a separate compartment from the other controller components shall be permitted to be used to meet the requirement of 8.1.1.2.6.1. *(See A.8.1.1.2.2.1.)*

8.1.1.2.7 Fuel tanks, float switches, and supervisory signals for interstitial space shall be tested quarterly for liquid intrusion.

8.1.1.2.8 Supervisory signal circuitry shall be tested annually for high cooling water temperature.

8.1.1.2.9 Fuel tanks shall be tested annually for water and foreign materials.

8.1.1.2.10 Fuel tank vents and overflow piping shall be inspected annually for any obstructions.

8.1.1.2.11 All flexible hoses and connections shall be inspected annually for cracks and leaks.

8.1.1.2.12 Engine crankcase breathers shall be inspected quarterly.

8.1.1.2.13 Exhaust systems, drain condensate traps, and silencers shall be inspected annually.

8.1.1.2.14 Back pressure on the engine turbos shall be measured annually.

Δ **8.1.1.2.15** Batteries shall be checked annually as follows:

(1) Test the specific gravity, state of charge, and charger rates of the batteries
(2) Clean the terminals of any corrosion
(3) Ensure that the cranking voltage exceeds 9 V on a 12 V system or 18 V on a 24 V system
(4) Ensure that only distilled water is used in batteries

Δ **8.1.1.2.16 Inspections of Controls and Power Wire Connections.**

N **8.1.1.2.16.1** All controls and power wiring connections shall be inspected annually and repaired as necessary to the extent that such work can be completed without opening an energized electric-motor-driven fire pump controller. *(See A.8.1.1.2.2.2.)*

N **8.1.1.2.16.2** The isolating switch in the fire pump controller that is located in a separate compartment from the other controller components shall be permitted to be used to meet the requirement of 8.1.1.2.16.1. *(See A.8.1.1.2.2.1.)*

8.1.1.2.17 Lubricating oil in engines shall be changed every 50 hours of operation or annually.

8.1.1.2.18 Lubricating oil filters shall be changed every 50 hours of operation or annually.

N **8.1.1.2.19** Fuel filter(s) shall be changed as needed, but at a minimum every 50 hours of operation or annually.

8.1.1.2.20 The condition of sacrificial anodes shall be inspected annually and replaced as necessary.

8.1.1.2.21 Circulating water filters shall be replaced annually.

8.1.1.2.22 The accuracy of pressure gauges and sensors shall be inspected annually and replaced or recalibrated when more than 5 percent out of calibration to the extent that such work can be completed without opening an energized electric-motor-driven fire pump controller. *(See A.8.1.1.2.2.2.)*

N **8.1.1.2.22.1** The isolating switch in the fire pump controller that is located in a separate compartment from the other controller components shall be permitted to be used to meet the requirement of 8.1.1.2.22. *(See A.8.1.1.2.2.1.)*

N **8.1.1.2.22.2** If replacement or recalibration is required, proper personal protective equipment in accordance with NFPA *70E* or an approved equivalent shall be used.

Δ **Table 8.1.1.2 Summary of Fire Pump Inspection, Testing, and Maintenance**

Item	Frequency	Reference
Inspection		
Alignment	Annually	8.3.6.4
Cable/wire insulation	Annually	8.1.1.2.5
Diesel engine system	Weekly	8.2.2(4)
Electric system	Weekly	8.2.2(3)
Engine crankcase breather	Quarterly	8.1.1.2.12
Exhaust system, drain condensate trap, and silencers	Annually	8.1.1.2.13
Flexible hoses and connections	Annually	8.1.1.2.11
Fuel tank vents and overflow	Annually	8.1.1.2.10
Plumbing parts — inside and outside of panels	Annually	8.1.1.2.6
Printed circuit board (PCB) corrosion	Annually	8.1.1.2.4
Pump	Weekly	8.2.2(2)
Pump house/room	Weekly	8.2.2(1)
Shaft movement or endplay while running	Annually	8.1.1.2.1
Steam pump system	Weekly	8.2.2(5)
Suction screens	Annually	8.3.3.15
Test		
Automatic transfer switch	Annually	8.3.3.12
Automatic transfer switch and emergency/standby generators	Per NFPA 110	8.3.6.1, 8.3.6.2
Diesel engine–driven fire pump (no flow)	Weekly	8.3.1.1
Diesel fuel testing	Annually	8.3.4.1
Electric motor–driven fire pump (no flow)	Weekly/monthly	8.3.1.2
Electronic control module (ECM)	Annually	8.3.3.16
Fire pump alarm signals	Annually	8.3.3.13
Flow meters	Annually	8.3.3.5.3
Fuel tank, float switch, and supervisory signal for interstitial space	Quarterly	8.1.1.2.7
Gauges, transducers, and other devices used for testing	Annually	8.3.3.5.2
Main pressure relief valve	Annually	8.3.3.11, 13.5.6.2.3
Pump house/room environmental conditions		8.3.6.3
Pump operation (no flow)	Weekly/monthly	8.3.2, 8.3.5
Pump performance (flow)	Annually	8.3.3, 8.3.5
Supervisory signal for high cooling water temperature	Annually	8.1.1.2.8
Maintenance		
Batteries	Annually	8.1.1.2.15
Circulating water filter	Annually	8.1.1.2.21
Control and power wiring connections	Annually	8.1.1.2 16
Controller and all other components of the pump assembly	Per manufacturer	8.5
Diesel active fuel maintenance system	Annually or per manufacturer	8.3.4.3
Diesel engine system	Per manufacturer	8.5
Electric motor and power system	Per manufacturer	8.5
Electrical connections	Annually	8.1.1.2.2
Engine lubricating oil	50 operating hours or annually	8.1.1.2.17
Engine oil filter	50 operating hours or annually	8.1.1.2.18
Fuel filter	50 operating hours or annually	8.1.1.2.19
Fuel tank — check for water and foreign materials	Annually	8.1.1.2.9
Measure back pressure on engine turbo	Annually	8.1.1.2.14
Power transmission components with elastomeric materials (including torsional couplings)	5 years or per manufacturer	8.1.1.2.23
Pressure gauges and sensors	Annually	8.1.1.2.22
Pump and motor bearings and coupling	Annually or as required	8.1.1.2.3
Sacrificial anode	Annually	8.1.1.2.20

Shaded text = Revisions.   Δ = Text deletions and figure/table revisions.   • = Section deletions.   *N* = New material.

N **8.1.1.2.23** Power transmitting components used in pump drives that include elastomeric materials, such as torsional couplings, shall be replaced every 5 years or as required by the component manufacturer for a specific elastomeric material.

8.1.2 Common Components and Valves. Common components and valves shall be inspected, tested, and maintained in accordance with Chapter 13.

8.1.3 Obstruction Investigations. The procedures outlined in Chapter 14 shall be followed where there is a need to conduct an obstruction investigation.

8.1.4* Auxiliary Equipment. The pump assembly auxiliary equipment shall include the following:

(1) Pump accessories as follows:

    (a) Pump shaft coupling
    (b) Automatic air release valve
    (c) Pressure gauges
    (d) Circulation relief valve (not used in conjunction with diesel engine drive with heat exchanger)

(2) Pump test device(s)
(3) Pump relief valve and piping (where maximum pump discharge pressure exceeds the rating of the system components or the driver is of variable speed)
(4) Alarm sensors and indicators
(5) Right-angle gear sets (for engine-driven vertical shaft turbine pumps)
(6) Pressure maintenance (jockey) pump and accessories

8.1.5 Water Supply to Pump Suction.

8.1.5.1 The suction supply for the fire pump shall provide the required flow at or above the lowest permissible suction pressure to meet the system demand.

8.1.5.2 Those installations for which NFPA 20 permitted negative suction gauge pressures at the time of pump installation, where the system demand still can be met by the pump and water supply, shall be considered to be in compliance with 8.1.5.

8.1.6 Energy Source. The energy sources for the pump driver shall supply the necessary brake horsepower of the driver so that the pump meets system demand.

8.1.7 Driver. The pump driver shall not overload beyond its rating (including any service factor allowance) when delivering the necessary brake horsepower.

8.1.8* Controller. Automatic and manual controllers for applying the energy source to the driver shall be capable of providing this operation for the type of pump used.

8.1.9 Impairments. The procedures outlined in Chapter 15 shall be followed where an impairment to protection occurs.

8.2 Inspection.

8.2.1 The purpose of inspection shall be to verify that the pump assembly appears to be in operating condition and is free from physical damage.

8.2.2* The pertinent visual observations specified in the following checklists shall be performed weekly:

(1) Pump house conditions are determined as follows:

    (a) Heat is adequate, not less than 40°F (4°C) for pump room with electric motor or diesel engine–driven pumps with engine heaters.
    (b) Heat is adequate, not less than 70°F (21°C) for pump room with diesel engine–driven pumps without engine heaters.
    (c) Ventilating louvers are free to operate.
    (d) Excessive water does not collect on the floor.
    (e) Coupling guard is in place.

(2) Pump system conditions are determined as follows:

    (a) Pump suction and discharge and bypass valves are fully open.
    (b) Piping is free of leaks.
    (c) Suction line pressure gauge reading is within acceptable range.
    (d) System line pressure gauge reading is within acceptable range.
    (e) Suction reservoir has the required water level.
    (f) Wet pit suction screens are unobstructed and in place.
    (g) Waterflow test valves are in the closed position, the hose connection valve is closed, and the line to test valves is free of water.

(3) Electrical system conditions are determined as follows:

    (a) Controller pilot light (power on) is illuminated.
    (b) Transfer switch normal pilot light is illuminated.
    (c) Isolating switch is closed — standby (emergency) source.
    (d) Reverse phase alarm pilot light is off, or normal phase rotation pilot light is on.
    (e) Oil level in vertical motor sight glass is within acceptable range.
    (f) Power to pressure maintenance (jockey) pump is provided.

(4) Diesel engine system conditions are determined as follows:

    (a) Fuel tank is at least two-thirds full.
    (b) Controller selector switch is in auto position.
    (c) Batteries' (2) voltage readings are within acceptable range.
    (d) Batteries' (2) charging current readings are within acceptable range.
    (e) Batteries' (2) pilot lights are on or battery failure (2) pilot lights are off.
    (f) All alarm pilot lights are off.
    (g) Engine running time meter is reading.
    (h) Oil level in right angle gear drive is within acceptable range.
    (i) Crankcase oil level is within acceptable range.
    (j) Cooling water level is within acceptable range.
    (k) Electrolyte level in batteries is within acceptable range.
    (l) Battery terminals are free from corrosion.
    (m) Water-jacket heater is operating.

(5)* Steam system conditions: Steam pressure gauge reading is within acceptable range.

8.3* Testing.

8.3.1 Frequency.

8.3.1.1* A no-flow test shall be conducted for diesel engine–driven fire pumps on a test frequency in accordance with 8.3.1.1.1 or 8.3.1.1.2.

8.3.1.1.1 Except as permitted in 8.3.1.1.2, a weekly test frequency shall be required.

8.3.1.1.2* The test frequency shall be permitted to be established by an approved risk analysis.

8.3.1.2* A no-flow test shall be conducted for electric motor–driven fire pumps on a test frequency in accordance with 8.3.1.2.1, 8.3.1.2.2, 8.3.1.2.3, or 8.3.1.2.4.

8.3.1.2.1 Except as permitted in 8.3.1.2.2 and 8.3.1.2.3, a weekly test frequency shall be required for the following electric fire pumps:

(1) Fire pumps that serve fire protection systems in buildings that are beyond the pumping capacity of the fire department
(2) Fire pumps with limited service controllers
(3) Vertical turbine fire pumps
(4) Fire pumps taking suction from ground level tanks or a water source that does not provide sufficient pressure to be of material value without the pump

8.3.1.2.2 A monthly test frequency shall be permitted for electric fire pumps not identified in 8.3.1.2.1.

8.3.1.2.3* A monthly test frequency shall be permitted for electric fire pump systems having a redundant fire pump.

8.3.1.2.4* The test frequency shall be permitted to be established by an approved risk analysis.

8.3.1.3 An annual flow test shall be conducted in accordance with 8.3.3.

8.3.2 No-Flow Test.

8.3.2.1 A no-flow test of fire pump assemblies shall be conducted in accordance with 8.3.2.

8.3.2.1.1 Except as permitted in 8.3.2.1.2 and 8.3.2.1.3, a main pressure relief valve (where installed) shall be permitted to weep but not discharge a significant quantity of water.

8.3.2.1.1.1 Except as required in 8.3.2.1.1.2, the circulation relief valve shall discharge a small flow of water.

8.3.2.1.1.2 The circulation relief valve shall not operate when the flow through the main pressure relief valve is greater than weeping.

8.3.2.1.2 For fire pump installations that were installed under a standard (1993 and earlier editions of NFPA 20) that did not prohibit a design that required operation of a pressure relief valve to keep the discharge pressure below the rating of the system components, the pressure relief valve shall be permitted to operate as designed during a no-flow test.

8.3.2.1.2.1* The pressure readings on the discharge and suction gauges shall be recorded, and a pressure difference that is greater than 95 percent of the rated pump pressure shall be investigated and corrected.

8.3.2.1.2.2* The discharge temperature of the water shall be monitored and the pump shut down if necessary to prevent exposing the pump and/or driver to excessive temperatures.

8.3.2.1.3 For positive displacement pumps, the pressure relief valve shall operate during a no-flow test.

8.3.2.1.3.1 Where the pressure relief valve is piped back to suction, the pump circulation relief valve shall not operate.

8.3.2.1.3.2 On electric motor and radiator cooled engine drives, a circulation pressure relief valve located downstream of the main pressure relief valve shall discharge sufficient water to prevent overheating of the pump.

8.3.2.2 The test shall be conducted by starting the pump automatically.

8.3.2.3 The electric pump shall run a minimum of 10 minutes.

8.3.2.4 The diesel pump shall run a minimum of 30 minutes.

8.3.2.5 A valve installed to open as a safety feature shall be permitted to discharge water.

8.3.2.6 An automatic timer that meets 8.3.2.6.1 through 8.3.2.6.3 shall be permitted to be substituted for the starting procedure.

8.3.2.6.1 A solenoid valve drain on the pressure control line shall be the initiating means for a pressure-actuated controller.

8.3.2.6.2 In a pressure-actuated controller, performance of this program timer shall be recorded as a pressure drop indication on the pressure recorder.

8.3.2.6.3 In a non-pressure-actuated controller, the test shall be permitted to be initiated by means other than a solenoid valve.

8.3.2.7 Qualified personnel shall be in attendance whenever the pump is in operation unless automated inspection and testing is performed in accordance with 8.3.2.10 including the provision for automated engine shutdown indicated in 8.3.2.10.3 for diesel engine drives.

8.3.2.7.1* The use of the automatic timer allowed in 8.3.2.6 shall not eliminate the requirement of 8.3.2.7 to have qualified personnel present during the test.

Δ 8.3.2.8 The pertinent visual observations or adjustments specified in the following checklists shall be conducted while the pump is idle:

(1) Record the system suction and discharge pressure gauge readings
(2) For pumps that use electronic pressure sensors to control the fire pump operation, record the current pressure and the highest and the lowest pressure shown on the fire pump controller event log where such information is available without having to open an energized electric motor–driven fire pump controller
(3) If the highest or lowest pressure is outside of the expected range, record all information from the event log that helps identify the abnormality

8.3.2.9* The pertinent visual observations or adjustments specified in the following checklists shall be conducted while the pump is running:

(1) Pump system procedure is as follows:

  (a) Record the pump starting pressure from the pressure switch or pressure transducer.
  (b) Record the system suction and discharge pressure gauge readings.
  (c) Inspect the pump packing glands for slight discharge.
  (d) Adjust gland nuts if necessary.
  (e) Inspect for unusual noise or vibration.

(f) Inspect packing boxes, bearings, or pump casing for overheating.

(g) Record pressure switch or pressure transducer reading and compare to the pump discharge gauge.

(h) For pumps that use electronic pressure sensors to control the fire pump operation, record the current pressure and the highest and the lowest pressure shown on the fire pump controller event log.

(i) For electric motor and radiator cooled diesel pumps, check the circulation relief valve for operation to discharge water.

(2) Electrical system procedure is as follows:

(a) Observe the time for motor to accelerate to full speed.

(b) Record the time controller is on first step (for reduced voltage or reduced current starting).

(c) Record the time pump runs after starting (for automatic stop controllers).

(3) Diesel engine system procedure is as follows:

(a) Observe the time for engine to crank.

(b) Observe the time for engine to reach running speed.

(c) Observe the engine oil pressure gauge, speed indicator, water, and oil temperature indicators periodically while engine is running.

(d) Record any abnormalities.

(e) Inspect the heat exchanger for cooling waterflow.

(4) Steam system procedure is as follows:

(a) Record the steam pressure gauge reading.

(b) Observe the time for turbine to reach running speed.

N 8.3.2.10 Remotely Monitored Automated Testing.

N 8.3.2.10.1 Remotely monitored automated testing performed in accordance with 4.6.6 shall be permitted for the no-flow test.

N 8.3.2.10.2 All of the pertinent observations or adjustments specified in the checklists described in 8.3.2.8 and 8.3.2.9 shall be performed.

N 8.3.2.10.2.1 Any abnormalities shall be recorded.

N 8.3.2.10.2.2 If, during the automated test, it becomes apparent that the packing gland nuts need to be adjusted as described in 8.3.2.9(1)(d), the need for adjustment shall be recorded and the necessary adjustment shall be made by qualified personnel.

N 8.3.2.10.3 The controller for a diesel engine–driven fire pump shall be equipped with automatic engine shutdown as referenced in 12.7.2.7 of NFPA 20.

N 8.3.2.10.4 Qualified personnel shall be able to respond to the pump location upon abnormal condition within 5 minutes.

8.3.3 Annual Flow Testing.

8.3.3.1* Except as permitted in 8.3.3.4, an annual test of each constant speed pump assembly shall be conducted by qualified personnel under no-flow (churn), rated flow, and 150 percent of the pump rated capacity flow of the fire pump by controlling the quantity of water discharged through approved test devices.

N 8.3.3.2* Except as permitted in 8.3.3.4, an annual test of each variable-speed pump assembly shall be conducted by qualified personnel under variable-speed control under no-flow (churn),

25 percent, 50 percent, 75 percent, 100 percent, 125 percent, and 150 percent of the rated pump capacity flow of the fire pump by controlling the quantity of water discharge through approved test devices.

N 8.3.3.3 Except as permitted in 8.3.3.4, an annual test of each variable speed pump assembly shall be conducted by qualified personnel under constant speed control under no-flow (churn), 100 percent rate, and 150 percent of the pump rated capacity flow of the fire pump by controlling the quantity of water discharged through approved test devices.

N 8.3.3.4 If available suction supplies do not allow flowing of 150 percent of the rated pump capacity, the fire pump shall be tested at flow rates at 100 percent of the rated pump flow rate, and at the maximum flow allowed at the lowest permissible suction pressure.

8.3.3.5 Test Equipment. Calibrated test equipment shall be provided to determine net pump pressures, rate of flow through the pump, and speed.

Δ 8.3.3.5.1 Gauges, transducers, and other devices used for measurement during the test shall bear a label with the latest date of calibration.

8.3.3.5.2 Gauges, transducers, and other devices, with the exception of flow meters, used for measurement during the test shall be calibrated a minimum of annually to an accuracy level of ±1 percent.

8.3.3.5.3* Flow meters shall be calibrated annually to an accuracy level of ±3 percent.

8.3.3.6 Discharge and sensing orifices that can be visually observed without disassembling equipment, piping, or valves shall be visually inspected and be free of damage and obstructions that could affect the accuracy of the measurement.

8.3.3.7 The sensing/measuring elements in a flow meter shall be calibrated in accordance with 8.3.3.5.

8.3.3.8 Discharge orifices shall be listed or constructed to a recognized standard with a known discharge coefficient.

8.3.3.9 The annual test shall be conducted as follows:

(1) The arrangement described in 8.3.3.9.1 or 8.3.3.9.2 shall be used at a minimum of every third year.

(2)* The arrangement described in 8.3.3.9.3 shall be permitted to be used 2 out of every 3 years.

8.3.3.9.1 Use of Pump Discharge via Hose Streams.

8.3.3.9.1.1 Pump suction and discharge pressures and the flow measurements of each hose stream shall determine the total pump output.

8.3.3.9.1.2* Prior to flow testing, the entity performing testing shall make the owner or their representative aware of the location, approximate flow rate, and duration of flow testing.

8.3.3.9.2 Use of Pump Discharge via Bypass Flowmeter to Drain or Suction Reservoir. Pump suction and discharge pressures and the flowmeter measurements shall determine the total pump output.

8.3.3.9.3 Use of Pump Discharge via Bypass Flowmeter to Pump Suction (Closed-Loop Metering).

8.3.3.9.3.1 Pump suction and discharge pressures and the flowmeter measurements shall determine the total pump output.

8.3.3.9.3.2 When testing includes recirculating water back to the fire pump suction, the temperature of the recirculating water shall be monitored to verify that it remains below temperatures that could result in equipment damage as defined by the pump and engine manufacturers.

8.3.3.9.3.3 If the test results are not consistent with the previous annual test, the test shall be repeated using the test arrangement described in 8.3.3.9.1.

8.3.3.9.3.4 If testing in accordance with 8.3.3.9.1 is not possible, a flowmeter calibration shall be performed and the test shall be repeated.

Δ **8.3.3.10** The pertinent visual observations, measurements, and adjustments specified in the following checklists shall be conducted annually while the pump is running and flowing water under the specified output condition:

(1) At no-flow condition (churn), the procedure is as follows:

    (a) Inspect the circulation relief valve for operation to discharge water

    (b) Inspect the pressure relief valve (if installed) for proper operation

(2) At each flow condition, the procedure is as follows:

    (a) Where an external means is provided on the controller, record the electric motor voltage and current (all lines)

    (b) Record the pump speed in rpm

    (c) Record the simultaneous (approximate) readings of pump suction and discharge pressures and pump discharge flow

(3)* For electric motor–driven pumps, do not shut down the pump until it has run for 10 minutes

(4) For diesel motor–driven pumps, do not shut down the pump until it has run for 30 minutes

8.3.3.11* For installations having a pressure relief valve, the operation of the relief valve shall be closely observed during each flow condition to determine whether the pump discharge pressure exceeds the normal operating pressure of the system components.

8.3.3.11.1* The pressure relief valve shall also be observed during each flow condition to determine whether the pressure relief valve closes at the proper pressure.

8.3.3.11.2 The pressure relief valve shall be closed during flow conditions if necessary to achieve minimum rated characteristics for the pump and reset to normal position at the conclusion of the pump test.

8.3.3.11.2.1 When it is necessary to close the relief valve to achieve minimum rated characteristics for the pump, the pump discharge control valve shall be closed if the pump churn pressure exceeds the system rated pressure.

8.3.3.11.3 When pressure relief valves are piped back to the fire pump suction, the temperature of the recirculating water shall be monitored to verify that it remains below temperatures

that could result in equipment damage as defined by the pump and engine manufacturers.

Δ **8.3.3.12** For installations having an automatic transfer switch, the following test shall be performed to ensure that the over-current protective devices (i.e., fuses or circuit breakers) do not open:

(1) Simulate a power failure condition while the pump is operating at peak load

(2) Verify that the transfer switch transfers power to the alternate power source

(3) While the pump is operating at peak load and alternate power, record the following to include in the pump test results:

    (a) The voltage where an external means is provided on the controller

    (b) The amperage where an external means is provided on the controller

    (c) The rpm

    (d) Suction pressure

    (e) Discharge pressure

(4) Verify that the pump continues to perform at peak horse-power load on the alternate power source for a minimum of 2 minutes

(5) Remove the power failure condition and verify that, after a time delay, the pump is reconnected to the normal power source

8.3.3.13* Alarm conditions shall be simulated by activating alarm circuits at alarm sensor locations and confirmed for proper operation.

8.3.3.13.1* Alarm sensors located within electric motor–driven fire pump controllers that cannot be accessed without opening an energized electric motor–driven fire pump controller shall be tested at an alternative location outside of the controller.

8.3.3.14 Safety. *(See also A.4.9.6.)*

8.3.3.14.1 Section 4.9 shall be followed for safety requirements while working near electric motor–driven fire pumps.

8.3.3.15* **Suction Screens.** After the waterflow portions of the annual test or fire protection system activations, the suction screens shall be inspected and cleared of any debris or obstructions.

8.3.3.16* Where engines utilize electronic fuel management control systems, the backup electronic control module (ECM) and the primary and redundant sensors for the ECM shall be tested annually.

8.3.4 Diesel Fuel Testing and Maintenance.

8.3.4.1 Diesel fuel shall be tested for degradation no less than annually.

8.3.4.1.1* Fuel degradation testing shall comply with ASTM D975, *Standard Specification for Diesel Fuel Oils,* or ASTM D6751, *Standard Specification for Biodiesel Fuel Blend Stock (B100) for Middle Distillate Fuels,* as approved by the engine manufacturer, using ASTM D7462, *Standard Test Method for Oxidation Stability of Biodiesel (B100) and Blends of Biodiesel with Middle Distillate Petroleum Fuel (Accelerated Method).*

8.3.4.2* If diesel fuel is found to be deficient in the testing required in 8.3.4.1.1, the fuel shall be reconditioned or replaced, the supply tank shall be cleaned internally, and the engine fuel filter(s) shall be changed.

8.3.4.2.1 After the restoration of the fuel and tank in 8.3.4.2, the fuel shall be retested every 6 months until experience indicates the fuel can be stored for a minimum of 1 year without degradation beyond that allowed in 8.3.4.1.1.

8.3.4.3 When provided, active fuel maintenance systems shall be listed for fire pump service.

8.3.4.3.1 Maintenance of active fuel maintenance systems shall be in accordance with the manufacturer's recommendations.

8.3.4.3.2 Maintenance of active fuel maintenance systems shall be performed at a minimum annual frequency for any portion of the system that the manufacturer does not provide a recommended maintenance frequency.

8.3.4.3.3 Where utilized, fuel additives shall be used and maintained in accordance with the active fuel maintenance system manufacturer's recommendations.

8.3.5 Positive Displacement Pumps. [20:14.2.6.4.3]

8.3.5.1 Except as provided in 8.3.5.1 through 8.3.5.7, positive displacement pumps shall be tested in accordance with 8.3.1 through 8.3.3.

8.3.5.2 The pump flow for positive displacement pumps shall be tested and determined to meet the specified rated performance criteria where only one performance point is required to establish positive displacement pump acceptability. [**20**:14.2.6.4.3.1]

8.3.5.3 The pump flow test for positive displacement pumps shall be accomplished using a flowmeter or orifice plate installed in a test loop back to the supply tank, to the inlet side of a positive displacement water pump, or to drain. [**20**:14.2.6.4.3.2]

8.3.5.4 The flowmeter reading or discharge pressure shall be recorded and shall be in accordance with the pump manufacturer's flow performance data. [**20**:14.2.6.4.3.3]

8.3.5.5 If orifice plates are used, the orifice size and corresponding discharge pressure to be maintained on the upstream side of the orifice plate shall be made available to the authority having jurisdiction. [**20**:14.2.6.4.3.4]

8.3.5.6 Flow rates shall be as specified while operating at the system design pressure. Tests shall be performed in accordance with HI 3.6, *Rotary Pump Tests*. [**20**:14.2.6.4.3.5]

8.3.5.7 Positive displacement pumps intended to pump liquids other than water shall be permitted to be tested with water; however, the pump performance will be affected, and manufacturer's calculations shall be provided showing the difference in viscosity between water and the system liquid. [**20**:14.2.6.4.3.6]

8.3.6 Other Tests.

8.3.6.1* Engine generator sets supplying emergency or standby power to fire pump assemblies shall be tested routinely in accordance with NFPA 110.

8.3.6.2 Automatic transfer switches shall be tested routinely and exercised in accordance with NFPA 110.

8.3.6.3 Tests of appropriate environmental pump room space conditions (e.g., heating, ventilation, illumination) shall be made to ensure proper manual or automatic operation of the associated equipment.

8.3.6.4* Parallel and angular alignment of the pump and driver shall be inspected during the annual test, and any misalignment shall be corrected.

8.3.7 Test Results and Evaluation.

8.3.7.1* Data Interpretation.

8.3.7.1.1 The interpretation of the flow test performance relative to the manufacturer's performance shall be the basis for determining performance of the pump assembly.

8.3.7.1.2 Qualified individuals shall interpret the test results.

8.3.7.1.3 Where applicable, speed and velocity pressure adjustments shall be applied to the net pressure and flow data obtained to determine compliance with 8.3.7.2.3(2).

8.3.7.2 Evaluation of Fire Pump Test Results.

8.3.7.2.1 The fire pump test results shall be evaluated in accordance with 8.3.7.2.2 through 8.3.7.2.9.

8.3.7.2.2 Increasing the engine speed beyond the rated speed of the pump shall not be permitted as a method for meeting the rated pump performance.

Δ **8.3.7.2.3** The fire pump test results shall be considered acceptable if all of the following conditions are satisfied:

(1) Fire pump meets the flow and pressure requirements of the most demanding system(s) being supplied by the fire pump based on owner-provided system design information
(2)* Fire pump supplies 100 percent of rated flow
(3)* The net pressure at each flow point is at least 95 percent of one of the following:

    (a) Original manufacturer's pump curve
    (b) Original unadjusted field test curve
    (c) Test curve generated from the fire pump nameplate

Δ **8.3.7.2.4*** The following actions shall be required upon failure to meet the criteria in 8.3.7.2.3:

(1) The owner shall be notified in writing of the unacceptable test results.
(2) An investigation shall be conducted into the cause of the unacceptable test results.
(3) Failure to provide the maximum system demand shall be deemed an impairment.
(4) Excessive vibration and/or excessively worn or loose components shall be deemed a deficiency.
(5) Degraded performance that still provides the maximum system demand shall be deemed a noncritical deficiency.
(6) The owner shall be notified in writing of corrections completed.

Δ **8.3.7.2.5** For electric motor–driven fire pumps operating at constant speed, the current at each flow rate test point and at each phase shall not exceed the product of the electric motor service factor and the full-load amperage rating of the motor.

Δ **8.3.7.2.6** Where the current at each flow rate test point and at each phase exceeds the product of the electric motor service factor and the full-load amperage rating of the motor, the source of the problem shall be identified and corrected.

Δ **8.3.7.2.7** For electric motor–driven fire pumps operating at varying voltage, the product of the test voltage and the current at each test point and on each phase shall not exceed the product of the voltage and the full-load current times the motor service factor.

Δ **8.3.7.2.8** Where the product of the test voltage and the current at each test point and on each phase exceeds the product of the voltage and the full-load current times the motor service factor, the source of the problem shall be identified and corrected.

8.3.7.2.9 Voltage readings at the motor within 5 percent below or 10 percent above the rated (i.e., nameplate) voltage shall be considered acceptable.

8.3.7.2.10 A written or electronic record of the results of the investigation and the corrective action shall be prepared and maintained by the owner.

8.4 Reports.

8.4.1* A complete written report of the fire pump test results shall be prepared for and retained by the owner.

8.4.1.1 At a minimum, the report shall contain the following information:

(1) All raw data necessary for a complete evaluation of the fire pump performance, including suction and discharge pressures, voltage and amperage readings, and pump speed at each flow rate tested
(2) The fire protection system demand as furnished by the owner
(3) Pump performance, whether satisfactory or unsatisfactory
(4) Deficiencies noted during the testing and identified during analysis, with recommendations to address deficiencies as appropriate

(5) Manufacturer's performance data, actual performance, and the available pump discharge curves required by this standard
(6) Time delay intervals associated with the pump's starting, stopping, and energy source transfer
(7) Where applicable, comparison with previous test results

8.5 Maintenance.

8.5.1* A preventive maintenance program shall be established on all components of the pump assembly in accordance with the manufacturer's recommendations or an approved alternative maintenance plan.

8.5.2 Records shall be maintained on all work performed on the pump, driver, controller, and auxiliary equipment.

8.5.3 The preventive maintenance program shall be initiated immediately after the pump assembly has passed acceptance tests.

8.6 Component Replacement Testing Requirements.

8.6.1 Whenever a component in a fire pump is adjusted, repaired, rebuilt, or replaced, the tests required to restore the system to service shall be performed in accordance with Table 8.6.1.

8.6.2 NFPA 20 shall be consulted for the minimum requirements for design, installation, and acceptance testing.

8.6.3 Replacement parts shall be provided that will maintain the listing for the fire pump component assembly whenever possible.

8.6.3.1 If the part is no longer available from the original equipment manufacturer, then an approved like part shall be permitted to be used.

Shaded text = Revisions.　Δ = Text deletions and figure/table revisions.　• = Section deletions.　**N** = New material.

△ Table 8.6.1 Summary of Component Action Requirements

Component	Adjust	Repair	Rebuild	Replace	Test Criteria
Fire Pump System					
Entire pump assembly				X	Perform acceptance test in accordance with NFPA 20
Impeller/rotating assembly		X		X	Perform acceptance test in accordance with NFPA 20
Casing		X		X	Perform acceptance test in accordance with NFPA 20 with alignment inspection
Bearings				X	Perform annual test in accordance with 8.3.3
Sleeves				X	Perform annual test in accordance with 8.3.3
Wear rings				X	Perform annual test in accordance with 8.3.3
Main shaft		X		X	Perform annual test in accordance with 8.3.3
Packing	X			X	Perform test in accordance with 8.3.2
Mechanical Transmission					
Gear right-angle drives		X	X	X	Perform acceptance test in accordance with NFPA 20
Drive coupling	X	X	X	X	Perform test in accordance with 8.3.3 with alignment inspection
Electrical System/Controller					
Entire controller				X	Perform acceptance test in accordance with NFPA 20
Electronic component or module that can prevent the controller from starting or running			X	X	Perform acceptance test in accordance with NFPA 20
Electronic component or module that will not prevent the controller from starting or running			X	X	Perform weekly test in accordance with 8.3.2
Plumbing part				X	Perform weekly test in accordance with 8.3.2
Isolating switch				X	Perform test in accordance with 8.3.2 and exercise six times
Circuit breaker	X				Perform six momentary starts in accordance with NFPA 20
Circuit breaker				X	Test in accordance with 8.3.3, including six starts at peak load and operate pump for a minimum of 1 hour
Electrical connections	X				Perform test in accordance with 8.3.2
Main contactor		X		X	Perform test in accordance with 8.3.3 with six starts
Power monitor				X	Perform six operations of the circuit breaker/ isolation switch disconnect (cycle the power on/ off)
Start relay				X	Perform test in accordance with 8.3.2 with six starts
Pressure switch	X			X	Perform test in accordance with 8.3.2 and exercise six times automatically
Pressure transducer	X			X	Perform six automatic no-load starts
Manual start or stop switch				X	Perform six operations under load
Transfer switch — load-carrying parts		X	X	X	Test in accordance with 8.3.3, including six starts at peak horsepower load, operate pump for a minimum of 1 hour, and transfer from normal power to emergency power and back one time
Transfer switch — no-load parts		X	X	X	Perform six no-load operations of transfer of power
Electric Motor Driver					
Electric motor		X	X	X	Perform acceptance test in accordance with NFPA 20 with alignment inspection
Motor bearings				X	Perform annual test in accordance with 8.3.3
Incoming power conductors				X	Test in accordance with 8.3.3 and operate pump for a minimum of 1 hour, including six starts at peak load
Diesel Engine Driver					
Entire engine			X	X	Perform acceptance test in accordance with NFPA 20 with alignment inspection
Fuel transfer pump	X		X	X	Perform test in accordance with 8.3.2

(continues)

Shaded text = Revisions.   **△** = Text deletions and figure/table revisions.   • = Section deletions.   *N* = New material.

Δ **Table 8.6.1** *Continued*

Component	Adjust	Repair	Rebuild	Replace	Test Criteria
Fuel injector pump or ECM	X			X	Perform test in accordance with 8.3.3
Fuel system filter		X		X	Perform test in accordance with 8.3.2
Combustion air intake system		X		X	Perform test in accordance with 8.3.2
Fuel tank		X		X	Perform test in accordance with 8.3.2
Cooling system		X	X	X	Perform test in accordance with 8.3.3
Batteries				X	Perform start/stop sequence from replaced battery in accordance with 8.3.2
Battery charger		X		X	Perform test in accordance with 8.3.2
Electric system		X		X	Perform test in accordance with 8.3.2
Lubrication filter/oil service		X		X	Perform test in accordance with 8.3.2
Steam Turbines					
Steam turbine		X		X	Perform acceptance test in accordance with NFPA 20
Steam regulator or source upgrade		X		X	Perform acceptance test in accordance with NFPA 20
Positive Displacement Pumps					
Entire pump				X	Perform acceptance test in accordance with NFPA 20
Rotors				X	Perform annual test in accordance with 8.3.3
Plungers				X	Perform annual test in accordance with 8.3.3
Shaft				X	Perform annual test in accordance with 8.3.3
Driver	X		X	X	Perform acceptance test in accordance with NFPA 20
Bearings				X	Perform annual test in accordance with 8.3.3
Seals				X	Perform test in accordance with 8.3.2
Pump House and Miscellaneous Components					
Baseplate		X			Perform test in accordance with 8.3.2 with alignment inspection
Baseplate				X	Perform test in accordance with 8.3.3 with alignment inspection
Foundation		X	X	X	Perform test in accordance with 8.3.2 with alignment inspection
Suction/discharge pipe		X		X	Perform visual inspection in accordance with 8.2.2(2)
Suction/discharge fittings		X		X	Perform visual inspection in accordance with 8.2.2(2)
Suction/discharge valves		X	X	X	Perform operational test in accordance with 13.3.3.1

Chapter 9   Water Storage Tanks

9.1* General.

9.1.1 Minimum Requirements.

9.1.1.1 This chapter shall provide the minimum requirements for the routine inspection, testing, and maintenance of water storage tanks dedicated to fire protection use.

9.1.1.2 Table 9.1.1.2 shall be used to determine the minimum required frequencies for inspection, testing, and maintenance.

9.1.2 Common Components and Valves. Common components and valves shall be inspected, tested, and maintained in accordance with Chapter 13.

9.1.3 Obstruction Investigations. The procedures outlined in Chapter 14 shall be followed where there is a need to conduct an obstruction investigation.

9.1.4 Impairments. The procedures outlined in Chapter 15 shall be followed where an impairment to protection occurs.

9.2 Inspection.

9.2.1 Water Level.

9.2.1.1* The water level in tanks equipped with supervised water level alarms that are supervised in accordance with *NFPA 72* shall be inspected quarterly.

9.2.1.2 The water level in tanks not equipped with supervised water level alarms connected to a constantly attended location shall be inspected monthly.

N **9.2.1.3 Water Level Verification.**

N **9.2.1.3.1** Inspection of water level shall be verified through the level indicator, where provided.

N **9.2.1.3.2*** The tank shall be at full or at the designed water level.

9.2.2 Heating System.

9.2.2.1 Tank heating systems installed on tanks equipped with low water temperature alarms supervised in accordance with *NFPA 72*, connected to a constantly attended location shall be inspected quarterly during the heating season.

Δ **Table 9.1.1.2 Summary of Water Storage Tank Inspection, Testing, and Maintenance**

Item	Frequency	Reference
Inspection		
Catwalks and ladders	Quarterly	9.2.4.1
Check valves		Chapter 13
Control valves		Chapter 13
Expansion joints	Annually	9.2.4.3
Foundation	Quarterly	9.2.4.1
Heating system — tanks with supervised low-temperature alarms connected to constantly attended location	Quarterly	9.2.2.1
Heating system — tanks without supervised low-temperature alarms connected to constantly attended location	Daily*	9.2.2.2
Hoops and grillage	Annually	9.2.4.4
Interior — all other tanks	5 years	9.2.5.1.2
Interior — steel tanks without corrosion protection	3 years	9.2.5.1.1
Painted, coated, or insulated surfaces	Annually	9.2.4.5
Support structure	Quarterly	9.2.4.1
Surrounding area	Quarterly	9.2.4.2
Tank — exterior	Quarterly	9.2.4.1
Temperature alarms — connected to constantly attended location	Quarterly*	9.2.3.2
Temperature alarms — not connected to constantly attended location	Weekly*	9.2.3.3
Vents	Quarterly	9.2.4.1
Water level — tanks equipped with supervised water-level alarms connected to constantly attended location	Quarterly	9.2.1.1
Water level — tanks without supervised water-level alarms connected to constantly attended location	Monthly	9.2.1.2
Test		
High-temperature limit switches	Prior to heating season	9.3.4
Level indicators	5 years	9.3.1
Low-water temperature alarms	Prior to heating season	9.3.3
Pressure gauges		Chapter 13
Tank heating system	Prior to heating season	9.3.2
Valve status test		Chapter 13
Water-level signals (high and low)	Annually	9.3.5
Maintenance		
Check valves		Chapter 13
Control valves		Chapter 13
Embankment-supported coated fabric (ESCF)	2 years or per manufacturer	9.4.6.2
Water level		9.4.2

*Cold weather/heating season only.

9.2.2.2 Tank heating systems without a supervised low temperature alarm connected to a constantly attended location shall be inspected daily during the heating season.

9.2.3 Water Temperature.

9.2.3.1 The temperature of water in tanks shall not be less than 40°F (4°C).

9.2.3.2 The temperature of water in tanks with low temperature alarms supervised in accordance with *NFPA 72*, connected to a constantly attended location shall be inspected and recorded quarterly during the heating season when the mean temperature is less than 40°F (4°C).

9.2.3.3 The temperature of water in tanks without low temperature alarms connected to a constantly attended location shall be inspected and recorded weekly during the heating season when the mean temperature is less than 40°F (4°C).

9.2.4 Exterior Inspection.

9.2.4.1* The exterior of the tank, supporting structure, vents, foundation, and catwalks or ladders, where provided, shall be inspected quarterly for signs of obvious damage or weakening.

9.2.4.2 The area surrounding the tank and supporting structure, where provided, shall be inspected quarterly to ensure that the following conditions are met:

(1) The area is free of combustible storage, trash, debris, brush, or material that could present a fire exposure hazard.

(2) The area is free of the accumulation of material on or near parts that could result in accelerated corrosion or rot.

(3) The tank and support are free of ice buildup.

(4) The exterior sides and top of embankments supporting coated fabric tanks are free of erosion.

9.2.4.3 Expansion joints, where provided, shall be inspected annually for leaks and cracks.

9.2.4.4 The hoops and grillage of wooden tanks shall be inspected annually.

9.2.4.5 Exterior painted, coated, or insulated surfaces of the tank and supporting structure, where provided, shall be inspected annually for signs of degradation.

9.2.5 Interior Inspection.

9.2.5.1 Frequency.

9.2.5.1.1* The interior of steel tanks without corrosion protection shall be inspected every 3 years.

9.2.5.1.2* The interior of all other types of tanks shall be inspected every 5 years.

9.2.5.2 Where interior inspection is made by means of underwater evaluation, silt shall first be removed from the tank floor.

9.2.5.3 The tank interior shall be inspected for signs of pitting, corrosion, spalling, rot, other forms of deterioration, waste materials and debris, aquatic growth, and local or general failure of interior coating.

9.2.5.4 Steel tanks exhibiting signs of interior pitting, corrosion, or failure of coating shall be tested in accordance with 9.2.6.

9.2.5.5* Tanks on ring-type foundations with sand in the middle shall be inspected for evidence of voids beneath the floor.

9.2.5.6 The heating system and components including piping shall be inspected.

9.2.5.7 The anti-vortex plate shall be inspected for deterioration or blockage.

9.2.6 Tests During Interior Inspection. Where a drained interior inspection of a steel tank is required by 9.2.5.4, the following tests shall be conducted:

(1) Evaluation of tank coatings shall be made in accordance with the adhesion test of ASTM D3359, *Standard Test Methods for Rating Adhesion by Tape Test*, generally referred to as the "cross-hatch test."

(2) Dry film thickness measurements shall be taken at random locations to determine the overall coating thickness.

(3) Nondestructive ultrasonic readings shall be taken to evaluate the wall thickness where there is evidence of pitting or corrosion.

(4) Interior surfaces shall be spot wet-sponge tested to detect pinholes, cracks, or other compromises in the coating. Special attention shall be given to sharp edges such as ladder rungs, nuts, and bolts.

(5) Tank bottoms shall be tested for metal loss and/or rust on the underside by use of ultrasonic testing where there is evidence of pitting or corrosion. Removal, visual inspection, and replacement of random floor coupons shall be an acceptable alternative to ultrasonic testing.

(6) Tanks with flat bottoms shall be vacuum-box tested at bottom seams in accordance with test procedures found in NFPA 22.

9.3 Testing.

9.3.1* Level indicators shall be tested every 5 years for accuracy and freedom of movement.

9.3.2 The tank heating system, where provided, shall be tested prior to the heating season to make certain it is in the proper working order.

9.3.3 Low water temperature signals, where provided, shall be tested prior to the heating season.

9.3.4* High water temperature limit switches on tank heating systems, where provided, shall be tested prior to the heating season.

9.3.5* High and low water level signals shall be tested annually.

9.4 Maintenance.

9.4.1 Voids discovered beneath the floors of tanks shall be filled by pumping in grout or accessing the sand and replenishing.

9.4.2 The tank shall be maintained full or at the designed water level.

9.4.3 The hatch covers in the roofs and the door at the top of the frostproof casing shall always be kept securely fastened with substantial catches as a protection against freezing and windstorm damage.

9.4.4 No waste materials, such as boards, paint cans, trim, or loose material, shall be left in the tank or on the surface of the tank.

9.4.5 Silt shall be removed during interior inspections or more frequently as needed to avoid accumulation to the level of the tank outlet.

9.4.6 Maintenance of Embankment-Supported Coated Fabric (ESCF) Suction Tanks.

9.4.6.1 The maintenance of ESCF tanks shall be completed in accordance with this section and the tank manufacturer's instructions.

9.4.6.2 The exposed surfaces of ESCF tanks shall be cleaned and painted every 2 years or in accordance with the manufacturer's instructions.

9.5 Automatic Tank Fill Valves.

9.5.1 Inspection.

9.5.1.1 Automatic tank fill valves shall be inspected in accordance with Table 9.5.1.1.

9.5.1.1.1 OS&Y isolation valves that are a part of the automatic fill valves shall be inspected in accordance with Chapter 13.

9.5.1.2 Valves secured with locks or electrically supervised in accordance with applicable NFPA standards shall be inspected monthly.

Δ **Table 9.5.1.1 Summary of Automatic Tank Fill Valve Inspection and Testing**

Item	Frequency	Reference
Inspection		
Enclosure (during cold weather)	Daily/weekly	Chapter 4
Exterior	Monthly	Chapter 13
Interior	Annually/5 years	Chapter 13
Strainers, filters, orifices (inspect)	5 years	Chapter 13
Test		
Automatic tank fill valve	Annually	9.5.3
Maintenance		
Strainers (clean)	Quarterly	9.5.2.3

9.5.1.3 The enclosure shall be inspected to verify that it is heated and secured.

9.5.2 Maintenance.

9.5.2.1 Maintenance of all automatic tank fill valves shall be conducted by a qualified person following the manufacturer's instructions in accordance with the procedure and policies of the authority having jurisdiction.

9.5.2.2 Rubber parts shall be replaced in accordance with the frequency required by the authority having jurisdiction and the manufacturer's instructions.

9.5.2.3 Strainers shall be cleaned quarterly.

9.5.3 Testing. All automatic tank fill valves shall be tested yearly in accordance with the following:

(1) The valve shall be actuated automatically by lowering the water level in the tank.
(2) The refill rate shall be measured and recorded.

9.6 Component Action Requirements.

9.6.1 Whenever a component in a water storage tank is adjusted, repaired, reconditioned, or replaced, the action required in Table 9.6.1 shall be performed.

9.6.2 Where the original installation standard is different from the cited standard, the use of the appropriate installing standard shall be permitted.

9.6.3 These actions shall not require a design review, which is outside the scope of this standard.

Shaded text = Revisions.   Δ = Text deletions and figure/table revisions.   • = Section deletions.   *N* = New material.

2020 Edition

Δ **Table 9.6.1   Summary of Component Action Requirements**

Component	Adjust	Repair/Recondition	Replace	Test Criteria
Tank Components				
Catwalks and ladders	X	X	X	Verify integrity in conformance with NFPA 22
Expansion joints	X	X	X	Verify integrity in conformance with NFPA 22
Heating system	X	X	X	Verify heating system is in conformance with NFPA 22
Hoops and grillage	X	X	X	Verify integrity in conformance with NFPA 22
Insulation		X	X	Verify integrity in conformance with NFPA 22
Overflow piping	X	X	X	Verify integrity in conformance with NFPA 22
Support structure		X	X	Verify integrity in conformance with NFPA 22
Tank exterior		X	X	Verify integrity in conformance with NFPA 22
Tank interior		X	X	Remove debris; verify integrity in conformance with NFPA 22
Alarm and Supervisory Components				
Enclosure temperature	X	X	X	Operational test for conformance with NFPA 22 and/or *NFPA 72*
High and low water level	X	X	X	Operational test for conformance with NFPA 22 and/or *NFPA 72* and the design water levels
Valve supervision	X	X	X	Operational test for conformance with NFPA 22 and/or *NFPA 72*
Water temperature	X	X	X	Operational test for conformance with NFPA 22 and/or *NFPA 72*
Fill and Discharge Components				
Automatic fill valves	X	X		Perform annual test in accordance with 9.5.3
Valves	X	X	X	See Chapter 13
Status Indicators				
Level indicators	X	X	X	Verify conformance with NFPA 22
Pressure gauges			X	Verify at 0 psi (0 bar) and at system working pressure

Chapter 10   Water Spray Fixed Systems

10.1* General.

10.1.1 Minimum Requirements.

10.1.1.1 This chapter shall provide the minimum requirements for the routine inspection, testing, and maintenance of water spray protection from fixed nozzle systems only.

10.1.1.2 Table 10.1.1.2 shall be used to determine the minimum required frequencies for inspection, testing, and maintenance.

10.1.2 Water Spray Protection. This chapter shall not cover water spray protection from portable nozzles, sprinkler systems, monitor nozzles, or other means of application.

10.1.3* Design and Installation. NFPA 15 shall be consulted to determine the requirements for design and installation, including acceptance testing.

10.1.4 Obstruction Investigations. The procedures outlined in Chapter 14 shall be followed where there is a need to conduct an obstruction investigation.

10.1.5 Common Components and Valves. Common components and valves shall be inspected, tested, and maintained in accordance with Chapter 13.

10.1.6* Impairments. The procedures outlined in Chapter 15 shall be followed where an impairment to protection occurs.

10.1.6.1 When a water spray fixed system or any portion thereof is out of service for any reason, notice shall be given to facility management, the local fire department, the on-site fire brigade, and other authorities having jurisdiction, as applicable.

10.1.6.2 A sign shall be posted at each fire department connection or system control valve indicating which portion of the system is out of service.

10.2 Inspection and Maintenance Procedures.

10.2.1 Components. The components described in this section shall be inspected and maintained at the frequency specified in Table 10.1.1.2 and in accordance with this standard and the manufacturer's instructions.

10.2.1.1 Items in areas that are inaccessible for safety considerations due to factors such as continuous process operations and energized electrical equipment shall be inspected during each scheduled shutdown but not more than every 18 months.

10.2.1.2 Inspections shall not be required for items in areas with no provision for access and that are not subject to the conditions noted in 10.2.3.1, 10.2.3.2, and 10.2.4.1.

Shaded text = Revisions.   Δ = Text deletions and figure/table revisions.   • = Section deletions.   *N* = New material.

△ **Table 10.1.1.2 Summary of Water Spray Fixed System Inspection, Testing, and Maintenance**

Item	Frequency	Reference
Inspection		
Backflow preventer		Chapter 13
Check valves		Chapter 13
Control valves		Chapter 13
Deluge valve		Chapter 13
Detection systems and components		NFPA 72
Detector check valves		Chapter 13
Drainage	Quarterly	10.2.7
Fire pump system		Chapter 8
Fittings	Annually	10.2.3, 10.2.3.1
Fittings (rubber-gasketed)	Annually and after each system activation	10.2.3.1
Gravity tanks		Chapter 9
Hangers, braces, and supports	Annually and after each system activation	10.2.3.2
Heat (deluge valve house)		Chapter 13
Nozzles	Annually and after each system activation	10.2.4
Piping	Annually and after each system activation	10.2.3.1
Pressure tank		Chapter 9
Strainers	Mainline — annually and after each system activation; Others — per manufacturer's instruction	10.2.6
Suction tanks		Chapter 9
Water supply piping		10.2.5.2
UHSWSS — controllers	Start of each shift	10.4.3
UHSWSS — detectors	Monthly	10.4.2
UHSWSS — valves	Start of each shift	10.4.4
Operational Test		
Backflow preventer		Chapter 13
Check valves		Chapter 13
Control valves		Chapter 13
Deluge valve		Chapter 13
Detection systems		NFPA 72
Detector check valve		Chapter 13
Fire pump system		Chapter 8
Gravity tanks		Chapter 9
Main drain test		Chapter 13
Manual release	Annually	10.3.5
Nozzles	Annually	Section 10.3
Pressure tank		Chapter 9
Strainers	Annually	10.2.6
Suction tanks		Chapter 9
Waterflow alarm		Chapter 5
Water spray system test		Chapter 13
Water supply flow test		Chapter 7
UHSWSS	Annually	Section 10.4
Valve status test		Chapter 13

(continues)

△ **Table 10.1.1.2** *Continued*

Item	Frequency	Reference
Maintenance		
Backflow preventer		Chapter 13
Check valves		Chapter 13
Control valves		Chapter 13
Deluge valve		Chapter 13
Deluge valve enclosures		Chapter 4
Detection systems		NFPA 72
Detector check valve		Chapter 13
Fire pump system		Chapter 8
Gravity tanks		10.2.9, Chapter 9
Pressure tank		10.2.9, Chapter 9
Strainers	Annually	10.2.1.4, 10.2.1.6, 10.2.6
Strainers (baskets/screen)	5 years	10.2.1.4, 10.2.1.7, A.10.2.6
Suction tanks		Chapter 9
Water spray nozzles	Annually	10.2.4

10.2.1.3 Items in areas that are inaccessible for safety considerations shall be tested at longer intervals in accordance with 13.4.4.2.3.2.

10.2.1.4 Other maintenance intervals shall be permitted, depending on the results of the visual inspection and operating tests.

10.2.1.5 Deluge valve enclosures shall be inspected in accordance with the provisions of Chapter 13.

10.2.1.6 Nozzle strainers shall be removed, inspected, and cleaned during the flushing procedure for the mainline strainer.

10.2.1.7 Mainline strainers shall be removed and inspected every 5 years for damaged and corroded parts.

10.2.2 Deluge Valves. Deluge valves shall be inspected, tested, and maintained in accordance with Chapter 13.

10.2.3* System Components. System piping, fittings, hangers, and supports shall be inspected and maintained to ensure continuity of water delivery to the spray nozzles at full waterflow and design pressure.

10.2.3.1* Piping and Fittings. System piping and fittings shall be inspected for the following:

(1) Mechanical damage (e.g., broken piping or cracked fittings)
(2) External conditions (e.g., missing or damaged paint or coatings, rust, and corrosion)
(3) Misalignment or trapped sections
(4) Condition of low-point drains (automatic or manual)
(5) Protection for rubber-gasketed fittings

10.2.3.2* Hangers, Braces, and Supports. Hangers, braces, and supports shall be inspected for the following and repaired or replaced as necessary:

(1) Condition (e.g., missing or damaged paint or coating, rust, and corrosion)
(2) Secure attachment to structural supports and piping
(3) Damaged or missing hangers, braces, and supports

10.2.4* Water Spray Nozzles.

10.2.4.1 Water spray nozzles shall be inspected and maintained to ensure that they are in place, continue to be aimed or pointed in the direction intended, and are free from external loading and corrosion.

10.2.4.2 Where caps or plugs are required, the inspection shall confirm they are in place and free to operate as intended.

10.2.4.3 Misaligned water spray nozzles shall be adjusted (aimed) by visual means, and the discharge patterns shall be inspected at the next scheduled flow test.

10.2.5 Water Supply.

10.2.5.1 The dependability of the water supply shall be ensured by regular inspection and maintenance, whether furnished by a municipal source, on-site storage tanks, a fire pump, or private underground piping systems.

10.2.5.2* Water supply piping shall be maintained free of internal obstructions.

10.2.6* Strainers.

10.2.6.1 Mainline strainers (basket or screen) shall be flushed until clear after each operation or flow test.

10.2.6.2 Individual water spray nozzle strainers shall be removed, cleaned, and inspected after each operation or flow test.

10.2.6.3 All strainers shall be inspected and cleaned in accordance with the manufacturer's instructions.

10.2.6.4 Damaged or corroded parts shall be replaced or repaired.

10.2.7 Drainage. The area beneath and surrounding a water spray fixed system shall be inspected visually on a quarterly basis to ensure that drainage facilities, such as trap sumps and drainage trenches, are not blocked and retention embankments or dikes are in good repair.

10.2.8 Fire Pumps. Chapter 8 shall be followed for inspection and maintenance requirements.

10.2.9 Water Tanks (Gravity, Pressure, or Suction Tanks, or Reservoirs). Chapter 9 shall be followed for inspection and maintenance requirements.

10.3 Operational Tests.

10.3.1 Performance.

10.3.1.1 Frequency of system tests shall be in accordance with Table 10.1.1.2.

10.3.1.2 Water spray fixed systems shall be serviced in accordance with this standard and with the manufacturer's instructions.

10.3.2* Test Preparation. Precautions shall be taken to prevent damage to property during the test.

10.3.3 Operational Test Performance. Operational tests shall be conducted to ensure that the water spray fixed systems respond as designed, both automatically and manually.

10.3.3.1* Response Time.

10.3.3.1.1 Under test conditions, the heat detection systems, where exposed to a heat test source, shall operate within 40 seconds.

10.3.3.1.2 Under test conditions, the flammable gas detection system, where exposed to a standard test gas concentration, shall operate within the time frame specified in the system design.

10.3.3.1.3 These response times shall be recorded.

10.3.3.2 Discharge Time. The time lapse between operation of detection systems and water delivery time to the protected area shall be recorded.

10.3.3.3* Discharge Patterns.

10.3.3.3.1* The water discharge patterns from all of the open spray nozzles shall be observed to ensure that patterns are not impeded by plugged nozzles, to ensure that nozzles are correctly positioned, and to ensure that obstructions do not prevent discharge patterns from wetting surfaces to be protected.

10.3.3.3.1.1 Where the nature of the protected property is such that water cannot be discharged, the nozzles shall be inspected for proper orientation and the system tested with air to ensure that the nozzles are not obstructed.

10.3.3.3.2 Where obstructions occur, the piping and nozzles shall be cleaned and the system retested.

10.3.3.4 Pressure Readings.

10.3.3.4.1 Pressure readings shall be recorded at the hydraulically most remote nozzle to ensure the waterflow has not been impeded by partially closed valves or by plugged strainers or piping.

10.3.3.4.2 A second pressure reading shall be recorded at the deluge valve to ensure the water supply is adequate.

10.3.3.4.3 Readings shall be compared to the hydraulic design pressures to ensure the original system design requirements are met and the water supply is adequate to meet the design requirements.

10.3.3.4.3.1 Where the hydraulically most remote nozzle is inaccessible, nozzles shall be permitted to be checked visually without taking a pressure reading on the most remote nozzle.

10.3.3.4.3.2 Where the reading taken at the riser indicates that the water supply has deteriorated, a gauge shall be placed on the hydraulically most remote nozzle and the results compared with the required design pressure.

10.3.4 Multiple Systems. The maximum number of systems expected to operate in case of fire shall be tested simultaneously to inspect the adequacy of the water supply.

10.3.5 Manual Operation. Manual actuation devices shall be operated annually.

10.3.6 Return to Service. After the full flow test, the water spray system shall be maintained and returned to service in accordance with the manufacturer's instructions.

10.3.6.1 Low Point Drains.

10.3.6.1.1 To prevent freezing and corrosion, all low point drains in aboveground piping shall be opened, the pipe drained, and the valves closed and plugs replaced.

10.3.6.1.2 Where weep holes are provided in lieu of low-point drains, they shall be inspected to ensure they are clear and unobstructed.

10.4 Ultra-High-Speed Water Spray System (UHSWSS) Operational Tests.

10.4.1 A full operational test, including measurements of response time, shall be conducted at intervals not exceeding 1 year.

10.4.1.1 Systems out of service shall be tested before being placed back in service.

10.4.2 All detectors shall be tested and inspected monthly for physical damage and accumulation of deposits on the lenses of optical detectors.

10.4.3 Controllers shall be inspected for faults at the start of each working shift.

10.4.4 Valves.

10.4.4.1 Valves on the water supply line shall be inspected at the start of each working shift to verify they are open.

10.4.4.2 Valves secured in the open position with a locking device or monitored by a signaling device that sounds a trouble signal at the deluge system control panel or other central location shall not require inspection.

10.4.5 Response Time.

10.4.5.1 The response time shall be verified during the operational test.

10.4.5.2 The response time shall be in accordance with the requirements of the system but not more than 100 milliseconds.

10.5 Component Action Requirements.

10.5.1 Whenever a component in a water spray fixed system is adjusted, repaired, reconditioned, or replaced, the action required in Table 10.5.1 shall be performed.

10.5.2 Where the original installation standard is different from the cited standard, the use of the appropriate installing standard shall be permitted.

10.5.3 The actions of 10.5.1 shall not require a design review, which is outside the scope of this standard.

Δ **Table 10.5.1 Summary of Component Action Requirements**

Component	Adjust	Repair/ Recondition	Replace	Required Action
Water Delivery Components				
Fire department connections				See Chapter 13
Manual release	X	X	X	(1) Operational test (2) Check for leaks at system working pressure (3) Test all alarms
Nozzles	X	X	X	Operational flow test
Pipe and fittings	X	X	X	Operational flow test
Alarm and Supervisory Components				
Detection system	X	X	X	Operational test for conformance with NFPA 15 and/or *NFPA 72*
Pressure-switch-type waterflow	X	X	X	Operational test using inspector's test connection
Valve supervisory device	X	X	X	Test for conformance with NFPA 15 and/or *NFPA 72*
Water motor gong	X	X	X	Operational test using inspector's test connection
Status-Indicating Components				
Gauges			X	Verify at 0 psi (0 bar) and system working pressure
Testing and Maintenance Components				
Auxiliary drains	X	X	X	(1) Inspect for leaks at system working pressure (2) Main drain test
Main drain	X	X	X	Full-flow main drain test
Structural Components				
Hanger/seismic bracing	X	X	X	Inspect for conformance with NFPA 15 and/or NFPA 13
Pipe stands	X	X	X	Inspect for conformance with NFPA 15 and/or NFPA 13
Informational Components				
Identification signs	X	X	X	Inspect for conformance with NFPA 15

Chapter 11   Foam-Water Sprinkler Systems

11.1 General.

11.1.1 Minimum Requirements.

11.1.1.1 This chapter shall provide the minimum requirements for the routine inspection, testing, and maintenance of foam-water sprinkler systems.

11.1.1.2 Table 11.1.1.2 shall be used to determine the minimum required frequencies for inspection, testing, and maintenance.

11.1.2 Other System Components. Fire pumps, water storage tanks, common components, and valves common to other types of water-based fire protection systems shall be inspected, tested, and maintained in accordance with Chapters 8, 9, and 13, respectively, and as specified in Table 11.1.1.2.

11.1.3 Foam-Water Sprinkler Systems.

11.1.3.1 This section shall apply to foam-water sprinkler systems as specified in NFPA 16.

11.1.3.2 This section shall not include systems detailed in NFPA 11.

11.1.4 Foam-Water Sprinkler System.

11.1.4.1 If during routine inspection and testing the foam-water sprinkler system is determined to have been altered or replaced (e.g., equipment replaced, relocated, or foam concentrate replaced), it shall be determined whether the system operates properly.

11.1.5 Obstruction Investigations. The procedures outlined in Chapter 14 shall be followed where there is a need to conduct an obstruction investigation.

11.1.6 Impairments. The procedures outlined in Chapter 15 shall be followed where an impairment to protection occurs.

11.2 Inspection. Systems shall be inspected in accordance with the frequency specified in Table 11.1.1.2.

11.2.1 Deluge Valves. Deluge valves shall be inspected in accordance with the provisions of Chapter 13.

11.2.2 System Piping and Fittings. System piping and fittings shall be inspected for the following:

(1) Mechanical damage (e.g., broken piping or cracked fittings)
(2) External conditions (e.g., missing or damaged paint or coatings, rust, and corrosion)
(3) Misalignment or trapped sections
(4) Low-point drains (automatic or manual)
(5) Location and condition of rubber-gasketed fittings

11.2.3 Hangers, Braces, and Supports. Hangers, braces, and supports shall be inspected for the following and repaired or replaced as necessary:

(1) Condition (e.g., missing or damaged paint or coating, rust, and corrosion)
(2) Secure attachment to structural supports and piping
(3) Damaged or missing hangers, braces, and supports

Δ **Table 11.1.1.2 Summary of Foam-Water Sprinkler System Inspection, Testing, and Maintenance**

System/Component	Frequency	Reference
Inspection		
Control valve(s)		Chapter 13
Deluge/preaction valve(s)		Chapter 13
Discharge device location (spray nozzle)	Monthly	11.2.4
Discharge device location (sprinkler)	Annually	11.2.4
Discharge device position (spray nozzle)	Monthly	11.2.4
Discharge device position (sprinkler)	Annually	11.2.4
Drainage in system area	Quarterly	11.2.7
Fire pump system		Chapter 8
Fittings corrosion	Annually	11.2.2
Fittings damage	Annually	11.2.2
Foam concentrate strainer(s)	Quarterly	11.2.6.4
Gauges		Chapter 13
Hangers/braces/supports	Annually	11.2.3
Pipe corrosion	Annually	11.2.2
Pipe damage	Annually	11.2.2
Proportioning system(s) — all	Monthly	11.2.8
Strainer(s) — Mainline	5 years	11.2.6.1
Water supply piping		11.2.5.1
Water supply tank(s)		Chapter 9
Waterflow alarm devices		Chapter 13
Test		
Backflow preventer(s)		Chapter 13
Complete foam-water sprinkler system(s) (operational test)	Annually	11.3.2, 11.3.3
Control valve(s)		Chapter 13
Deluge/preaction valve(s)		Chapter 13
Discharge device location	Annually	11.3.2.6
Discharge device obstruction	Annually	11.3.2.6
Discharge device position	Annually	11.3.2.6
Fire pump system		Chapter 8
Foam-water solution	Annually	11.3.5
Manual actuation device(s)	Annually	11.3.4
Valve status test		Chapter 13
Water supply flow test		Chapter 7
Water supply tank(s)		Chapter 9
Waterflow alarm devices		Chapter 13
Maintenance		
Backflow preventer(s)		Chapter 13
Bladder tank type		
Foam concentrate tank — hydrostatic test	10 years	11.4.5.2
Sight glass	10 years	11.4.5.1
Check valve(s)		Chapter 13
Control valve(s)		Chapter 13
Deluge/preaction valves		Chapter 13
Detector check valve(s)		Chapter 13
Fire pump system		Chapter 8
Foam concentrate pump operation	Monthly	11.4.7.1

(continues)

Shaded text = Revisions.   Δ = Text deletions and figure/table revisions.   • = Section deletions.   *N* = New material.

△ Table 11.1.1.2 *Continued*

System/Component	Frequency	Reference
Foam concentrate samples	Per manufacturer's recommendation	11.4.2
Foam concentrate strainer(s)	Quarterly	Section 11.4
In-line balanced pressure type		
Balancing valve diaphragm	5 years	11.4.8.3
Foam concentrate pump(s)	5 years*	11.4.8.2
Foam concentrate tank	10 years	11.4.8.4
Line type		
Foam concentrate tank — corrosion and pickup pipes	10 years	11.4.6.1
Foam concentrate tank — drain and flush	10 years	11.4.6.2
Pressure vacuum vents	5 years	11.4.9
Proportioning system(s) standard pressure type		
Ball drip (automatic type) drain valves	5 years	11.4.4.1
Corrosion and hydrostatic test	10 years	11.4.4.4
Foam concentrate tank — drain and flush	10 years	11.4.4.2
Standard balanced pressure type		
Balancing valve diaphragm	5 years	11.4.7.3
Foam concentrate pump(s)	5 years*	11.4.7.2
Foam concentrate tank	10 years	11.4.7.4
Strainer(s) — mainline	5 years	11.2.6.1
Water supply	Annually	11.2.5.2
Water supply tank(s)		Chapter 9

*Also refer to manufacturer's instructions and frequency. Maintenance intervals other than preventive maintenance are not provided, as they depend on the results of the visual inspections and operational tests. For foam-water sprinkler systems in aircraft hangars, refer to the inspection, test, and maintenance requirements of Table 11.1.1 in NFPA 409.

11.2.4* Foam-Water Discharge Devices.

11.2.4.1 Foam-water discharge devices shall be inspected visually and maintained to ensure that they are in place, continue to be aimed or pointed in the direction intended in the system design, and are free from external loading and corrosion.

11.2.4.2 Where caps or plugs are required, the inspection shall confirm they are in place and free to operate as intended.

11.2.4.3 Misaligned discharge devices shall be adjusted (aimed) by visual means, and the discharge patterns shall be inspected at the next scheduled flow test.

11.2.4.4* Inspection shall verify that unlisted combinations of discharge devices and foam concentrate have not been substituted.

11.2.5 Water Supply.

11.2.5.1 The dependability of the water supply shall be ensured by regular inspection and maintenance, whether furnished by a municipal source, on-site storage tanks, a fire pump, or private underground piping systems.

11.2.5.2* Water supply piping shall be maintained free of internal obstructions.

11.2.6 Strainers.

11.2.6.1 Mainline and individual discharge device strainers (basket or screen) shall be inspected every 5 years for damaged and corroded parts.

11.2.6.2 Other maintenance intervals shall be permitted, depending on the results of the visual inspection and operating tests.

11.2.6.3 Discharge device strainers shall be removed, inspected, and cleaned during the flushing procedure for the mainline strainer.

11.2.6.4 Foam concentrate strainers shall be inspected visually to ensure the blowdown valve is closed and plugged.

11.2.6.5 Baskets or screens shall be removed and inspected after each operation or flow test.

11.2.7 Drainage. The area beneath and surrounding a foam-water spray system shall be inspected to ensure that drainage facilities, such as trap sumps and drainage trenches, are not blocked, and retention embankments or dikes are in good repair.

11.2.8* Proportioning Systems.

11.2.8.1 The components of the various proportioning systems described in 11.2.8 shall be inspected in accordance with the frequency specified in Table 11.1.1.2.

11.2.8.2 Valves specified to be inspected shall be permitted to be open or closed, depending on specific functions within each foam-water sprinkler system.

11.2.8.3 The position (open or closed) of valves shall be verified in accordance with specified operating conditions.

11.2.8.4* Inspection of the concentrate tank shall include verification that the quantity of foam concentrate satisfies the requirements of the original design.

11.2.8.5 Additional inspection requirements shall be performed as detailed for the proportioning systems specified in 11.2.8.

11.2.8.5.1 Standard Pressure Proportioner.

11.2.8.5.1.1* The pressure shall be removed before the inspection to prevent injury.

11.2.8.5.1.2 The inspection shall verify the following:

(1) Ball drip valves (automatic drains) are free and opened.
(2) External corrosion on foam concentrate storage tanks is not present.

11.2.8.5.2 Bladder Tank Proportioner.

11.2.8.5.2.1* The pressure shall be removed before the inspection to prevent injury.

11.2.8.5.2.2 The inspection shall include the following:

(1) Water control valves to foam concentrate tank
(2) An inspection for external corrosion on foam concentrate storage tanks
(3) An inspection for the presence of foam in the water surrounding the bladder (annual)

11.2.8.5.3 Line Proportioner. The inspection shall include the following:

(1)* Strainers
(2)* Verification that pressure vacuum vent is operating freely
(3) An inspection for external corrosion on foam concentrate storage tanks

11.2.8.5.4 Standard Balanced Pressure Proportioner. The inspection shall include the following:

(1)* Strainers
(2)* Verification that pressure vacuum vent is operating freely
(3) Verification that gauges are in good operating condition
(4) Verification that sensing line valves are open
(5) Verification that power is available to foam liquid pump

11.2.8.5.5 In-Line Balanced Pressure Proportioner. The inspection shall include the following:

(1)* Strainers
(2)* Verification that pressure vacuum vent is operating freely
(3) Verification that gauges are in good working condition
(4) Verification that sensing line valves at pump unit and individual proportioner stations are open
(5) Verification that power is available to foam liquid pump

11.2.8.5.6 Orifice Plate Proportioner. The inspection shall include the following:

(1)* Strainers
(2)* Verification that pressure vacuum vent is operating freely
(3) Verification that gauges are in good working condition
(4) Verification that power is available to foam liquid pump

11.3* Operational Tests. Frequency of system tests shall be in accordance with Table 11.1.1.2.

11.3.1* Test Preparation. Precautions shall be taken to prevent damage to property during the test.

11.3.2* Operational Test Performance.

11.3.2.1 Operational tests shall be conducted to ensure that the foam-water sprinkler system(s) responds as designed, both automatically and manually.

11.3.2.2 The test procedures shall simulate anticipated emergency events so the response of the foam-water sprinkler system(s) can be evaluated.

11.3.2.3 Where discharge from the system discharge devices would create a hazardous condition or conflict with local requirements, an approved alternate method to achieve full flow conditions shall be permitted.

11.3.2.4 Response Time. Under test conditions, the automatic fire detection systems, when exposed to a test source, shall operate within the requirements of *NFPA 72* for the type of detector provided, and the response time shall be recorded.

11.3.2.5 Discharge Time. The time lapse between operation of detection systems and water delivery time to the protected area shall be recorded for open discharge devices.

11.3.2.6 Discharge Patterns.

11.3.2.6.1 The discharge patterns from all of the open spray devices shall be observed to ensure that patterns are not impeded by plugged discharge devices and to ensure that discharge devices are correctly positioned and that obstructions do not prevent discharge patterns from covering surfaces to be protected.

11.3.2.6.2 Where obstructions occur, the piping and discharge devices shall be cleaned and the system retested.

11.3.2.6.3 Discharge devices shall be permitted to be of different orifice sizes and types.

11.3.2.7* Pressure Readings.

11.3.2.7.1 Pressure readings shall be recorded at the highest, most remote discharge device.

11.3.2.7.2 It shall be permissible to test the full flow discharge from foam-water deluge systems using water only in lieu of foam.

11.3.2.7.3 A second pressure reading shall be recorded at the main control valve.

11.3.2.7.4 Readings shall be compared to the hydraulic design pressures to ensure the original system design requirements are met.

11.3.3 Multiple Systems. The maximum number of systems expected to operate in case of fire shall be tested simultaneously to inspect the adequacy of the water supply and concentrate pump.

11.3.4 Manual Actuation Devices. Manual actuation devices shall be tested annually.

11.3.5 Concentration Testing.

11.3.5.1 During the operational test, a foam sample shall be taken.

11.3.5.2 Where approved by the authority having jurisdiction, simulated foam concentrates or alternative test systems shall be permitted to be substituted for actual foam concentrate, but system pressures and flows shall remain as described above and meet manufacturer's system requirements and recommendations. [**16:**8.4.1.6]

11.3.5.3 The foam sample shall be inspected by refractometric or other methods to verify concentration of the solution.

11.3.5.4 The foam concentrate induction rate of a proportioner, expressed as a percentage of the foam solution flow (water plus foam concentrate), shall be within minus 0 percent to plus 30 percent of the manufacturer's listed concentration, or plus 1 percentage point, whichever is less. [**16:**8.4.1.4]

11.3.6 Return to Service. After the full flow test, the foam-water sprinkler shall be returned to service and the foam concentrate tank shall be replenished to design level.

11.4* Maintenance.

11.4.1 Maintenance of foam-water sprinkler systems shall be in accordance with the requirements of those chapters covering the specific component parts.

11.4.2 Foam Concentrate Samples. Samples of foam concentrates shall be sent to the manufacturer or qualified laboratory for quality condition testing at the frequency recommended by the manufacturer.

11.4.3 Foam Components. Maintenance of specific foam components shall be in accordance with 11.4.4 through 11.4.8.

11.4.4 Standard Pressure Proportioner.

11.4.4.1 The ball drip (automatic-type) drain valves shall be disassembled, cleaned, and reassembled.

11.4.4.2* The foam liquid storage tank shall be drained of foam liquid and flushed.

11.4.4.3 Foam liquid shall be permitted to be salvaged and reused.

11.4.4.4 The foam liquid tank shall be inspected for internal and external corrosion and hydrostatically tested to the specified working pressure.

11.4.5 Bladder Tank Proportioner.

11.4.5.1 Sight glass, where provided, shall be removed and cleaned.

11.4.5.2* The foam concentrate bladder tank shall be hydrostatically tested at system working pressure.

N 11.4.5.2.1 The hydrostatic test shall not create a pressure differential across the diaphragm.

N 11.4.5.2.2 While under system working pressure, the exterior of the foam concentration bladder tank shall be inspected for leaks.

11.4.6 Line Proportioner.

11.4.6.1 The foam concentrate tank shall be inspected for internal corrosion.

11.4.6.2 Pickup pipes inside the tank shall be inspected for corrosion, separation, or plugging.

11.4.6.3 The foam concentrate tank shall be drained and flushed.

11.4.6.4 Foam concentrate shall be permitted to be salvaged and reused.

11.4.7 Standard Balanced Pressure Proportioner.

11.4.7.1 Pump Operation.

11.4.7.1.1 The foam concentrate pump shall be operated.

11.4.7.1.2 Foam concentrate shall be circulated back to the tank.

11.4.7.2 Servicing. Foam pumps, drive train, and drivers shall be serviced in accordance with the manufacturer's instructions and frequency but not at intervals of more than 5 years.

11.4.7.3 Flushing. The diaphragm balancing valve shall be flushed through the diaphragm section with water or foam concentrate until fluid appears clear or new.

11.4.7.4 Corrosion and Sediment.

11.4.7.4.1 The foam concentrate tank shall be inspected internally for corrosion and sediment.

11.4.7.4.2 Excessive sediment shall require draining and flushing of the tank.

11.4.8 In-Line Balanced Pressure Proportioner.

11.4.8.1 Pump Operation.

11.4.8.1.1 The foam concentrate pump shall be operated.

11.4.8.1.2 Foam concentrate shall be circulated back to the tank.

11.4.8.2 Servicing. Foam pumps, drive train, and drivers shall be serviced in accordance with the manufacturer's instructions and frequency but not at intervals of more than 5 years.

11.4.8.3 Flushing. The diaphragm balancing valve shall be flushed through the diaphragm section with water or foam concentrate until fluid appears clear or new.

11.4.8.4 Corrosion and Sediment.

11.4.8.4.1 The foam concentrate tank shall be inspected internally for corrosion and sediment.

11.4.8.4.2 Excessive sediment shall require draining and flushing of the tank.

11.4.9 Pressure Vacuum Vents. The procedures specified in 11.4.9.1 through 11.4.9.13 shall be performed on pressure vacuum vents every 5 years.

11.4.9.1 The vent shall be removed from the expansion dome.

11.4.9.2 The vent shall be inspected to ensure that the opening is not blocked and that dirt or other foreign objects do not enter the tank.

11.4.9.3 The vent bonnet shall be removed.

11.4.9.4 The vacuum valve and pressure valve shall be lifted out.

11.4.9.5 The vent body shall be flushed internally, and the vacuum valve and the pressure valve shall be washed thoroughly.

11.4.9.6 The vent shall be inspected to ensure that the screen is not clogged, and the use of any hard, pointed objects to clear the screen shall be avoided.

11.4.9.7 If the liquid has become excessively gummy or solidified, the vent body and parts shall be soaked in hot soapy water.

11.4.9.8 The vent body shall be turned upside down and drained thoroughly.

11.4.9.9 Parts shall be dried by placing them in a warm and dry area or by using an air hose.

11.4.9.10 Parts shall be sprayed with a light Teflon® coating, and the vent shall be reassembled.

11.4.9.11 The use of any type of oil for lubrication purposes shall not be permitted.

11.4.9.12 The vent bonnet shall be replaced, and the vent shall be turned upside down slowly a few times to ensure proper freedom of the movable parts.

11.4.9.13 The vent shall be attached to the liquid storage tank expansion dome.

11.5 Component Action Requirements.

11.5.1 Whenever a component in a foam-water sprinkler system is adjusted, repaired, reconditioned, or replaced, the action required in Table 11.5.1 shall be performed.

11.5.2 Where the original installation standard is different from the cited standard, the use of the appropriate installing standard shall be permitted.

11.5.3 The actions of 11.5.1 and 11.5.2 shall not require a design review, which is outside the scope of this standard.

Δ **Table 11.5.1 Summary of Component Action Requirements**

Component	Adjust	Repair/ Recondition	Replace	Required Action
Water Delivery Components				
Discharge devices	X		X	(1) Inspect for leaks at system working pressure (2) Inspect for impairments at orifice
Fire department connections	X	X	X	See Chapter 13
Manual release	X	X	X	(1) Operational test (2) Inspect for leaks at system working pressure (3) Test all alarms
Pipe and fittings on closed-head system	X	X	X	Hydrostatic test in conformance with NFPA 16
Pipe and fittings on open-head system	X	X	X	Operational flow test
Foam Components				
Ball drip (automatic-type) drain valves				See Chapter 13
Bladder tank	X	X	X	Inspect water jacket for presence of foam concentrate
Foam concentrate	X		X	Submit a sample for laboratory analysis for conformance with manufacturer's specifications
Foam concentrate pump				See Chapter 8
Foam concentrate strainer(s)				See Chapter 13
Foam concentrate tank	X	X	X	Inspect for condition; repair as appropriate
Proportioning system(s)	X	X	X	Conduct flow test and inspect proportioning by refractometer test or equivalent
Water supply tank(s)				See Chapter 9
Alarm and Supervisory Components				
Detection system	X	X	X	Operational test for conformance with NFPA 16 and/or *NFPA 72*
Pressure-switch-type waterflow	X	X	X	Operational test using inspector's test connection
Valve supervisory device			X	Test for conformance with NFPA 16 and/or *NFPA 72*
Vane-type waterflow	X	X	X	Operational test using inspector's test connection
Water motor gong			X	Operational test using inspector's test connection
Status-Indicating Components				
Gauges	X		X	Verify at 0 psi (0 bar) and system working pressure; see Chapter 13 regarding calibration
Testing and Maintenance Components				
Auxiliary drains	X	X	X	Inspect for leaks at system working pressure
Inspector's test connection	X	X	X	Inspect for leaks at system working pressure
Main drain	X	X	X	Full-flow main drain test
Structural Components				
Hanger/seismic bracing	X	X	X	Inspect for conformance with NFPA 16 and/or NFPA 13
Pipe stands	X	X	X	Inspect for conformance with NFPA 16 and/or NFPA 13
Informational Components				
General information sign	X	X	X	Inspect for conformance with NFPA 16 and/or NFPA 13
Hydraulic information sign	X	X	X	Inspect for conformance with NFPA 16 and/or NFPA 13
Valve signs	X	X	X	Inspect for conformance with NFPA 16 and/or NFPA 13

Chapter 12   Water Mist Systems

12.1 General.

12.1.1 Minimum Requirements.

12.1.1.1 This chapter shall provide the minimum requirements for the routine inspection, testing, and maintenance of water mist systems only.

Δ **12.1.1.2** Table 12.1.1.2 shall be used to determine the minimum required infrequencies for inspection, testing, and maintenance.

12.1.2 Common Components and Valves. Where inspection, testing, and maintenance criteria for common components and valves are not specified in Chapter 12, the requirements of Chapter 13 shall apply.

N **12.1.3 Impairments.** The procedures outlined in Chapter 15 shall be followed where an impairment to protection occurs.

N **12.1.4 Hose Connections.** Hose connections shall be inspected, tested, and maintained in accordance with Chapters 6 and 13.

N **12.2 Inspection.**

N **12.2.1 Water Mist Nozzles.**

12.2.1.1 Water mist nozzles shall be inspected from the floor level annually.

12.2.1.1.1 Any water mist nozzle that shows signs of any of the following shall be replaced:

(1) Leakage
(2) Corrosion
(3) Physical damage
(4) Loss of fluid in the glass bulb heat responsive element
(5)* Loading
(6) Painting, unless painted by the water mist nozzle manufacturer

12.2.1.1.2 Any water mist nozzle that has been installed in the incorrect orientation shall be corrected by repositioning the branch line, drop, or sprig, or shall be replaced.

12.2.1.1.3 Water mist nozzles with glass bulbs shall be replaced if the bulbs are partially or fully empty of fluid.

12.2.1.1.4 Water mist nozzles installed in concealed spaces such as above suspended ceilings shall not require inspection.

12.2.1.1.5 Water mist nozzles installed in areas that are inaccessible for safety considerations due to process operations shall be inspected during each scheduled shutdown.

12.2.1.1.6 Stock, furnishings, or equipment closer to the water mist nozzle than permitted by the clearance specified in the manufacturer's installation instructions shall be corrected.

N **12.2.1.1.7** Open nozzles shall be removed, inspected, and cleaned during the flushing procedure for the mainline strainer.

12.2.1.2 The supply of spare automatic water mist nozzles shall be inspected annually for the correct number and type of water mist nozzles as required by NFPA 750.

N **12.2.2 Strainers and Filters.**

N **12.2.2.1** Mainline strainers and filters shall be flushed until clear after each operation or flow test.

N **12.2.2.2** Individual water mist nozzle strainers and filters shall be inspected and cleaned after each operation or flow test.

N **12.2.2.3** All strainers and filters shall be inspected and cleaned in accordance with the manufacturer's instructions.

N **12.2.2.4** Damaged or corroded parts or assemblies shall be replaced or repaired.

N **12.2.3 System Piping, Tubing, and Fittings.**

N **12.2.3.1** Water mist system distribution piping, tubing, and fittings shall be inspected annually from the floor level.

N **12.2.3.2** Piping, tubing, and fittings shall be free of mechanical damage, leakage, and corrosion.

N **12.2.3.3** Water mist system distribution piping shall not be subjected to external loads by materials either resting on the pipe or hung from the pipe.

N **12.2.3.4** Piping, tubing, and fittings installed in concealed spaces such as above suspended ceilings shall not require inspection.

N **12.2.3.5** Piping, tubing, and fittings installed in areas that are inaccessible for safety considerations due to process operations shall be inspected during each scheduled shutdown.

N **12.2.4 Hangers, Braces, and Supports.** *(See also A.5.2.3.)*

N **12.2.4.1** Water mist system distribution pipe hangers, braces, and supports shall be inspected annually from the floor level.

N **12.2.4.2** Hangers, braces, and supports shall not be damaged, loose, or unattached.

N **12.2.4.3** Hangers, braces, and supports that are damaged, loose, or unattached shall be replaced or refastened.

N **12.2.4.4*** Hangers, braces, and supports installed in concealed spaces such as above suspended ceilings shall not require inspection.

N **12.2.4.5** Hangers, braces, and supports installed in areas that are inaccessible for safety considerations due to process operations shall be inspected during each scheduled shutdown.

N **12.2.5 High Pressure Storage Cylinder Assemblies (Gas and Water).**

N **12.2.5.1** All cylinders and mounting brackets shall be fastened securely in accordance with the manufacturer's requirements.

N **12.2.5.1.1** Quarterly, compressed gas cylinders shall be inspected for proper securement.

N **12.2.5.1.2** Annually, high pressure water cylinders shall be inspected for proper securement.

N **12.2.5.2*** Compressed gas cylinders continuously in service without discharging shall be given a complete external visual inspection every 5 years or more frequently if required.

N **12.2.5.2.1** The visual inspection shall be in accordance with Section 3 of CGA C-6, *Standard for Visual Inspection of Steel Compressed Gas Cylinders*, except that the cylinders need not be emptied or stamped while under pressure.

Shaded text = Revisions.   Δ = Text deletions and figure/table revisions.   • = Section deletions.   *N* = New material.

2020 Edition

N **Table 12.1.1.2 Summary of Water Mist System Inspection, Testing, and Maintenance**

Item	Frequency	Reference
Inspection		
Additive storage cylinders	Quarterly/semiannually	12.2.7
Air compressors and receivers		Chapter 13
Backflow preventers		Chapter 13
Compressed gas storage cylinders, hoses, support, and restraint	Quarterly/annually/every 5 years	12.2.5.1.1, 12.2.5.2, 12.2.5.3, 12.2.5.9
Compressed gas storage cylinder valve and pressure	Semiannually/annually	12.2.5.4, 12.2.5.4.1, 12.2.5.4.2, 12.2.5.8
Control equipment		*NFPA 72*
Detection systems		*NFPA 72*
Enclosure features, interlocks	Semiannually	12.2.11
Fire pump system		Chapter 8
Gauges (piping system)		Chapter 13
Hangers, braces, and supports	Annually and after each system discharge or activation	12.2.4
Internal piping conditions		Chapter 14
Nozzles	Annually and after each system discharge or activation	12.2.1
Pneumatically operated valves and tubing	Semiannually	12.2.6
Pneumatically operated standby pumps	Monthly	12.2.9
Strainers and filters	After each system discharge or activation	12.2.2
System control valves		Chapter 13
System piping, tubing, and fittings	Annually and after each system discharge or activation	12.2.3
Water recirculation tanks	Monthly/quarterly/annually	12.2.8
Water storage cylinders (high pressure)	Quarterly/semiannually/ annually	12.2.5.1.2, 12.2.5.4, 12.2.5.4.3, 12.2.5.5, 12.2.5.6, 12.2.5.7, 12.2.5.8
Water storage tanks		Chapter 9
Water supply	Quarterly/annually	12.2.10
Testing		
Additives and injection system	Annually	12.3.4, 12.3.5
Air compressors and receivers	Annually	Chapter 13
Backflow preventers		Chapter 13
Compressed gas storage cylinder	5–12 years	12.3.6
Control equipment		12.3.7
Detection systems		12.3.8
Fire pump system		Chapter 8, 12.3.9
Gauges (piping system)		Chapter 13
Hoses	5 years	12.3.10
Interlocks	Annually	12.3.11
Nozzles, automatic	At 10 years and every 5 years thereafter	12.3.1.2
Nozzles, automatic (harsh environments)	At 5 years and every 5 years thereafter	12.3.1.3
Nozzles, open	At 10 years and every 5 years thereafter	12.3.2.3

(continues)

Shaded text = Revisions.   **Δ** = Text deletions and figure/table revisions.   • = Section deletions.   **N** = New material.

N **Table 12.1.1.2**   *Continued*

Item	Frequency	Reference
Nozzles, open (harsh environments)	Annually	12.3.2.2
Pneumatic valves	Semiannually	12.3.12
Pneumatic valve solenoid releases	Annually	12.3.13
Pneumatically operated standby pumps	Annually	12.3.14
Strainers and filters	Annually	12.3.3
System control valves	Annually	12.3.15
Water mist system	Annually	12.3.16
Water recirculation tanks	Annually	12.3.17
Water storage cylinders (high pressure)	5–12 years	12.3.18
Water storage tanks		12.3.19
Water supply	Annually	12.3.20
Maintenance		
Air compressors and receivers		Chapter 13
Backflow preventers		Chapter 13
Control equipment		*NFPA 72*
Detection systems		*NFPA 72*
Fire pump system		Chapter 8
Pneumatically operated standby pumps	Every 5 years	12.4.3
Strainers and filters	Annually and after each system discharge	12.2.2
Water mist system	Annually	12.4.1
Water tanks	Annually	12.4.1

N **12.2.5.2.2** Inspections shall be made only by competent personnel.

N **12.2.5.2.3** The inspection results shall be recorded on both of the following:

(1) A record tag permanently attached to each cylinder
(2) A suitable inspection report

N **12.2.5.2.3.1** A completed copy of the inspection report shall be furnished to the owner of the system or an authorized representative.

N **12.2.5.2.3.2** These records shall be retained by the owner for the life of the system.

N **12.2.5.3** Annually, the cylinder shall be visually inspected for the proper specification, capacity, and pressure rating.

N **12.2.5.4** The pressure in the high-pressure storage containers shall be within the water mist manufacturer's specifications.

N **12.2.5.4.1** Pressure in compressed gas cylinders that are electrically supervised and monitored shall be inspected, at a minimum, semiannually, or in accordance with the manufacturer's specifications.

N **12.2.5.4.2** Pressure in compressed gas cylinders that are not electrically supervised and monitored shall be inspected, at a minimum, monthly, or in accordance with the manufacturer's specifications.

N **12.2.5.4.3** The cylinder pressure on the discharge side of a high-pressure water storage container shall be inspected annually.

N **12.2.5.5** The water level in the high-pressure storage containers shall be within the water mist manufacturer's specifications.

N **12.2.5.5.1** Unsupervised water levels in high-pressure cylinders shall be inspected quarterly.

N **12.2.5.5.2** Supervised water levels in high-pressure cylinders shall be inspected semiannually.

N **12.2.5.6** Annually, the vent plugs on high-pressure water storage containers shall be visually inspected to ensure the vent is not ruptured or open.

N **12.2.5.7** Annually, the filter on high-pressure water storage containers shall be visually inspected to ensure it is clean.

N **12.2.5.8** All manually operated indicating control valves shall be visually inspected to confirm that they are in proper position, at a minimum, semiannually, or in accordance with manufacturer's specifications.

N **12.2.5.9** Annually, all hoses used as a part of the system shall be visually inspected for damage.

N **12.2.6 Pneumatic Valves and Tubing.** Pneumatically operated valves and pneumatic tubing shall be visually inspected, at a minimum, semiannually, or in accordance with the manufacturer's specifications.

N **12.2.7 Additive Storage Cylinders.**

N **12.2.7.1** Quarterly, the storage cylinder shall be visually inspected for external corrosion or damage.

N **12.2.7.2** Semiannually, the quantity of the additive agent shall be inspected.

N **12.2.8 Water Recirculation Tanks.**

N **12.2.8.1** All tank attachments and supports shall be secured in accordance with the manufacturer's requirements.

N **12.2.8.2** The water level in recirculation tanks shall be within the water mist manufacturer's specifications.

N **12.2.8.2.1** Unsupervised water levels in recirculation tanks shall be inspected monthly.

N **12.2.8.2.2** Supervised water levels in recirculation tanks shall be inspected quarterly.

N **12.2.8.3** Annually, the water quality shall be inspected and drained, flushed, and refilled as necessary.

N **12.2.8.4** Annually, the filters, strainers, and cyclone separator shall be visually inspected and cleaned as necessary.

N **12.2.9 Pneumatically Operated Standby Pumps.**

N **12.2.9.1** Monthly, the moisture trap shall be visually inspected and emptied.

N **12.2.9.2** Monthly, the compressed gas supply and inlet air pressure shall be visually inspected in accordance with the manufacturer's specifications.

N **12.2.9.3** Monthly, the outlet water (standby) pressure shall be visually inspected in accordance with the manufacturer's specifications.

N **12.2.9.4** Monthly, the oil level on air regulator units shall be visually inspected in accordance with the manufacturer's specifications.

N **12.2.10 Water Supply.**

N **12.2.10.1** Quarterly, the water supply pressure shall be visually inspected to determine that it is within the water mist manufacturer's specifications.

N **12.2.10.2** The water quality shall be inspected semiannually for the first year and then annually thereafter.

N **12.2.11 Enclosures and Interlocks.** Semiannually, the integrity of the enclosure and interlocks shall be inspected.

N **12.3 Testing.**

N **12.3.1 Nozzles, Automatic.**

12.3.1.1* Where required by this section, sample automatic water mist nozzles shall be submitted to a recognized testing laboratory acceptable to the authority having jurisdiction for functional testing.

12.3.1.2 Automatic water mist nozzles that have been installed for 10 years shall be replaced, or representative samples shall be tested and then retested at 5-year intervals.

12.3.1.3* Where water mist nozzles are subjected to harsh environments, including corrosive atmospheres and corrosive water supplies, they shall be either replaced or representative samples tested on a 5-year basis.

12.3.1.4* A representative sample of water mist nozzles for testing per 12.3.1.2 or 12.3.1.3 shall consist of a minimum of four water mist nozzles or 1 percent of the number of water mist nozzles per individual water mist nozzle sample, whichever is greater.

12.3.1.5* Where one water mist nozzle within a representative sample fails to meet the test requirement, all water mist nozzles within the area represented by that sample shall be replaced.

N **12.3.1.6** Automatic water mist nozzles that need to be replaced shall be in accordance with the requirements of 12.4.2.

N **12.3.2 Nozzles, Open.**

N **12.3.2.1** Water mist nozzles installed to protect application areas without protective coverings shall be capable to operate and protect the hazard with an overspray residue in the event of a fire.

N **12.3.2.2*** Where water mist nozzles are subjected to environments with residues, including corrosive atmospheres and corrosive water supplies, they shall be either replaced or representative samples tested on a 1-year basis. *(See also A.12.3.1.3.)*

N **12.3.2.3** Where the nature of the protected property is such that water cannot be discharged annually as indicated in 12.3.16.5 and not subject to the conditions in 12.3.2.2, open water mist nozzles that have been in service for 10 years shall be either replaced or representative samples shall be tested and then retested at 5-year intervals. *(See A.12.3.2.2.)*

N **12.3.2.4** A representative sample of water mist nozzles for testing per 12.2.10.2 shall consist of a minimum of three water mist nozzles or 1 percent of the number of water mist nozzles per individual water mist nozzle sample, whichever is greater.

N **12.3.2.5*** Where one water mist nozzle within a representative sample fails to meet the test requirement, all water mist nozzles within the area represented by that sample shall be replaced.

N **12.3.3 Strainers and Filters.** Mainline strainers (basket or screen) shall be flushed until clear after each operation or flow test.

N **12.3.4 Additives.** Samples of the additive shall be submitted in accordance with the manufacturer's recommended sampling procedures for evaluation of quality to its specification.

N **12.3.5 Operational Test Performance with Additives.**

N **12.3.5.1** Operational tests shall be conducted to ensure the injection rate of the additive for the water mist system responds as designed, both automatically and manually.

N **12.3.5.2** The test procedures shall simulate anticipated emergency events so the response of the water mist system can be evaluated.

N **12.3.5.3** Where a discharge from the system discharge devices would create a hazardous condition or conflict with local requirements, an approved alternate method to achieve full flow conditions shall be permitted.

N **12.3.5.4** It shall be permissible to test the full flow discharge from the water mist system with additive using water only in lieu of the additive.

N **12.3.5.5** Under test conditions, the automatic fire detection systems, when exposed to a test source, shall operate within the requirements of NFPA 72 for the type of detector provided, and the response time shall be recorded.

N 12.3.5.6 The time lapse between operation of detection systems and water delivery time to the protected area shall be recorded for open discharge devices.

N 12.3.6 Compressed Gas Storage Cylinders.

N 12.3.6.1 Gas cylinders designed in accordance with U.S. Department of Transportation (DOT), Canadian Transport Commission (CTC), or similar containers shall not be recharged without retesting if more than 5 years have elapsed since the date of last test.

N 12.3.6.2 A completed copy of the test report shall be furnished to the owner of the system or an authorized representative.

N 12.3.6.3 These records shall be retained by the owner for the life of the system.

N 12.3.7 Control Equipment.

N 12.3.7.1 Operational tests shall be conducted to ensure the control equipment for the water mist system responds as designed, both automatically and manually.

N 12.3.7.2 Annual operational testing shall be conducted in accordance with the requirements of *NFPA 72*.

N 12.3.7.3 Where a discharge from the system discharge devices would create a hazardous condition or conflict with local requirements, an approved alternate method to achieve full flow conditions shall be permitted.

N 12.3.8 Detection Systems.

N 12.3.8.1 Operational tests shall be conducted to ensure the control equipment for the water mist system responds as designed, both automatically and manually.

N 12.3.8.2 Conduct annual operational testing of the initiating devices for detection in accordance with the requirements of *NFPA 72*.

N 12.3.8.3 Under test conditions, the automatic fire detection systems, when exposed to a test source, shall operate within the requirements of *NFPA 72* for the type of detector provided, and the response time shall be recorded.

N 12.3.8.4 The time lapse between operation of detection systems and water delivery time to the protected area shall be recorded for open discharge devices.

N 12.3.9 Fire Pumps and Drivers.

N 12.3.9.1 Fire pumps shall be tested in accordance with the requirements of Section 8.3.

N 12.3.9.2 Water mist systems that are powered by or operated by pressurized gas (normally air or nitrogen) cylinders or pressure vessels shall be tested quarterly or determined by an approved risk analysis in accordance with the manufacturer's specifications using pressurized gas and water from either the primary cylinders or pressure vessels and/or tanks or by using temporary/test cylinders or tanks to verify nozzle flows (no blockage, fully developed spray pattern) upon operation.

N 12.3.10 Hoses.

N 12.3.10.1 All hose shall be tested every 5 years.

N 12.3.10.2 All hose shall be tested at 1½ times the maximum container pressure at 130°F (54.4°C).

N 12.3.10.3 The hose testing procedure shall be as follows:

(1) The hose is removed from any attachment.
(2) The hose assembly is then placed in a protective enclosure designed to permit visual observation of the test.
(3) The hose must be completely filled with water before testing.
(4) Pressure then is applied at a rate-of-pressure rise to reach the test pressure within 1 minute. The test pressure is then maintained for 1 full minute. Observations are then made to note any distortion or leakage.
(5) If the test pressure has not dropped or if the couplings have not moved, the pressure is released. The hose assembly is considered to have passed the hydrostatic test if no permanent distortion has taken place.
(6) Hose assembly passing the test must be completely dried internally. If heat is used for drying, the temperature must not exceed the manufacturer's specifications.
(7) Hose assemblies failing a hydrostatic test must be marked and destroyed and be replaced with new assemblies.
(8) Each hose assembly passing the hydrostatic test is marked to show the date of test.

N 12.3.11 Interlocks.

N 12.3.11.1 Annual testing to confirm the operation of the interlock for ventilation shall be conducted, if required.

N 12.3.11.2 Annual testing to confirm the operation of the interlock for fuel or lubrication systems shall be conducted, if required.

N 12.3.12 Pneumatic Valves.

N 12.3.12.1 Operational tests shall be conducted to ensure the pneumatic valves for the water mist system respond as designed, both automatically and manually.

N 12.3.12.2 Semiannual testing of the following pneumatic valves shall be conducted for operation in accordance with the manufacturer's instructions:

(1) Slave valves
(2) Valves intended to cycle on–off

N 12.3.12.3 All pneumatic cylinder release valves shall be reset after testing.

N 12.3.13 Pneumatic Valve Solenoid Releases. All pneumatic cylinder release valves shall be reset after testing.

N 12.3.13.1 Operational tests shall be conducted to ensure the pneumatic valve solenoid releases for the water mist system responds as designed, both automatically and manually.

N 12.3.13.2 Annual testing of the following pneumatic solenoid valve releases shall be conducted for operation in accordance with the manufacturer's instructions:

(1) Electric release
(2) Manual release

N 12.3.14 Pneumatically Operated Standby Pumps.

N 12.3.14.1 Pumps (booster pumps, jockey pumps or transfer pumps) used in the water mist system that are not main pressure pumps shall be operated to demonstrate support of their design function for the main pressure pumps.

N 12.3.14.2 Standby pumps shall be operated at least annually to demonstrate their system flow support when the main pressure pumps are tested.

N 12.3.15 System Control Valves. Each control valve for a zone of protection by the water mist system shall be operated annually through its full range and returned to its normal position.

N 12.3.16 Water Mist System. Water mist systems shall be operated annually in accordance with the manufacturer's instructions.

N 12.3.16.1 Test Preparation. Precautions shall be taken to prevent damage to property during the test. *(See also A.10.3.2.)*

N 12.3.16.2 Operational Test Performance. Operational tests shall be conducted to ensure the water mist system responds as designed, both automatically and manually.

N 12.3.16.2.1 Where the nature of the protected property is such that water cannot be discharged into the occupancy or onto the hazard, an operational test shall be conducted from a test connection with an orifice equivalent to the friction loss for the total number of nozzles.

N 12.3.16.3* Response Time.

N 12.3.16.3.1 Under test conditions, the detection systems, shall operate with the specifications from the acceptance test and 12.3.7.

N 12.3.16.3.2 The response times shall be recorded.

N 12.3.16.4 Discharge Time. The time lapse between operation of detection systems and water delivery time to the protected area shall be recorded.

N 12.3.16.5* Discharge Patterns.

N 12.3.16.5.1 The water discharge patterns from all of the open water mist nozzles shall be observed to ensure that patterns are not impeded by plugged nozzles, to ensure that nozzles are correctly positioned, and to ensure that obstructions do not prevent discharge patterns from fully developing. *(See also 13.4.4.2.3.1.)*

N 12.3.16.5.2 Where the nature of the protected property is such that water cannot be discharged, the nozzles shall be inspected for proper orientation and the system tested with air to ensure that the nozzles are not obstructed.

N 12.3.16.5.3 Where obstructions occur, the piping and nozzles shall be cleaned and the system retested.

N 12.3.16.6 Pressure Readings.

N 12.3.16.6.1 Pressure readings shall be recorded at the hydraulically most remote nozzle or test connection to ensure the water flow has not been impeded by partially closed valves or by plugged strainers or piping.

N 12.3.16.6.2 For water mist systems with a deluge valve, a second pressure reading shall be recorded at the deluge valve to ensure the water supply is adequate.

N 12.3.16.6.3 Readings shall be compared to the hydraulic design pressures to ensure the original system design requirements are met and the water supply is adequate to meet the design requirements.

N 12.3.16.6.3.1 Where the hydraulically most remote nozzle is inaccessible, nozzles shall be permitted to be checked visually without taking a pressure reading on the most remote nozzle.

N 12.3.16.6.3.2 Where the reading taken at the riser indicates that the water supply has deteriorated, a gauge shall be placed on the hydraulically most remote nozzle and the results compared with the required design pressure.

N 12.3.16.7 Multiple Systems. The maximum number of systems expected to operate in case of fire shall be tested simultaneously to inspect the adequacy of the water supply.

N 12.3.16.8 Return to Service. After the full flow test, the water mist system shall be returned to service in accordance with the manufacturer's instructions.

N 12.3.17 Water Recirculation Tanks.

N 12.3.17.1 Operational tests shall be conducted to ensure water recirculation tanks for the water mist system responds as designed, both automatically and manually.

N 12.3.17.2 Annual testing shall be conducted for operation in accordance with the manufacturer's instructions:

(1) Float-operated valves
(2) Backflow prevention device, when present

N 12.3.17.3 Pressure reading shall be recorded at the outlet of the recirculation tank during the operational discharge test of the water mist system.

N 12.3.18 Water Storage Cylinders (High Pressure).

N 12.3.18.1* Water cylinders used with high pressure for power to deliver the water mist, or those that become pressurized at activation or water delivery or as the water source for a water mist system shall be tested in accordance with applicable current pressure vessel standard or code.

N 12.3.18.2 Water cylinders designed in accordance with U.S. Department of Transportation (DOT), Canadian Transport Commission (CTC), or similar containers shall not be recharged without retesting if more than 5 years have elapsed since the date of last test.

N 12.3.18.3 A completed copy of the test report shall be furnished to the owner of the system or an authorized representative.

N 12.3.18.4 The records shall be retained by the owner for the life of the system.

N 12.3.19 Water Storage Tanks. Water storage tanks or cylinders shall be tested in accordance with the requirements of Section 9.3.

N 12.3.20 Water Supply. Annual testing shall be conducted in accordance with Section 7.3 to verify the source:

(1) Pressure
(2) Flow
(3) Quantity
(4) Duration

12.4 Maintenance.

Δ 12.4.1 General.

12.4.1.1 Maintenance shall be performed to keep the system equipment operable or to make repairs.

12.4.1.1.1 Where required by the manufacturer, maintenance shall be performed on devices not described in this standard.

12.4.1.2 As-built system installation drawings, original acceptance test records, and device manufacturer's maintenance bulletins shall be retained to assist in the proper care of the system and its components.

12.4.1.3 Replacement components shall be in accordance with the manufacturer's specifications and the original system design.

12.4.1.4 Spare components shall be accessible and shall be stored in a manner to prevent damage or contamination.

12.4.1.5* After each system operation, a representative sample of operated water mist nozzles in the activated zone shall be inspected.

12.4.1.6 After each system operation due to fire, the system filters and strainers shall be cleaned or replaced.

Δ **12.4.1.7** Annually, a water tank used to supply a water mist system shall be drained and refilled.

N **12.4.1.8** Annually, a water mist system with open nozzles shall be flushed.

12.4.2 Water Mist Nozzles.

12.4.2.1* Replacement water mist nozzles shall have the proper characteristics for the application intended, including the nozzle model and temperature rating.

12.4.2.2 Only new water mist nozzles shall be used to replace existing water mist nozzles.

12.4.2.3* A supply of spare water mist nozzles (never fewer than three) shall be maintained on the premises so that any water mist nozzles that have operated or been damaged in any way can be promptly replaced.

12.4.2.3.1 The water mist nozzles shall correspond to the manufacturer(s), models, and temperature ratings of the water mist nozzles in the property.

12.4.2.3.2 The automatic water mist nozzles shall be kept in a cabinet located where the temperature will at no time exceed 100°F (38°C).

12.4.2.3.3 The stock of spare thermally activated nozzles shall include all types and ratings installed and shall be as follows:

(1) For systems having fewer than 50 nozzles, not fewer than 3 nozzles

(2) For systems having 50 to 300 nozzles, not fewer than 6 nozzles

(3) For systems having 301 to 1000 nozzles, not fewer than 12 nozzles

(4) For systems having over 1000 nozzles, not fewer than 24 nozzles

12.4.2.4* Where required by the manufacturer, a special water mist nozzle wrench shall be provided and kept in the cabinet to be used for the removal and installation of nozzles.

12.4.2.4.1 One water mist nozzle wrench shall be provided for each type of nozzle installed.

12.4.2.5 Protective Coverings.

12.4.2.5.1 Water mist nozzles protecting spray areas and mixing rooms in resin application areas installed with protective coverings shall continue to be protected against overspray residue so that they will operate in the event of fire.

12.4.2.5.2* Water mist nozzles installed as described in 12.4.2.5.1 shall be protected using cellophane bags having a thickness of 0.003 in. (0.076 mm) or less or thin paper bags.

12.4.2.5.3 Coverings shall be replaced periodically so that heavy deposits of residue do not accumulate.

12.4.2.6 Water mist nozzles shall not be altered in any respect or have any type of ornamentation, paint, or coatings applied after shipment from the manufacturer.

12.4.2.7 Automatic water mist nozzles used for protecting commercial-type cooking equipment and ventilating systems shall be replaced annually.

12.4.2.7.1 Where automatic water mist nozzles are used and annual examination shows no buildup of grease or other material on the nozzles, the nozzles shall not be required to be replaced.

N **12.4.3 Pneumatically Operated Standby Pumps.** Pneumatically operated standby pumps shall be rebuilt every 5 years or as specified by the manufacturer.

12.5 Training.

12.5.1 All persons who might be expected to inspect, test, maintain, or operate water mist systems shall be trained thoroughly in the functions they are expected to perform.

12.5.2 Refresher training shall be provided as recommended by the manufacturer or by the authority having jurisdiction.

Chapter 13   Common Components and Valves

13.1* General.

13.1.1 Minimum Requirements.

13.1.1.1 This chapter shall provide the minimum requirements for the routine inspection, testing, and maintenance of common components and valves.

13.1.1.2 Table 13.1.1.2 shall be used to determine the minimum required frequencies for inspection, testing, and maintenance.

13.2 General Provisions.

13.2.1 The property owner or designated representative shall have manufacturers' literature available to provide specific instructions for inspecting, testing, and maintaining the valves and associated equipment.

• **13.2.2*** All system valves shall be protected from physical damage and shall be accessible.

• **13.2.3* Main Drain Test.** A main drain test shall be conducted annually for each water supply lead-in to a building water-based fire protection system to determine whether there has been a change in the condition of the water supply.

13.2.3.1 Where the lead-in to a building supplies a header or manifold serving multiple systems, a single main drain test shall be permitted.

13.2.3.2 In systems where the sole water supply is through a backflow preventer and/or pressure-reducing valves, the main drain test of at least one system downstream of the device shall be conducted on a quarterly basis.

△ **Table 13.1.1.2 Summary of Valves, Valve Components, and Trim Inspection, Testing, and Maintenance**

Item	Frequency	Reference
Inspection		
Alarm Valves		
Exterior	Quarterly	13.4.1.1
Interior	5 years	13.4.1.2
Strainers, filters, orifices	5 years	13.4.1.2
Backflow Prevention Assemblies		
Reduced pressure	Weekly	13.7.1
Reduced-pressure detectors	Weekly	13.7.1
Interior	5 years	13.7.1.3
Check Valves		
Interior	5 years	13.4.2.1
Control Valves		
All valves except locked or supervised	Weekly	13.3.2.1
Locked or supervised	Monthly	13.3.2.1.1
Electrically supervised	Quarterly	13.3.2.1.2
Dry Pipe Valves/		
* Quick-Opening Devices*		
Enclosure (during cold weather)		Chapter 4
Exterior	Monthly	13.4.5.1.2
Interior	Annually	13.4.5.1.3
Strainers, filters, orifices	5 years	13.4.5.1.4
Low temperature alarm	Annually	Chapter 4
Deluge Valves		
Enclosure (during cold weather)	Daily/weekly	Chapter 4
Exterior	Monthly	13.4.4.1.1
Interior	Annually/5 years	13.4.4.1.2
Strainers, filters, orifices	5 years	13.4.4.1.3
Fire Department Connections	Quarterly	13.8.1
Gauges	Monthly/quarterly	13.2.5
Hose Valves	Quarterly	13.6.1
Preaction Valves		
Enclosure (during cold weather)		Chapter 4
Exterior	Monthly	13.4.3.1.1
Interior	Annually/5 years	13.4.3.1.2
Strainers, filters, orifices	5 years	13.4.3.1.3
Pressure-Regulating and Relief Valves		
Master pressure-regulating	Weekly	13.5.4.1
Sprinkler system pressure-reducing	Quarterly	13.5.1.1
Hose connection pressure-regulating	Annually	13.5.2.1
Hose rack pressure-regulating	Annually	13.5.3.1
Fire pump circulation relief	With no flow test	13.5.6.1
Fire pump main pressure-relief	With fire pump test	13.5.6.2.1
Valve Supervisory Signal Initiating Device	Quarterly	13.3.2.1.3
Supervisory Signal Devices (except valve supervisory switches)	Quarterly	13.2.6.1
Testing		
Backflow Prevention Assemblies	Annually	13.7.2
Control Valves		
Operation and position	Annually	13.3.3.1
Valve status test	After the control valve closed and reopened	13.3.3.4
Supervisory	Semiannually	13.3.3.5
Deluge Valves		
Trip test	Annually/3 years	13.4.4.2.3

(continues)

Shaded text = Revisions.   △ = Text deletions and figure/table revisions.   • = Section deletions.   *N* = New material.

Δ **Table 13.1.1.2**   *Continued*

Item	Frequency	Reference
Dry Pipe Valves/		
Quick-Opening Devices		
Air leakage	3 years	13.4.5.2.9
Priming water	Quarterly	13.4.5.2.1
Low air pressure alarm	Annually	13.4.5.2.6
Quick-opening devices	Quarterly	13.4.5.2.4
Trip test	Annually	13.4.5.2.2
Full-flow trip test	3 years	13.4.5.2.2.2
Gauges	5 years	13.2.5.2
Main Drains	Annually/quarterly	13.2.3
Preaction Valves		
Priming water	Quarterly	13.4.3.2.1
Low air pressure alarms	Quarterly	13.4.3.2.11
Trip test	Annually/3 years	13.4.3.2.2 and 13.4.3.2.3
Air leakage	3 years	13.4.3.2.6
Low temperature alarm	Annually	13.4.3.2.12
Pressure-Regulating and Relief Valves		
Master pressure-regulating	Quarterly/annually	13.5.4.2 and 13.5.4.3
Sprinkler systems pressure-reducing	Annually/5 years	13.5.1.3 and 13.5.1.2
Hose connection pressure-regulating	Annually/5 years	13.5.2.3 and 13.5.2.2
Hose rack pressure-regulating	Annually/5 years	13.5.3.3 and 13.5.3.2
Fire pump circulation relief	With churn test	13.5.6.1.2
Fire pump pressure relief valves	With fire pump test	13.5.6.2.2
Hose Valves	Annually/3 years	13.6.2
Waterflow Alarms	Quarterly/semiannually	13.2.4
Supervisory Signal Devices (except valve supervisory switches)	Annually	13.2.6.2
Maintenance		
Alarm Valves	Per manufacturer	13.4.1.3
Backflow Prevention Assemblies	Per manufacturer	13.7.3
Check Valves	Per manufacturer	13.4.2.2
Control Valves (outside screw and yoke)	Annually	13.3.4
Deluge Valves	Annually/5 years	13.4.4.3
Dry Pipe Valves/	Annually	13.4.5.3
Quick-Opening Devices		
Hose Valves	As needed	13.6.3
Preaction Valves	Annually/5 years	13.4.3.3

13.2.3.3 When there is a 10 percent reduction in full flow pressure when compared to the original acceptance test or previously performed tests, the cause of the reduction shall be identified and corrected if necessary.

13.2.4 Waterflow Alarm Devices.

N **13.2.4.1** Activation of the waterflow alarm device shall result in an audible alarm within 5 minutes after such flow begins and until such flow stops.

N **13.2.4.2** Activation of the initiating device shall occur within 90 seconds of waterflow at the alarm-initiating device when flow occurs that is equal to or greater than that from a single sprinkler of the smallest orifice size installed in the system. [**72:**17.13.2]

13.2.4.3 Mechanical Waterflow Alarm Devices, Including, but Not Limited to, Water Motor Gongs.

13.2.4.3.1 Mechanical waterflow alarm devices shall be inspected quarterly to verify that they are free of physical damage

13.2.4.3.2 Mechanical waterflow alarm devices shall be tested quarterly.

13.2.4.4 Vane-Type, Paddle-Type, and Pressure-Switch-Type Waterflow Devices.

13.2.4.4.1 Vane-type, paddle-type, and pressure-switch-type waterflow alarm devices shall be inspected quarterly to verify that they are free of physical damage.

Shaded text = Revisions.   Δ = Text deletions and figure/table revisions.   • = Section deletions.   *N* = New material.

2020 Edition

13.2.4.4.2 Vane-type, paddle-type, and pressure-switch-type waterflow alarm devices shall be tested semiannually.

13.2.4.5 Testing waterflow alarm devices on wet pipe systems shall be accomplished by opening the inspector's test valve or by using the automated test equipment in accordance with 4.6.6.

13.2.4.6 Where freezing weather conditions or other circumstances prohibits the use of the inspector's test valve, the bypass connection shall be permitted to be used.

13.2.4.7 Fire pumps shall not be taken out of service during testing unless constantly attended by qualified personnel, or all impairment procedures contained in Chapter 15 are followed.

13.2.4.8* Testing waterflow alarm devices on dry pipe, preaction, or deluge systems shall be accomplished by using the bypass connection.

13.2.5 Gauges.

13.2.5.1* Inspections.

13.2.5.1.1* Gauges shall be inspected monthly to verify that the gauges are operable and not physically damaged.

13.2.5.1.2 Gauges monitoring water pressure shall be inspected quarterly to verify that normal water supply pressure is being maintained.

13.2.5.1.3 Gauges monitoring air or nitrogen pressure shall be inspected monthly to verify that normal air or nitrogen pressure are being maintained.

13.2.5.1.3.1 The gauge on the quick-opening device, if provided, shall indicate the same pressure as the gauge on the system side of the dry pipe valve.

13.2.5.1.3.2 Where air pressure supervision is connected to a constantly attended location, gauges shall be inspected quarterly.

13.2.5.1.4* For dry pipe or preaction systems protecting freezers with an air pressure gauge(s) on the air line(s) between the compressor and the dry pipe or preaction valve, the air pressure gauge near the compressor shall be compared monthly to the pressure gauge above the dry pipe or preaction valve.

13.2.5.1.4.1 When the gauge near the compressor is reading higher than the gauge near the dry pipe valve, the air line in service shall be taken out of service and the alternate air line shall be opened to equalize the pressure.

13.2.5.1.4.2 An air line taken out of service in accordance with 13.2.5.1.4.1 shall be internally inspected, removed of all ice blockage, and reassembled for use as a future alternate air line.

13.2.5.2 Gauges shall be replaced every 5 years or tested every 5 years by comparison with a calibrated gauge.

13.2.5.3 Gauges not accurate to within 3 percent of the full scale shall be recalibrated or replaced.

13.2.6 Supervisory Signal Devices (except valve supervisory switches).

13.2.6.1 Supervisory signal devices shall be inspected quarterly to verify that they are free of physical damage.

13.2.6.2 Supervisory signal devices shall be tested annually in accordance with the manufacturer's instructions.

13.2.7 Records. Records shall be maintained in accordance with Section 4.3.

13.3 Control Valves in Water-Based Fire Protection Systems.

13.3.1* Each control valve shall be identified and have a sign indicating the system or portion of the system it controls.

13.3.1.1 Systems that have more than one control valve that must be closed to work on a system shall have a sign on each affected valve referring to the existence and location of other valves.

13.3.1.2* When a normally open valve is closed, the procedures established in Chapter 15 shall be followed.

13.3.1.3 Each normally open valve shall be secured by means of a seal or a lock or shall be electrically supervised in accordance with the applicable NFPA standards.

13.3.1.4 Normally closed valves shall be secured by means of a seal or shall be electrically supervised in accordance with the applicable NFPA standard.

13.3.1.5 Sealing or electrical supervision shall not be required for hose valves.

13.3.2 Inspection.

13.3.2.1 All valves shall be inspected weekly.

13.3.2.1.1 Valves secured with locks or supervised in accordance with applicable NFPA standards shall be permitted to be inspected monthly.

13.3.2.1.2 Valves that are electrically supervised shall be permitted to be inspected quarterly.

13.3.2.1.3 Control valve supervisory alarm devices shall be inspected quarterly to verify that they are free of physical damage.

13.3.2.1.4 After any alterations or repairs, an inspection shall be made by the property owner or designated representative to ensure that the system is in service and all valves are in the normal position and properly sealed, locked, or electrically supervised.

13.3.2.2* The valve inspection shall verify that the valves are in the following condition:

(1) In the normal open or closed position
(2)* Sealed, locked, or supervised
(3) Accessible
(4) Post indicator valves (PIVs) are provided with correct wrenches
(5) Free from external leaks
(6) Provided with applicable identification

13.3.3 Testing.

13.3.3.1 Each control valve shall be operated annually through its full range and returned to its normal position.

13.3.3.2* Post indicator valves shall be opened until spring or torsion is felt in the rod, indicating that the rod has not become detached from the valve.

13.3.3.2.1 This test shall be conducted every time the valve is closed.

13.3.3.3 Post indicator and outside screw and yoke valves shall be backed a one-quarter turn from the fully open position to prevent jamming.

13.3.3.4 A valve status test shall be conducted any time the control valve is closed and reopened at system riser.

13.3.3.5* Valve Supervisory Switches.

13.3.3.5.1 Valve supervisory switches shall be tested semiannually.

13.3.3.5.2 A distinctive signal shall indicate movement from the valve's normal position during either the first two revolutions of a handwheel or when the stem of the valve has moved one-fifth of the distance from its normal position.

13.3.3.5.3 The signal shall not be restored at any valve position except the normal position.

13.3.4 Maintenance.

13.3.4.1 The operating stems of outside screw and yoke valves shall be lubricated annually.

13.3.4.2 The valve then shall be completely closed and reopened to test its operation and distribute the lubricant.

13.4 System Valves.

13.4.1 Inspection of Alarm Valves. Alarm valves shall be inspected as described in 13.4.1.1 and 13.4.1.2.

13.4.1.1* Alarm valves and system riser check valves shall be externally inspected quarterly and shall verify the following:

(1) The gauges indicate normal supply water pressure is being maintained.
(2) The valves and trim are free of physical damage.
(3) All valves are in the appropriate open or closed position.
(4) The retarding chamber or alarm drains are not leaking.

13.4.1.2* Alarm valves and their associated strainers, filters, and restriction orifices shall be inspected internally every 5 years unless tests indicate a greater frequency is necessary.

13.4.1.3 Maintenance.

13.4.1.3.1 Internal components shall be cleaned/repaired as necessary in accordance with the manufacturer's instructions.

13.4.1.3.2 The system shall be returned to service in accordance with the manufacturer's instructions.

13.4.2 Check Valves.

13.4.2.1 Inspection. Valves shall be inspected internally every 5 years to verify that all of the valve's components operate correctly.

13.4.2.2 Maintenance. Internal components shall be cleaned, repaired, or replaced as necessary in accordance with the manufacturer's instructions.

13.4.3 Preaction Valves.

13.4.3.1 Inspection.

13.4.3.1.1 The preaction valve shall be externally inspected monthly to verify the following:

(1) The valve is free from physical damage.
(2) All trim valves are in the appropriate open or closed position.

(3) The valve seat is not leaking.
(4) Electrical components are in service.

13.4.3.1.2 The interior of the preaction valve and the condition of detection devices shall be inspected annually when the trip test is conducted.

13.4.3.1.2.1 Internal inspection of valves that can be reset without removal of a faceplate shall be permitted to be conducted every 5 years.

13.4.3.1.3 Strainers, filters, restricted orifices, and diaphragm chambers shall be inspected internally every 5 years unless tests indicate a greater frequency is necessary.

13.4.3.1.4 Preaction systems with auxiliary drains shall require a sign at the valve indicating the number of auxiliary drains and the location of each individual drain.

13.4.3.2 Testing.

13.4.3.2.1* The priming water level in supervised preaction systems shall be tested quarterly for compliance with the manufacturer's instructions.

13.4.3.2.2 Except for preaction systems covered by 13.4.3.2.5, every 3 years the preaction valve shall be trip tested with the control valve fully open.

13.4.3.2.3 During those years when full flow testing in accordance with 13.4.3.2.2 is not required, the preaction valve shall be trip tested with the control valve partially open.

N **13.4.3.2.4*** Preaction valve flow tests shall incorporate full functionality of the system as a unit, including automatic and manual activation.

13.4.3.2.5 Preaction valves protecting freezers shall be trip tested in a manner that does not introduce moisture into the piping in the freezer.

13.4.3.2.6 Preaction systems shall be tested once every 3 years for air leakage, using one of the following test methods:

(1) Perform a pressure test at 40 psi (3.2 bar) for 2 hours. The system shall be permitted to lose up to 3 psi (0.2 bar) during the duration of the test. Air leaks shall be addressed if the system loses more than 3 psi (0.2 bar) during this test.
(2) With the system at normal system pressure, shut off the air source (compressor or shop air) for 4 hours. If the low air pressure alarm goes off within this period, the air leaks shall be addressed.

13.4.3.2.7 Manual Operation. Manual actuation devices shall be operated annually.

13.4.3.2.8 Return to Service. After the annual trip test, the preaction system shall be returned to service in accordance with the manufacturer's instructions.

13.4.3.2.9 Grease or other sealing materials shall not be applied to the seating surfaces of preaction valves.

13.4.3.2.10* Records indicating the date the preaction valve was last tripped and the tripping time, as well as the individual and organization conducting the test, shall be maintained at a location or in a manner readily available for review by the authority having jurisdiction.

Shaded text = Revisions.   Δ = Text deletions and figure/table revisions.   • = Section deletions.   *N* = New material.

2020 Edition

13.4.3.2.11 Low air pressure alarms, if provided, shall be tested quarterly in accordance with the manufacturer's instructions.

13.4.3.2.12 Low temperature alarms, if installed in valve enclosures, shall be tested annually at the beginning of the heating season.

13.4.3.2.13 Automatic air pressure maintenance devices, if provided, shall be tested yearly at the time of the annual preaction valve trip test, in accordance with the manufacturer's instructions.

13.4.3.3 Maintenance.

13.4.3.3.1 Leaks causing drops in supervisory pressure sufficient to sound warning alarms and electrical malfunctions causing alarms to sound shall be located and repaired.

13.4.3.3.2 During the annual trip test, the interior of the preaction valve shall be cleaned thoroughly and the parts replaced or repaired as necessary.

13.4.3.3.2.1 Interior cleaning and parts replacement or repair shall be permitted every 5 years for valves that can be reset without removal of a faceplate.

13.4.3.3.3* Auxiliary drains in preaction systems shall be operated after each system operation and before the onset of freezing conditions (and thereafter as needed).

13.4.3.3.4 Additional maintenance as required by the manufacturer's instructions shall be provided.

13.4.4 Deluge Valves.

13.4.4.1 Inspection.

13.4.4.1.1 The deluge valve shall be externally inspected monthly to verify the following:

(1) The valve is free from physical damage.
(2) All trim valves are in the appropriate open or closed position.
(3) The valve seat is not leaking.
(4) Electrical components are in service.

13.4.4.1.2 The interior of the deluge valve and the condition of detection devices shall be inspected annually when the trip test is conducted.

13.4.4.1.2.1 Internal inspection of valves that can be reset without removal of a faceplate shall be permitted to be conducted every 5 years.

13.4.4.1.3 Strainers, filters, restricted orifices, and diaphragm chambers shall be inspected internally every 5 years unless tests indicate a greater frequency is necessary.

13.4.4.2 Testing.

13.4.4.2.1 Deluge valve flow tests shall incorporate full functionality of the system as a unit, including automatic and manual activation.

13.4.4.2.2 Protection shall be provided for any devices or equipment subject to damage by system discharge during flow tests.

13.4.4.2.3* Except as provided by 13.4.4.2.3.1 and 13.4.4.2.3.2, each deluge valve shall be trip tested annually at full flow in warm weather and in accordance with the manufacturer's instructions.

13.4.4.2.3.1* Where the nature of the protected property is such that water cannot be discharged for test purposes, an annual trip test shall be permitted to be conducted in a manner that does not necessitate discharge in the protected area.

13.4.4.2.3.2 Where the nature of the protected property is such that water cannot be discharged unless protected equipment is shut down (e.g., energized electrical equipment), a full flow system test shall be conducted at the next scheduled shutdown.

13.4.4.2.3.3 For full flow tests in accordance with 13.4.4.2.3.2, the test frequency shall not exceed 3 years.

13.4.4.2.4 During the annual full flow test, the water discharge patterns from all of the open spray nozzles or sprinklers shall be observed to ensure that patterns are not impeded by plugged nozzles, that nozzles are correctly positioned, and that obstructions do not prevent discharge patterns from wetting surfaces to be protected.

13.4.4.2.4.1 Where the nature of the protected property is such that water cannot be discharged, the nozzles or open sprinklers shall be inspected for correct orientation.

13.4.4.2.4.2 Where the nature of the protected property is such that water cannot be discharged unless protected equipment is shut down (e.g., energized electrical equipment), all open spray nozzles or sprinklers shall be inspected in accordance with 13.4.4.2.4 during the full flow system test conducted at the next scheduled shutdown.

13.4.4.2.4.3 Where misalignment or obstructions occur, the piping and sprinklers or nozzles shall be adjusted and/or cleaned to correct the condition, and the system shall be retested.

13.4.4.2.5 Full flow deluge valve tests, in accordance with 13.4.4.2.3 and 13.4.4.2.3.2, shall be conducted with the deluge system control valve fully open.

13.4.4.2.6 Deluge valve trip tests, in accordance with 13.4.4.2.3.1, shall be permitted to be conducted with the deluge system control valve partially open.

13.4.4.2.7 Deluge System Pressure Readings.

13.4.4.2.7.1 Pressure readings shall be recorded at the hydraulically most remote nozzle or sprinkler.

13.4.4.2.7.2 A second pressure reading shall be recorded at the deluge valve.

13.4.4.2.7.3 These readings shall be compared to the hydraulic design pressures to ensure the original system design requirements are met by the water supply.

13.4.4.2.7.4 Where the hydraulically most remote nozzle or sprinkler is inaccessible, nozzles or sprinklers in other than foam-water sprinkler systems shall be permitted to be inspected visually without taking a pressure reading on the most remote nozzle or sprinkler.

13.4.4.2.7.5 Where the reading taken at the riser indicates that the water supply has deteriorated, a gauge shall be placed on the hydraulically most remote nozzle or sprinkler and the results compared with the required design pressure.

13.4.4.2.8 Multiple Systems. The maximum number of systems expected to operate in case of fire shall be tested simultaneously to inspect the adequacy of the water supply.

13.4.4.2.9 Manual Operation. Manual actuation devices shall be operated annually.

13.4.4.2.10 Return to Service. After the annual trip test, the system shall be returned to service in accordance with the manufacturer's instructions.

13.4.4.2.11 Grease or other sealing materials shall not be applied to the seating surfaces of deluge valves.

13.4.4.2.12* Records indicating the date the deluge valve was last tripped and the tripping time, as well as the individual and organization conducting the test, shall be maintained at a location or in a manner readily available for review by the authority having jurisdiction.

13.4.4.2.13 Low air pressure supervisory devices, if provided on the detection system, shall be tested quarterly in accordance with the manufacturer's instructions.

13.4.4.2.14 Low temperature alarms, if installed in valve enclosures, shall be tested annually at the beginning of the heating season.

13.4.4.2.15 Automatic air pressure maintenance devices, if provided on the detection system, shall be tested yearly at the time of the annual deluge valve trip test, in accordance with the manufacturer's instructions.

13.4.4.3 Maintenance.

13.4.4.3.1 Leaks causing drops in supervisory pressure sufficient to sound warning alarms and electrical malfunctions causing alarms to sound shall be located and repaired.

13.4.4.3.2 During the annual trip test, the interior of the deluge valve shall be cleaned thoroughly and the parts replaced or repaired as necessary.

13.4.4.3.2.1 Interior cleaning and parts replacement or repair shall be permitted every 5 years for valves that can be reset without removal of a faceplate.

13.4.4.3.3* Auxiliary drains in deluge systems shall be operated after each system operation and before the onset of freezing conditions (and thereafter as needed).

13.4.4.3.4 Additional maintenance as required by the manufacturer's instructions shall be provided.

13.4.5 Dry Pipe Valves/Quick-Opening Devices.

13.4.5.1 Inspection.

13.4.5.1.1 Systems with auxiliary drains shall require a sign at the dry valve indicating the number of auxiliary drains and the location of each individual drain.

13.4.5.1.2 The dry pipe valve shall be externally inspected monthly to verify the following:

(1) The valve is free of physical damage.

(2) All trim valves are in the appropriate open or closed position.

(3) The intermediate chamber is not leaking.

13.4.5.1.3 The interior of the dry pipe valve shall be inspected annually when the trip test is conducted.

13.4.5.1.4 Strainers, filters, and restricted orifices shall be inspected internally every 5 years unless tests indicate a greater frequency is necessary.

13.4.5.2 Testing.

13.4.5.2.1* The priming water level shall be tested quarterly.

13.4.5.2.2* Each dry pipe valve shall be trip tested annually during warm weather.

13.4.5.2.2.1 Dry pipe valves protecting freezers shall be trip tested in a manner that does not introduce moisture into the piping in the freezers.

13.4.5.2.2.2* Every 3 years and whenever the system is altered, the dry pipe valve shall be trip tested with the control valve fully open and the quick-opening device, if provided, in service.

13.4.5.2.2.3* During those years when full flow testing in accordance with 13.4.5.2.2.2 is not required, each dry pipe valve shall be trip tested with the control valve partially open.

13.4.5.2.2.4 When refilling a dry system, the air supply shall be capable of restoring normal air pressure in the system within 30 minutes.

13.4.5.2.2.5 The requirements of 13.4.5.2.2.4 shall not apply in refrigerated spaces maintained below 5°F (–15°C), where normal system air pressure shall be permitted to be restored within 60 minutes.

13.4.5.2.3 Grease or other sealing materials shall not be applied to the seating surfaces of dry pipe valves.

13.4.5.2.4* Quick-opening devices, if provided, shall be tested quarterly.

13.4.5.2.5 A tag or card that shows the date on which the dry pipe valve was last tripped, and the name of the person and organization conducting the test, shall be attached to the valve.

13.4.5.2.5.1 Separate records of initial air and water pressure, tripping air pressure, and dry pipe valve operating conditions shall be maintained on the premises for comparison with previous test results.

13.4.5.2.5.2 Records of dry pipe valve tripping time and water transit delivery time to the inspector's test connection shall be maintained for full flow trip tests.

13.4.5.2.6 Low air pressure alarms, if provided, shall be tested annually in accordance with the manufacturer's instructions.

13.4.5.2.7 Low temperature alarms, if installed in valve enclosures, shall be tested annually at the beginning of the heating season.

13.4.5.2.8 Automatic air pressure maintenance devices, if provided, shall be tested annually during the dry pipe valve trip test in accordance with the manufacturer's instructions.

Shaded text = Revisions.   Δ = Text deletions and figure/table revisions.   • = Section deletions.   *N* = New material.

2020 Edition

13.4.5.2.9 Dry pipe systems shall be tested once every 3 years for gas leakage, using one of the following test methods:

(1) A gas (air or nitrogen) pressure test at 40 psi (3.2 bar) shall be performed for 2 hours.

    (a) The system shall be permitted to lose up to 3 psi (0.2 bar) during the duration of the test.

    (b) Gas leaks shall be addressed if the system loses more than 3 psi (0.2 bar) during this test.

(2) With the system at normal system pressure, the gas source (nitrogen supply, compressor, or shop air) shall be shut off for 4 hours. If the low pressure alarm goes off within this period, the leaks shall be addressed.

13.4.5.3 Maintenance.

13.4.5.3.1 During the annual trip test, the interior of the dry pipe valve shall be cleaned thoroughly, and parts replaced or repaired as necessary.

13.4.5.3.2* Auxiliary drains in dry pipe sprinkler systems shall be drained after each operation of the system, before the onset of freezing weather conditions, and thereafter as needed.

13.5 Pressure-Reducing Valves and Relief Valves.

13.5.1 Inspection and Testing of Sprinkler Pressure-Reducing Valves. Sprinkler pressure-reducing valves shall be inspected and tested as described in 13.5.1.1 and 13.5.1.2.

13.5.1.1 All valves shall be inspected quarterly to verify that the valves are in the following condition:

(1) In the open position
(2) Not leaking
(3) Maintaining downstream pressures in accordance with the design criteria
(4) Handwheels installed and unbroken

13.5.1.2 A full flow test shall be conducted on each valve at 5-year intervals and shall be compared to previous test results.

13.5.1.2.1 Adjustments shall be made in accordance with the manufacturer's instructions.

13.5.1.3 A partial flow test adequate to move the valve from its seat shall be conducted annually.

13.5.2 Hose Connection Pressure-Regulating Devices.

13.5.2.1 All devices shall be inspected annually to verify the following:

(1) The handwheel is not broken or missing.
(2) The outlet hose threads are not damaged.
(3) No leaks are present.
(4) The hose adapter and the cap are not missing.

13.5.2.2* A full flow test shall be conducted on each device at 5-year intervals and shall be compared to previous test results.

13.5.2.2.1 Adjustments shall be made in accordance with the manufacturer's instructions.

13.5.2.3 A partial flow test for pressure-reducing valves adequate to move the device from its seat shall be conducted annually.

13.5.3 Hose Rack Assembly Pressure-Regulating Devices.

13.5.3.1 All devices shall be inspected annually to verify the following:

(1) The handwheel is not missing or broken.
(2) No leaks are present.

13.5.3.2 A full flow test shall be conducted on each device at 5-year intervals and compared to previous test results.

13.5.3.2.1 Adjustments shall be made in accordance with the manufacturer's instructions.

13.5.3.3 A partial flow test for pressure-reducing valves adequate to move the device from its seat shall be conducted annually.

13.5.4 Master Pressure-Regulating Devices.

13.5.4.1 Devices shall be inspected weekly to verify that the devices are in the following condition:

(1)* Normal downstream pressures are maintained.
(2) Normal supply pressure is maintained.
(3) Devices and associated trim components are free of physical damage and are not leaking.

13.5.4.2* A partial flow test adequate to move the valve from its seat shall be conducted quarterly.

13.5.4.3 A full flow test shall be conducted on each valve annually and shall be compared to previous test results.

13.5.4.4 When valve adjustments are necessary, they shall be made in accordance with the manufacturer's instructions.

13.5.5 Pressure-Reducing Valves.

13.5.5.1 All pressure-reducing valves installed on fire protection systems not covered by 13.5.1, 13.5.2, 13.5.3, or 13.5.4 shall be inspected in accordance with 13.5.1.1.

13.5.5.2 All pressure-reducing valves installed on fire protection systems not covered by 13.5.1, 13.5.2, 13.5.3, or 13.5.4 shall be tested in accordance with 13.5.1.2.

13.5.6 Fire Pump Relief Valves.

13.5.6.1 Circulation Relief Valves.

13.5.6.1.1 Where installed, circulation relief valves shall be inspected on the same frequency as the no-flow (churn) test.

13.5.6.1.2 The inspection shall verify that water flows through the valve when the fire pump is operating at shutoff pressure (i.e., churn) to prevent the pump from overheating.

13.5.6.1.3 On completion of any fire pump test, the closure of the circulation relief valve shall be verified.

13.5.6.2 Main Pressure Relief Valve.

13.5.6.2.1 Where installed, main pressure relief valves shall be inspected during any fire pump test.

13.5.6.2.2 The inspection shall verify that the pressure downstream of the relief valve fittings in the fire pump discharge piping does not exceed the pressure for which the system components are rated.

13.5.6.2.3 During the annual fire pump flow test, the pressure relief valve shall be verified to be correctly adjusted and set to relieve at the correct pressure and to close below that pressure setting.

13.5.7 Maintenance. All damaged or missing components noted during the inspections specified in 13.6.1 through 13.6.2.2 shall be repaired or replaced in accordance with the manufacturer's instructions.

13.6 Hose Valves.

13.6.1 Inspection.

13.6.1.1 Hose valves shall be inspected quarterly to verify that the valves are in the following condition:

(1) Hose caps are in place and not damaged.
(2) Hose threads are not damaged.
(3) Valve handles are present and not damaged.
(4) Gaskets are not damaged or showing signs of deterioration.
(5) No leaks are present.
(6) Valves are not obstructed or otherwise not capable of normal operation.

13.6.1.2 Hose valves shall be inspected to ensure that hose caps are in place and not damaged.

13.6.1.3 Hose threads shall be inspected for damage.

13.6.1.4 Valve handles shall be present and not damaged.

13.6.1.5 Gaskets shall be inspected for damage or deterioration.

13.6.1.6 Hose valves shall be inspected for leaks.

13.6.1.7 Hose valves shall be inspected to ensure no obstructions are present.

13.6.1.8 Hose valves shall be inspected to ensure that restricting devices are present.

13.6.2 Testing.

13.6.2.1* Class I and Class III standpipe system hose valves shall be tested annually by fully opening and closing the valves.

13.6.2.1.1 Class I and Class III standpipe system hose valves that are difficult to operate or leak shall be repaired or replaced.

13.6.2.2* Hose valves on hose stations attached to sprinkler systems and Class II standpipe systems shall be tested every 3 years by opening and closing the valves.

13.6.2.2.1 Hose valves on hose stations attached to sprinkler systems and Class II standpipe systems that are difficult to operate or leak shall be repaired or replaced.

13.6.3 Maintenance. Hose valves that do not operate smoothly or open fully shall be lubricated, repaired, or replaced.

13.7 Backflow Prevention Assemblies.

13.7.1 Inspection. Inspection of backflow prevention assemblies shall be as described in 13.7.1.1 through 13.7.1.3.

13.7.1.1 Reduced-pressure assemblies and reduced-pressure detector assemblies shall be inspected weekly to ensure that the differential-sensing valve relief port is not continuously discharging.

13.7.1.2 After any testing or repair, an inspection by the property owner or designated representative shall be made to ensure that the system is in service and all isolation valves are in the normal open position and properly locked or electrically supervised.

13.7.1.3* Backflow prevention assemblies shall be inspected internally every 5 years to verify that all components operate correctly, move freely, and are in good condition.

13.7.2 Testing.

13.7.2.1* All backflow preventers installed in fire protection system piping shall be exercised annually by conducting a forward flow test at a minimum flow rate of the system demand.

13.7.2.1.1 Where water rationing is enforced during shortages lasting more than 1 year, an internal inspection of the backflow preventer to ensure the check valves will fully open shall be permitted in lieu of conducting the annual forward flow test.

13.7.2.1.2 The forward flow test shall not be required where annual fire pump testing causes the system flow rate to flow through the backflow preventer device.

13.7.2.2 Where hydrants or inside hose stations are located downstream of the backflow preventer, the forward flow test shall include hose stream demand.

13.7.2.3 Where connections do not permit verification of the forward flow test at the minimum flow rate of system demand, tests shall be conducted at the maximum flow rate possible.

13.7.3 Maintenance. Maintenance of all backflow prevention assemblies shall be conducted by a qualified individual following the manufacturer's instructions in accordance with the procedure and policies of the authority having jurisdiction.

13.8 Fire Department Connections.

13.8.1 Fire department connections shall be inspected quarterly to verify the following:

(1) Fire department connections are visible and accessible.
(2) Couplings or swivels are not damaged and rotate smoothly.
(3) Plugs or caps are in place and undamaged.
(4) Gaskets are in place.
(5) Identification signs are in place.
(6) Check valve is not leaking.
(7) Automatic drain valve is in place and operating properly.
(8) Fire department connection clapper(s) is in place and operating properly.
(9)* Interior of the connection is inspected for obstructions.
(10) Visible piping supplying the fire department connection is undamaged.

13.8.2 Interior inspections shall be conducted annually if approved locking caps or locking plugs are installed.

13.8.3 Components shall be repaired or replaced as necessary in accordance with the manufacturer's instructions.

13.8.4 Any obstructions that are present shall be removed.

13.8.5 The piping from the fire department connection to the fire department check valve shall be hydrostatically tested at 150 psi (10 bar) for 2 hours at least once every 5 years.

13.9 Automatic Detection Equipment.

13.9.1 Automatic detection equipment used to actuate water-based fire protection systems shall be inspected, tested, and maintained in accordance with *NFPA 72.*

Shaded text = Revisions.   Δ = Text deletions and figure/table revisions.   • = Section deletions.   *N* = New material.

2020 Edition

13.9.2 Automatic detection equipment used to actuate water-based fire protection systems that is not covered by *NFPA 72* shall be inspected, tested, and maintained to ensure that the detectors are in place, securely fastened, and protected from corrosion, weather, and mechanical damage and to ensure that the communication wiring, control panels, or pneumatic tubing system is functional.

13.10 Air Compressors and Nitrogen Generators.

Δ **13.10.1 General.**

N **13.10.1.1** Air compressors and nitrogen generators dedicated to water-based fire protection systems shall be inspected, tested, and maintained in accordance with 13.10.2, 13.10.3, and 13.10.4.

13.10.1.2 Air compressors not dedicated to water-based fire protection systems shall be inspected, tested, and maintained in accordance with the manufacturer's instructions.

13.10.2 Inspection. Air compressors and nitrogen generators dedicated to water-based fire protection systems shall be inspected monthly to verify the following:

(1) Air compressor or nitrogen generator is free of physical damage.
(2) Power wiring to the air compressor is intact and free of physical damage.
(3) Piping from the air compressor or nitrogen generator to the fire protection system is intact and free of physical damage.
(4) The means of anchoring the air compressor or nitrogen generator to the structure or to the system piping is secure, tight, and free of physical damage.
(5) Air compressors requiring oil have the required amount of oil in the oil reservoir.

13.10.3 Testing. Air compressors or nitrogen generator dedicated to water-based fire protection systems shall be tested annually to verify the following:

(1) Air compressor or nitrogen generator operates as intended on the proper drop of air pressure in the fire protection system.
(2)* Air compressor or nitrogen generator restores normal supervisory pressure in the fire protection system in the required time frame.
(3) Air compressor does not overheat while running.

13.10.4 Maintenance.

13.10.4.1 Air compressors or nitrogen generators dedicated to water-based fire protection systems shall be maintained in accordance with the manufacturer's instructions.

13.10.4.2 Compressors requiring oil shall have the oil replaced on an annual basis unless the manufacturer's instructions require more frequent replacement.

13.11 Component Testing Requirements.

13.11.1 Whenever a valve, valve component, and/or valve trim is adjusted, repaired, reconditioned, or replaced, the action required in Table 13.11.1 shall be performed.

13.11.2 Where the original installation standard is different from the cited standard, the use of the appropriate installing standard shall be permitted.

13.11.3* These actions shall not require a design review.

Δ **Table 13.11.1 Summary of Component Action Requirements**

Component	Adjust	Repair/ Recondition	Replace	Inspection, Test, and Maintenance Procedures
Water delivery components				
Post indicator and wall indicator valves	X	X	X	(1) Inspect for leaks at system pressure (2) Perform full operational test conforming to 13.3.3.1 (3) Perform spring torsion inspection conforming to 13.3.3.2 (4) Verify target visibility at shut and full open position (5) Test supervisory device (6) Valve status test
Control valves other than post indicator and wall indicator valves	X	X	X	(1) Inspect for leaks at system pressure (2) Perform full operational test conforming to 13.3.3.1 (3) Valves to be backed one-quarter turn from fully open to prevent jamming in accordance with 13.3.3.3 (4) Verify supervisory device (5) Valve status test
Alarm check valve	X	X	X	(1) Inspect for leaks at system pressure per 13.4.1 (2) Test all alarms and supervisory signals affected by the alarm valve (3) Valve status test
Dry pipe valve	X	X	X	(1) Inspect for leaks at system pressure (2) Trip test per 13.4.5.2 (3) Inspect condition of valve seat (4) Test all dry pipe system alarms and supervisory signals (5) Valve status test
Deluge/preaction valve	X	X	X	(1) Inspect for leaks at system pressure per 13.4.4/13.4.3 (2) Trip test (3) Inspect condition of valve seat (4) Test all deluge/preaction system alarms and supervisory signals (5) Valve status test
Quick-opening device	X	X	X	(1) Inspect for leaks at system pressure per 13.4.5.2.9 (2) Trip test (3) Valve status test
Pressure-regulating device — hose valves	X	X	X	(1) Inspect for leaks at system pressure per 13.5.2 (2) Full flow test (3) Valve status test
Pressure-regulating devices — other than hose valves	X	X	X	(1) Inspect for leaks at system pressure per Section 13.5 (2) Test pressure setting with full flow and without flow (3) Test supervisory device and alarm (4) Valve status test
Hose valve	X	X	X	(1) Inspect for leaks at system pressure per Section 13.6 (2) Valve status test

(continues)

Shaded text = Revisions.   Δ = Text deletions and figure/table revisions.   • = Section deletions.   *N* = New material.

2020 Edition

Δ **Table 13.11.1**   *Continued*

Component	Adjust	Repair/ Recondition	Replace	Inspection, Test, and Maintenance Procedures
Backflow prevention device	X	X	X	(1) Inspect for leaks at system pressure per Section 13.7 (2) Forward flow test per 13.7.2.1 (3) Test supervisory device and alarm (4) Valve status test
Check valves	X	X	X	(1) Inspect for leaks at system pressure per 13.4.2 (2) Inspect for leaking through check valve (3) Valve status test
Fire department connection	X	X		(1) Inspect for leaks at system pressure per Section 13.8 (2) Valve status test
Fire department connection — sprinkler system(s)			X	(1) Isolate and hydrostatic test for 2 hours at 150 psi (10 bar) (2) Valve status test
Fire department connection — other than sprinkler system(s)			X	(1) Isolate and hydrostatic test for 2 hours at 50 psi (3.5 bar) above the normal working pressure [200 psi (14 bar) minimum] (2) Valve status test
Strainers	X	X	X	Inspect and clean in accordance with manufacturer's instructions
Main drain valves	X	X	X	Main drain test per 13.2.3
Gauges			X	Calibrate per 13.2.5
Alarm and supervisory components				
Alarm device	X	X	X	Test for conformance with NFPA 13 and/or *NFPA 72*
Supervisory device	X	X	X	Test for conformance with NFPA 13 and/or *NFPA 72*
System protection components				
Pressure relief valve — fire pump installation	X	X	X	See 8.3.3.11 and 13.5.6
Pressure relief valve — other than fire pump installation			X	Verify relief valve is listed or approved for the application and set to the correct pressure
Informational components				
Identification signs	X	X	X	Inspect for compliance with NFPA 13 and 13.3.1

Chapter 14   Internal Piping Condition and Obstruction Investigation

14.1* General. This chapter shall provide the minimum requirements for conducting investigations of fire protection system piping for possible sources of materials that could cause pipe blockage or internal corrosion of system components.

14.2 Assessment of Internal Condition of Piping.

14.2.1* An assessment of the internal condition of piping shall be conducted on a frequency determined by 14.2.1.1 or 14.2.1.2 for the purpose of inspecting for the presence of foreign organic and inorganic material.

14.2.1.1 An assessment of the internal condition of piping shall be conducted at a minimum of every 5 years or in accord-ance with 14.2.1.2 for the purpose of inspecting for the presence of foreign organic and inorganic material.

14.2.1.2* Where an assessment frequency has been established by an approved risk analysis, the assessment shall be performed at a frequency determined by the approved risk analysis.

14.2.1.3 Tubercules or slime, if found, shall be tested for indications of microbiologically influenced corrosion (MIC).

14.2.1.4* If the presence of sufficient foreign organic or inorganic material is found to obstruct pipe or sprinklers, an obstruction investigation shall be conducted as described in Section 14.3.

14.2.1.5 Nonmetallic pipe shall not be required to comply with Section 14.2.

14.2.2* In buildings having multiple wet pipe systems, every other system shall have an assessment of the internal condition of piping as described in 14.2.1.

14.2.2.1 During the next inspection frequency required by 14.2.1.1 or 14.2.1.2, the alternate systems not assessed during the previous assessment shall be assessed as described in 14.2.1.

14.2.2.2 If foreign organic and/or inorganic material is found in any system in a building, all systems shall be assessed.

14.3 Obstruction Investigation and Prevention.

14.3.1* An obstruction investigation shall be conducted for system or yard main piping wherever any of the following conditions exist:

(1) Defective intake for fire pumps taking suction from open bodies of water
(2) The discharge of obstructive material during routine water tests
(3) Foreign materials in fire pumps, in dry pipe valves, or in check valves
(4) Foreign material in water during drain tests or plugging of inspector's test connection(s)
(5) Unknown materials are heard in the system piping during draining, refilling, or otherwise flowing water through the system
(6) Plugged sprinklers
(7) The presence of sufficient foreign organic or inorganic material is found in the pipe
(8) Failure to flush yard piping or surrounding public mains following new installations or repairs
(9) A record of broken public mains in the vicinity
(10) Abnormally frequent false tripping of a dry pipe valve(s)
(11) A system that is returned to service after an extended shutdown (greater than 1 year)
(12) There is reason to believe that the sprinkler system contains sodium silicate or highly corrosive fluxes in copper systems
(13) A system has been supplied with raw water via the fire department connection
(14) Pinhole leaks
(15) A 50 percent increase in the time it takes water to travel to the inspector's test connection from the time the valve trips during a full flow trip test of a dry pipe sprinkler system when compared to the original system acceptance test

14.3.2* Systems shall be examined for internal obstructions where conditions exist that could cause obstructed piping.

14.3.2.1 If the condition has not been corrected or the condition is one that could result in obstruction of the piping despite any previous flushing procedures that have been performed, the system shall be examined for internal obstructions every 5 years.

14.3.2.2* Internal examination shall be performed at the following minimum four points:

(1) System valve
(2) Riser
(3) Cross main
(4) Branch line

14.3.2.3* Alternative nondestructive examination methods shall be permitted.

14.3.3* If an obstruction investigation indicates the presence of sufficient material to obstruct pipe or sprinklers, a complete flushing program shall be conducted by qualified personnel.

14.3.4 Tubercules or slime, if found during an obstruction investigation, shall be tested for indications of microbiologically influenced corrosion (MIC).

14.4 Ice Obstruction. Dry pipe or preaction sprinkler system piping that protects or passes through refrigerated spaces maintained at temperatures below 32°F (0°C) shall be inspected internally on an annual basis for ice obstructions at the point where the piping enters the refrigerated area.

14.4.1 Alternative nondestructive examinations shall be permitted.

14.4.2 All penetrations into the refrigerated spaces shall be inspected and, if an ice obstruction is found, additional pipe shall be examined to ensure that no additional ice obstructions or ice blockages exist.

Chapter 15   Impairments

15.1 General.

15.1.1 Minimum Requirements.

Δ **15.1.1.1** This chapter shall provide the minimum requirements for a fire protection system impairment program.

15.1.1.2 Measures shall be taken during the impairment to ensure that increased risks are minimized and the duration of the impairment is limited.

15.2 Impairment Coordinator.

15.2.1 The property owner or designated representative shall assign an impairment coordinator to comply with the requirements of this chapter.

15.2.2 In the absence of a specific designee, the property owner or designated representative shall be considered the impairment coordinator.

15.2.3 Where the lease, written use agreement, or management contract specifically grants the authority for inspection, testing, and maintenance of the fire protection system(s) to the tenant, management firm, or managing individual, the tenant, management firm, or managing individual shall assign a person as impairment coordinator.

15.3 Tag Impairment System.

15.3.1* A tag shall be used to indicate that a system, or part thereof, has been removed from service.

15.3.2* The tag shall be posted at each fire department connection and the system control valve, and other locations required by the authority having jurisdiction, indicating which system, or part thereof, has been removed from service.

15.4 Impaired Equipment.

15.4.1 The impaired equipment shall be considered to be the water-based fire protection system, or part thereof, that is removed from service.

15.4.2 The impaired equipment shall include, but shall not be limited to, the following:

(1) Sprinkler systems
(2) Standpipe systems
(3) Fire hose systems
(4) Underground fire service mains
(5) Fire pumps
(6) Water storage tanks
(7) Water spray fixed systems
(8) Foam-water sprinkler systems
(9) Water mist systems
(10) Fire service control valves
(11) Water supply

15.5* Preplanned Impairment Programs.

15.5.1 All preplanned impairments shall be authorized by the impairment coordinator.

15.5.2 Before authorization is given, the impairment coordinator shall be responsible for verifying that the following procedures have been implemented:

(1) The extent and expected duration of the impairment have been determined.
(2) The areas or buildings involved have been inspected and the increased risks determined.
(3) Recommendations to mitigate any increased risks have been submitted to management or the property owner or designated representative.
(4) Where a fire protection system is out of service for more than 10 hours in a 24-hour period, the impairment coordinator shall arrange for one of the following:

    (a) Evacuation of the building or portion of the building affected by the system out of service
    (b)* An approved fire watch
    (c)* Establishment of a temporary water supply
    (d)* Establishment and implementation of an approved program to eliminate potential ignition sources and limit the amount of fuel available to the fire

(5) The fire department has been notified.
(6) The insurance carrier, the alarm company, property owner or designated representative, and other authorities having jurisdiction have been notified.
(7) The supervisors in the areas to be affected have been notified.
(8) A tag impairment system has been implemented. *(See Section 15.3.)*
(9) All necessary tools and materials have been assembled on the impairment site.

15.6* Emergency Impairments.

15.6.1 Emergency impairments shall include, but are not limited to, interruption of water supply, frozen or ruptured piping, and equipment failure, and includes impairments found during inspection, testing, or maintenance activities.

15.6.2* The coordinator shall implement the steps outlined in Section 15.5.

15.7* Restoring Systems to Service. When all impaired equipment is restored to normal working order, the impairment coordinator shall verify that the following procedures have been implemented:

(1) Any necessary inspections and tests have been conducted to verify that affected systems are operational. The appro-

priate chapter of this standard shall be consulted for guidance on the type of inspection and test required.
(2) Supervisors have been advised that protection is restored.
(3) The fire department has been advised that protection is restored.
(4) The property owner or designated representative, insurance carrier, alarm company, and other authorities having jurisdiction have been advised that protection is restored.
(5) The impairment tag has been removed.

Chapter 16 Special Requirements from Other NFPA Documents

16.1 General.

16.1.1 Application.

16.1.1.1* This chapter shall include the inspection, testing, and maintenance requirements for water-based fire protection systems found in other NFPA standards that are different from those included in this standard.

16.1.1.2* The requirements of this chapter shall be extracted from the other referenced standards.

16.1.1.3 Where the requirements of the referenced standard differ from the requirements of this standard, the referenced standard shall take precedence.

16.1.2 Definitions. For terms not defined in Chapter 3, the definitions of the reference standard shall apply.

16.2 Small Residential Board and Care Occupancies.

16.2.1 The requirements in this section shall only apply to residential board and care facilities with sprinkler systems installed in accordance with NFPA 13D as described in NFPA *101*.

16.2.1.1 Systems installed in accordance with NFPA 13D shall be inspected, tested, and maintained in accordance with NFPA *101*.

Annex A Explanatory Material

Annex A is not a part of the requirements of this NFPA document but is included for informational purposes only. This annex contains explanatory material, numbered to correspond with the applicable text paragraphs.

A.1.1.1.2 This standard does not address all of the inspection, testing, and maintenance requirements of the electrical components of a water-based fire protection system that are addressed by *NFPA 72*. However, there are times when a single inspection or test can meet the requirements of both NFPA 25 and *NFPA 72* (e.g., operation of a tamper switch). This standard does not necessarily require that two separate inspections or tests be conducted on the same component, provided the inspection or test meets the requirements of both standards and the individual performing the inspection or test is qualified to perform the inspection or test required by both standards.

Δ **A.1.1.3** Generally accepted NFPA installation practices for water-based fire protection systems relevant to this standard are found in the following:

(1) NFPA 13
(2) NFPA 13R

(3)   NFPA 14
(4)   NFPA 15
(5)   NFPA 16
(6)   NFPA 20
(7)   NFPA 22
(8)   NFPA 24
(9)   NFPA 750

△ A.1.1.3.1 The requirement to evaluate the adequacy of the design of the installed system or the capability of the fire protection system to protect the building or its contents is not a part of the periodic inspection, testing, and maintenance requirements of this standard. Examples of items not covered by this standard include the evaluation of unsprinklered areas and the spacing of sprinklers. However, such evaluation is the responsibility of the property owner or designated representative as indicated in 4.1.6, 4.1.7, and the Hazard Evaluation Form in Annex E.

A.1.1.4 For systems originally installed in accordance with one of these standards, the repair, replacement, alteration, or extension of such systems should also be performed in accordance with that same standard. When original installations are based on other applicable codes or standards, repair, replacement, alteration, or extension practices should be conducted in accordance with those other applicable codes or standards.

A.1.2 History has shown that the performance reliability of a water-based fire protection system under fire-related conditions increases where comprehensive inspection, testing, and maintenance procedures are enforced. Diligence during an inspection is important. The inspection, testing, and maintenance of some items in the standard might not be practical or possible, depending on existing conditions. The inspector should use good judgment when making inspections.

A.1.3 An entire program of quality control includes, but is not limited to, maintenance of equipment, inspection frequency, testing of equipment, on-site fire brigades, loss control provisions, and personnel training. Personnel training can be used as an alternative even if a specific frequency differs from that specified in this standard.

A.1.4 The liter and bar units, which are not part of but are recognized by SI, commonly are used in international fire protection. These units are provided in Table A.1.4 with their conversion factors.

A.3.2.1 Approved. The National Fire Protection Association does not approve, inspect, or certify any installations, procedures, equipment, or materials; nor does it approve or evaluate

testing laboratories. In determining the acceptability of installations, procedures, equipment, or materials, the authority having jurisdiction may base acceptance on compliance with NFPA or other appropriate standards. In the absence of such standards, said authority may require evidence of proper installation, procedure, or use. The authority having jurisdiction may also refer to the listings or labeling practices of an organization that is concerned with product evaluations and is thus in a position to determine compliance with appropriate standards for the current production of listed items.

A.3.2.2 Authority Having Jurisdiction (AHJ). The phrase "authority having jurisdiction," or its acronym AHJ, is used in NFPA documents in a broad manner, since jurisdictions and approval agencies vary, as do their responsibilities. Where public safety is primary, the authority having jurisdiction may be a federal, state, local, or other regional department or individual such as a fire chief; fire marshal; chief of a fire prevention bureau, labor department, or health department; building official; electrical inspector; or others having statutory authority. For insurance purposes, an insurance inspection department, rating bureau, or other insurance company representative may be the authority having jurisdiction. In many circumstances, the property owner or his or her designated agent assumes the role of the authority having jurisdiction; at government installations, the commanding officer or departmental official may be the authority having jurisdiction.

A.3.2.3 Listed. The means for identifying listed equipment may vary for each organization concerned with product evaluation; some organizations do not recognize equipment as listed unless it is also labeled. The authority having jurisdiction should utilize the system employed by the listing organization to identify a listed product.

A.3.3.2 Alarm Receiving Facility. This can include proprietary supervising stations, central supervising stations, remote supervising stations, or public fire service communications centers.

A.3.3.4 Automatic Detection Equipment. Water spray systems can use fixed temperature, rate-of-rise, rate-compensation fixed temperature, optical devices, flammable gas detectors, or products of combustion detectors.

A.3.3.5 Automatic Operation. This operation includes, but is not limited to, heat, rate of heat rise, smoke, or pressure change.

A.3.3.8 Deficiency. Depending on the nature and significance of the deficiency, it can result in a system impairment. Critical deficiencies will adversely impact performance but without the need for the implementing impairment procedures. Noncritical deficiencies have the potential to impact performance.

Table A.3.3.8 provides examples for classifying conditions needing repair or correction that are identified during the inspection, testing, and maintenance of water-based suppression systems. The conditions are classified as an impairment, critical deficiency, or noncritical deficiency. The table is not all-inclusive but is included to provide guidance in responding to these conditions. For example, an impairment should be addressed promptly by either immediately correcting the condition or implementing the impairment procedures found in Chapter 15. Critical and noncritical deficiencies should be corrected as soon as practical after considering the nature and severity of the risk. It should be noted that many jurisdictions

△ Table A.1.4 Metric Conversions

Name of Unit	Unit Symbol	Conversion Factor
liter	L	1 gal = 3.785 L
liter per minute per square meter	$L/min \cdot m^2$	1 gpm/ft^2 = 40.746 $L/min \cdot m^2$
cubic decimeter	dm^3	1 gal = 3.785 dm^3
pascal	Pa	1 psi = 6894.757 Pa
bar	bar	1 psi = 0.0689 bar
bar	bar	1 bar = 10^5 Pa

Note: For additional conversions and information, see IEEE/ASTM-SI-10, *American National Standard for Metric Practice*.

have requirements for the timely correction of impairments and/or deficiencies.

The table does not take into account every variation of the conditions needing repair or correction. For example, a single lightly painted sprinkler in a large warehouse might be noncritical in its risk while a single painted sprinkler in a battery-charging station might be considered a critical deficiency or perhaps an impairment. In addition, the nature of the hazard or the life safety exposure of the occupancy should be considered when assigning a classification. The table should be used with good judgment and could require input from the authority having jurisdiction.

A.3.3.11.2 Sectional Drain. An example of a sectional drain is a drain located beyond a floor control valve on a multistory building.

A.3.3.13 Fire Hydrant. See Figure A.3.3.13(a) and Figure A.3.3.13(b).

A.3.3.13.1 Dry Barrel Hydrant (Frostproof Hydrant). A drain is located at the bottom of the barrel above the control valve seat for proper drainage after operation to prevent freezing. See Figure A.3.3.13.1.

N **A.3.3.13.2 Dry Hydrant.** See Figure A.3.3.13.2. [1142, 2017]

A.3.3.13.3 Monitor Nozzle Hydrant. See Figure A.3.3.13.3.

A.3.3.13.4 Wall Hydrant. See Figure A.3.3.13.4.

A.3.3.13.5 Wet Barrel Hydrant. See Figure A.3.3.13.5.

A.3.3.14 Foam Concentrate. For the purpose of this document, *foam concentrate* and *concentrate* are used interchangeably.

A.3.3.17 Hose House. See Figure A.3.3.17(a) through Figure A.3.3.17(c).

A.3.3.20.1 Conventional Pin Rack. See Figure A.3.3.20.1.

A.3.3.20.2 Horizontal Rack. See Figure A.3.3.20.2.

A.3.3.20.3 Hose Reel. See Figure A.3.3.20.3.

A.3.3.20.4 Semiautomatic Hose Rack Assembly. See Figure A.3.3.20.4.

A.3.3.22 Impairment. The use of the phrase *fire protection system or unit* is a broad reference to those terms used in titles of Chapters 5 through 12. Some fire protection features are referred to as systems in the installation standards (e.g., sprinkler,

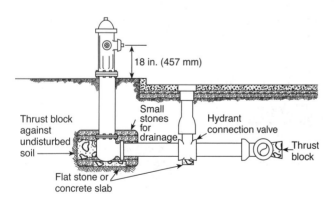

FIGURE A.3.3.13(a)   Typical Fire Hydrant Connection.

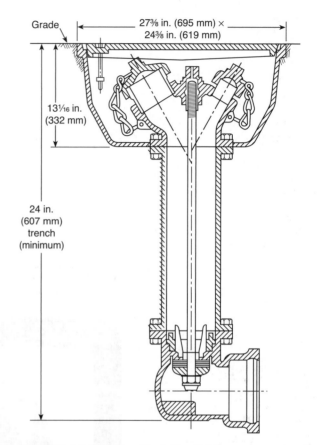

FIGURE A.3.3.13(b)   Flush-Type Hydrant.

standpipe, water spray, foam-water, and water mist), or are referred to as units (e.g., fire pumps), and others use neither term (e.g., private service fire mains and water tanks). For the purpose of this standard, the term *unit* refers to a fire pump and its connections required by NFPA 20, or a water storage tank and its connections required by NFPA 22, or a private service fire main and its connections required by NFPA 24. The use of the term *unit* in the definitions of impairment, deficiency, critical deficiency, and noncritical deficiency is not referring to an individual component such as a sprinkler, valve, fitting, switch, piece of pipe, and so forth.

Temporarily shutting down a system as part of performing the routine inspection, testing, and maintenance on that system while under constant attendance by qualified personnel, and where the system can be restored to service quickly, should not be considered an impairment. Good judgment should be considered for the hazards presented.

A.3.3.22.1 Emergency Impairment. Examples of emergency impairments might include a ruptured pipe, an operated sprinkler, or an interruption of the water supply to the system.

A.3.3.25 Inspection, Testing, and Maintenance Service. This program includes logging and retention of relevant records. Any portion or all of the inspection, testing, and maintenance can be contracted with an inspection, testing, and maintenance service. Similarly, any portion or all of the inspection, testing, and maintenance can be performed by qualified personnel employed by the property owner or designated representative.

Δ Table A.3.3.8 Water-Based Fire Protection System Inspection and Testing Findings

Item	Finding	Reference	Impairment	Critical Deficiency	Noncritical Deficiency
Chapter 5: Sprinkler Systems — Inspection					
All sprinklers	Leaking — spraying or running water	5.2.1.1.1	X		
All sprinklers	Leaking — dripping water	5.2.1.1.1		X	
All sprinklers	Foreign material attached or suspended from	5.2.1.1.1	X		
All sprinklers	Minimum clearance to storage not maintained	5.2.1.2		X	
All sprinklers	Lightly loaded	5.2.1.1.1			X
Standard-response sprinklers in nonresidential occupancies	One sprinkler and less than 50% of sprinklers in compartment is heavily loaded or corroded; painted operating element, bulb, deflector, or coverplate; improper orientation; glass bulb has lost fluid; damaged	5.2.1.1.1		X	
Standard-response sprinklers in nonresidential occupancies	Two or more sprinklers in compartment are heavily loaded or corroded; painted operating element, bulb, deflector, or coverplate; improper orientation; glass bulb has lost fluid; damaged	5.2.1.1.1	X		
Fast-response element, quick-response, electrically operated, residential sprinklers and standard-response in residential occupancies	One or more sprinklers heavily loaded or corroded; painted operating element, bulb, deflector, or coverplate; improper orientation; glass bulb has lost fluid; damaged	5.2.1.1.1	X		
Coverplates	Concealed sprinkler coverplates caulked or glued to ceiling	5.2.1.1.1	X		
Escutcheons and coverplates	Missing recessed or flush escutcheons, concealed coverplate with deflector and operating element in correct position	5.2.1.1.5			X
Escutcheons and coverplates	Missing recessed or flush escutcheons, concealed coverplate with deflector and operating element not in correct position	5.2.1.1.5	X		
Escutcheons	Recessed or flush escutcheons caulked or glued to ceiling	5.2.1.1.1		X	
Spare sprinkler cabinet	Cabinet missing, temperature, above maximum permitted, not proper number and type, missing wrench for each type	5.2.1.4	Table 5.4.1.5.2		X
Pipe and fittings	Leaking — slowly dripping and/or moisture on surface	5.2.2.1		X	
Pipe and fittings	Leaking — spraying or running water	5.2.2.1	X		
Pipe and fittings	Critical mechanical damage	5.2.2.1		X	
Hangers and seismic braces	Loose	5.2.3.2			X
Hangers and seismic braces	Damaged or unattached	5.2.3.2		X	
Gauges	Not operating or damaged	13.2.5.1.1			X
Gauges	Not showing normal water/air pressure	13.2.5.1.2, 13.7.5.1.3		X	
Gauges	Freezer — system pressure lower than compressor	13.2.5.1.4	X		
Alarm devices	Physical damage	5.2.4			X
Hydraulic design information sign	Not attached properly, illegible or missing	5.2.5			X
Information sign	Not attached, illegible, or missing	5.2.7			X
General information sign	Not attached, illegible, or missing	5.2.8			X
Antifreeze information sign	Not attached, illegible, or missing	5.2.9			X
Heat tape	Not in accordance with manufacturer's instructions	5.2.6		X	
Chapter 5: Sprinkler Systems — Testing					
Gauges	Not replaced or calibrated in 5 years, not accurate within 3% of scale	13.2.5.2/13.2.5.3			X
Alarm devices	Water motor and gong not functioning	5.3.3.1		X	

(continues)

Shaded text = Revisions.   Δ = Text deletions and figure/table revisions.   • = Section deletions.   *N* = New material.

2020 Edition

Δ **Table A.3.3.8**   *Continued*

Item	Finding	Reference	Impairment	Critical Deficiency	Noncritical Deficiency
Alarm devices	Pressure-switch- or vane-type switch not functioning or no alarm	5.3.3.2		X	
Antifreeze systems	Mixture and concentration does not meet requirements of 5.3.3.4.1 and 5.3.3(1)(a)	5.3.4		X	
Antifreeze systems	Concentration is inadequate to prevent freezing	Table A.5.3.4.4.1(1), 5.3.4.2.1, and Figure A.5.3.4	X		
Main drain	More than 10% drop in full flow pressure	13.2.3.3		X	
Assessment of internal condition	Assessment revealed presence of MIC, zebra mussels, rust, or scale	14.2.1		X	
Sprinklers	Sprinkler(s) fail laboratory testing	5.3.1	X	X	
Chapter 6: Standpipe and Hose Systems — Inspection					
Pipe and fittings	Leaking — slowly dripping and/or moisture on surface	6.2.4		X	
Pipe and fittings	Leaking — spraying or running water	6.2.4	X		
Pipe and fittings	Critical mechanical damage	6.2.4		X	
Hangers and supports	Damaged or missing	6.2.4		X	
Hose	Cuts, couplings not of compatible threads	6.2.5, NFPA 1962		X	
Hose	Deterioration, no gasket or damaged gaskets	6.2.5, NFPA 1962		X	
Hose	Mildew present, corrosion present, hose not connected	6.2.5, NFPA 1962			X
Hose nozzle	Missing, broken parts or thread gasket damaged	6.2.6, NFPA 1962		X	
Hose storage	Hose not properly racked or rolled, nozzle clip missing, nozzle not contained, damaged, obstructed	6.2.7, NFPA 1962		X	
Cabinet	Corroded or damaged parts, not easy to open, not accessible, not identified, door glazing in poor condition, lock not functioning in break glass type, valve, hose nozzle, fire extinguisher, etc.; not readily accessible	6.2.8, NFPA 1962		X	
Hydraulic design information sign	Missing	6.2.2			X
Chapter 6: Standpipe and Hose Systems — Testing					
Hose storage device	Rack will not swing out of cabinet at least 90 degrees	6.2.7, NFPA 1962			X
Standpipe system	Test results did not provide design pressure at required flow	6.3.1		X	
Hydrostatic test of manual and semiautomatic dry standpipe systems	Leakage in inside piping	6.3.2.1			X
Main drain	More than 10% drop in full flow pressure	13.2.3.3		X	
Assessment of internal condition	Assessment revealed presence of MIC, zebra mussels, rust, or scale	14.2.1		X	
Chapter 7: Private Fire Service Mains — Inspection					
Exposed piping	Leaking — slowly dripping, and/or moisture on surface	7.2.2.1.2		X	
Exposed piping	Leaking — spraying or running water	7.2.2.1.2	X		
Exposed piping	Mechanical damage, corroded, not properly restrained	7.2.2.1.2		X	
Mainline strainers	Plugged, fouled	7.2.2.3.2	X		
Mainline strainers	Corroded	7.2.2.3.2		X	
Dry barrel, wet barrel, and wall hydrant	Inaccessible, barrel contains ice, cracks in barrel	7.2.2.4, 7.2.2.5	X		
Dry barrel, wet barrel, and wall hydrant	Barrel contains water, improper drainage from barrel, leaks at outlets or top of hydrant	7.2.2.4, 7.2.2.5		X	

(continues)

Shaded text = Revisions.   Δ = Text deletions and figure/table revisions.   • = Section deletions.   *N* = New material.

Δ **Table A.3.3.8** *Continued*

Item	Finding	Reference	Impairment	Critical Deficiency	Noncritical Deficiency
Dry barrel, wet barrel, and wall hydrant	Tightness of outlets, worn nozzle threads, worn operating nut, missing wrench	7.2.2.4, 7.2.2.5			X
Monitor nozzles	Damaged, corroded, leaking	7.2.2.7		X	
Hose/hydrant houses	Inaccessible	7.2.2.8	X		
Hose/hydrant houses	Damaged	7.2.2.8		X	
Hose/hydrant houses	Not fully equipped	7.2.2.8			X
Chapter 7: Private Fire Service Mains — Testing					
Underground and exposed piping	Test results show deterioration in water supply when compared to previous results	7.3.1.1		X	
Dry barrel and wall hydrant	Hydrant did not flow clear or did not drain within 60 minutes	7.3.2.1, 7.3.2.4			X
Monitor nozzles	Did not flow acceptable amount of water, did not operate throughout their full range	7.3.3		X	
Chapter 8: Fire Pumps — Inspection					
Pump house/room	Ventilating louvers not free to operate	8.2.2(1)(c)		X	
Pump house/room	Heat not adequate, temperature less than 40°F (4°C)	8.2.2(1)(a)	X		
Pump house/room	Heat not adequate, temperature less than 70°F (21°C) for diesel pumps without engine heaters	8.2.2(1)(b)	X		
Pump house/room	Heat not adequate, temperature less than 40°F (4°C), not as recommended by the engine manufacturer, for diesel pumps with engine heaters	8.2.2(1)(a) and (b)	X		
Pump house/room	Excessive water on floor	8.2.2(1)(d)		X	
Pump house/room	Coupling guard not in place	8.2.2(1)(e)		X	
Pump system	Suction, discharge, or bypass valves not fully open, pipe leaking, suction line and system line pressure not normal, wet pit suction screens obstructed	8.2.2(2)(a–f)	X		
Pump system	Waterflow test valves open, hose connection valve open, test line contains water	8.2.2(2)(g)		X	
Pump system suction	Reservoir empty	8.2.2(2)	X		
Pump system	Suction reservoir does not have required water level, wet pit suction screens missing	8.2.2(2)		X	
Electrical power to pump system	No electrical power — controller pilot light not illuminated, transfer switch pilot light not illuminated, isolating switch not closed, reverse phase alarm pilot light on or normal phase light is off	8.2.2(3)	X		
Electrical power to pump system	Electrical power is provided — controller pilot light not illuminated, transfer switch pilot light not illuminated, reverse phase alarm pilot light on, normal phase light is not illuminated	8.2.2(3)			X
Electric pump system	Oil level in vertical motor sight glass not normal	8.2.2(3)(e)		X	
Pressure maintenance (jockey) pump	No power	8.2.2(3)(f)			X
Diesel engine system	Alarm pilot lights are on	8.2.2(4)(f)		X	
Diesel engine system	Battery charging current not normal	8.2.2(4)(d)		X	
Diesel engine system	Battery failure pilot lights on	8.2.2(4)(e)		X	
Diesel engine system	Battery pilot lights off	8.2.2(4)(e)		X	
Diesel engine system	Battery terminals corroded	8.2.2(4)(l)		X	
Diesel engine system	Battery voltage readings not normal	8.2.2(4)(c)		X	

(continues)

Shaded text = Revisions.   Δ = Text deletions and figure/table revisions.   • = Section deletions.   *N* = New material.

2020 Edition

Δ **Table A.3.3.8** *Continued*

Item	Finding	Reference	Impairment	Critical Deficiency	Noncritical Deficiency
Diesel engine system	Controller selector switch not in auto position	8.2.2(4)(b)	X		
Diesel engine system	Cooling water level not normal	8.2.2(4)(j)			X
Diesel engine system	Cooling water level not visible	8.2.2(4)(j)		X	
Diesel engine system	Crankcase oil level not normal	8.2.2(4)(i)			X
Diesel engine system	Crankcase oil level below low level	8.2.2(4)(i)	X		
Diesel engine system	Electrolyte level in batteries not normal	8.2.2(4)(k)			X
Diesel engine system	Electrolyte level in batteries below top of battery plates	8.2.2(4)(k)		X	
Diesel engine system	Engine running time meter not reading	8.2.2(4)(g)			X
Diesel engine system	Fuel tank less than two-thirds full	8.2.2(4)(a)		X	
Diesel engine system	Fuel tank empty	8.2.2(4)(a)	X		
Diesel engine system	Water-jacket heater not operating	8.2.2(4)(m)		X	
Diesel engine system	Oil level in right angle gear drive not normal (not at level mark but visible in sight glass)	8.2.2(4)(h)			X
Diesel engine system	Oil level in right angle gear drive below low level (not visible in sight glass or below one finger knuckle for inspection hole)	8.2.2(4)(h)		X	
Diesel engine system	Battery terminals corroded	8.2.2(4)(l)		X	
Steam system	Steam pressure gauge reading not normal	8.2.2(5)		X	
Chapter 8: Fire Pumps — Testing					
Fire pump test	Pump did not start automatically	8.3.2.2	X		
	Pump failed to run for 10 minutes	8.3.2.3	X		
	Pump failed to run for 30 minutes	8.3.2.4	X		
Fire pump test — pump system	System suction and discharge gauge reading, or pump starting pressure outside the acceptable range	8.3.2.9(1)		X	
Fire pump test — pump system	Pump packing gland discharge not acceptable, unusual noise or vibration, packing boxes, bearings, or pump casing overheating	8.3.2.9(1)		X	
Fire pump test — electrical-motor-driven system	Time for motor to accelerate to full speed, time controller is on first step, or time pump runs after starting not acceptable	8.3.2.9(2)	X		
Fire pump test — diesel-engine-driven system	Time for engine to crank and time for engine to reach running speed not acceptable (engine to reach rated speed within 20 seconds per 11.2.7.1 of NFPA 20, 2019 edition)	8.3.2.9(3)		X	
Fire pump test — diesel-engine-driven system	Low rpm	8.3.2.9(3)	X		
Fire pump test — diesel-engine-driven system	Low oil pressure, high temperature, high cooling water pressure	8.3.2.9(3)		X	
Fire pump test — diesel-engine-driven system	Time for engine to crank and time for engine to reach running speed not acceptable, low rpm, low oil pressure, high temperature, high cooling water pressure	8.3.2		X	
Fire pump test — steam system	Gauge reading and time for turbine to reach running speed not acceptable	8.3.2.9(4)			X
Fire pump annual test	Circulation relief valve and/or pressure relief valve did not work properly at churn condition	8.3.3.10(1)		X	
Fire pump annual test	Pressure relief valve did not work properly at each flow condition	8.3.3.11		X	

(continues)

Δ **Table A.3.3.8** *Continued*

Item	Finding	Reference	Impairment	Critical Deficiency	Noncritical Deficiency
Fire pump annual test (with transfer switch)	Overcurrent protective devices opened when simulating a power failure condition at peak load, power not transferred to alternate source, pump did not continue to perform at peak load, pump did not reconnect to normal power after removing power failure condition	8.3.3.12	X		
Fire pump annual test	Alarms did not properly operate	8.3.3.13		X	
Pump house/room	Heating, lighting, ventilating systems did not pass test	8.2.2		X	
Fire pump annual test	Parallel or angular alignment not correct	8.3.6.4		X	
Fire pump annual test	Flow test does not meet most demanding system flow and pressure requirements	8.3.7.2.3(1)	X		
Fire pump annual test	Flow test results not within 5% of acceptance test or nameplate	8.3.7.2.3(2)			X
Fire pump annual test	Voltage readings at motor not within 5% below or 10% above rated (nameplate)	8.3.7.2.9		X	
Diesel fuel annual test	Diesel fuel tested for degradation and failed	8.3.4	X		
Chapter 9: Water Storage Tanks — Inspection					
Water level	Water level and/or condition not correct	9.2.1		X	
Water level	Tank is empty	9.2.1	X		
Heating system	Heating system not operational, water temperature below 40°F (4°C)	9.2.2		X	
Heating system	Water temperature at or below 32°F (0°C)	9.2.2	X		
Exterior	Tank exterior, supporting structure, vents, foundation, catwalks, or ladders where provided damaged	9.2.4.1			X
Exterior	Area around tank has fire exposure hazard in form of combustible storage, trash, debris, brush, or material	9.2.4.2			X
Exterior	Accumulation of material on or near parts that could result in accelerated corrosion or rot	9.2.4.2			X
Exterior	Ice buildup on tank and support	9.2.4.2		X	
Exterior	Erosion exists on exterior sides or top of embankments supporting coated fabric tanks	9.2.4.2			X
Exterior	Expansion joints leaking or cracking	9.2.4.3		X	
Exterior	Hoops and grilles of wooden tanks in poor condition	9.2.4.4			X
Exterior	Exterior painted, coated, or insulated surfaces of tanks or supporting structure degraded	9.2.4.5			X
Interior	Pitting, corrosion, spalling, rot, other forms of deterioration, waste materials exist, aquatic growth, local or general failure of interior coating	9.2.5.3			X
Interior	Voids beneath floor, with sand in middle of tanks on ring-type foundations	9.2.5.5			X
Interior	Heating system components or piping in poor condition but working	9.2.5.6			X
Interior	Heating system components or heating system piping in poor condition and not working	9.2.5.6	X		

(continues)

Shaded text = Revisions.   Δ = Text deletions and figure/table revisions.   • = Section deletions.   *N* = New material.

2020 Edition

Δ **Table A.3.3.8**   *Continued*

Item	Finding	Reference	Impairment	Critical Deficiency	Noncritical Deficiency
Interior	Blockage of antivortex plate	9.2.5.7	X		
Interior	Deterioration of antivortex plate	9.2.5.7		X	
Chapter 9: Water Storage Tanks — Testing					
Interior testing	Tank coating did not pass adhesion, coating thickness, or wet sponge test	9.2.6			X
Interior testing	Tank walls and bottoms did not pass ultrasonic test	9.2.6			X
Interior testing	Tank bottom seams did not pass vacuum-box test	9.2.6			X
Level indicator	Level indicator lacked freedom of movement, or not accurate	9.3.1		X	
Heating system	Not in working order	9.3.2		X	
Low-temperature alarm	Low-water-temperature alarm did not pass test	9.3.3		X	
High-temperature alarm	High-water-temperature limit switch did not pass test	9.3.4			X
Water level alarm	High- and low-water-level alarms did not pass test	9.3.5		X	
Gauges	Not tested in 5 years, not accurate within 3% of scale	13.2.5.2, 13.2.5.3			X
Chapter 10: Water Spray Fixed Systems — Inspection					
Pipe and fittings	Mechanical damage, missing or damaged paint or coating, rusted or corroded, not properly aligned or trapped sections, low point drains not functioning, improper location of rubber-gasketed fittings	10.2.3.1		X	
Hangers and seismic braces	Damaged or missing, not securely attached to structural or piping, missing or damaged paint or coating, rusted or corroded	10.2.3.2		X	
Water spray nozzles	Discharge devices missing, not properly positioned or pointed in design direction, loaded or corroded	10.2.4.1		X	
Water spray nozzles	Missing caps or plugs if required, or not free to operate as intended	10.2.4.2		X	
Strainers	Strainer plugged or fouled	10.2.6	X		
Strainers	Strainer damaged or corroded	10.2.6			X
Drainage	Trap sumps and drainage trenches blocked, retention embankments or dikes in disrepair	10.2.7			X
Ultra-high-speed	Detectors have physical damage or deposits on lenses of optical detectors	10.4.2		X	
Ultra-high-speed	Controllers found to have faults	10.4.3		X	
Chapter 10: Water Spray Fixed Systems — Testing					
Operational test	Heat detection system did not operate within 40 seconds, flammable gas detection system did not operate within 20 seconds	10.3.3.1	X		
Operational test	Nozzles plugged	10.3.3.3.1	X		
Operational test	Nozzles not correctly positioned	10.3.3.3.1		X	
Operational test	Pressure readings not comparable to original design requirements	10.3.3.4.		X	
Operational test	Manual actuation devices did not work properly	10.3.5	X		
Main drain	More than 10% drop in full flow pressure	13.2.3.3		X	
Ultra-high-speed operational test	Response time was more than 100 milliseconds	10.4.5.2	X		
Assessment of the internal condition	Inspection revealed presence of MIC, zebra mussels, rust, and scale	14.2.1		X	

(continues)

Δ Table A.3.3.8   *Continued*

Item	Finding	Reference	Impairment	Critical Deficiency	Noncritical Deficiency
Chapter 11: Foam-Water Sprinkler Systems — Inspection					
Alarm devices	Physical damage apparent	5.2.4			X
Pipe and fittings	Mechanical damage, missing or damaged paint or coating, rusted or corroded, not properly aligned or trapped sections, low point drains not functioning, improper location or poor condition of rubber-gasketed fittings	11.2.2		X	
Hangers and seismic braces	Damaged or missing, not securely attached to structural or piping, missing or damaged paint or coating, rusted or corroded	11.2.3		X	
Foam-water discharge devices	Discharge devices missing	11.2.4.1	X		
Foam-water discharge devices	Discharge devices not properly positioned or pointed in design direction, loaded or corroded	11.2.4.1		X	
Foam-water discharge devices	Not free to operate as intended	11.2.4.2		X	
Foam-water discharge devices	Missing caps or plugs if required	11.2.4.2		X	
Foam-water discharge devices	Incorrect foam concentrate for application and devices	11.2.4.4		X	
Foam concentrate strainers	Blowdown valve open or not plugged	11.2.6.4		X	
Drainage	Trap sumps and drainage trenches blocked, retention embankments or dikes in disrepair	11.2.7			X
Proportioning systems (all)	Proportioning system valves not in correct open/closed position in accordance with specified operating conditions	11.2.8.3	X		
Proportioning systems (all)	Concentrate tank does not have correct quantity required by original design	11.2.8.4		X	
Proportioning systems (all)	Concentrate tank empty	11.2.8.4	X		
Standard pressure proportioner	Automatic drains (ball drip valves) not free or open, external corrosion on foam concentrate tanks	11.2.8.5.1			X
Bladder tank proportioner	Water control valve to foam concentrate in "closed" position	11.2.8.5.2	X		
Bladder tank proportioner	Foam in water surrounding bladder	11.2.8.5.2	X		
Bladder tank proportioner	External corrosion on foam concentrate tank	11.2.8.5.2			X
Line proportioner	Strainer damaged, corroded, pressure vacuum vent not operating freely	11.2.8.5.3		X	
Line proportioner	Strainer plugged or fouled	11.2.8.5.3	X		
Line proportioner	External corrosion on foam concentrate tank	11.2.8.5.3			X
Standard balanced pressure proportioner	Sensing line valves not open, no power to foam liquid pump	11.2.8.5.4	X		
Standard balanced pressure proportioner	Strainer damaged, corroded, plugged, or fouled, pressure vacuum vent not operating freely, gauges damaged or not showing proper pressures	11.2.8.5.4		X	
In-line balanced pressure proportioner	Sensing line valves at pump unit or individual proportioner stations not open, no power to foam liquid pump	11.2.8.5.5	X		
In-line balanced pressure proportioner	Strainer damaged, corroded, pressure vacuum vent not operating freely, gauges damaged or not showing proper pressures	11.2.8.5.5		X	
In-line balanced pressure proportioner	Strainer plugged or fouled	11.2.8.5.5	X		
Orifice plate proportioner	No power to foam liquid pump	11.2.8.5.6	X		

(continues)

Shaded text = Revisions.   Δ = Text deletions and figure/table revisions.   • = Section deletions.   *N* = New material.

2020 Edition

Δ **Table A.3.3.8**   *Continued*

Item	Finding	Reference	Impairment	Critical Deficiency	Noncritical Deficiency
Orifice plate proportioner	Strainer damaged, corroded, pressure vacuum vent not operating freely, gauges damaged or not showing proper pressures	11.2.8.5.6		X	
Orifice plate proportioner	Strainer plugged or fouled	11.2.8.5.6	X		
Foam concentrate	Fails quality testing	11.4.2		X	
Chapter 11: Foam-Water Sprinkler Systems — Testing					
Alarm devices	Water motor and gong not functioning	13.2.4.1		X	
Alarm devices	Pressure switch or vane-type switch not functioning or no alarm	13.2.4.2		X	
Operational test	Fire detection system did not operate within requirements of *NFPA 72*	11.3.2.4		X	
Operational test	Nozzles plugged	11.3.2.6.1	X		
Operational test	Nozzles not correctly positioned	11.3.2.6.1		X	
Operational test	Pressure readings not comparable to original design requirements	11.3.2.7		X	
Operational test	Manual actuation devices not working properly	11.3.4	X		
Operational test	Foam sample failed concentration test	11.3.5	X		
Main drain	More than 10% drop in full flow pressure	13.2.3.3		X	
Assessment of internal condition	Inspection revealed presence of MIC, zebra mussels, rust, and scale	14.2.1		X	
Chapter 13: Valves, Valve Components, and Trim — Inspection					
Gauges	Not operating or damaged	13.2.5.1			
Gauges	Not showing normal water/air pressure	13.2.5.1		X	
Control valve	Improper closed position	13.3.2.2	X		
Control valve	Improper open position, leaking	13.3.2.2		X	
Control valve	Not accessible, no appropriate wrench if required, no identification	13.3.2.2			X
Control valve	Not sealed, locked, or supervised	13.3.2.2		X	
Alarm valve	External physical damage, trim valves not in appropriate open or closed position, retard chamber or alarm drain leaking	13.4.1.1		X	
Valve enclosure	Upon visual observation, enclosure not maintaining minimum 40°F (4°C) temperature	4.1.2.5		X	
Valve enclosure	Low-temperature alarms (if installed) are physically damaged	4.1.2.5.1, 4.1.2.5.2		X	
Preaction valve and deluge valve	External physical damage, trim valves not in appropriate open or closed position, valve seat leaking	13.4.3.1.1, 13.4.4.1.1		X	
Preaction valve and deluge valve	Electrical components not in service	13.4.3.1.1, 13.4.4.1.1	X		
Dry pipe valve/quick-opening device	External physical damage, trim valves not in appropriate open or closed position, intermediate chamber leaking	13.4.5.1.2		X	
Sprinkler pressure-reducing control valves	Not in open position	13.5.1.1	X		
Sprinkler pressure-reducing control valves	Not maintaining downstream pressures in accordance with design criteria	13.5.1.1		X	
Sprinkler pressure-reducing control valves	Leaking, valve damaged, hand wheel missing or broken	13.5.1.1		X	
Hose connection pressure-reducing valves	Hand wheel broken or missing, hose threads damaged, leaking, reducer missing	13.5.2.1		X	
Hose connection pressure-reducing valves	Cap missing	13.5.2.1			X
Hose rack assembly pressure-reducing valve	Hand wheel broken or missing, leaking	13.5.3.1		X	

(continues)

Shaded text = Revisions.   Δ = Text deletions and figure/table revisions.   • = Section deletions.   *N* = New material.

△ **Table A.3.3.8**   *Continued*

Item	Finding	Reference	Impairment	Critical Deficiency	Noncritical Deficiency
Hose valves	Leaking, visible obstructions, caps, hose threads, valve handle, cap gasket, no restricting device, damaged, or in poor condition	13.6.1		X	
Hose valves	Hose threads not compatible	6.2.5.1	X		
Backflow prevention assemblies	Reduced-pressure assemblies, differential-sensing valve relief port continuously discharging	13.7.1.1		X	
Fire department connection	Not accessible, damaged couplings, or clapper not operating properly or missing	13.8.1	X		
Fire department connection	Couplings and swivels damaged, do not rotate smoothly, check valve leaking, automatic drain not operating properly or missing	13.8.1		X	
Fire department connection	Missing identification sign	13.8.1			X
Chapter 13: Valves, Valve Components, and Trim — Testing					
Main drain	More than 10% drop in full flow pressure	13.2.3.3		X	
Alarm devices	Water motor and gong not functioning	5.3.3.1, 13.2.4.3.2		X	
Alarm devices	Pressure switch or vane-type switch not functioning, no alarm	5.3.3.2, 13.2.4.4.2		X	
Gauges	Not replaced or calibrated in 5 years, not accurate within 3% of scale	13.2.5.2, 13.2.5.3			X
Control valve	Valve not operating through its full range	13.3.3.1		X	
Control valve	No spring or torsion felt in rod when opening post indicator valve	13.3.3.2	X		
Supervisory switches	No signal from two revolutions of hand-wheel from normal position or when stem has moved one-fifth of distance from normal position, signal restored in position other than normal	13.3.3.5.2		X	
Preaction valve	Priming water level not correct	13.4.3.2.1		X	
Preaction valve	Three-year air leakage test failed	13.4.3.2.6		X	
Deluge valve	Annual full flow trip test revealed plugged nozzles, manual actuation devices did not operate properly	13.4.4.2.4	X		
Deluge valve	Pressure reading at hydraulically most remote nozzle and/or at valve not compatible with original design values	13.4.4.2.7		X	
Preaction valve	Low air pressure switch did not send signal, no alarm	13.4.3.2.11		X	
Preaction and deluge valve	Low-temperature switch did not send signal, no alarm	13.4.3.2.12, 13.4.4.2.14		X	
Preaction valve	Automatic air maintenance device did not pass test	13.4.3.2.13			X
Dry pipe valve	Priming water level not correct	13.4.5.2.1		X	
Dry pipe valve	Does not trip during test	13.4.5.2.2	X		
Dry pipe valve	Test results not comparable with previous results	13.4.5.2.2		X	
Quick-opening device	Quick-opening device did not pass test	13.4.5.2.4		X	
Dry pipe valve	Low air pressure switch did not send signal, no alarm	13.4.5.2.6		X	
Dry pipe valve	Low-temperature switch did not send signal, no alarm	13.4.5.2.7		X	
Dry pipe valve	Automatic air maintenance device did not pass test	13.4.5.2.8		X	
Dry pipe system	Three-year leakage test failed	13.4.5.2.9		X	
Sprinkler pressure-reducing control valves	Test results not comparable to previous results	13.5.1.2		X	
Hose connection pressure-regulating valves	Test results not comparable to previous results	13.5.2.2		X	

(continues)

Δ **Table A.3.3.8**   *Continued*

Item	Finding	Reference	Impairment	Critical Deficiency	Noncritical Deficiency
Hose rack assembly pressure-regulating valve	Test results not comparable to previous results	13.5.3.2		X	
Hose valves (Class I and Class III standpipe system)	Annual test revealed valve leaking or difficult to operate	13.6.2.1.1		X	
Hose valves (Class II standpipe system)	Test revealed valve leaking or difficult to operate	13.6.2.2.1		X	
Backflow prevention assemblies	Did not pass minimum flow requirement for forward flow test	13.7.2.1	X		
Air compressors and nitrogen generators	Unit does not start at required air pressure, does not restore normal supervisory air pressure in required time frame, unit overheats while operating	13.10.3		X	

N **A.3.3.26 Lowest Permissible Suction Pressure.** The lowest pressure permitted by the authority having jurisdiction will likely be upstream of the backflow prevention device or at the connection to the water utility main. The permissible pressure at the pump suction could be lower than the limit stated by the authority having jurisdiction and could be determined by adding the friction loss and pressure elevation change between the cited location and the fire pump suction. [**20**, 2019]

A.3.3.27 Maintenance. As used in this standard, the term *maintenance* does not include repair activities. Such activities are expressly identified by the term *repair*.

A.3.3.29.1 Monitor Nozzle. Monitor nozzles can be used to protect large amounts of combustible materials, aircraft, tank farms, and any other special hazard. See Figure A.3.3.29.1(a) and Figure A.3.3.29.1(b).

A.3.3.29.2 Water Spray Nozzle. The selection of the type and size of spray nozzles should have been made with proper consideration given to factors such as physical character of the hazard involved, draft or wind conditions, material likely to be burning, and the general purpose of the system.

High velocity spray nozzles, generally used in piped installations, discharge in the form of a spray-filled cone. Low velocity spray nozzles usually deliver a much finer spray in the form of either a spray-filled spheroid or cone. Due to differences in the size of orifices or waterways in the various nozzles and the range of water particle sizes produced by each type, nozzles of one type cannot ordinarily be substituted for those of another type in an individual installation without seriously affecting fire extinguishment. In general, the higher the velocity and the coarser the size of the water droplets, the greater the effective "reach" or range of the spray.

Another type of water spray nozzle uses the deflector principle of the standard sprinkler. The angle of the spray discharge cones is governed by the design of the deflector. Some manufacturers make spray nozzles of this type individually automatic by constructing them with heat-responsive elements as used in standard automatic sprinklers.

A.3.3.32 Pressure-Regulating Device. Examples include pressure-reducing valves, pressure control valves, and pressure-restricting devices.

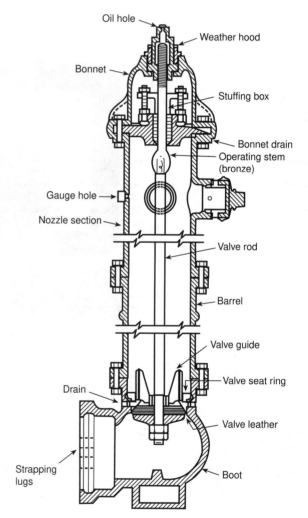

FIGURE A.3.3.13.1   Dry Barrel Hydrant.

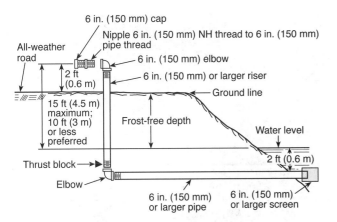

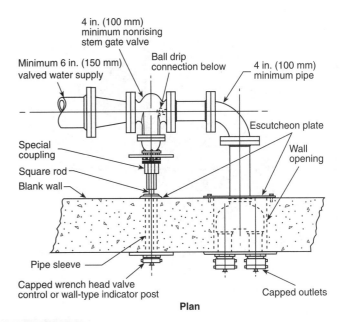

N FIGURE A.3.3.13.2   **Exploded View of Dry Hydrant Construction. [1142:Figure A.8.3.2(b)]**

FIGURE A.3.3.13.4   **Wall Hydrant.**

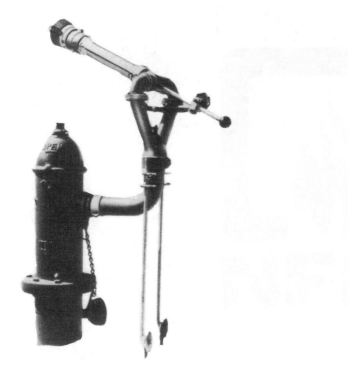

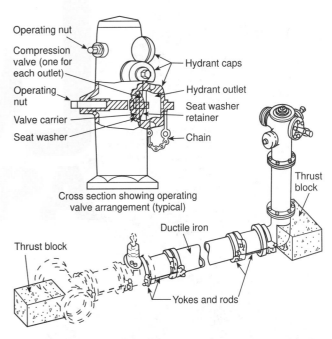

FIGURE A.3.3.13.3   **Hydrant with Monitor Nozzle.**

FIGURE A.3.3.13.5   **Wet Barrel Hydrant.** *(Courtesy of the Los Angeles Department of Water and Power.)*

A.3.3.34 Pressure Vacuum Vent. At rest (static condition), this device is closed to prevent free breathing of the foam concentrate storage tank. See Figure A.3.3.34.

A.3.3.35 Proportioner. See Figure A.3.3.35.

A.3.3.35.1 Bladder Tank Proportioner. Operation is the same as a standard pressure proportioner, except that, because of the separation of the foam concentrate and water, this system can be used with all foam concentrates, regardless of specific gravity. See Figure A.3.3.35.1.

A.3.3.35.2 In-Line Balanced Pressure Proportioner. Balancing of water and liquid takes place at individual proportioners located in the system riser or in segments of multiple systems. See Figure A.3.3.35.2.

A.3.3.35.3 Line Proportioner. See Figure A.3.3.35.3.

A.3.3.35.4 Standard Balanced Pressure Proportioner. Water and foam concentrate-sensing lines are directed to the balancing valve and maintain the foam liquid at a pressure equal to that of the water pressure. The two equal pressures are fed to the proportioner proper and are mixed at a predetermined rate. See Figure A.3.3.35.4.

FIGURE A.3.3.17(a)   Hose House of Five-Sided Design for Installation over Private Hydrant.

FIGURE A.3.3.17(b)   Steel Hose House of Compact Dimensions for Installation over Private Hydrant. House is shown closed; top lifts up, and doors on front side open for complete accessibility.

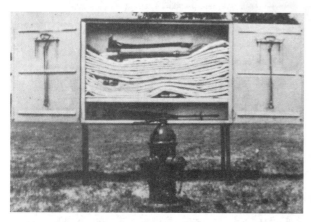

FIGURE A.3.3.17(c)   Hose House That Can Be Installed on Legs, As Pictured, or on Wall Near, but Not Directly over, Private Hydrant.

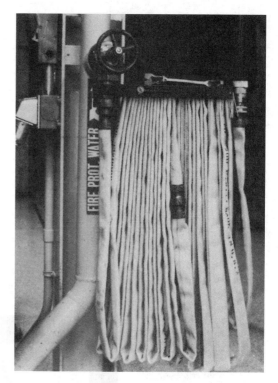

FIGURE A.3.3.20.1   Conventional Pin Rack.

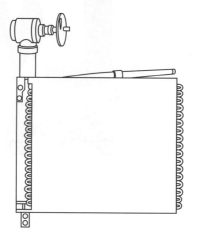

FIGURE A.3.3.20.2   Horizontal Rack.

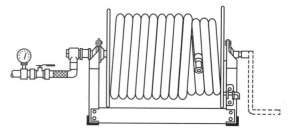

FIGURE A.3.3.20.3   Constant Flow Hose Reel.

Shaded text = Revisions.   **Δ** = Text deletions and figure/table revisions.   • = Section deletions.   ***N*** = New material.

FIGURE A.3.3.20.4   Semiautomatic Hose Rack Assembly.

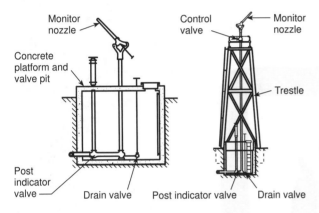

FIGURE A.3.3.29.1(a)   Standard Monitor Nozzles; Gear Control Nozzles Also Are Permitted.

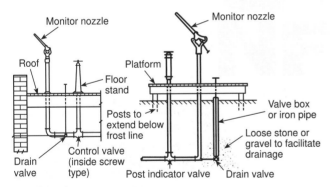

FIGURE A.3.3.29.1(b)   Alternative Arrangement of Standard Monitor Nozzles.

A.3.3.35.5 Standard Pressure Proportioner. Pressurized concentrate then is forced through an orifice back into the flowing water stream. This type of system is applicable for use with foam concentrates having a specific gravity substantially higher than water. It is not applicable for use with foam concentrates with a specific gravity at or near that of water. See Figure A.3.3.35.5.

A.3.3.42.2 Control Mode Specific Application (CMSA) Sprinkler. A large drop sprinkler is a type of CMSA sprinkler that is capable of producing characteristic large water droplets and

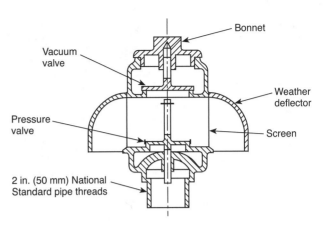

FIGURE A.3.3.34   Pressure Vacuum Vent.

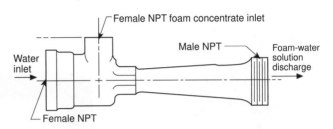

FIGURE A.3.3.35   Proportioner.

that is listed for its capability to provide fire control of specific high-challenge fire hazards. [13, 2019]

A.3.3.43 Standpipe System. This is accomplished by means of connections to water supply systems or by means of pumps, tanks, and other equipment necessary to provide an adequate supply of water to the hose connections.

A.3.3.45 Strainer. There are two types of strainers. Pipeline strainers are used in water supply connections. These are capable of removing from the water all solids of sufficient size to obstruct the spray nozzles [1/8 in. (3.2 mm) perforations usually are suitable]. Pipeline strainer designs should incorporate a flushout connection or should be capable of flushing through the main drain.

Individual strainers for spray nozzles, where needed, are capable of removing from the water all solids of sufficient size to obstruct the spray nozzle that they serve.

A.3.3.48 Testing. These tests follow up on the original acceptance test at intervals specified in the appropriate chapter of this standard.

A.3.3.50 Valve Status Test Connection. These connections can include the main drain, fire pump test header, backflow preventer forward flow test connection, fire hydrant, and other similar locations. In the absence of the aforementioned devices, an inspector's test connection might be used.

A.3.3.51 Water Spray. Water spray fixed systems are usually applied to special fire protection problems, since the protection can be specifically designed to provide for fire control, extinguishment, or exposure protection. Water spray fixed systems are permitted to be independent of, or supplementary to, other forms of protection.

Shaded text = Revisions.   Δ = Text deletions and figure/table revisions.   • = Section deletions.   N = New material.

2020 Edition

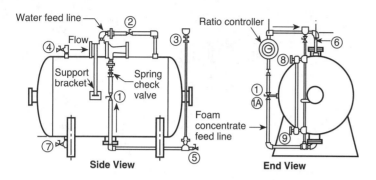

Valve description		Normal position	
Valve no.	Description	Manual system	Auto system
1	Concentrate shutoff	Closed	Closed
1A	Auto. conc. shutoff	N/A	Closed
2	Water pres. shutoff	Open	Open
3	Fill cup shutoff	Closed	Closed
4	Tank water vent	Closed	Closed
5	Diaph. conc. vent	Closed	Closed
6	Water fill	Closed	Closed
7	Concentrate drain/fill	Closed	Closed
8	Upr. sight gauge (opt.)	Closed	Closed
9	Lwr. sight gauge (opt.)	Closed	Closed

FIGURE A.3.3.35.1   Bladder Tank Proportioner.

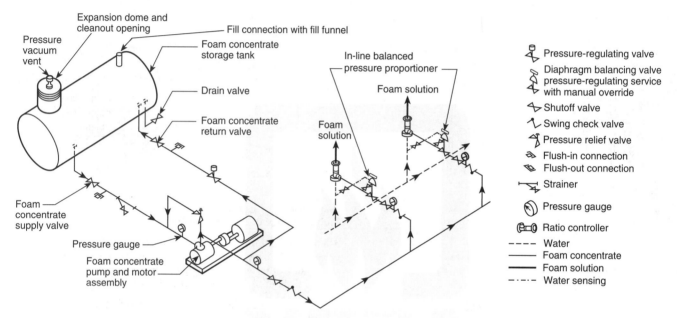

FIGURE A.3.3.35.2   In-Line Balanced Pressure Proportioner.

A.3.5.1 Control Valve. Experience has shown that closed valves are the primary cause of failure of water-based fire protection systems in protected occupancies. Control valves do not include hose valves, inspector's test valves, drain valves, trim valves for dry pipe, preaction and deluge valves, check valves, or relief valves.

A.3.5.2 Deluge Valve. Each deluge valve is intended to be capable of automatic and manual operation.

A.3.5.5.1 Master Pressure-Reducing Valve. Master pressure-reducing valves are typically found downstream of a fire pump's discharge.

A.3.6.2.4 No Flow (Churn, Shutoff). A small discharge of water is required to prevent the pump from overheating when operating under no flow (churn) conditions. [20, 2019]

A.3.6.2.5 Peak Load. The maximum power requirements for a centrifugal pump typically occur when the pump is operating between 130 percent and 150 percent of the rated flow. The required power could continue to increase beyond 150 percent of rated flow, but NFPA 20 does not require testing beyond 150 percent of rated flow. The peak load can be determined by looking at the horsepower curve on the fire pump curve supplied by the pump manufacturer. [20, 2019]

A.3.6.2.6.2 Net Pressure (Differential Pressure). The net pressure (differential pressure) includes the difference in velocity head correction (pressure) from the pump discharge to the pump suction. In many cases, the difference in suction and discharge velocity head correction (pressure) is small and can be ignored without adversely affecting the evaluation of the pump performance. [20, 2019]

A.3.6.3 Private Fire Service Main. See Figure A.3.6.3.

A.3.6.4 Sprinkler System. As applied to the definition of a sprinkler system, each system riser serving a portion of a single floor of a facility or where individual floor control valves are used in a multistory building should be considered a separate sprinkler system. Multiple sprinkler systems can be supplied by a common supply main. [13, 2019]

A.3.6.4.6 Wet Pipe Sprinkler System. Hose connections [1½ in. (40 mm) hose, valves, and nozzles] supplied by sprin-

Shaded text = Revisions.   Δ = Text deletions and figure/table revisions.   • = Section deletions.   *N* = New material.

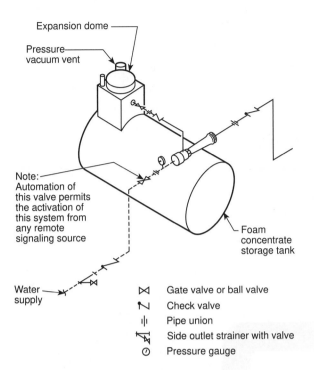

Expansion dome

Pressure vacuum vent

Note: Automation of this valve permits the activation of this system from any remote signaling source

Water supply

Foam concentrate storage tank

⋈	Gate valve or ball valve
N	Check valve
⊣⊢	Pipe union
⋈⃫	Side outlet strainer with valve
⊘	Pressure gauge

FIGURE A.3.3.35.3   Line Proportioner.

kler system piping are considered components of the sprinkler system.

A.3.6.6 Water Spray System. Automatic systems can be actuated by separate detection equipment installed in the same area as the water spray nozzles or by the water spray nozzles using an operating element. In some cases, the automatic detector can also be located in another area. [15, 2017]

A.3.7.1 Frequency. The frequencies in NFPA 25 are intended to establish an optimal time between tasks that are required by this document. When scheduling conflicts or other conditions do not allow the tasks to be performed on a strict calendar schedule, it is important that the required task frequencies be identified and complied with according to the variances described in the frequency definitions. When the required task frequencies have not been followed, it should be noted on the inspection report, the task should be performed, and the task frequencies should be followed for all future tasks. The variances should not be used to "skip" tasks or to perform fewer tasks than called for in this document.

A.4.1.1 Any portion or all of the inspection, testing, and maintenance can be permitted to be contracted with an inspection, testing, and maintenance service. When an inspection, testing, and maintenance service company agrees to perform inspections and tests at a specific frequency required by this standard, the inspection, testing, and maintenance service company should perform all inspections and tests that are required more frequently than the specified frequency. For example, the ITM service provider agrees to perform required inspections and tests on an annual basis. Those inspections and tests required on a daily, weekly, quarterly, and semiannual frequency should also be performed during the annual inspections and tests.

A.4.1.1.2.1 Water-based systems rely on the adequacy and ongoing maintenance of drainage systems such as roof drains

storm drains and floor drains, during flowing water as part of testing systems. These systems are often used for other purposes than fire system testing and are not part of the fire protection system. They are often designed and maintained as part of building plumbing systems.

A.4.1.1.3 Examples of designated representatives can include the occupant, management firm, or managing individual through specific provisions in the lease, written use agreement, or management contract.

A.4.1.2 In areas that have the potential for freezing temperatures below the level that can be adequately protected by an allowable antifreeze solution, supplemental heat can be provided when temperatures fall below the level of the antifreeze solution. Other means of freeze protection for water-filled piping, including heated valve enclosures, heat tracing, insulation, or other methods, are allowed by the applicable installation standard. Installation standards require heat tracing protecting fire protection piping against freezing to be supervised.

A.4.1.2.1 In order to ensure compliance, the owner should verify that windows, skylights, doors, ventilators, other openings and closures, concealed spaces, unused attics, stair towers, roof houses, and low spaces under buildings do not expose water-filled piping to freezing. This should occur prior to the onset of cold weather and periodically thereafter.

N **A.4.1.2.2** There are locations where water-filled piping was approved for installation and temperatures cannot be maintained at 40°F (4°C). For example, NFPA 13 permits water-filled piping in areas where temperatures are less than 40°F (4°C) and heat loss calculations verify that the system will not freeze.

A.4.1.3 The components are not required to be open or exposed. Doors, removable panels, or valve pits can be permitted to satisfy the need for accessibility. Such equipment should not be obstructed by features such as walls, ducts, columns, direct burial, or stock storage.

Δ **A.4.1.5** Needed corrections and repairs should be classified as an impairment, critical deficiency, or noncritical deficiency according to the effect on the fire protection system and the nature of the hazard protected.

Impairments are the highest priority problem found during inspection, testing, and maintenance and should be corrected as soon as possible. The fire protection system cannot provide an adequate response to a fire, and implementation of impairment procedures outlined in Chapter 15 is required until the impairment is corrected.

Critical deficiencies need to be corrected in a timely fashion. The fire protection system is still capable of performing, but its performance can be impacted and the implementation of impairment procedures might not be needed. However, special consideration must be given to the hazard in the determination of the classification. A deficiency that is critical for one hazard might be an impairment in another.

Noncritical deficiencies do not affect the performance of the fire protection system but should be corrected in a reasonable time period so that the system can be properly inspected, tested, and maintained.

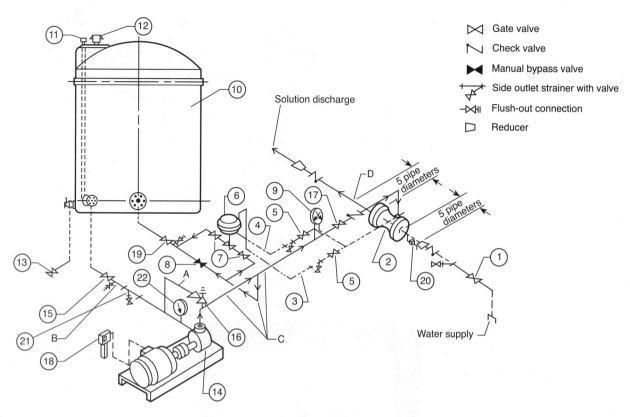

Legend:
1 Water supply valve (normally closed)
2 Ratio controller
3 Water balance line — minimum ³⁄₁₆ in. (5 mm) I.D. pipe or tubing recommended
4 Concentrate balance line — minimum ³⁄₁₆ in. (5 mm) I.D. pipe or tubing recommended
5 Sensing line valves (normally open)
6 Diaphragm control valve — automatic pressure balance — must be in vertical position
7 Block valves (normally open)
8 Manual bypass valve (normally open)
9 Water and concentrate pressure gauge (duplex)
10 Foam concentrate storage tank
11 Concentrate storage tank fill connection
12 Pressure vacuum vent
13 Concentrate storage tank drain valve (normally closed)
14 Foam concentrate pump and motor
15 Concentrate pump supply valve (normally open)
16 Pressure relief valve (setting as required by system)
17 Concentrate pump discharge valve (normally open)
18 Electric motor starter and switch

19 Concentrate return line valve (normally open)
20 Ball drip valve — ¾ in. (20 mm) (install in horizontal position)
21 Strainer with valved side outlet
22 Compound gauge

Operation:
Start concentrate pump (18). Open water supply valve (1). Open concentrate pump discharge valve (17). Equal gauge readings then maintained at (9) by the automatic valve (6). For manual operation, valves (7) can be closed and equal gauge readings maintained by regulating valve (8) manually.

System Automation:
By automating certain valves, the balanced pressure proportioning system can be activated from any remote signaling source.

• Water supply valve (1), normally closed, to be automatically operated;
• Concentrate pump discharge valve (17), normally closed, to be automatically operated;
• Electric motor starter switch (18) to be automatically operated.

FIGURE A.3.3.35.4   Standard Balanced Pressure Proportioner.

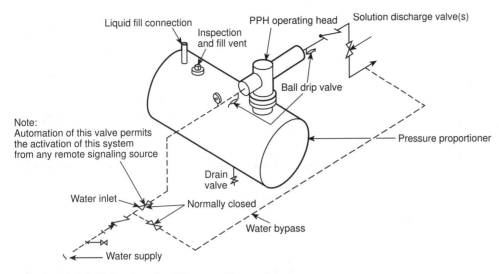

FIGURE A.3.3.35.5   Standard Pressure Proportioner.

Assembly occupancies, health care facilities, prisons, high-rise buildings, other occupancies where the life safety exposure is significant, or facilities that cannot be evacuated in a timely manner require special consideration. As an example, a nonfunctioning waterflow alarm might be considered a critical deficiency in a storage warehouse but an impairment in a hospital.

High-hazard occupancies where early response to a fire is critical also require special consideration. A small number of painted sprinklers could be considered an impairment for a system protecting a high-hazard occupancy but might be considered a critical deficiency in a metal working shop.

Classifications of needed corrections and repairs are shown in Table A.3.3.8.

A.4.1.5.1 System deficiencies not explained by normal wear and tear, such as hydraulic shock, can often be indicators of system problems and should be investigated and evaluated by a qualified person or engineer. Failure to address these issues could lead to catastrophic failure. Examples of deficiencies that can be caused by issues beyond normal wear and tear are as follows:

(1) Pressure gauge deficiencies as follows:

    (a) Gauge not returning to zero
    (b) Gauge off scale
    (c) Gauge with bent needle

(2) Support devices deficiencies as follows:

    (a) Bent hangers and/or rods
    (b) Hangers pulled out/off structure
    (c) Indication of pipe or hanger movement such as the following:

        i. Hanger scrape marks on pipe, exposed pipe surface where pipe and hangers are painted
        ii. Firestop material damaged at pipe penetration of fire-rated assembly

(3) Unexplained system damage as follows:

    (a) Unexplained system damage beyond normal wear and tear
    (b) Bent or broken shafts on valves

    (c) Bent or broken valve clappers
    (d) Unexplained leakage at branch lines, cross main, or feed main piping
    (e) Unexplained leakage at closed nipples
    (f) Loose bolts on flanges and couplings

(4) Fire pump deficiencies as follows:

    (a) Fire pump driver out of alignment
    (b) Vibration of fire pump and/or driver
    (c) Unusual sprinkler system piping noises (sharp report, loud bang)

N A.4.1.5.1.1 For an example of a reference source containing a list of links to manufacturers' information regarding components that are recalled or part of a replacement program, see www.nfsa.org.

N A.4.1.5.1.2 Remedies for equipment under recall include entrance into a program for scheduled replacement. Such replacement or remedial product should be installed in accordance with the manufacturer's instructions and the appropriate NFPA installation standards. A recalled product is a product subject to a statute or administrative regulation specifically requiring the manufacturer, importer, distributor, wholesaler, or retailer of a product, or any combination of such entities, to recall the product, or a product voluntarily recalled by a combination of such entities.

A.4.1.6 The inspections and tests specified in this standard do not address the adequacy of design criteria or the capability of the fire protection system to protect the building or its contents. It is assumed that the original system design and installation were appropriate for the occupancy and use of the building and were approved by all applicable authorities having jurisdiction. If no changes to the water supply or to the building or its use have transpired since it was originally occupied, no evaluation is required. If changes are contemplated, it is the owner's responsibility to arrange for the evaluation of the fire protection system(s). In such a case, Figure A.4.1.6 provides an example of a questionnaire that the owner could use. Where the inspections and tests specified in the standard have been contracted to a qualified inspection provider or contractor, it is not the role of the inspector or contractor to determine if any

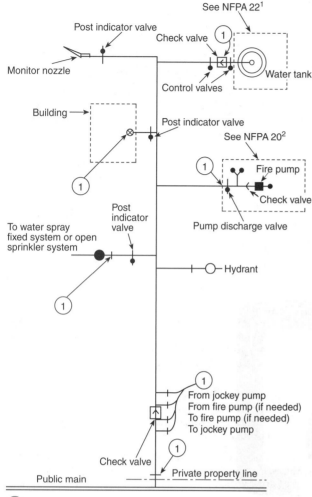

(1) End of private fire service main

Note: The piping (aboveground or buried) shown is specific as to the end of the private fire service main, and this schematic is only for illustrative purposes beyond the end of the fire service main. Details of valves and their location requirements are covered in the specific standard involved.
1. See NFPA 22, *Standard for Water Tanks for Private Fire Protection.*
2. See NFPA 20, *Standard for the Installation of Stationary Pumps for Fire Protection.*

△ **FIGURE A.3.6.3   Typical Private Fire Service Main.** [24:Figure A.3.3.13]

changes have been made or the subsequent evaluation of the fire protection system. The evaluation of any building changes should be conducted before any proposed change is incorporated and should utilize the appropriate installation standard and input from applicable authorities having jurisdiction.

Fire protection systems should not be removed from service when the building is not in use; however, where a system that has been out of service for a prolonged period (such as in the case of idle or vacant properties) is returned to service, it is recommended that a responsible and experienced contractor be retained to perform all inspections and tests.

△ **A.4.1.6.2** Fire protection systems are designed and installed based on a specific set of circumstances and building uses. For example, the volume of water needed for a sprinkler system to control a fire in the built environment is based upon the intended use of the facility known at the time the sprinkler system was designed and installed. Revisions to properties used for storage represent one of the most common scenarios that impact the ability of systems to provide adequate protection. Some of the most common changes include raising the storage height, changing the storage method arrangement such as adding racks, installing solid shelves in rack structures or decreasing the aisle widths between racks. Changes in product packaging with the use of foam inserts, bubble wrap, or other plastics or encapsulated storage can significantly increase the fire hazard. Changing from wood pallets to plastic pallets, converting to the use of plastic bin boxes, or revising or adding material handling systems such as conveyors could severely impact the effectiveness of the fire protection systems.

△ **A.4.1.7** Annex E for an example of a hazard evaluation form. A hazard evaluation is not part of a system inspection.

N **A.4.1.9** Systems installed in accordance with the 2007 and subsequent editions of NFPA 13 should have a general information sign. It is not the intent of the committee for a system to have both the information sign required by NFPA 25 and the general information sign required by NFPA 13. The information sign required by this standard is intended to be provided for systems installed prior to the 2007 edition of NFPA 13. Systems installed under the 2007 and subsequent editions of NFPA 13 should have a general information sign.

△ **A.4.3.1** Typical records include, but are not limited to, valve inspections; flow, drain, and pump tests; and trip tests of dry pipe, deluge, and preaction valves.

Acceptance test records should be retained for the life of the system or its special components. Subsequent test records should be retained for a period of 1 year after the next test. The comparison determines deterioration of system performance or condition and the need for further testing or maintenance.

A.4.3.1.2 Computer programs that file inspection and test results should provide a means of comparing current and past results and should indicate the need for corrective maintenance or further testing.

A.4.3.3 See Section B.3 for information regarding sample forms.

A.4.5 Inspection and periodic testing determine what, if any, maintenance actions are required to maintain the operability of a water-based fire protection system. The standard establishes minimum inspection/testing frequencies, responsibilities, test routines, and reporting procedures but does not define precise limits of anomalies where maintenance actions are required.

Substandard conditions, such as a closed valve, subnormal water pressure, loss of building heat or power, or obstruction of sprinklers, nozzles, detectors, or hose stations, can delay or prevent system actuation and impede manual fire-fighting operations.

Owner's Questionnaire

A. Is the building occupied?   ❏ Yes   ❏ No

B. Has the occupancy and hazard of contents remained the same since the last inspection?   ❏ Yes   ❏ No

C. Are all fire protection systems in service?   ❏ Yes   ❏ No

D. Has the system remained in service without modification since the last inspection?   ❏ Yes   ❏ No

E. Was the system free of actuation of devices or alarms since the last inspection?   ❏ Yes   ❏ No

Explain any "no" answers:

_____

_____

_____

_____

_____

_____   _____
Owner or Designated Representative (print)   Signature and Date

© 2019 National Fire Protection Association   NFPA 25

N **FIGURE A.4.1.6   Owner's Questionnaire.**

A.4.6.4 The types of tests required for each protection system and its components, and the specialized equipment required for testing, are detailed in the appropriate chapter.

As referred to in 4.3.4, original records should include, at a minimum, the contractor's material and test certificate, "as-built" drawings and calculations, and any other required or pertinent test reports. These documents establish the conditions under which the systems were first installed and offer some insight to the design intent, installation standards used, and water supply present at the time of installation. Original records are instrumental in determining any subsequent changes or modifications to the buildings or system.

Δ A.4.6.5 Examples of subsystems or components include fire pumps, drivers or controllers, pressure-regulating devices, detection systems and controls, alarm check, and dry pipe, deluge, and preaction valves. The required tests for components are contained in the corresponding chapter in tables titled "Summary of [Component] Inspection, Testing, and Maintenance."

A.4.6.6 Some devices, such as waterflow alarm devices, can be tested automatically. Some things to consider include the following:

(1) Not all tests required by NFPA 25 are suitable for automatic testing.
(2) Periodic visual inspection, including the use of video, should be performed.

Δ A.4.6.6.2 Transducers, temperature sensors, automatic and remotely operated valves, including motorized valves, and solenoids are examples of some of the equipment that could be used in an automated inspection. The list of items above is a partial list and should not be considered an exclusive list of equipment and methodologies.

A.4.6.6.4.2 The visual observation should be coordinated with the automatic testing. Appropriate remote visual observation might satisfy this requirement.

N **A.4.6.6.7** Certain devices, meters, and equipment that can be used to perform inspection and testing procedures from a distant location are not integral to the system and don't affect system performance. Automated inspection and testing devices and equipment, such as a digital camera, can be in the riser room or attached to the system externally but are not an integral part of the system. Such devices do not need to be listed.

A.4.7 Section 4.7 provides the option to adopt a performance-based test and inspection method as an alternative means of compliance with 4.6.2. The prescriptive test and requirements contained in this standard are essentially qualitative. In addition, this standard is applied equally to systems where a system failure might be acceptable and to systems where preventing system failure is an extremely high priority. It is appropriate to adjust reliability requirements in performance-based ITM accordingly. One suggested means to complete a performance-based program can be found in the second edition (2007) of *SFPE Engineering Guide to Performance-Based Fire Protection.*

Δ A.4.7.1 As noted in A.4.7, this standard is applied equally to systems where a system failure might be acceptable and to systems where preventing system failure is an extremely high priority. Goals should be adjusted accordingly.

Sprinkler systems can be used as an example for establishing a baseline. The overall performance of sprinkler systems is documented and can be used as a starting point to establish a baseline for reliability. However, the performance level of sprinkler systems maintained in accordance with this standard is not currently well documented, and the reliability baseline should be adjusted upward using an adjustment factor agreeable to the approving authority.

Once a baseline for reliability is established, it should be adjusted upward or downward based on, as a minimum, the following issues:

(1) Building criticality
(2) System/component preventive maintenance programs
(3) Consequences of system maloperation such as the following:

    (a) Immediate loss of and/or damage to facilities, equipment, and contents
    (b) Business interruption
    (c) Increased hazard to fire fighters
    (d) Impact on adjacent facilities
    (e) Economic impact on community

(4) System/component repair history
(5) Building/service conditions

Once a baseline acceptable to the approving authority has been determined, equivalent or superior levels of performance can be demonstrated through qualitative and/or quantitative performance-based analyses. This section provides a basis for implementing and monitoring a quantitative performance-based program acceptable under this option (providing approval is obtained from the authority having jurisdiction).

The concept of a quantitative performance-based testing and inspection program is to establish the requirements and frequencies at which inspection and testing must be performed to achieve an acceptable level of operational reliability. The goal is to balance the inspection/test frequency with the reliability of the system or component. Ideally, a quantitative performance-based inspection program will adjust test/inspection frequencies commensurate with historical documented equipment performance and desired reliability. Frequencies of test/inspection under a quantitative performance-based program can be extended or reduced from the prescriptive test requirements contained in this standard when continued testing has been documented indicating a higher or lower degree of reliability compared to the authority having jurisdiction's expectations of performance. Additional program attributes that should be considered when adjusting test/inspection frequencies include the following:

(1) System/component preventive maintenance programs
(2) Consequences of system maloperation
(3) System/component repair history
(4) Building/service conditions

Fundamental to implementing a quantitative performance-based program is that adjusted test and inspection frequencies must be technically defensible to the authority having jurisdiction and supported by evidence of higher or lower reliability. Data collection and retention must be established so that the data utilized to alter frequencies are representative, statistically valid, and evaluated against firm criteria. Frequencies should not be arbitrarily extended or reduced without a suitable basis and rationale. It must be noted that transitioning to a quantitative performance-based program might require additional

expenditures of resources in order to collect and analyze failure data, coordinate review efforts, replace program documents, and seek approval from the authority having jurisdiction. Information on how to estimate the reliability of fire protection systems can be found in Chapter 74, "Reliability, Availability, and Maintainability," of the fifth edition (2016) of the *SFPE Handbook of Fire Protection Engineering*.

Failure Rate Calculation. A quantitative performance-based program requires that a maximum allowable failure rate be established and approved by the authority having jurisdiction in advance of implementation. The use of historical system/component fire system inspection records can be utilized to determine failure rates. One method of calculating the failure rate of a fire system is based on the following equation:

[A.4.7.1a]

$$FSFR(t) = \frac{NF}{(NC)(t)}$$

where:
$FSFR$ = fire system failure rate (failures per year)
  t = time interval of review (years)
 NF = number of failures
NC = total number of fire systems inspected or tested

Example. Data are collected for 50 fire pump weekly tests over a 5-year period. The testing is conducted, as described in 8.3.1. A review of the data has identified five failures:

Total components: 280

Data collection period: 5 years

Total failures: 5

[A.4.7.1b]

$$FSFR = \frac{5}{280 \times 5} = 0.003/\text{year}$$

A fundamental requirement of a quantitative performance-based program is the continual monitoring of fire system/component failure rates and determining whether they exceed the maximum allowable failure rates as agreed upon with the authority having jurisdiction. The process used to complete this review should be documented and repeatable.

Coupled with this ongoing review is a requirement for a formalized method of increasing or decreasing the frequency of testing/inspection when systems exhibit either a higher than expected failure rate or an increase in reliability as a result of a decrease in failures, or both. A formal process for reviewing the failure rates and increasing or decreasing the frequency of testing must be well documented.

Concurrence of the authority having jurisdiction on the process used to determine test frequencies should be obtained in advance of any alterations to the test program. The frequency required for future tests might be reduced to the next inspection frequency and maintained there for a period equaling the initial data review or until the ongoing review indicates that the failure rate is no longer being exceeded — for example, going from annual to semiannual testing when the failure rate exceeds the authority having jurisdiction's

Shaded text = Revisions. **Δ** = Text deletions and figure/table revisions. • = Section deletions. **N** = New material.

expectations or from annual to every 18 months when the failure trend indicates an increase in reliability.

References.

Edward K. Budnick, P.E., "Automatic Sprinkler System Reliability," *Fire Protection Engineering*, Society of Fire Protection Engineers, SFPE Winter 2001.

Fire Protection Equipment Surveillance Optimization and Maintenance Guide, Electric Power Research Institute, July 2003.

Kenneth W. Dungan, P.E., "Performance-Based Inspection, Testing, and Maintenance," *Fire Protection Engineering*, SFPE, Quarter 4, 2016.

William E. Koffel, P.E., *Reliability of Automatic Sprinkler Systems*, Alliance for Fire Safety.

NFPA's Future in Performance Based Codes and Standards, July 1995.

NFPA Performance Based Codes and Standards Primer, December 1999.

A.4.9.5 Most places using or storing hazardous materials have stations set up for employees where material safety data sheets (MSDSs) are stored. The inspector should be familiar with the types of materials present and the appropriate actions to take in an emergency.

Δ **A.4.9.6 WARNING:** NFPA 20 includes electrical requirements that discourage the installation of a disconnect means in the power supply to electric motor-driven fire pumps. This is intended to ensure the availability of power to the fire pumps. Where equipment connected to those circuits is serviced or maintained, the service person could be subject to unusual exposure to electrical and other hazards. It could be necessary to establish special safe work practices and to use safeguards or personal protective clothing, or both. See also NFPA *70E* for additional safety guidance.

N **A.4.9.6.2** NFPA *70E* helps establish an overall electrical safety program. It is not the intent of 4.9.6.2 to restrict the use of other electrical safety programs that are recognized and established by a jurisdiction. For jurisdictions that do not recognize the provisions of NFPA *70E*, other approved electrical safety programs could be acceptable. The acceptance of an equivalent standard or program to NFPA *70E* must be approved by the authority having jurisdiction.

A.5.2 The provisions of the standard are intended to apply to routine inspections. In the event of a fire, a post-fire inspection should be made of all sprinklers within the fire area. In situations where the fire was quickly controlled or extinguished by one or two sprinklers, it might be necessary only to replace the activated sprinklers. Care should be taken that the replacement sprinklers are of the same make and model or that they have compatible performance characteristics (*see 5.4.1.2*). Soot-covered sprinklers should be replaced because deposits can result in corrosion of operating parts. In the event of a substantial fire, special consideration should be given to replacing the first ring of sprinklers surrounding the operated sprinklers because of the potential for excessive thermal exposure, which could weaken the response mechanisms.

N **A.5.2.1.1** The coverplates of concealed sprinklers do not need to be removed for inspection. Where the inspection of coverplates for concealed sprinklers reveals possible signs of leakage, damage, corrosion, or other adverse conditions, those coverplates should be removed to facilitate a closer inspection of the concealed sprinkler.

A.5.2.1.1.1 The conditions described in this section can have a detrimental effect on the performance of sprinklers by adversely impacting water distribution patterns, insulating thermal elements delaying operation, or otherwise rendering the sprinkler inoperable or ineffectual.

Severely corroded or loaded sprinklers should be reported as a deficiency or impairment as part of the visual inspection and designated to be replaced. Such sprinklers could be affected in their distribution or other performance characteristics not addressed by routine sample testing.

Corrosion found on the seat, or built up on the deflector that could affect the spray pattern, or a buildup on the operating elements that could affect the operation can have a detrimental effect on the performance of the sprinkler. Sprinklers having limited corrosion or loading that does not impact the water distribution characteristics can continue to be used if the samples are selected for testing in accordance with 5.3.1 based on worst-case conditions and if the samples successfully pass the tests. Surface discoloration that does not impact the performance of the sprinkler should not warrant replacement or testing.

Multiple sprinkler operations within a facility without a fire might be a sign of exposure to excessive temperatures, sprinkler damage, or excessive corrosion of similar sprinklers installed in that facility. Consideration should be given to replacing sprinklers that are considered representative of the operated sprinklers.

Glass bulbs in sprinklers exposed to sunlight or installed in cold environments such as walk-in coolers and freezers might lose or change their temperature classification color due to the environment. This loss of color should not be confused with loss of fluid in the glass bulb. Tests have shown that this loss or change of color in the bulb does not affect the operation or any other performance characteristics of the sprinkler, and these sprinklers can be allowed to remain in service. The tests also showed that when sprinklers installed in cold environments were subjected to temperatures above 60°F (15.5°C), the fluid color returned.

In lieu of replacing sprinklers that are loaded with a coating of dust, it is permitted to clean sprinklers with compressed air or a vacuum, provided that the equipment does not touch the sprinkler.

A.5.2.1.1.3 Examples include spaces above ceilings, whether the ceilings are lay-in tile or gypsum board, areas under theater stages, pipe chases, and other inaccessible areas, even if access panels or hatches are provided into the areas.

Where temporary listed membrane ceilings are installed, NFPA 13 allows sprinkler protection to be omitted below the "drop out" membrane ceiling. These areas should be inspected during periods when the membrane ceiling is not present.

Where finished ceiling areas around installed pendent sprinklers show signs of water damage, further investigation should be conducted and the building owner or representative should be notified.

A.5.2.1.2 NFPA 13 in the storage definitions defines clearance as the distance from the top of storage to the ceiling sprinkler deflectors. Other obstruction rules are impractical to enforce under this standard. However, if obstructions that might cause a concern are present, the owner is advised to have an engineering evaluation performed.

A.5.2.1.2.1 The 18 in. (457 mm) clearance rule generally applies to standard pendent, upright and sidewall spray sprinklers, extended coverage upright and pendent sprinklers, and residential sprinklers.

A.5.2.1.2.3 The special sprinklers that the minimum 36 in. (915 mm) clearance rule generally applies to includes large drop sprinklers, CMSA sprinklers, and early suppression fast-response (ESFR) sprinklers.

A.5.2.1.2.6 The purpose of maintaining a minimum clearance is to ensure water discharge is not obstructed. There are certain installations where this can be achieved by other means. Examples include library stacks, record storage, and where sprinklers are installed in aisles in between storage shelving. Clearance is also not needed for shelving along perimeter walls since this does not cause an obstruction. NFPA 13 allows a clearance less than 18 in. (457 mm) where full-scale fire tests demonstrate an acceptable sprinkler discharge pattern. Also, where sufficient shielding of the sprinkler spray pattern has resulted in an increase in the hazard classification to Extra Hazard Group 2, a clearance less than 18 in. (457 mm) might be acceptable.

A.5.2.1.3 Sprinkler spray patterns should not be obstructed by temporary or nonpermanent obstructions such as signs, banners, or decorations. While it is impractical for an inspector to know all of the various obstruction rules for all the different types of sprinklers, the inspector can observe when temporary or nonpermanent obstructions have been installed that could block or obstruct a sprinkler's spray pattern. Temporary or nonpermanent obstructions that appear to be obstructions to sprinkler spray patterns should be removed or repositioned so they are not an obstruction.

A.5.2.2 The conditions described in 5.2.2 can have a detrimental effect on the performance and life of pipe by affecting corrosion rates or pipe integrity or otherwise rendering the pipe ineffectual.

A.5.2.2.1 Surface corrosion not impacting the integrity of the piping strength or raising concern of potential leakage should not warrant the replacement of piping. A degree of judgment should be exercised in the determination of the extent of corrosion that would necessitate replacement.

A.5.2.2.3 Examples include some floor/ceiling or roof/ceiling assemblies, areas under theater stages, pipe chases, and other inaccessible areas.

A.5.2.3 The conditions described in this section can have a detrimental effect on the performance of hangers and braces by allowing failures if the components become loose.

A.5.2.3.3 Examples of hangers and seismic braces installed in concealed areas include some floor/ceiling or roof/ceiling assemblies, areas under theater stages, pipe chases, and other inaccessible areas.

A.5.2.5 The hydraulic design information sign should be secured to the riser with durable wire, chain, or equivalent. *(See Figure A.5.2.5.)*

This system as shown on _____ company

print no. _____ dated _____

for _____

at _____ contract no. _____

is designed to discharge at a rate of _____

gpm per ft^2 (L/min per m^2) of floor area over a maximum

area of _____ ft^2 (m^2) when supplied

with water at a rate of _____ gpm (L/min)

at _____ psi (bar) at the base of the riser.

Hose stream allowance of _____

gpm (L/min) is included in the above.

FIGURE A.5.2.5   Sample Hydraulic Design Information Sign.

△ **A.5.2.8** The sign referenced in 5.2.8 should satisfy the requirements of 4.1.9 and 5.2.7. See Figure A.5.2.8.

A.5.3.1 The sprinkler performance testing described in this section is considered routine testing to determine if the installed sprinklers have maintained a level of sensitivity that would allow them to operate as expected during a fire event. Nonroutine testing should be conducted to address unusual conditions not associated with the routine test cycles mandated within this standard. Due to the nature of nonroutine testing, specific tests cannot be identified in this standard. The type of tests to be conducted and the number and location of samples to be submitted should be appropriate to the problem discovered or being investigated and based on consultation with the manufacturer, listing agency, and the authority having jurisdiction.

Examples of documents that can be used to determine the installation date include the Contractor's Material and Test Certificate for Aboveground Piping or the Certificate of Occupancy. Where documentation of the installation date is not available, the start date for the in-service performance testing interval should be based upon the sprinkler's manufacture date.

△ **A.5.3.1.1** Sprinklers should be first given a visual inspection in accordance with 5.2.1.1.1 to determine if replacement is required. Sprinklers that have passed the visual inspection should then be laboratory tested for sensitivity and functionality. The waterway should clear when sensitivity/functionality tested at 7 psi (0.5 bar) or the minimum listed operating pressure for dry sprinklers.

The thermal sensitivity should be such that the RTI does not exceed 350 (meters-seconds)$^{1/2}$ for standard-response sprinklers, 65 (meters-seconds)$^{1/2}$ for quick-response and residential sprinklers and 50 (meters-seconds)$^{1/2}$ for ESFR sprinklers.

SPRINKLER SYSTEM — GENERAL INFORMATION
for

_____

_____

_____

Pipe schedule system	❏ Yes	❏ No
High-piled storage	❏ Yes	❏ No
Rack storage:	❏ Yes	❏ No

Commodity class:_____

Max. storage height _____ ft m

Aisle width (min.) _____ ft m

Encapsulation	❏ Yes	❏ No
Solid shelving:	❏ Yes	❏ No
Flammable/ combustible liquids:	❏ Yes	❏ No
Other storage:	❏ Yes	❏ No

_____

Hazardous materials:	❏ Yes	❏ No
Idle pallets:	❏ Yes	❏ No
Antifreeze systems	❏ Yes	❏ No

Location: _____

Dry or aux systems	❏ Yes	❏ No

Location:_____

Date:_____

Flow test data:

Static: _____ psi bar

Resid: _____ psi bar

Flow: _____ gpm lpm

Pitot: _____ psi bar

Date:_____

Location: _____

_____

Location of aux/low point drains:

_____

_____

_____

Dry pipe/double interlock preaction valve
test results
_____

Original main drain test results:

Static: _____ psi bar

Residual: _____ psi bar

Venting valve location: _____

Where injection systems are used to treat MIC or corrosion:

Type of chemical:_____ Concentration: _____ For proper disposal, see:

_____

Name of contractor or designer: _____

Address: _____

Phone: _____

_N_ **FIGURE A.5.2.8   Sprinkler System General Information. [13:Figure A.28.6]**

Sprinklers that have been installed for a number of years should not be expected to have all of the performance qualities of a new sprinkler. However, if there is any question about their continued satisfactory performance, the sprinklers should be replaced.

A.5.3.1.1.1.3 Sprinklers defined as fast response have a thermal element with an RTI of 50 (meters-seconds)$^{1/2}$ or less. A quick-response sprinkler, residential sprinkler, and early suppression fast-response (ESFR) sprinklers are examples of fast-response sprinklers.

A.5.3.1.1.1.4 Due to solder migration caused by the high temperatures to which these devices are exposed, it is important to test them every 5 years. Because of this phenomenon, the operating temperature can vary over a wide range.

A.5.3.1.1.1.6 See 3.3.42.4.

△ A.5.3.1.1.2 Examples of these environments are paper mills, packing houses, tanneries, alkali plants, organic fertilizer plants, foundries, forge shops, fumigation areas, pickle and vinegar works, stables, storage battery rooms, electroplating rooms, galvanizing rooms, steam rooms of all descriptions including moist vapor dry kilns, salt storage rooms, locomotive sheds or houses, driveways, areas exposed to outside weather, around bleaching equipment in flour mills, and portions of any area where corrosive vapors prevail.

A.5.3.1.2 Within an environment, similar sidewall, upright, and pendent sprinklers produced by the same manufacturer could be considered part of the same sample, but additional sprinklers would be included within the sample if produced by a different manufacturer.

The sample sprinklers sent for testing can represent any group of sprinklers that is practical, keeping in mind that if one sprinkler in the sample set fails, then all sprinklers that the sample represents should be replaced. The following is an example of sample sprinklers chosen for testing:

Example:

A warehouse has five overhead systems with 300 sprinklers per system, and an office area with 200 sprinklers. The warehouse sprinklers are all subject to the same ambient environment and all of the office area sprinklers are subjected to the same ambient environment.

Sample Option #1: All warehouse sprinklers as one sample set (1% of 1500 = 15 sprinklers).

All office sprinklers as one sample set (1% of 200 = 2, but a minimum of 4 sprinklers must be tested).

Total of 19 sprinklers tested.

Sample Option #2: Each warehouse system sample set (1% of 300 = 3, but a minimum of 4 sprinklers must be tested, 4 × 5 = 20 sprinklers).

All office sprinklers as one sample set (1% of 200 = 2, but a minimum of 4 sprinklers must be tested).

Total of 24 sprinklers tested.

As shown, the number of sprinklers to be tested would be different depending on the sample chosen.

A.5.3.3.2 Data concerning reliability of electrical waterflow switches indicate no appreciable change in failure rates for those tested quarterly and those tested semiannually. Mechanical motor gongs, however, have additional mechanical and environmental failure modes and need to be tested more often.

△ A.5.3.4 Sampling from the top and bottom of the system helps to determine if the solution has settled. Antifreeze solutions are heavier than water. If the antifreeze compound is separating from the water due to poor mixing, it will exhibit a higher concentration in the lower portion of the system than in the upper portion of the system. If the concentration is acceptable near the top, but too low near the water connection, it might mean that the system is becoming diluted near the water supply. If the concentration is either too high or too low in both the samples, it might mean that the wrong concentration was added to the system.

Two or three times during the freezing season, test samples can be drawn from test valve B as shown in Figure 8.6.3.1 of NFPA 13, especially if the water portion of the system has been drained for maintenance or repairs. A small hydrometer can be used so that a small sample is sufficient. Where water appears at valve B, or where the sample indicates that the solution has become weakened, the entire system should be emptied and refilled with acceptable solution as previously described.

See Figure A.5.3.4 for expected minimum air temperatures in 48 of the United States and parts of Canada where the lowest one-day mean temperature can be used as one method of determining the minimum reasonable air temperature. In situations where the piping containing the antifreeze solution is protected in some way from exposure to the outside air, higher minimum temperatures can be anticipated.

Where systems are drained in order to be refilled, it is not typically necessary to drain drops. Most systems with drops have insufficient volume to cause a problem, even if slightly higher concentration solutions collect in the drops. For drops in excess of 36 in. (915 mm), consideration should be given to draining drops if there is evidence that unacceptably high concentrations of antifreeze have collected in these long drops.

When emptying and refilling antifreeze solutions, every attempt should be made to recycle the old solution with the antifreeze manufacturer rather than discard it.

A.5.3.4.3.1 Where inspecting antifreeze systems employing listed CPVC piping, the solution should be verified to be glycerine based.

A.5.3.4.4.1 All antifreeze systems installed after September 30, 2012, are assumed to meet the minimum requirements of NFPA 13, 2013 edition. For systems installed after September 30, 2012, that do not meet the requirements of the 2013 edition of NFPA 13, consideration should be given to applying 5.3.4.4.1.

A.5.3.4.4.1(1) The use of factory premixed solutions is required because solutions that are not mixed properly have a possibility of separating from the water, allowing the pure concentrate (which is heavier than water) to drop out of solution and collect in drops or low points of the system. Such concentrations are combustible and could present problems during fires. The properties of glycerine are shown in Table A.5.3.4.4.1(1).

A.5.3.4.4.1(2) Antifreeze solutions with a maximum concentration of 38 percent glycerine or 30 percent propylene glycol

Shaded text = Revisions. **△** = Text deletions and figure/table revisions. • = Section deletions. **N** = New material.

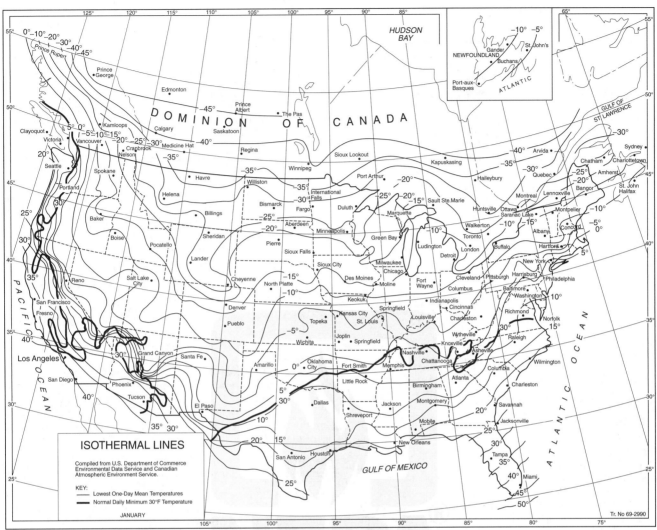

FIGURE A.5.3.4   Isothermal Lines — Lowest One-Day Mean Temperature (°F). [24:Figure A.10.5.1]

do not require a deterministic hazard analysis. The risk assessment should be prepared by individual(s) who can demonstrate an ability to prepare a risk assessment by education and experience and who can demonstrate an understanding of the issues associated with antifreeze sprinkler systems, including the available related fire tests. For additional information regarding the risk assessment process, documentation to be submitted, and the AHJ's role, refer to NFPA 551 and the SFPE *Engineering Guide: Fire Risk Assessment.*

Propylene glycol and glycerine antifreeze solutions discharged from sprinklers have the potential to ignite under certain conditions. Research testing has indicated that several variables might influence the potential for large-scale ignition of the antifreeze solution discharged from a sprinkler. These variables include, but are not limited to, the concentration of antifreeze solution, sprinkler discharge characteristics, inlet pressure at the sprinkler, ceiling height, and size of fire at the time of sprinkler discharge. All relevant data and information should be carefully reviewed and considered in the determinis-

tic risk assessment. As appropriate, the risk assessment should consider factors such as the following:

(1) Occupancy use group per NFPA 13
(2) Ceiling height
(3) Antifreeze solution concentration and type
(4) Maximum system pressure (normal static pressures)
(5) Sprinkler type, including K-factor
(6) Potential and actual fuel load (Christmas trees)
(7) Type of structure (construction types)
(8) Size of structure
(9) Ability of the sprinkler system to control the fire
(10) Occupied spaces versus unoccupied spaces such as trash enclosures and dust collectors as follows:

    (a) Adjacent occupancies (spaces adjacent to the area protected by antifreeze systems)

    (b) Separation between areas protected with an antifreeze system and other areas

    (c) Ventilation of areas protected with an antifreeze system to prevent damage to adjacent areas

    (d) Duration of antifreeze discharge

Shaded text = Revisions.   Δ = Text deletions and figure/table revisions.   • = Section deletions.   *N* = New material.

2020 Edition

Table A.5.3.4.4.1(1) Properties of Glycerine and Propylene Glycol

Material	Solution (% by Volume)	Specific Gravity at 77°F (25°C)	Freezing Point	
			°F	°C
Glycerine (C.P. or U.S.P. grade)	0	1.000	32	0
	5	1.014	31	–0.5
	10	1.029	28	–2.2
	15	1.043	25	–3.9
	20	1.059	20	–6.7
	25	1.071	16	–8.9
	30	1.087	10	–12
	35	1.100	4	–15.5
	40	1.114	–2	–19
	45	1.130	–11	–24
	50	1.141	–19	–28
Propylene glycol	0	1.000	32	0
	5	1.004	26	–3
	10	1.008	25	–4
	15	1.012	22	–6
	20	1.016	19	–7
	25	1.020	15	–10
	30	1.024	11	–12
	35	1.028	2	–17
	40	1.032	–6	–21

Tests summarized in Table A.5.3.4.4.1(2) show that large-scale ignition of the sprinkler spray did not occur in tests with 50 percent glycerine and 40 percent propylene glycol antifreeze solutions discharging onto a fire having a nominal heat release rate (HRR) of 1.4 MW. A deterministic risk assessment that demonstrates that the heat release rate for reasonably credible fire scenarios will be less than 1.4 MW at the time of sprinkler activation should be acceptable. The risk assessment should also address issues associated with management of change, such as change in occupancy and temporary fuel loads. A natural Christmas tree can result in an HRR well above 1.4 MW at the time of sprinkler activation. In addition to the variables identified previously, the deterministic risk assessment should include occupancy, quantity of solution, impact on life safety, and potential increase in heat release rate.

The following is a list of research reports that have been issued by the Fire Protection Research Foundation (FPRF) related to the use of antifreeze in sprinkler systems that should be considered in the development of the deterministic risk assessment:

(1) *Antifreeze Systems in Home Fire Sprinkler Systems — Literature Review and Research Plan,* Fire Protection Research Foundation, June 2010.
(2) *Antifreeze Systems in Home Fire Sprinkler Systems — Phase II Final Report,* Fire Protection Research Foundation, December 2010.

(3) *Antifreeze Solutions Supplied through Spray Sprinklers — Interim Report,* Fire Protection Research Foundation, February 2012.

Table A.5.3.4.4.1(2) provides an overview of the testing conducted by the FPRF.

A.5.4.1.2 To help in the replacement of like sprinklers, unique sprinkler identification numbers (SINs) are provided on all sprinklers manufactured after January 1, 2001. The SIN accounts for differences in orifice size, deflector characteristics, pressure rating, and thermal sensitivity.

A.5.4.1.2.1 Old-style sprinklers are permitted to replace existing old-style sprinklers. Old-style sprinklers should not be used to replace standard sprinklers without a complete engineering review of the system. The old-style sprinkler is the type manufactured before 1953. It discharges approximately 40 percent of the water upward to the ceiling, and it can be installed in either the upright or pendent position.

A.5.4.1.2.2 It is recognized that the flow and pressure available to the replacement sprinkler might be less than its current flow and pressure requirement.

A.5.4.1.4 It is imperative that any replacement sprinkler have the same characteristics as the sprinkler being replaced. If the same temperature range, response characteristics, spacing requirements, flow rates, and K-factors cannot be obtained, a sprinkler with similar characteristics should be used, and the system should be evaluated to verify the sprinkler is appropriate for the intended use. With regard to response characteristics, matching identical response time index (RTI) and conductivity factors are not necessary unless special design considerations are given for those specific values.

A.5.4.1.5 A minimum of two sprinklers of each type and temperature rating installed should be provided.

A.5.4.1.5.5 One sprinkler wrench design can be appropriate for many types of sprinklers, and multiple wrenches of the same design should not be required.

A.5.4.1.5.6.1 The minimum information in the list contained in the spare sprinkler cabinet should be marked with the following:

(1) General description of the sprinkler, including upright, pendent, residential, ESFR, and so forth
(2) Quantity of sprinklers to be maintained in the spare sprinkler cabinet

An example of the list is shown in Figure A.5.4.1.5.6.1.

A.5.4.1.6 Corrosion-resistant or specially coated sprinklers should be installed in locations where chemicals, moisture, or other corrosive vapors exist.

A.5.4.1.9.1 Typical sandwich bags purchased in a grocery store are generally plastic, not cellophane. Plastic bags have a tendency to shrink and adhere to the sprinkler prior to sprinkler activation, creating the potential for disruption of sprinkler spray patterns. Bags placed over sprinklers need to be true cellophane or paper.

A.5.4.2 Conversion of dry pipe systems to wet pipe systems on a seasonal basis causes corrosion and accumulation of foreign matter in the pipe system and loss of alarm service.

Shaded text = Revisions.   **Δ** = Text deletions and figure/table revisions.   • = Section deletions.   **N** = New material.

Table A.5.3.4.4.1(2) FPRF Testing Summary

Topic	Information
Scope of sprinklers tested	The following sprinklers were used during the residential sprinkler research program described in the report dated December 2010: (1) Residential pendent style having nominal K-factors of 3.1, 4.9, and 7.4 gpm/psi$^{1/2}$ (2) Residential concealed pendent style having a nominal K-factor of 4.9 gpm/psi$^{1/2}$ (3) Residential sidewall style having nominal K-factors of 4.2 and 5.5 gpm/psi$^{1/2}$ The following sprinklers were used during the spray sprinkler research program described in the report dated February 2012: (1) Residential pendent style having a nominal K-factor of 3.1 gpm/psi$^{1/2}$ (2) Standard spray pendent style having nominal K-factors of 2.8, 4.2, 5.6, and 8.0 gpm/psi$^{1/2}$ (3) Standard spray concealed pendent style having a nominal K-factor of 5.6 gpm/psi$^{1/2}$ (4) Standard spray upright style having a nominal K-factor of 5.6 gpm/psi$^{1/2}$ (5) Standard spray extended coverage pendent style having a nominal K-factor of 5.6 gpm/psi$^{1/2}$
Antifreeze solution concentration	<50% glycerine and <40% propylene glycol antifreeze solutions — solutions were not tested. 50% glycerine and 40% propylene glycol antifreeze solutions — large-scale ignition of the sprinkler spray did not occur in tests with sprinkler discharge onto a fire having a nominal heat release rate (HRR) of 1.4 MW. Large-scale ignition of the sprinkler spray occurred in multiple tests with sprinkler discharge onto a fire having a nominal HRR of 3.0 MW. 55% glycerine and 45% propylene glycol antifreeze solutions — large-scale ignition of the sprinkler spray occurred in tests with sprinkler discharge onto a fire having a nominal HRR of 1.4 MW. >55% glycerine and >45% propylene glycol antifreeze solutions — large-scale ignition of the sprinkler spray occurred in tests with sprinkler discharge onto a fire having an HRR of less than 500 kW. 70% glycerine and 60% propylene glycol antifreeze solutions — maximum antifreeze solution concentrations tested.
Sprinkler inlet pressure	Large-scale ignition of the sprinkler discharge spray was not observed when the sprinkler inlet pressure was 50 psi or less for tests using 50% glycerine or 40% propylene glycol.
Ceiling height	When discharging 50% glycerine and 40% propylene glycol antifreeze solutions onto fires having an HRR of 1.4 MW, no large-scale ignition of the sprinkler spray was observed with ceiling heights up to 20 ft. When discharging 50% glycerine and 40% propylene glycol antifreeze solutions onto fires having an HRR of 3.0 MW, large-scale ignition of the sprinkler spray was observed at a ceiling height of 20 ft.
Fire control	The test results described in the test reports of December 2010 and February 2012 indicated that discharging glycerine and propylene glycol antifreeze solutions onto a fire can temporarily increase the fire size until water is discharged. As a part of the residential sprinkler research described in report dated December 2010, tests were conducted to evaluate the effectiveness of residential sprinklers to control fires involving furniture and simulated furniture. The results of these tests indicated that 50% glycerine and 40% propylene glycol antifreeze solutions demonstrated the ability to control the furniture-type fires in a manner similar to water. For standard spray–type sprinklers, no tests were conducted to investigate the ability of these sprinklers to control the types and sizes of fires that these sprinklers are intended to protect.

A.5.4.3 Certain sprinkler systems, such as those installed aboard ships, are maintained under pressure by a small freshwater supply but are supplied by a raw water source following system activation. In these systems, the effects of raw water are minimized by draining and refilling with freshwater. For systems on ships, flushing within 45 days or the vessel's next port of call, whichever is longer, is considered acceptable.

A.6.2.2 The design information sign should be secured with durable wire, chain, or equivalent to the water supply control valve for automatic or semiautomatic standpipe systems and at an approved location for manual systems. See Figure A.6.2.2 for sample hydraulic information sign.

A.6.3.1.1 The hydraulically most remote hose connections in a building are generally at a roof manifold, if provided, or at the top of a stair leading to the roof. In a multizone system, the testing means is generally at a test header at grade or at a suction tank on higher floors.

A.6.3.1.2 When the standpipe system was accepted, NFPA 14 required that each additional standpipe be flowed to simulate the hydraulic calculations. Typically, the lowest hose valve was used to create this simultaneous flow so hoses wouldn't have to be run all the way down each standpipe.

Sprinklers Contained in this Cabinet			
Sprinkler Identification, SIN	General Description	Temperature Rating, °F	Sprinkler Quantity Maintained
TY9128	Extended Coverage, K-25, upright	165	6
VK494	Residential concealed pendent	155	6
Issued: 8/31/19	Revised:		

Δ **FIGURE A.5.4.1.5.6.1   Sample List. [13:Figure A.16.2.7.7.1]**

Location of the two hydraulically most remote hose connections: _____

Design flow rate for the connections identified above: _____

Design residual inlet and outlet pressures for the connections identified above: _____

Design static pressure and design system demand (i.e., flow and residual pressure) at the system control valve, or at the pump discharge flange where a pump is installed, and at each fire department connection: _____

FIGURE A.6.2.2   Sample Hydraulic Sign. [14:Figure A.6.8]

A.6.3.1.2.1 Since the pressures at each standpipe aren't required to be balanced by NFPA 14 or this standard, any hose valve on the standpipe can be flowed to achieve the additional 250 gpm (950 L/min) needed. It might be more convenient to use a hose valve on an upper level rather than the lowest one on the standpipe.

A.6.3.1.2.2 In some instances it isn't reasonable to attach a hose to a standpipe to provide this additional flow point. The authority having jurisdiction can allow the additional flow be made at other outlets on the standpipe system, such as from another standpipe, or from the fire pump test header. Although the results of having the flow points somewhere else in the standpipe system won't match the hydraulic calculations, the test will still prove that the most remote standpipe can provide the necessary flow and pressure required for fire department use while simultaneously flowing the full system demand.

A.6.3.2.1 The intent of 6.3.2.1 is to ascertain whether the system retains its integrity under fire conditions. Minimum leakage existing only under test pressure is not cause for repair.

A.7.2.2 The requirements in 7.2.2 outline inspection intervals, conditions to be inspected, and corrective actions necessary for private fire service mains and associated equipment.

A.7.2.2.2 Generally, underground piping cannot be inspected on a routine basis. However, flow testing can reveal the condition of underground piping and should be conducted in accordance with Section 7.3.

A.7.2.2.3 Any flow in excess of the flow through the main drain connection should be considered significant.

N **A.7.2.2.6** There could be a need for more frequent inspections due to freezing and droughts. Particular attention should be given to streams and ponds where frequent removal of debris, dredging or excavation of silt, and protection from erosion might be required.

The pond should be maintained as free of aquatic growth as possible. At times it might be necessary to drain the pond to control this growth. Helpful information is available from such sources as the county agricultural extension agent or the U.S. Department of Agriculture. [**1142**, 2017]

N **A.7.2.2.6.5** Dry hydrants can be checked and tested by actual drafting as part of the fire department training program. If the tests do not produce the design flow, the fire department should determine what the problem is. It could be necessary to back flush the system to clear leaves and other debris. When a dry hydrant is back flushed, pump pressures should not exceed 20 psi. [**1142**, 2017]

Δ **A.7.3.1** Full flow tests of underground piping can be accomplished by methods including, but not limited to, flow through yard hydrants, fire department connections once the check valve has been removed, main drain connections, and hose connections. The flow test should be conducted in accordance with NFPA 291.

•

A.7.4.2.2 The intent of 7.4.2.2 is to maintain adequate space for use of hydrants during a fire emergency. The amount of space needed depends on the configuration as well as the type and size of accessory equipment, such as hose, wrenches, and other devices that could be used.

A.7.5.3 Private fire service mains might not include a main drain connection; therefore, other equivalent means of flow such as an installed fire hydrant can be used.

A.8.1 A fire pump assembly provides waterflow and pressure for private fire protection. The assembly includes the water supply suction and discharge piping and valving; pump; electric, diesel, or steam turbine driver and control; and the auxiliary equipment appurtenant thereto.

A.8.1.1.2 Alternative Inspection, Testing, and Maintenance Procedures. In the absence of manufacturer's recommendations for preventive maintenance, Table A.8.1.1.2 can be used for alternative requirements.

A.8.1.1.2.1 Shaft movement should be less than ⅛ in. (3 mm).

N **A.8.1.1.2.2.1** Where available, a disconnect switch upstream of the fire pump controller can be opened and the isolated electrical connections inside the electric-motor-driven controller inspected. In some cases the fire pump controller cannot be isolated without shutting off power to the building, and shutting off power to the building could be impractical.

N **A.8.1.1.2.2.2** Some manufacturers are including an isolation switch upstream of all controller components in an isolated sub-cabinet as part of the controller. This permits de-energizing the circuit boards and other controller components and allows the controller to be opened for ITM activities.

Shaded text = Revisions.   Δ = Text deletions and figure/table revisions.   • = Section deletions.   *N* = New material.

Δ **Table A.8.1.1.2 Alternative Fire Pump Inspection, Testing, and Maintenance Procedures**

Complete as Applicable	Visual Inspection	Inspect	Change	Clean	Test	Frequency
Pump System						
Pump bearings		X				Annually
Lubricate pump bearings			X			As needed
Inspect pump shaft end play		X				Annually
Inspect accuracy of pressure gauges and sensors		X	X			Annually (replace or recalibrate when 5% out of calibration)
Inspect pump coupling alignment		X				Annually
Wet pit suction screens		X		X		After each pump operation
Mechanical Transmission						
Lubricate coupling/flexible connecting shaft (driveshaft)		X				Annually
Lubricate right-angle gear drive		X				Annually
Electrical System						
Exercise isolating switch and circuit breaker					X	Monthly
Trip circuit breaker (if mechanism provided)					X	Annually
Operate manual starting means (electrical)					X	Semiannually
Inspect and operate emergency manual starting means (without power)	X				X	Annually
Lubricate mechanical moving parts (excluding starters and relays)		X				Annually
Calibrate pressure switch settings*		X				Annually
Grease motor bearings		X				Annually
			X			Annually or as needed
Any corrosion on printed circuit boards (PCBs)*	X					Annually
Any cracked cable/wire insulation*	X					Annually
Any leaks in plumbing parts*	X					Annually
Any signs of water on electrical parts*	X					Annually
Diesel Engine System						
Fuel						
Tank level	X	X				Weekly
Tank float switch	X				X	Weekly
Solenoid valve operation	X				X	Weekly
Strainer, filter, or dirt leg, or combination thereof				X		Quarterly
Water and foreign material in tank				X		Annually
Water in system		X		X		Weekly
Flexible hoses and connectors	X					Weekly
Tank vents and overflow piping unobstructed		X			X	Annually
Piping	X					Annually
Lubrication system						
Oil level	X	X				Weekly
Oil change			X			50 hours or annually
Oil filter(s)			X			50 hours or annually
Lube oil heater		X				Weekly
Crankcase breather	X		X	X		Quarterly
Cooling system						
Level	X	X				Weekly
Antifreeze protection level					X	Semiannually
Antifreeze		X				Annually
Adequate cooling water to heat exchanger		X				Weekly
Rod out heat exchanger				X		Annually
Water pump(s)	X					Weekly
Condition of flexible hoses and connections	X	X				Weekly

(continues)

Shaded text = Revisions.   Δ = Text deletions and figure/table revisions.   • = Section deletions.   *N* = New material.

2020 Edition

Δ **Table A.8.1.1.2**   *Continued*

Complete as Applicable	Visual Inspection	Inspect	Change	Clean	Test	Frequency
Jacket water heater		X				Weekly
Inspect duct work, clean louvers (combustion air)	X	X	X			Annually
Water strainer				X		Quarterly
Exhaust system						
Leakage	X	X				Weekly
Drain condensate trap		X				Weekly
Insulation and fire hazards	X					Quarterly
Excessive back pressure					X	Annually
Exhaust system hangers and supports	X					Annually
Flexible exhaust section	X					Semiannually
Battery system						
Electrolyte level		X				Weekly
Terminals clean and tight	X	X				Quarterly
Case exterior clean and dry	X	X				Monthly
Specific gravity or state of charge					X	Monthly
Charger and charge rate	X					Monthly
Equalize charge		X				Monthly
Clean terminals				X		Annually
Cranking voltage exceeds 9 volts on a 12 volt system or 18 volts on a 24 volt system		X				Weekly
Electrical system						
General inspection	X					Weekly
Tighten control and power wiring connections		X				Annually
Wire chafing where subject to movement	X	X				Quarterly
Operation of safeties and alarms		X			X	Semiannually
Boxes, panels, and cabinets				X		Semiannually
Circuit breakers or fuses	X	X				Monthly
Circuit breakers or fuses			X			Biennially
Voltmeter and ammeter for accuracy (5%)		X				Annually
Any corrosion on printed circuit boards (PCBs)	X					Annually
Any cracked cable/wire insulation	X					Annually
Any leaks in plumbing parts	X					Annually
Any signs of water on electrical parts	X					Annually

*Required only where the extent of such work can be completed without the opening of energized electric motor-driven fire pump controller.

A.8.1.4 Types of centrifugal fire pumps include single and multistage units of horizontal or vertical shaft design. Listed fire pumps have rated capacities of 25 gpm to 5000 gpm (95 L/min to 18,925 L/min), with a net pressure range from approximately 40 psi to 400 psi (2.75 bar to 27.6 bar).

(1) *Horizontal Split Case.* This pump has a double suction impeller with an inboard and outboard bearing and is used with a positive suction supply. A variation of this design can be mounted with the shaft in a vertical plane. *[See Figure A.8.1.4(a).]*

(2) *End Suction and Vertical In-Line.* This pump can have either a horizontal or vertical shaft with a single suction impeller and a single bearing at the drive end. *[See Figure A.8.1.4(b).]*

(3) *Vertical Shaft, Turbine Type.* This pump has multiple impellers and is suspended from the pump head by a column pipe that also serves as a support for the shaft and bearings. This pump is necessary where a suction lift is needed, such as from an underground reservoir, well, river, or lake. *[See Figure A.8.1.4(c).]*

A.8.1.8 Controllers include air-, hydraulic-, or electric-operated units. These units can take power from the energy source for their operation, or the power can be obtained elsewhere. Controllers used with electric power sources can apply the source to the driver in one (across-the-line) or two (reduced voltage or current) steps. Controllers can be used with automatic and manual transfer switches to select the available electric power source where more than one is provided.

A.8.2.2 See Table A.8.2.2 and Figure A.8.2.2.

A.8.2.2(5) Visual indicators other than pilot lights can be used for the same purpose.

A.8.3 The purpose of testing the pump assembly is to ensure automatic or manual operation upon demand and continuous delivery of the required system output. An additional purpose is to detect deficiencies of the pump assembly not evident by inspection.

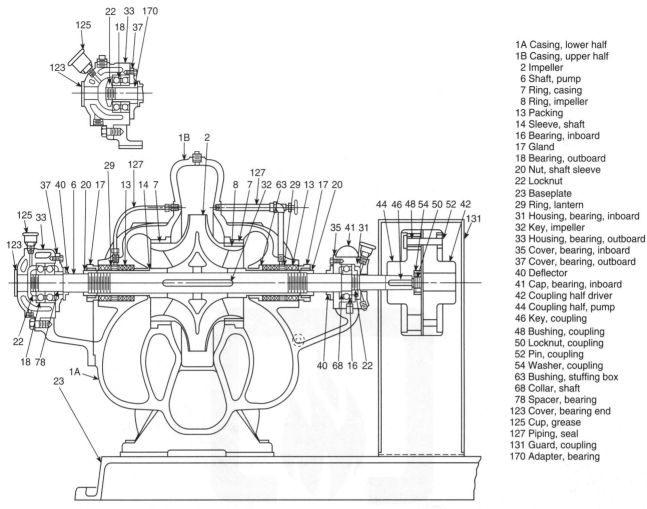

1A Casing, lower half
1B Casing, upper half
2 Impeller
6 Shaft, pump
7 Ring, casing
8 Ring, impeller
13 Packing
14 Sleeve, shaft
16 Bearing, inboard
17 Gland
18 Bearing, outboard
20 Nut, shaft sleeve
22 Locknut
23 Baseplate
29 Ring, lantern
31 Housing, bearing, inboard
32 Key, impeller
33 Housing, bearing, outboard
35 Cover, bearing, inboard
37 Cover, bearing, outboard
40 Deflector
41 Cap, bearing, inboard
42 Coupling half driver
44 Coupling half, pump
46 Key, coupling
48 Bushing, coupling
50 Locknut, coupling
52 Pin, coupling
54 Washer, coupling
63 Bushing, stuffing box
68 Collar, shaft
78 Spacer, bearing
123 Cover, bearing end
125 Cup, grease
127 Piping, seal
131 Guard, coupling
170 Adapter, bearing

The numbers used in this figure do not necessarily represent standard part numbers used by any manufacturer.

FIGURE A.8.1.4(a)   Impeller Between Bearings, Separately Coupled, Single-Stage Axial (Horizontal) Split Case. *(Courtesy of Hydraulic Institute, Parsippany, NJ, www.Pumps.org.)*

A.8.3.1.1 Fire pump systems conforming to the 1999 and more recent editions of NFPA 20 should be designed so that the pressure relief valve has a minimum flow (to verify pressure relief valve is properly set and operating) at churn and only allows a larger flow under abnormal conditions (i.e., engine overspeed or failure of a variable speed pressure limiting control). In situations where the discharge from the relief valve is piped back to the pump suction, the fire pump imparts more energy into the water when recirculating the water through the pump than when the pump is operating at churn (no flow). Since the 1999 edition of NFPA 20 a circulation relief valve has been required downstream of the pressure relief valve whenever the pressure relief valve is piped back to the pump suction. Improperly installed and/or operating circulation relief valves can result in unacceptably high water temperature, especially when recirculating the water to the pump suction. High water temperatures can affect the operation of a diesel engine drive. Modern engines, due to EPA requirements, are more sensitive to cooling water temperatures. For fire pump systems conforming to editions of NFPA 20 prior to 1999 that were installed with a pressure relief valve piped back to suction without a circulation relief valve installed downstream of the pressure relief valve, installation of a circulation relief valve is needed. The test can be conducted without a circulation relief valve by taking suction and discharge pressure gauge readings quickly while there is no flow into the fire protection system, then creating a small flow by opening an inspector's test connection, alarm bypass or main drain downstream of the pump to prevent the pump from overheating during the rest of the test. However, if the first pump starts while it is unattended without water flowing into the fire protection system, it is likely to be damaged.

A.8.3.1.1.2 The risk analysis should be prepared and reviewed by qualified people. Increased test frequencies might be desirable when high impact losses could result from an uncontrolled fire. Examples where increased fire pump test frequencies can be considered could include high piled storage facilities and buildings where the predominant occupancy is protected by an extra hazard density sprinkler system.

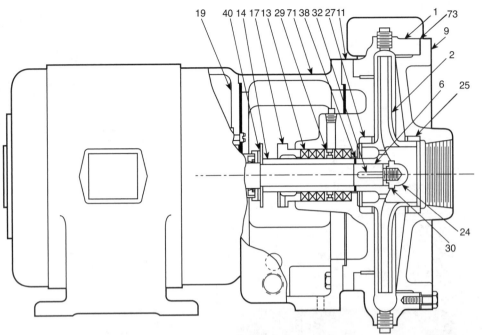

1 Casing
2 Impeller
6 Shaft
9 Cover, suction
11 Cover, stuffing box
13 Packing
14 Sleeve, shaft
17 Gland
19 Frame
24 Nut, impeller
25 Ring, suction cover
27 Ring, stuffing box cover
29 Ring, lantern
30 Gasket, impeller nut
32 Key, impeller
38 Gasket, shaft sleeve
40 Deflector
71 Adapter
73 Gasket

The numbers used in this figure do not necessarily represent standard part numbers used by any manufacturer.

FIGURE A.8.1.4(b)   **Overhung Impeller, Close-Coupled, Single-Stage, End Suction.** *(Courtesy of the Hydraulic Institute, Parsippany, NJ, www.Pumps.org.)*

Test frequency has been a heavily discussed and researched topic for several years, and is still continuing to be researched. A set of data was submitted in 2008 by a group of owners and maintainers of large numbers of fire pumps. This data was presented to the committee as indicating a decreased test frequency on electric fire pumps did not "significantly" impact "reliability"; however, "reliability" as used in the discussion of the data presentation was actually the failure rate, and did not take into account the effect of test frequency on the fire pump reliability (i.e., the time between failure and discovery of the failure affects reliability). Subsequently, the NFPA Research Council commissioned research, and the resultant "Fire Pump Field Data Collection and Analysis Report" in 2011 (available for download at www.nfpa.org/Foundation) reported that electric fire pumps tested weekly had a failure rate of approximately 0.64 per year. Assuming a failure rate independent of the test frequency, and assuming that on the average the impairment occurs at the midpoint of the test interval, this failure rate provides approximately 99.4 percent reliability with weekly testing and approximately 97.3 percent reliability with monthly testing. Diesel engine fire pumps tested weekly had a failure rate of approximately 1.02 per year. Assuming a failure rate independent of the test frequency and assuming that on the average the impairment occurs at the midpoint of the test interval, this failure rate provides approximately 99.1 percent reliability with weekly testing and approximately 96.0 percent reliability with monthly testing.

Based on this data, the lower reliability has not been determined to be acceptable for all facilities. Decisions to decrease test frequency must be based on more than cost savings. A reliability/risk analysis to decrease test frequency should take into account the risk associated with life safety, property values, hazards, and business interruption at the protected property.

Fire pump redundancy can impact overall fire system reliability and be used in a reliability/risk analysis.

A.8.3.1.2 For pressure relief valve operation, see 8.3.1.1.

A.8.3.1.2.3 For systems where multiple fire pumps are required to meet the system demand, a one-for-one redundancy is not necessary (i.e., one backup pump for two or more primary pumps meets the intent of this section).

A.8.3.1.2.4 The risk analysis should be prepared and reviewed by qualified people. Increased test frequencies can be desirable when high impact losses could result from an uncontrolled fire. Examples where increased fire pump test frequencies can be considered could include high piled storage facilities and buildings where the predominant occupancy is protected by an extra hazard density sprinkler system.

A.8.3.2.1.2.1 An excessive pressure differential might indicate that the pressure relief valve is wide open and not properly regulating the pressure. Excessively high flow rates through the pressure relief valve can cause failure of the fire protection system and can overload a diesel engine drive and result in destruction of the engine.

A.8.3.2.1.2.2 High water temperatures can cause diesel engines to overheat and fail.

A.8.3.2.7.1 An automatic timer allows a person who has been instructed on what to watch for and record during this test to monitor the test and request assistance should any issues arise.

A.8.3.2.9 See Table A.8.3.2.9.

A.8.3.3.1 Minimum flow for a pump is the churn pressure.

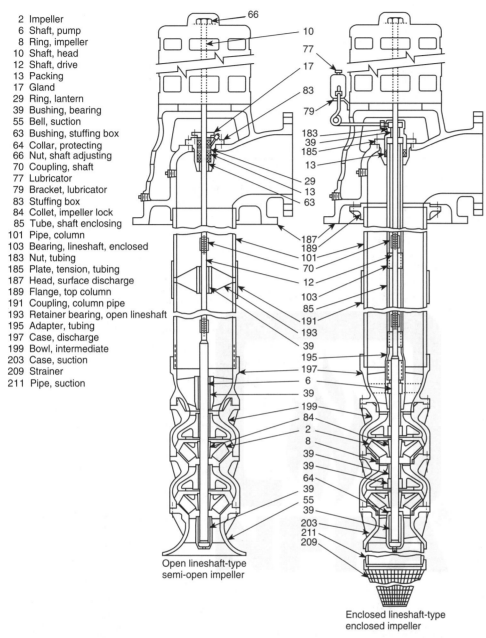

2 Impeller
6 Shaft, pump
8 Ring, impeller
10 Shaft, head
12 Shaft, drive
13 Packing
17 Gland
29 Ring, lantern
39 Bushing, bearing
55 Bell, suction
63 Bushing, stuffing box
64 Collar, protecting
66 Nut, shaft adjusting
70 Coupling, shaft
77 Lubricator
79 Bracket, lubricator
83 Stuffing box
84 Collet, impeller lock
85 Tube, shaft enclosing
101 Pipe, column
103 Bearing, lineshaft, enclosed
183 Nut, tubing
185 Plate, tension, tubing
187 Head, surface discharge
189 Flange, top column
191 Coupling, column pipe
193 Retainer bearing, open lineshaft
195 Adapter, tubing
197 Case, discharge
199 Bowl, intermediate
203 Case, suction
209 Strainer
211 Pipe, suction

Open lineshaft-type
semi-open impeller

Enclosed lineshaft-type
enclosed impeller

The cross-sectional views illustrate the largest possible number of parts in their proper relationship and some
construction modifications but do not necessarily represent recommended design.

FIGURE A.8.1.4(c)   Turbine-Type, Vertical, Multistage, Deep Well. *(Courtesy of the Hydraulic Institute, Parsippany, NJ, www.Pumps.org.)*

Table A.8.2.2 Observations — Before Pumping

Item	Before Pump Is Operated
Horizontal pumps	1. Inspect drip pockets under packing glands for proper drainage. Standing water in drip pockets is the most common cause of bearing failure.
	2. Inspect packing adjustment — approximately one drop per second is necessary to keep packing lubricated.
	3. Observe suction and discharge gauges. Readings higher than suction pressure indicate leakage back from system pressure through either the fire pump or jockey pump.

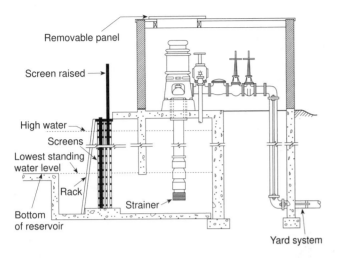

FIGURE A.8.2.2 Wet Pit Suction Screen Installation.

N A.8.3.3.2 Unless otherwise specified by the pump manufacturer and the controller manufacturer, two separate tests are required for variable-speed pumps: one test under variable-speed control and one test under constant-speed control. Operation and setting of relief valves that are required for variable-speed pumps should be done in accordance with the requirements of Chapter 13.

N A.8.3.3.5.3 When using a flow meter piped back to suction, the requirement for annual calibration applies to the sensing devices on the flow meter. When the test discharges water downstream of the flow meter, the flow discharge should be measured and used to calibrate the flow meter.

A.8.3.3.9(2) The method described in 8.3.3.9.3 is not considered as complete as those in 8.3.3.9.1 and 8.3.3.9.2, because it does not test the adequacy of the water supply for compliance with the requirements of 8.1.6 at the suction flange.

Δ A.8.3.3.9.1.2 Whether using a play pipe, water diffuser, or other discharge device, damage can be caused by the water stream, or can be caused by inadequate drainage in the area of the discharge

A.8.3.3.10(3) It is not the intent to discharge water for the full 1-hour test duration, provided all flow tests can be conducted in less time and efforts are taken to prevent the pump from overheating.

A.8.3.3.11 A pressure relief valve that opens during a flow condition is discharging water that is not measured by the recording device(s). It can be necessary to temporarily close the pressure relief valve to achieve favorable pump test results. At the conclusion of the pump test, the pressure relief valve must be readjusted to relieve pressures in excess of the normal operating pressure of the system components.

If the pressure relief valve is open during the flowing conditions due to the fact that the pressure is too high for the components in the fire protection system, the discharge control valve should be closed prior to closing the pressure relief valve to make sure that the fire protection system is not overpressurized. After the test, the valve must be opened again.

A.8.3.3.11.1 A pressure relief valve that is open during a flow condition will affect test results.

A.8.3.3.13 It is not the intent to verify that all the alarm conditions required by NFPA 20 (e.g., low oil pressure, high coolant temperature, failure of engine to start, engine overspeed) transmit individually to a remote location, as long as these alarms, where provided, can be individually verified at the fire pump controller.

Table A.8.3.2.9 Observations — While Pumping

Item		While Pump Is Operating
Horizontal pumps	1.	Read suction and discharge gauges — difference between these readings indicates churn pressure, which should match churn pressure as shown on fire pump nameplate.
	2.	Observe packing glands for proper leakage for cooling of packing.
	3.	Observe discharge from casing relief valve — adequate flow keeps pump case from overheating.
Vertical pumps	1.	Read discharge gauge — add distance to water level in feet (or meters) and divide by 2.31 to compute psi (30.47 to compute bar). This total must match churn pressure as shown on fire pump nameplate.
	2.	Observe packing glands for proper leakage for cooling of packing.
	3.	Observe discharge from casing relief valve — adequate flow keeps pump case from overheating.
Diesel engines	1.	Observe discharge of cooling water from heat exchanger — if not adequate, inspect strainer in cooling system for obstructions. If still not adequate, adjust pressure-reducing valve for correct flow.
	2.	Inspect engine instrument panel for correct speed, oil pressure, water temperature, and ammeter charging rate.
	3.	Inspect battery terminal connections for corrosion and clean if necessary.
	4.	After pump has stopped running, inspect intake screens, if provided; replace diesel system pressure recorder chart; and rewind if necessary.

Shaded text = Revisions.   Δ = Text deletions and figure/table revisions.   • = Section deletions.   *N* = New material.

A.8.3.3.13.1 Testing at an alternative location can include completion of a test at an external fire alarm monitor module used to monitor the sensors within the fire pump controller.

A.8.3.3.15 During periods of unusual water supply conditions such as floods, inspection should be on a daily basis.

A.8.3.3.16 *ECM and Sensor Testing.* To verify the operation of the alternate ECM with the stop, the ECM selector switch should be moved to the alternate ECM position. Repositioning of this should cause an alarm on the fire pump controller. Then the engine is started; it should operate normally with all functions. Next, the engine is shut down, switched back to the primary ECM, and restarted briefly to verify that correct switchback has been accomplished.

To verify the operation of the redundant sensor, with the engine running, the wires are disconnected from the primary sensor. There should be no change in the engine operation. The wires are then reconnected to the sensor, then disconnected from the redundant sensor. There should be no change in the engine operation. The wires should next be reconnected to the sensor. This process is repeated for all primary and redundant sensors on the engines. It should be noted whether disconnecting and reconnecting of wires to the sensors can be done while the engine is not running, then starting the engine after each disconnecting and reconnecting of the wires to verify engine operation.

A.8.3.4.1.1 Commercial distillate fuel oils used in modern diesel engines are subject to various detrimental effects from storage. The origin of the crude oil, refinement processing techniques, ·time of year, and geographical consumption location all influence the determination of fuel blend formulas. Naturally occurring gums, waxes, soluble metallic soaps, water, dirt, blends, and temperature all contribute to the degradation of the fuel as it is handled and stored. These effects begin at the time of fuel refinement and continue until consumption. Proper maintenance of stored distillate fuel is critical for engine operation, efficiency, and longevity.

Storage tanks should be kept water-free. Water contributes to steel tank corrosion and the development of microbiological growth where fuel and water interface. This and the metals of the system provide elements that react with fuel to form certain gels or organic acids, resulting in clogging of filters and system corrosion. Scheduled fuel maintenance helps to reduce fuel degradation. Fuel maintenance filtration can remove contaminants and water and maintain fuel conditions to provide reliability and efficiency for standby fire pump engines. Fuel maintenance and testing should begin the day of installation and first fill.

A.8.3.4.2 Where environmental or fuel quality conditions result in degradation of the fuel while stored in the supply tank, from items such as water, micro-organisms and particulates, or destabilization, active fuel maintenance systems permanently installed on the fuel storage tanks have proven to be successful at maintaining fuel quality. An active fuel maintenance system will maintain the fuel quality in the tank, therefore preventing the fuel from going through possible cycles of degradation, risking engine reliability, and then requiring reconditioning.

A.8.3.6.1 Routine tests required by NFPA 110 and conducted in accordance with NFPA 110 should be performed to utilize the generator for standby power for a fire pump. During the annual fire pump test, a generator test is required by 8.3.3.9 of this standard. Except for 8.3.3.9, the testing requirements for the standby generator reside in NFPA 110.

△ A.8.3.6.4 A pump and driver shipped from the factory with both machines mounted on a common baseplate, are accurately aligned before shipment. All baseplates are flexible to some extent and, therefore, should not be relied upon to maintain the factory alignment. Realignment is necessary after the complete unit has been leveled on the foundation and again after the grout has set and foundation bolts have been tightened. The alignment should be checked after the unit is piped and rechecked periodically. To facilitate accurate field alignment, most manufacturers either do not dowel the pumps or drivers on the baseplates before shipment or, at most, dowel the pump only.

After the pump and driver unit has been placed on the foundation, the coupling halves should be disconnected. The coupling should not be reconnected until the alignment operations have been completed.

The purpose of the flexible coupling is to compensate for temperature changes and to permit end movement of the shafts without interference with each other while transmitting power from the driver to the pump.

There are two forms of misalignment between the pump shaft and the driver shaft are as follows:

(1) *Angular misalignment.* Shafts with axes concentric but not parallel
(2) *Parallel misalignment.* Shafts with axes parallel but not concentric

The faces of the coupling halves should be spaced within the manufacturer's recommendations and far enough apart so that they cannot strike each other when the driver rotor is moved hard over toward the pump. Due allowance should be made for wear of the thrust bearings. The necessary tools for an approximate check of the alignment of a flexible coupling are a straight edge and a taper gauge or a set of feeler gauges.

A check for angular alignment is made by inserting the taper gauge or feelers at four points between the coupling faces and comparing the distance between the faces at four points spaced at 90 degree intervals around the coupling *[see Figure A.8.3.6.4(a)]*. The unit will be in angular alignment when the measurements show that the coupling faces are the same distance apart at all points.

A check for parallel alignment is made by placing a straight edge across both coupling rims at the top, bottom, and at both sides *[see Figure A.8.3.6.4(b)]*. The unit will be in parallel alignment when the straight edge rests evenly on the coupling rim at all positions. Allowance might be necessary for temperature changes and for coupling halves that are not of the same outside diameter. Care must be taken to have the straight edge parallel to the axes of the shafts.

Angular and parallel misalignment are corrected by means of shims under the motor mounting feet. After each change, it is necessary to recheck the alignment of the coupling halves. Adjustment in one direction can disturb adjustments already made in another direction. It should not be necessary to adjust the shims under the pump.

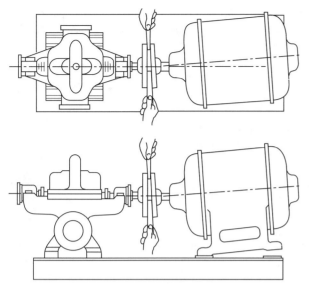

FIGURE A.8.3.6.4(a) **Checking Angular Alignment.** *(Courtesy of the Hydraulic Institute, Parsippany, NJ, www.Pumps.org.)*

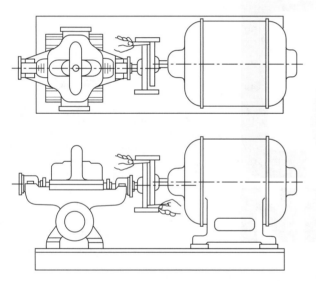

FIGURE A.8.3.6.4(b) **Checking Parallel Alignment.** *(Courtesy of the Hydraulic Institute, Parsippany, NJ, www.Pumps.org.)*

The permissible amount of misalignment will vary with the type of pump and driver; and coupling manufacturer, model, and size. [**20:** A.6.5]

A.8.3.7.1 Where the information is available, the test plot should be compared with the original acceptance test plot. It should be recognized that the acceptance test plot could exceed the minimum acceptable pump requirements as indicated by the rated characteristics for the pump. While a reduction in output is a matter of concern, this condition should be evaluated in light of meeting the rated characteristics for the pump. *[See Figure A.8.3.7.2.3(2)(a).]*

The test equipment should be of high quality and accuracy. All equipment should have been calibrated within the last 12 months by an approved calibration facility. Where possible, the calibration facility should provide documentation indicating the instrument reading against the calibrated reading. Instruments that pass the calibration test should be labeled by the calibration facility with the name of the facility and the date of the test.

Pressure gauges should have an accuracy not greater than 1 percent of full scale. To prevent damage to a pressure gauge utilizing a Bourdon tube mechanism, it should not be used where the expected test pressure is greater than 75 percent of the test gauge scale. Some digital gauges can be subjected to twice the full scale pressure without damage. The manufacturer's recommendations should be consulted for the proper use of the gauge. To be able to easily read an analog gauge, the diameter of the face of the analog gauge should be greater than 3 in. (76 mm). Pressure snubbers should be used for all gauges to minimize needle fluctuation. All gauges used in the test should be such that a gauge with the lowest full scale pressure is used. For example, a 300 psi (20.7 bar) gauge should not be used to measure a 20 psi (1.4 bar) pitot pressure.

Equipment other than pressure gauges, such as volt/ammeters, tachometers, and flowmeters, should be calibrated to the manufacturer's specifications. The readings from equipment with this level of accuracy and calibration can be used without adjustment for accuracy.

A.8.3.7.2.3(2) Figure A.8.3.7.2.3(2)(a) shows a pump test result plotted on linear graph paper adjusted to rated speed and compared to an original pump performance test and the manufacturer's test curve. Suction pressure and discharge pressure are also plotted, which when compared to previous results can aid in determining if a degraded pump discharge is the result of a decreased water supply. Also note that adjusted results of this test closely overlap, which is a good indication that the internal parts of the pump are functioning well (i.e., the pump is performing at or above 95 percent of the original design specifications per the manufacturer's performance curve).

Figure A.8.3.7.2.3(2)(b) shows an unadjusted pump test result plotted on linear graph paper and compared (plotted) with fire system demands. This is the actual tested performance and shows how the pump will perform in an emergency. This curve clearly shows whether the actual pump discharge can meet fire system demands. Suction pressure and discharge pressure are also plotted. The suction curve can be compared to previous results to aid in determining if a degraded pump discharge is the result of a decreased water supply.

N **A.8.3.7.2.3(3)** While pressures that exceed the original unadjusted field test curve or fire pump nameplate are considered acceptable, the test could be flawed and should be thoroughly reviewed by a qualified person.

A.8.3.7.2.4 See Annex C.

A.8.4.1 For a sample pump test form, see Figure A.8.4.1.

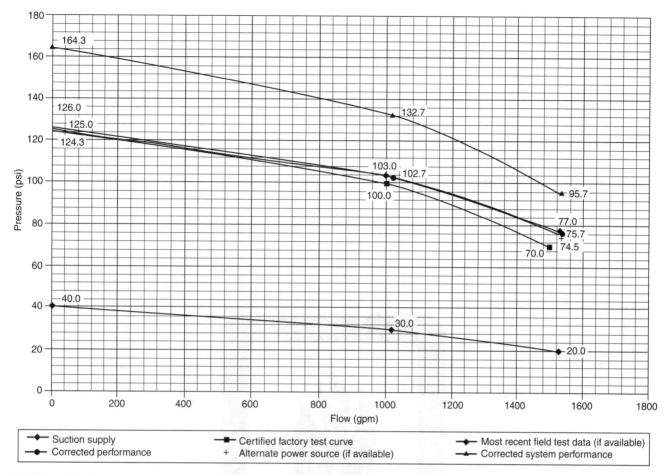

FIGURE A.8.3.7.2.3(2)(a)   Fire Pump Performance Curve — Corrected Data.

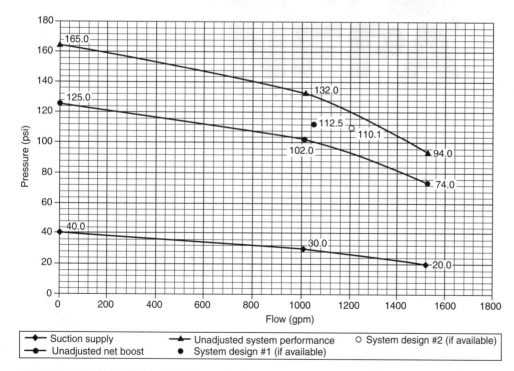

FIGURE A.8.3.7.2.3(2)(b)   Fire Pump Performance Curve — Unadjusted Data.

Sample Centrifugal Fire Pump Annual Test Form

Information on this form covers the minimum requirements of NFPA 25, 2020 edition, for performing an annual test on centrifugal fire pumps with electric motor or diesel engine drivers. A separate form is required for each pump operating simultaneously. This form does not cover other periodic inspections, testing, and maintenance required by NFPA 25.

Owner: _____

Owner's address: _____
_____

Pump location: _____

Property address: _____
_____

Date of test: _____

Maximum demand(s) of fire protection system(s) _____ gpm at _____ psi for _____ minutes at fire pump discharge

System demand information supplied by: _____

Pump type: Horizontal ❑ Vertical ❑ Inline ❑ Other (specify) _____

Manufacturer: _____ Model or type: _____ Shop/serial number _____

Pump rated for _____ gpm at _____ psi at _____ RPM, net discharge pressure _____ psi at 150% _____ psi at churn

Pump suction size _____ in. Discharge size _____ in. Suction from _____

If suction from tank, tank diameter _____ ft, height _____ ft, net capacity _____ gpm

Driver: _____ Electric motor _____ Diesel engine _____ Steam turbine

Manufacturer: _____ Shop/serial number: _____ Model or type: _____

Rated horsepower: _____ Rated speed: _____ If electric motor, rated voltage _____ Operating voltage _____

Rated amps _____ Phase cycles _____ Service factor _____

Controller manufacturer: _____

Shop/serial number: _____ Model or type: _____

Controller rated _____ HP _____ VAC

Does controller rated HP & VAC match motor? .... ❑ Yes ❑ No

Transfer switch? .... ❑ Yes ❑ No

Transfer switch rated _____ HP _____ VAC

Does controller rate HP & VAC match motor? .... ❑ Yes ❑ No ❑ N/A

Pressure maintenance (jockey) pump on system? .... ❑ Yes ❑ No ❑ Manual ❑ Automatic

Manufacturer: _____ Shop/serial number: _____

Model or type: _____ ❑ Centrifugal or ❑ Positive displacement?

Pressure relief valve provided on jockey pump discharge? .... ❑ Yes ❑ No ❑ N/A

Jockey pump rated for _____ gpm at _____ psi at _____ RPM _____ HP

Jockey pump suction size _____ in. Discharge size _____ in.

Jockey pump controller manufacturer: _____

Shop/serial number: _____ Model or type: _____

Jockey pump controller rated _____ HP _____ VAC

Does jockey pump controller rated HP & VAC match motor? .... ❑ Yes ❑ No

Note: All blanks are to be filled in. All questions are to be answered Yes, No, or Not Applicable. All "No" answers are to be explained in the comments portion of this form.

I. People Present

A. Owner or owner's representative? .... ❑ Yes ❑ No

B. Other attendees? .... ❑ Yes ❑ No

II. Electric Wiring

A. Was any defect noted in the electric wiring? .... ❑ Yes ❑ No ❑ N/A

III. Annual Flow Test

A. Is a copy of the manufacturer's certified pump test curve attached? .... ❑ Yes ❑ No

B. Test results compared to the following: 1. The manufacturer's certified pump test curve? .... ❑ Yes ❑ No

2. The nameplate? .... ❑ Yes ❑ No

C. Gauges and other test equipment calibrated? .... ❑ Yes ❑ No

D. No vibrations that could potentially damage any fire pump component? .... ❑ Yes ❑ No ❑ N/A

E. The fire pump performed at all conditions without objectionable overheating of any component? ... ❑ Yes ❑ No ❑ N/A

© 2019 National Fire Protection Association

(NFPA 25, p. 1 of 4)

△ **FIGURE A.8.4.1   Sample Annual Centrifugal Pump Test Form.**

Shaded text = Revisions.   △ = Text deletions and figure/table revisions.   • = Section deletions.   *N* = New material.

F. For each test, record the required information for each load condition using the following formulas (or other acceptable methods) and tables:

$$P_{Net} = P_{Discharge} - P_{Suction}$$
$$Q = 29.83 \, cd^2 P^{0.5}$$
$$Pv = 0.43352 V^2/(2g) = (Q^2)/(890.47 D^4)$$

where

P_{Net}	= Net pump pressure (psi)	P	= Pressure measured on gauge (pitot)
$P_{Discharge}$	= Total pressure at the pump discharge (psi)	Pv	= Velocity pressure (psi)
$P_{Suction}$	= Total pressure at the pump suction (psi)	V	= Velocity of liquid (ft/sec)
Q	= Flow through a circular orifice (gpm)	g	= Gravitational constant (32.174 ft/sec)
c	= Nozzle discharge coefficient	D	= Internal pipe diameter (in.)
d	= Nozzle orifice diameter (in.)		

Nozzle size (in.)_____
Nozzle coef. _____

Test	Pump speed (rpm)	Suction pressure (psi)	Discharge pressure (psi)	Pitot readings (psi) 1	2	3	4	5	6	Flow (gpm)	Net pressure (psi)	RPM adjusted net pressure	RPM adjusted flow (gpm)	Suction velocity pressure (psi)[1]	Discharge velocity pressure (psi)[1]	Velocity adjusted pressure (psi)[1]	Oil pressure (psi)[2]	Exhaust back pressure (in. Hg)[2]	Diesel water temperature[2]	Cooling loop pressure (psi)[2]
0%																				
25%																				
50%																				
75%																				
100%																				
125%																				
150%																				
0%																				
100%																				
150%																				

Pump is ❏ constant speed ❏ variable speed

Notes:
(1) Velocity pressure adjustments provide a more accurate analysis in most cases and as a minimum should be included whenever the pump suction and discharge diameters are different and the pump fails by a narrow margin. The actual internal diameter of the pump suction and discharge should be obtained from the manufacturer.
(2) These readings are applicable to diesel engine pumps only. Recording these readings is not specifically required in Chapter 14.

For electric motor–driven pumps also record the following:

Test	Voltage			Amperes		
	L1-L2	L2-L3	L1-L3	L1	L2	L3
0%						
25%						
50%						
75%						
100%						
125%						
150%						
0%						
100%						
150%						

G. For electric motors operating at rated voltage and frequency, is the ampere demand less than or equal to the product of the full load ampere rating times the allowable service factor as stamped on the motor nameplate? .... ❏ Yes ❏ No ❏ N/A
H. For electric motors operating under varying voltage, determine the following:
   1. Was the product of the actual voltage and current demand less than or equal to the product of the rated full load current times the rated voltage times the allowable service factor? .... ❏ Yes ❏ No ❏ N/A
   2. Was the voltage always less than 5 percent above the rated voltage during the test? .... ❏ Yes ❏ No ❏ N/A
   3. Was the voltage always less than 10 percent above the rated voltage during the test? .... ❏ Yes ❏ No ❏ N/A
I. Did engine-driven units operate without any signs of overload or stress? .... ❏ Yes ❏ No ❏ N/A
J. Was the engine overspeed emergency shutdown tested? .... ❏ Yes ❏ No ❏ N/A
K. Was the governor set to properly regulate the engine speed at rated pump speed? .... ❏ Yes ❏ No ❏ N/A

© 2019 National Fire Protection Association

(NFPA 25, p. 2 of 4)

Δ **FIGURE A.8.4.1** *Continued*

Shaded text = Revisions. Δ = Text deletions and figure/table revisions. • = Section deletions. *N* = New material.

2020 Edition

L. Did the gear drive assembly operate without excessive objectionable noise, vibration, or heating? .... ❏ Yes ❏ No ❏ N/A

M. Was the fire pump unit started and brought up to rated speed without interruption under the conditions of a discharge equal to peak load? .... ❏ Yes ❏ No ❏ N/A

N. Did the fire pump performance equal a minimum of 95 percent of the manufacturer's factory curve within the accuracy limits of the test equipment? .... ❏ Yes ❏ No ❏ N/A

O. Did the electric motor pumps pass phase reversal test on normal and alternate (if provided) power? .... ❏ Yes ❏ No ❏ N/A

IV. Multiple Pump Operation

A. _____ fire pumps are required to operate ❏ in series ❏ in parallel ❏ N/A to meet the maximum fire protection demand.

B. Record the following information for each of the _____ pumps operating simultaneously.

Nozzle size (in.) _____
Nozzle coef. _____

Test	Pump speed (rpm)	Suction pressure (psi)	Discharge pressure (psi)	Pitot readings (psi) 1	2	3	4	5	6	7	8	9	10	11	12	Oil pressure (psi)	Total flow (gpm)	Flow through net pressure	RPM adjusted flow (psi)	RPM adjusted flow (psi)	Suction velocity pressure (psi)	Suction velocity pressure (psi)	Velocity adjusted net pressure (psi)
0%																							
25%																							
50%																							
75%																							
100%																							
125%																							
150%																							
0%																							
100%																							
150%																							

Pump is ❏ constant speed   ❏ variable speed

C. Did the fire pump performance equal a minimum of 95 percent of the manufacturer's factory curve within the accuracy limits of the test equipment during the multiple test? .... ❏ Yes ❏ No ❏ N/A

V. Main Pressure Relief Valve

A. Is a main pressure relief valve installed on the fire pump discharge? ❏ Yes ❏ No

B. During variable speed performance testing, what was the flow rate through the main pressure relief valve at churn?
❏ No flow ❏ Weeping flow ❏ More than weeping flow ❏ Substantial flow ❏ N/A

C. During variable speed performance testing, what was the flow rate though the main pressure relief valve at rated flow?
❏ No flow ❏ Weeping flow ❏ More than weeping flow ❏ Substantial flow ❏ N/A

D. During constant speed performance testing, what was the flow rate though the main pressure relief valve at rated churn?
❏ No flow ❏ Weeping flow ❏ More than weeping flow ❏ Substantial flow ❏ N/A

E. During constant speed performance testing, what was the flow rate though the main pressure relief valve at rated flow?
❏ No flow ❏ Weeping flow ❏ More than weeping flow ❏ Substantial flow ❏ N/A

F. After resetting the pressure relief valve after performance testing, under variable speed operation, what was the flow rate through the main pressure relief valve at churn? ❏ No flow ❏ Weeping flow ❏ More than weeping flow ❏ Substantial flow ❏ N/A

G. After resetting the pressure relief valve after performance testing, under constant speed operation, what was the flow rate through the main pressure relief valve at churn? ❏ No flow ❏ Weeping flow ❏ More than weeping flow ❏ Substantial flow ❏ N/A
What was the fire pump discharge pressure? _____ psi.

H. After resetting the pressure relief valve after performance testing, under constant speed operation, at what flow rate did the pressure relief valve substantially close? _____ gpm. What was the fire pump discharge pressure when the pressure relief valve was substantially closed? _____ psi.

I. Is the maximum discharge pressure adjusted for elevation, and with the pressure relief operational, less than the pressure rating of the system components for elevation? ❏ Yes ❏ No ❏ N/A

VI. Controller Test

A. Did the pump start from automatic sources? .... ❏ Yes ❏ No ❏ N/A

B. Was each automatic starting feature tested at least once? .... ❏ Yes ❏ No ❏ N/A

C. Did the pump start manually? .... ❏ Yes ❏ No ❏ N/A

D. Was the pump run for at least 5 minutes during each of the operations in Parts A, B, and C above? .... ❏ Yes ❏ No ❏ N/A
(Note: An engine driver is not required to run for 5 minutes at full speed between successive starts until the cumulative cranking time of successive starts reaches 45 seconds.)

E. Were the starting operations divided between both sets of batteries for engine-driven controllers? .... ❏ Yes ❏ No ❏ N/A

F. Were both ECMs tested if supported? .... ❏ Yes ❏ No ❏ N/A

G. Was the engine tested and RPM set on both ECMs at rated flow and full load? .... ❏ Yes ❏ No ❏ N/A

H. Were all alarm functions, including ECM alarms for fuel injection failure, low fuel pressure, and any primary sensor failure, tested at the engine? .... ❏ Yes ❏ No ❏ N/A

© 2019 National Fire Protection Association   (NFPA 25, p. 3 of 4)

△ **FIGURE A.8.4.1**   *Continued*

Shaded text = Revisions.   △ = Text deletions and figure/table revisions.   • = Section deletions.   *N* = New material.

I. Electric Driven Pump Controllers
    1. Did all overcurrent protective devices (including the controller circuit breaker) hold during the tests? .... ❏ Yes ❏ No ❏ N/A
    2. Was the fire pump started at least once from each power service and run for at least 5 minutes? .... ❏ Yes ❏ No ❏ N/A
    3. Upon simulation of a power failure, while the pump is operating at peak load, did the transfer switch transfer from the
       normal to the emergency source without opening overcurrent protection devices on either line? .... ❏ Yes ❏ No ❏ N/A
    4. When normal power was restored, did retransfer from emergency to normal power occur without overcurrent protection
       devices opening on either line? .... ❏ Yes ❏ No ❏ N/A
    5. Were at least 1 automatic and 1 manual starts performed with the pump connected to the alternate source? .... ❏ Yes ❏ No ❏ N/A
J. Were all signal conditions simulated demonstrating satisfactory operation? .... ❏ Yes ❏ No ❏ N/A
K. Did the pump run for at least the minimum time required by this standard? .... ❏ Yes ❏ No ❏ N/A
    NOTE: Run time includes all time the driver was turning the impellar, i.e., no-flow and flow conditions.

VII. Water Storage Tank ❏ Yes ❏ No
    A. Tank capacity_____ gallons, height _____ ft, diameter _____ ft
    B. Break tank ❏ Yes ❏ No ❏ N/A   Required break tank fill rate _____ gpm ❏ N/A
    C. Did refill rate maintain tank level when flowing 150 percent of rated capacity? ❏ Yes ❏ No ❏ N/A
    D. A water refill rate of_____ gpm was ❏ field verified by flowing _____ gpm through the fire pump with a starting water level of _____ ft _____ in.
       and an ending water level of_____ ft _____ in. after flowing for _____ minutes, ❏ field verified by raising the water level from _____ ft_____ in.
       to _____ ft _____ in. in minutes, ❏ field verified by other means (specify) _____
    E. Was the automatic refill assembly operated? .... ❏ Yes ❏ No ❏ N/A

VIII. Test Evaluation
    A. Did the pump performance equal that indicated on the manufacturer's certified shop test under all load conditions? .... ❏ Yes ❏ No
    B. Did the pump discharge equal or exceed the maximum fire protection system demand? .... ❏ Yes ❏ No
    C. Did the pump performance meet the requirements of NFPA 25?.. ❏ Yes ❏ No

IX. Tester Information
Tester: _____
Company: _____
Company address: _____

I state that the information on this form is correct at the time and place of my test, and that all equipment tested was left in operational condition upon
completion of this test except as noted in the comments section below.
Signature of tester: _____ Date: _____ License or certification number if applicable: _____

X. Comments *(Any "No" answers, test failures, or other problems must be explained — use additional sheets if necessary.)*
_____
_____
_____
_____
_____
_____

NFPA 25 Annual Fire Pump Test Form

Legend:
Factory curve
RPM adjusted net
Pump suction
Pump discharge
Net pump

(Y-axis: Pressure in PSI, 0–200; X-axis: Flow rate in GPM, 0–1600)

© 2019 National Fire Protection Association   (NFPA 25, p. 4 of 4)

Δ **FIGURE A.8.4.1**   *Continued*

Shaded text = Revisions.   Δ = Text deletions and figure/table revisions.   • = Section deletions.   ***N*** = New material.   2020 Edition

A.8.5.1 Where the manufacturer's preventive maintenance requirements are not provided, refer to Table A.8.1.1.2.

It is important to provide proper bearing lubrication and to keep bearings clean. Some bearings are the sealed type and need no relubrication. Couplings with rubber drive parts do not need lubrication; other types generally do. The following practices are recommended:

(1) Lubricant fittings should be cleaned before relubricating with grease.
(2) The proper amount of lubricant should be used. Too much lubricant results in churning, causing excessive power loss and overheating.
(3) The correct lubricant should be used.

Engine Maintenance. Engines should be kept clean, dry, and well lubricated. The proper oil level in the crankcase should be maintained.

Battery Maintenance. Only distilled water should be used in battery cells. Plates should be kept submerged at all times. An automatic battery charger is not a substitute for proper maintenance of the battery and charger. Periodic inspection ensures that the charger is operating correctly, the water level in the battery is adequate, and the battery is holding its proper charge.

Fuel Supply Maintenance. The fuel storage tank should be kept at least two-thirds full. Fuel should be maintained free of water and foreign material by draining water and foreign material from the tank sump annually. This necessitates draining approximately 5 gal (19 L).

Temperature Maintenance. The temperature of the pump room, pump house, or area where engines are installed should never be less than the minimum recommended by the engine manufacturer. The manufacturer's temperature recommendations for water and oil heaters should be followed.

A.9.1 One source of information on the inspection and maintenance of steel gravity and suction tanks is the AWWA *Manual of Water Supply Practices — M42 Steel Water-Storage Tanks*, Part III and Annex C.

A.9.2.1.1 More frequent inspections should be made where extreme conditions, such as freezing temperatures or arid climate, can increase the probability of adversely affecting the stored water.

Supervisory water level alarms installed on tanks provide notification that the tank water level is above or below an acceptable level. The water level of the tank is the main concern as opposed to the condition of the water. For convenience, inspection of the condition of the water can take place concurrently with the water level inspection.

N **A.9.2.1.3.2** The designed water level should be based on the fire protection system having the largest stored water volume requirement based on its demand and required duration as defined by the appropriate referenced standards. The designed water level is often used as the set point for operation of the tank fill valve.

A.9.2.4.1 Lightning protection systems, where provided, should be inspected, tested, and maintained in accordance with NFPA 780.

A.9.2.5.1.1 To aid in the inspection and evaluation of test results, it is a good idea for the property owner or designated

representative to stencil the last known date of an interior paint job on the exterior of the tank in a conspicuous place. A typical place is near one of the manways at eye level.

A.9.2.5.1.2 If written verification of interior corrosion protection for a tank per NFPA 22 cannot be provided by the building owner, the interior of the tank should be inspected every 3 years.

A.9.2.5.5 This inspection can be performed by looking for dents on the tank floor. Additionally, walking on the tank floor and looking for buckling of the floor will identify problem areas.

A.9.3.1 The testing procedure for listed mercury gauges is as follows.

To determine that the mercury gauge is accurate, the gauge should be tested every 5 years as follows [steps (1) through (7) coincide with Figure A.9.3.1]:

(1) Overflow the tank.
(2) Close valve F. Open test cock D. The mercury will drop quickly into the mercury pot. If it does not drop, there is an obstruction that needs to be removed from the pipe or pot between the test cock and the gauge glass.
(3) If the mercury does lower at once, close cock D and open valve F. If the mercury responds immediately and comes to rest promptly opposite the "FULL" mark on the gauge board, the instrument is functioning properly.
(4) If the mercury column does not respond promptly and indicate the correct reading during the test, there probably are air pockets or obstructions in the water connecting pipe. Open cock D. Water should flow out forcibly. Allow water to flow through cock D until all air is expelled and rusty water from the tank riser appears. Close cock D. The gauge now likely will read correctly. If air separates from the water in the 1 in. (25 mm) pipe due to being enclosed in a buried tile conduit with steam pipes, the air can be removed automatically by installing a ¾ in. (20 mm) air trap at the high point of the piping. The air trap usually can be installed most easily in a tee connected by a short piece of pipe at E, with a plug in the top of the tee so that mercury can be added in the future, if necessary, without removing the trap. If there are inaccessible pockets in the piping, as where located below grade or under concrete floors, the air can be removed only through petcock D.
(5) If, in step (4), the water does not flow forcibly through cock D, there is an obstruction that needs to be removed from the outlet of the test cock or from the water pipe between the test cock and the tank riser.
(6) If there is water on top of the mercury column in the gauge glass, it will provide inaccurate readings and should be removed. First, lower the mercury into the pot as in step (2). Close cock D and remove plug G. Open valve F very slowly, causing the mercury to rise slowly and the water above it to drain through plug G. Close valve F quickly when mercury appears at plug G, but have a receptacle ready to catch any mercury that drains out. Replace plug G. Replace any escaped mercury in the pot.
(7) After testing, leave valve F open, except under the following conditions: If it is necessary to prevent forcing mercury and water into the mercury catcher, the controlling valve F can be permitted to be closed when filling the tank but should be left open after the tank is filled. In cases where the gauge is subjected to continual fluctua-

tion of pressure, it could be necessary to keep the gauge shut off except when it needs to be read. Otherwise, it could be necessary to remove water frequently from the top of the mercury column as in step (5).

△ A.9.3.4 The manufacturer's instructions should be consulted for guidance on testing. In some situations, it might not be possible to test the actual initiating device. In such cases, only the circuitry should be tested.

△ A.9.3.5 See A.9.3.4.

A.10.1 The effectiveness and reliability of water spray fixed systems depends on maintenance of the integrity of hydraulic characteristics, water control valves, deluge valves and their fire detection/actuation systems, pipe hangers, and prevention of obstructions to nozzle discharge patterns.

Water spray fixed systems are most commonly used to protect processing equipment and structures, flammable liquid and gas vessels, piping, and equipment such as transformers, oil switches, and motors. They also have been shown to be effective on many combustible solids.

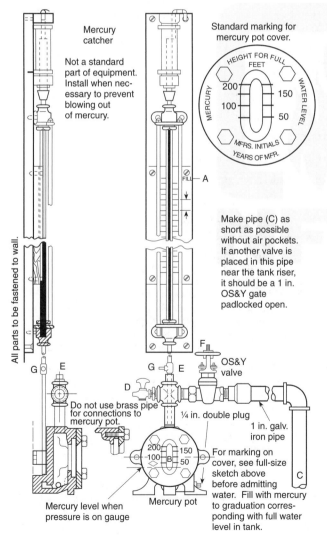

Note: For SI units, 1 in. = 25.4 mm.

FIGURE A.9.3.1   Mercury Gauge.

Many of the components and subsystems found in a water spray system require the same inspection, test, and maintenance procedures where they are used in automatic sprinkler systems and other fixed water-based fire protection systems. Other chapters of this standard should be consulted for particulars on required inspection and maintenance.

A.10.1.3 Insulation acting in lieu of water spray protection is expected to protect a vessel or structure for the duration of the exposure. The insulation is to prevent the temperature from exceeding 850°F (454°C) for structural members and 650°F (393°C) for vessels. If the insulation is missing, the structure or vessel is not considered to be protected, regardless of water spray protection or insulation on other surfaces. To re-establish the proper protection, the insulation should be replaced or the water spray protection should be extended, using the appropriate density.

A.10.1.6 The inspection, testing, and maintenance of water spray fixed systems can involve or result in a system that is out of service. Also see Chapter 15.

A.10.2.3 The operation of the water spray system is dependent on the integrity of the piping, which should be kept free of mechanical damage. The pipe should not be used for support of ladders, stock, or other material. Where piping is subject to a corrosive atmosphere, a protective corrosion-resistant coating should be provided and maintained. Where the age or service conditions warrant, an internal examination of the piping should be made. Where it is necessary to flush all or part of the piping system, this work should be done by sprinkler contractors or other qualified workers.

A.10.2.3.1 Rubber-gasketed fittings in the fire areas are inspected to determine whether they are protected by the water spray or other approved means. Unless properly protected, fire could cause loss of the rubber gasket following excessive leakage in a fire situation.

A.10.2.3.2 Hangers and supports are designed to support and restrain the piping from severe movement when the water supply operates and to provide adequate pipe slope for drainage of water from the piping after the water spray system is shut down. Hangers should be kept in good repair. Broken or loose hangers can put undue strain on piping and fittings, cause pipe breaks, and interfere with proper drainage of the pipe. Broken or loose hangers should be replaced or refastened.

A.10.2.4 Systems need inspection to ensure water spray nozzles effectively discharge water unobstructed onto surfaces to be protected from radiant heat (exposure protection) or onto flaming surfaces to extinguish or control combustion. Factors affecting the proper placement of water spray nozzles include the following:

(1) Changes or additions to the protected area that obstruct existing nozzles or require additional coverage for compliance
(2) Removal of equipment from the protected area that results in nozzle placement at excessive distances from the hazard
(3) Mechanical damage or previous flow tests that have caused nozzles to be misdirected
(4) A change in the hazard being protected that requires more or different nozzles to provide adequate coverage for compliance

Shaded text = Revisions.   △ = Text deletions and figure/table revisions.   • = Section deletions.   *N* = New material.

2020 Edition

Spray nozzles can be permitted to be placed in any position necessary to obtain proper coverage of the protected area. Positioning of nozzles with respect to surfaces to be protected, or to fires to be controlled or extinguished, should be guided by the particular nozzle design and the character of water spray produced. In positioning nozzles, care should be taken that the water spray does not miss the targeted surface and reduce the efficiency or calculated discharge rate.

A.10.2.5.2 Water supply piping should be free of internal obstructions that can be caused by debris (e.g., rocks, mud, tubercles) or by closed or partially closed control valves. See Chapter 5 for inspection and maintenance requirements.

A.10.2.6 Mainline strainers should be removed and inspected for damaged and corroded parts every 5 years.

A.10.3.2 The property owner or designated representative should take care to prevent damage to equipment or the structure during the test. Damage could be caused by the system discharge or by runoff from the test site. It should be verified that there is adequate and unobstructed drainage. Equipment should be removed or covered as necessary to prevent damage. Means such as curbing or sandbagging should be used to prevent entry of the water.

A.10.3.3.1 Test methods are as follows:

(1) Some detection circuits can be permitted to be deliberately desensitized in order to override unusual ambient conditions. In such cases, the response required in 10.3.3.1 can be permitted to be exceeded.
(2) Testing of integrating tubing systems can be permitted to be related to this test by means of a standard pressure impulse test specified by the listing laboratory.
(3) One method of testing heat detection uses a radiant heat surface at a temperature of 300°F (149°C) and a capacity of 350 watts at a distance of 1 in. (25 mm) but not more than 2 in. (50 mm) from the nearest part of the detector. This method of testing with an electric test set should not be used in hazardous locations. Other test methods can be permitted to be employed, but the results should be obtained under these conditions.

A.10.3.3.3 Spray nozzles can be of different sizes and types. Some are more subject to internal obstructions than others.

A.10.3.3.3.1 See 13.4.4.2.3.1.

A.11.2.4 Directional-type foam-water discharge devices are quite often located in heavy traffic areas and are more apt to be dislocated compared to ordinary sprinkler locations. Of particular concern are low-level discharge devices in loading racks in and around low-level tankage and monitor-mounted devices that have been pushed out of the way for convenience. Inspection frequency might have to be increased accordingly.

A.11.2.4.4 Discharge devices are listed or approved for particular foam concentrates.

A.11.2.5.2 Water supply piping should be free of internal obstructions that can be caused by debris (e.g., rocks, mud, tubercles) or by closed or partially closed control valves. See Chapter 5 for inspection and maintenance requirements.

A.11.2.8 Proportioning systems might or might not include foam concentrate pumps. If pumps are part of the proportioning system, the driver, pump, and gear reducer should be inspected in accordance with the manufacturer's recommenda-

tions, and the inspection can include items such as lubrication, fuel, filters, oil levels, and clutches.

A.11.2.8.4 In some cases, an adequate supply of foam liquid is available without a full tank. This is particularly true of foam liquid stored in nonmetallic tanks. If liquid is stored in metallic tanks, the proper liquid level should be one-half the distance into the expansion dome.

A.11.2.8.5.1.1 The standard pressure proportioner is a pressure vessel. Although under normal standby conditions this type of proportioning system should not be pressurized, some installations allow for inadvertent pressurization. Pressure should be removed before inspection.

A.11.2.8.5.2.1 The bladder tank proportioner is a pressure vessel. Where inspecting for a full liquid tank, the manufacturer's instructions should be followed. If inspected incorrectly, the tank sight gauges could indicate a full tank when the tank actually is empty of foam liquid. Some foam liquids, due to their viscosity, might not indicate true levels of foam liquid in the tank where inspected via the sight glass.

CAUTION: Depending on system configuration, this type of proportioner system might be pressurized or nonpressurized under normal conditions. Pressure should be removed before inspection.

A.11.2.8.5.3(1) See 11.2.6.1.

A.11.2.8.5.3(2) See Figure A.3.3.34.

A.11.2.8.5.4(1) See 11.2.6.1.

A.11.2.8.5.4(2) See Figure A.3.3.34.

A.11.2.8.5.5(1) See 11.2.6.1.

A.11.2.8.5.5(2) See Figure A.3.3.34.

A.11.2.8.5.6(1) See 11.2.6.1.

A.11.2.8.5.6(2) See Figure A.3.3.34.

△ **A.11.3** Operational tests generally should be comprised of the following:

(1) A detection/actuation test with no flow to verify that all components such as automated valves, foam and water pumps, and alarms operate properly
(2) A water-only flow test to inspect piping continuity, discharge patterns, pressures, and line flushing
(3) A foam flow test to verify solution concentration
(4) Resetting of system to its normal standby condition, including draining of lines and filling of foam liquid tank

A.11.3.1 The property owner or designated representative should take care to prevent damage to equipment or the structure during the test. Damage could be caused by the system discharge or by runoff from the test site. It should be verified that there is adequate and unobstructed drainage. Equipment should be removed or covered as necessary to prevent damage. Means such as curbing or sandbagging should be used to prevent entry of the foam-water solution.

A.11.3.2 An alternative method for achieving flow can be permitted to be an installation as shown in Figure A.11.3.2. This type of testing does not verify system pipe conditions or discharge device performance but only the water supply, foam concentrate supply, and proportioning accuracy.

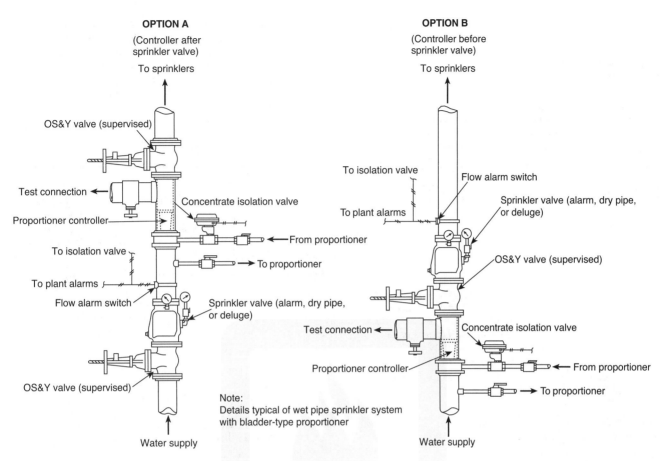

FIGURE A.11.3.2   Foam System/Test Header Combination.

△ **A.11.3.2.7** Specific foam concentrates typically are listed or approved with specific sprinklers. Part of the approval and listing is a minimum sprinkler operating pressure. Sprinkler operating pressure affects foam quality, discharge patterns, and fire extinguishment (control) capabilities. Discharge pressures less than this specified minimum pressure should be corrected immediately; therefore, it is necessary to test under full flow conditions.

● **A.11.4** The maintenance items specified in the body of this standard are in addition to the typical inspection and test procedures indicated. Foam-water sprinkler systems are, as are all fire protection systems, designed to be basically maintenance free. There are, however, some areas that need special attention. Foam concentrate shelf life varies between liquids and is affected by factors such as heat, cold, dilution, contamination, and many others. As with all systems, common sense dictates those maintenance-sensitive areas that should be given attention. Routine testing and inspection generally dictate the need for additional maintenance items. Those maintenance items specified are key procedures that should be performed routinely.

A.11.4.4.2 Foam concentrates tend to settle out over time. Depending on the specific characteristics of the foam concentrate, sedimentation accumulates in the bottom of the storage vessel. This sediment can affect proportioning and foam concentrate integrity. Some concentrates tend to settle out more rapidly than others. If the annual samples indicate excessive sediment, flushing the tank could be required more frequently.

A.11.4.5.2 When hydrostatically testing bladder tanks, the generation of a pressure differential across the diaphragm could cause damage to the diaphragm. Tanks should be filled with agent to no less than the normal fill capacity and air should be vented from inside and outside the bladder before pressurizing.

A.12.2.1.1.1(5) In lieu of replacing water mist nozzles that are loaded with a coating of dust, it is permitted to clean the nozzles with compressed air or by a vacuum provided that the equipment does not touch the nozzle.

N **A.12.2.4.4** Examples of hangers and seismic braces installed in concealed areas include some floor/ceiling or roof/ceiling assemblies, pipe chases, and other inaccessible areas.

N **A.12.2.5.2** These guidelines apply only to the external inspection of containers continuously in service in the water mist system and should not be confused with the DOT retest requirements for visual inspection described in 49 CFR.

Proper recordkeeping is an important part of every inspection. The inspector should be guided by the following outline to ensure that the minimum information is recorded:

(1)   Record tag. A record tag should be attached to every container being inspected for future reference. The record tag should be marked with the date of inspection

(month/year), name of individuals(s) and company performing the inspection, container serial number, condition of the container (paint, corrosion, dents, gouges, etc.), and disposition.

(2) Inspection report. The inspection report should record the date of inspection (month/year), name of individual(s) and company performing the inspection, DOT specification number, container serial number, date of manufacture, date of previous inspection and/or test, type of protective coating, surface condition (corrosion, dents, gouges, fire damage, etc.), and disposition (satisfactory, repaint, repair, scrap, etc.). A sample of a suitable inspection report form can be found in Appendix A of CGA C-6, *Standard for Visual Inspection of Steel Compressed Gas Cylinders.*

A.12.3.1.1 Water mist nozzles should be first given a visual inspection for signs of mechanical damage, cleaning, painting, leakage in service, or severe loading or corrosion, all of which are causes for immediate replacement.

Automatic nozzles that have passed the visual inspection should be laboratory tested for sensitivity (RTI), functionality, and K-factor. Thermal sensitivity should be not less than that permitted in post-corrosion testing of new automatic water mist nozzles of the same type. Automatic water mist nozzles should be tested for functionality at their minimum operating pressure specified by the manufacturer. Automatic water mist nozzles should have a K-factor within ±5 percent of the value published by the manufacturer.

Some example testing standards include EN 12259-1, *Fixed firefighting systems – Components for sprinkler and water spray systems – Part 1: Sprinklers*; UL 2167, *Standard for Water Mist Nozzles for Fire Protection Service*; and FM Approvals Standard 5560, *Water Mist Systems.*

Water mist nozzles that have been in service for a number of years should not be expected to have all of the performance measurements of a new water mist nozzle. However, if there is any question about their continued satisfactory performance, the water mist nozzles should be replaced.

A.12.3.1.3 These environments include outdoor weather conditions and portions of any area where corrosive vapors prevail. Harsh water environments include water supplies that are chemically reactive. An example of a corrosive atmosphere is a marine environment. The testing requirements for these types of environments are also described in the International Maritime Organization's MSC.1/Circular 1432, *Guidelines for the Maintenance and Inspection of Fire Protection Systems and Appliances.*

A.12.3.1.4 Within the area represented by the selected sample, water mist nozzles of the same design produced by the same manufacturer can be considered part of the same sample, but additional water mist nozzles would need to be selected if produced by a different manufacturer.

N **A.12.3.1.5** When acceptable to the authority having jurisdiction, in lieu of replacement of all the water mist nozzles within the area represented, additional representative samples could be tested to assess the performance of the water mist nozzles in that area.

N **A.12.3.2.2** Water mist nozzles should be first given a visual inspection for signs of mechanical damage, cleaning, painting, or severe loading or corrosion, all of which are causes for immediate replacement.

Open nozzles that have passed the visual inspection should be laboratory tested for functionality and K-factor. Open water mist nozzles with blow-off caps and/or dust plugs should be tested for functionality at their minimum operating pressure specified by the manufacturer. Open water mist nozzles should have a K-factor within ±5 percent of the value published by the manufacturer.

Some example testing standards include EN 12259-1, *Fixed firefighting systems – Components for sprinkler and water spray systems – Part 1: Sprinklers*; UL 2167, *Standard for Water Mist Nozzles for Fire Protection Service*; and FM Approvals Standard 5560, *Water Mist Systems.*

Water mist nozzles that have been in service for a number of years should not be expected to have all of the same performance measurements of a new water mist nozzle. However, if there is any question about their continued satisfactory performance, the water mist nozzles should be replaced.

N **A.12.3.2.5** Where acceptable to the authority having jurisdiction, in lieu of replacement of all the water mist nozzles within the area represented, additional representative samples could be tested to assess the performance of the water mist nozzles in that area.

N **A.12.3.16.3** Test methods are as follows:

(1) Some detection circuits can be permitted to be deliberately desensitized in order to override unusual ambient conditions. In such cases, the response required in 12.3.16.3 can be permitted to be exceeded.

(2) Testing of integrating tubing systems can be permitted to be related to this test by means of a standard pressure impulse test specified by the listing laboratory.

One method of testing heat detection uses a radiant heat surface at a temperature of 300°F (149°C) and a capacity of 350 watts at a distance of 1 in. (25 mm) but not more than 2 in. (50 mm) from the nearest part of the detector. This method of testing with an electric test set should not be used in hazardous locations. Other test methods can be permitted to be employed, but the results should be obtained under these conditions.

N **A.12.3.16.5** Water mist nozzles can be of different sizes and types. Some might be more susceptible to internal obstructions than others.

N **A.12.3.18.1** A source for test requirements is the most current FSSA Cylinder Service Guide. There are the same requirements that are applicable to cylinders, pressure tanks or pressure vessels used for pressurized gas agents.

A.12.4.1.5 The representative sample should include 10 percent of the water mist nozzles in the activated zone. If contamination of filters or strainers is found on inspection, it is recommended that all nozzles within the activated zone be inspected.

A.12.4.2.1 Each water mist nozzle has unique requirements for protection applications and end-use limitations.

A.12.4.2.3 A minimum of two water mist nozzles of each type and temperature rating installed should be provided.

A.12.4.2.4 Other types of wrenches could damage the water mist nozzles.

A.12.4.2.5.2 Typical sandwich bags purchased in a grocery store are generally plastic, not cellophane. Plastic bags have a tendency to shrink and adhere to the nozzles prior to nozzle activation, creating the potential for disruption of nozzle spray pattern. Bags placed over nozzles need to be cellophane or paper.

A.13.1 *Alarm Valves.* Alarm valves are installed in water-based fire protection systems to sound a fire alarm when a flow of water from the system equals or exceeds the flow of a single discharge device. A retarding chamber, which minimizes false alarms due to surges and fluctuating water supply pressure, can be supplied with the alarm valve.

Backflow Prevention Devices. Backflow prevention devices are used to prevent water in a fire protection system from entering the public water supply due to a reverse flow of water, thermal expansion, hydraulic shock, back pressure, or back siphonage. *[See Figure A.13.1(a).]*

Ball Valves. Ball valves are manually operated through their full range of open to closed positions with a one-quarter turn.

Butterfly Valves. Butterfly valves are water supply control valves with gear operators to assist in opening and closing. Butterfly valves can be of the wafer or grooved-end type. *[See Figure A.13.1(b).]*

Check Valves. Check valves allow waterflow in one direction only. *[See Figure A.13.1(c).]*

DCA. A double check assembly (DCA) consists of two independently operating spring-loaded check valves. The assembly includes two resilient-seated isolation valves and four test cocks required for testing.

DCDA. A double check detector assembly (DCDA) is hydraulically balanced to include a metered bypass assembly to detect system leakage. The main valve assembly and bypass assembly afford equal levels of backflow prevention and are each equipped with two resilient-seated isolation valves and four test cocks required for testing.

Deluge Valves. Deluge valves hold water at the valve until actuated by the operation of a detection system or manual release. *[See Figure A.13.1(d).]*

Drip Valves. Drip valves automatically drain condensation or small amounts of water that have leaked into system piping or valves. Drip valves close when exposed to system pressure.

Dry Pipe Valves. Dry pipe valves control the flow of water to areas that could be exposed to freezing conditions. Water is held at the valve by air pressure in the system piping. When the air pressure is reduced, the valve operates and floods the system. *[See Figure A.13.1(e) and Figure A.13.1(f).]*

Indicating Valves. Indicating valves provide a dependable, visible indication of the open position, even at a distance.

Indicator Posts. Indicator posts include wall and underground types and are intended for use in operating inside screwed pattern gate valves and for indicating the position of the gates in the valves. *[See Figure A.13.1(g).]*

NRS Gate Valves, OS&Y Gate Valves. Nonrising stem (NRS) gate valves are used underground with indicator posts attached or as roadway box valves (curb-box installation). Outside screw and yoke (OS&Y) gate valves are used indoors and in pits outdoors. The valve stem moves out when the valve is open and moves in when it is closed. The stem indicates the position of the valve. *[See Figure A.13.1(h) and Figure A.13.1(i).]*

RPA. A reduced-pressure zone principle assembly (RPA) consists of two independently spring-loaded check valves separated by a differential-sensing valve. The differential-sensing valve includes a relief port to atmosphere that discharges excess water resulting from supply system fluctuations. The assembly includes two resilient-seated isolation valves and four test cocks required for testing.

RPDA. A reduced-pressure detector assembly (RPDA) is hydraulically balanced to include a metered bypass assembly to detect system leakage. The main valve assembly and bypass assembly afford equal levels of backflow prevention, and each assembly is equipped with two resilient-seated isolation valves and four test cocks required for testing.

Strainers. Strainers are used for protection against clogging of water discharge openings.

Waterflow Detector Check Valves. Detector-type check valves allow flow in one direction only and have provisions for the connection of a bypass meter around the check valve. *[See Figure A.13.1(c).]*

A.13.2.2 The valves are not required to be exposed. Doors, removable panels, or valve pits can be permitted to satisfy this requirement. Such equipment should not be obstructed by features such as walls, ducts, columns, direct burial, or stock storage.

△ **A.13.2.3** Main drains are installed on system risers for one principal reason: to drain water from the overhead piping after the system is shut off. This allows the contractor or plant maintenance department to perform work on the system or to replace nozzles after a fire or other incident involving system operation.

Data collected from the suction gauges during a fire pump flow test that test the water supply would satisfy the requirements for a main drain test.

These drains also are used to determine whether there is a major reduction in waterflow to the system, such as could be caused by a major obstruction, a dropped gate, a valve that is almost fully closed, or a check valve clapper stuck to the valve seat.

A satisfactory main drain test (i.e., one that reflects the results of previous tests) does not necessarily indicate an unobstructed passage, nor does it prove that all valves in the upstream flow of water are fully opened. However, these tests provide a reasonable level of confidence that the water supply has not been compromised.

The main drain test is conducted in the following manner:

(1) Record the pressure indicated by the supply water gauge.
(2) Close the alarm control valve on alarm valves.
(3) Fully open the main drain valve.
(4) After the flow has stabilized, record the residual (flowing) pressure indicated by the water supply gauge.
(5) Close the main drain valve slowly.

A.13.2.4.8 Opening the inspector's test connection can cause the system to trip accidentally.

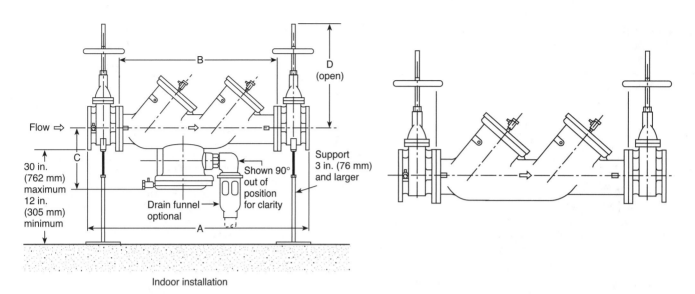

FIGURE A.13.1(a)   Reduced-Pressure Backflow Preventers (left) and Double Check Valve Assemblies (right).

A.13.2.5.1 The inspection frequencies identified in this section apply to all systems and devices covered by this standard.

A.13.2.5.1.1 "Normal water supply pressure" could be a pressure reading that is too high or too low relative to what reasonably would be expected based on system design information, knowledge of the connected water supply, and/or reading data based on past inspections. "Normal" pressure includes pressure expected to be found on a system in order to adequately supply the supplied fire sprinkler system. For example, a gauge reading a pressure close to or below a sprinkler system's demand listed on the design placard would not be expected to be normal because as, the system could have a water supply issue. Normal water supply pressure on a gauge above an alarm or system check valve might be higher than that of a gauge below as a result of trapped pressure surges. This can be typical in buildings with trapped air located close to metal deck roofs without air conditioning. Gridded systems also have a high probability of excess pressure development, which is why NFPA 13 requires relief valves on such systems.

Due to the high probability of excess pressure buildup, gridded wet pipe systems should be provided with a relief valve not less than ¼ in. (6.3 mm) in accordance with NFPA 13. It is normal, though, that the pressure above the alarm or system check valve is typically higher than that of the water supply as a result of trapped pressure surges.

A.13.2.5.1.4 See Figure A.13.2.5.1.4.

A.13.3.1 Signs identifying underground fire service main control valves in roadway boxes should indicate the direction of valve opening, the distance and direction of the valve from the sign location (if the valve is subject to being covered by snow or ice), and the location of the wrench if not located with the sign.

A.13.3.1.2 Valves that normally are closed during cold weather should be removed and replaced with devices that provide continuous fire protection service.

FIGURE A.13.1(b)   Butterfly Post Indicator Valve. *(Courtesy of Henry Pratt Co.)*

A.13.3.2.2 Valves should be kept free of snow, ice, storage, or other obstructions so that access is ensured.

A.13.3.2.2(2) The purpose of the valve sealing program is as follows:

(1) The presence of a seal on a control valve is a deterrent to closing a valve indiscriminately without obtaining the proper authority.
(2) A broken or missing seal on a valve is cause for the plant inspector to verify that protection is not impaired and to notify superiors of the fact that a valve could have been closed without following procedures.

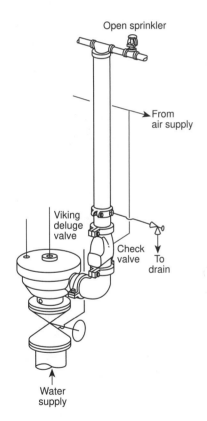

FIGURE A.13.1(c)   Detector Check Valve.

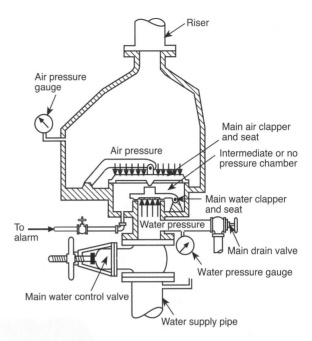

FIGURE A.13.1(e)   Dry Pipe Valve.

FIGURE A.13.1(d)   Deluge Valve.

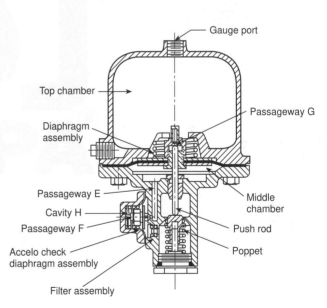

FIGURE A.13.1(f)   Dry Pipe System Accelerator. *(Courtesy of The Reliable Automatic Sprinkler Co., Inc.)*

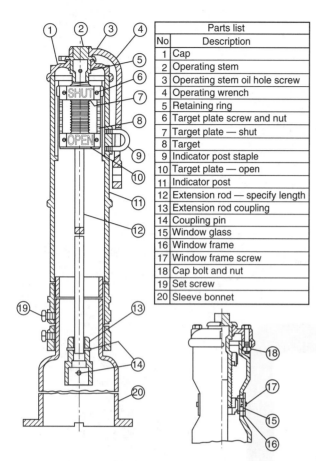

Parts list	
No	Description
1	Cap
2	Operating stem
3	Operating stem oil hole screw
4	Operating wrench
5	Retaining ring
6	Target plate screw and nut
7	Target plate — shut
8	Target
9	Indicator post staple
10	Target plate — open
11	Indicator post
12	Extension rod — specify length
13	Extension rod coupling
14	Coupling pin
15	Window glass
16	Window frame
17	Window frame screw
18	Cap bolt and nut
19	Set screw
20	Sleeve bonnet

FIGURE A.13.1(g)   Vertical Indicator Post.

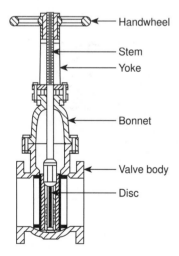

FIGURE A.13.1(h)   OS&Y Gate Valve.

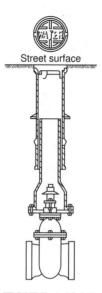

FIGURE A.13.1(i)   Nonindicating-Type Gate Valve.

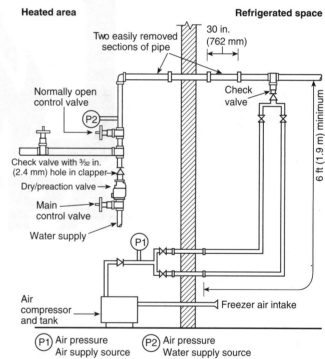

Notes:
1. Check valve with ³⁄₃₂ in. (2.4 mm) hole in clapper not required if prime water not used.
2. Supply air to be connection to top or side of system pipe.
3. Each removable air line should be a minimum of 1 in. (25 mm) diameter and minimum of 6 ft (1.9 m) long.

FIGURE A.13.2.5.1.4   Refrigerator Area Sprinkler System Used to Minimize Chances of Developing Ice Plugs.

   Shaded text = Revisions.   △ = Text deletions and figure/table revisions.   • = Section deletions.   **N** = New material.

A.13.3.3.2 A proper wrench needs to be used for this test. Using an improper wrench such as a pipe wrench has resulted in damage to the operating nut. The use of break over bars and extensions on the wrench can damage the valve and/or the post. If the valve cannot be closed and reopened using the proper wrench with reasonable force, then some maintenance and/or repairs are necessary so the valve can be operated when needed in a fire event. These "spring tests" are made to verify that a post indicator valve is fully open. If an operator feels the valve is fully open, he or she should push in the "open" direction. The handle usually moves a short distance (approximately a one-quarter turn) and "springs" back toward the operator in a subtle move when released. This spring occurs when the valve gate pulls up tight against the top of its casting and the valve shaft (being fairly long) twists slightly. The spring indicates that the valve is fully opened and that the gate is attached to the handle. If the gate is jammed due to a foreign particle, the handle is not likely to spring back. If the gate is loose from the handle, the handle continues to turn in the "open" direction with little resistance.

A.13.3.3.5 For further information, see *NFPA 72*.

A.13.4.1.1 A higher pressure reading on the system gauge is normal in variable pressure water supplies. Pressure over 175 psi (12.1 bar) can be caused by fire pump tests or thermal expansion and should be investigated and corrected.

A.13.4.1.2 The system should be drained for internal inspection of valve components as follows:

(1) Close the control valve
(2) Open the main drain valve
(3) Open the inspector's test valve
(4) Wait for the sound of draining water to cease and for all gauges to indicate 0 psi (0 bar) before removing the handhole cover or dismantling any component

A.13.4.3.2.1 High priming water levels can adversely affect the operation of supervisory air. Test the water level as follows:

(1) Open the priming level test valve.
(2) If water flows, drain it.
(3) Close the valve when water stops flowing and air discharges.
(4) If air discharges when the valve is opened, the priming water level could be too low. To add priming water, refer to the manufacturer's instructions.

N **A.13.4.3.2.4** It is necessary that the full flow test incorporate the full functionality of the system, which would include any solenoid valves or other actuation devices. It was common practice in the past to test the detection system or manual pull station up to the solenoid valve or actuator and to separately test the preaction valve and system after the solenoid valve or actuator. The detectors on the system can be tested separately as long as the functional test includes activation of the actuator or solenoid when it receives an actual or simulated signal.

A.13.4.3.2.10 Methods of recording maintenance include tags attached at each riser, records retained at each building, and records retained at one building in a complex.

A.13.4.3.3.3 Suitable facilities should be provided to dispose of drained water. Low points equipped with a single valve should be drained as follows:

(1) Open the low-point drain valve slowly.

(2) Close the drain valve as soon as water ceases to discharge, and allow time for additional accumulation above the valve.
(3) Repeat this procedure until water ceases to discharge.
(4) Replace plug or nipple and cap as necessary.

Low points equipped with dual valves should be drained as follows:

(1) Close the upper valve.
(2) Open the lower valve, and drain the accumulated water.
(3) Close the lower valve, open the upper valve, and allow time for additional water accumulation.
(4) Repeat this procedure until water ceases to discharge.
(5) Replace plug or nipple and cap in lower valve.

Removing water from a deluge system is an essential part of a good maintenance program. Failure to keep these systems free of water can result in damage and expensive repairs to both the system and the building. A program for monitoring the condition of the system and the operation of the auxiliary drains should be instituted. Auxiliary drains should be operated on a daily basis after a system operation until several days pass with no discharge of water from the drain valve. Thereafter, it might be possible to decrease the frequency to weekly or longer intervals, depending on the volume of water discharged. Likewise, when preparing for cold weather, the auxiliary drains should be operated daily, with the frequency of operation decreasing depending on the discharge of accumulated water. In many cases, the frequency of the operation can decrease significantly if a system is shown to be dry.

A.13.4.4.2.3 Deluge valves in areas subject to freezing should be trip tested in the spring to allow time before the onset of cold weather for all water that has entered the system or condensation to drain to low points or back to the valve.

A.13.4.4.2.3.1 It is necessary that the full flow test incorporate the full functionality of the system, which would include any solenoid valves or other actuation devices. It was a common practice in the past to test the detection system or manual pull station up to the solenoid valve or actuator and to separately test the deluge valve and system after the solenoid valve or actuator. The detectors on the system can be tested separately as long as the functional test includes activation of the actuator or solenoid when it receives an actual or simulated signal.

A.13.4.4.2.12 Methods of recording maintenance include tags attached at each riser, records retained at each building, and records retained at one building in a complex.

A.13.4.4.3.3 Suitable facilities should be provided to dispose of drained water. Low points equipped with a single valve should be drained as follows:

(1) Open the low-point drain valve slowly.
(2) Close the drain valve as soon as water ceases to discharge, and allow time for additional accumulation above the valve.
(3) Repeat this procedure until water ceases to discharge.
(4) Replace plug or nipple and cap as necessary.

Low points equipped with dual valves should be drained as follows:

(1) Close the upper valve.
(2) Open the lower valve, and drain the accumulated water.
(3) Close the lower valve, open the upper valve, and allow time for additional water accumulation.

(4) Repeat this procedure until water ceases to discharge.
(5) Replace plug or nipple and cap in lower valve.

Removing water from a preaction system is an essential part of a good maintenance program. Failure to keep these systems free of water can result in damage and expensive repairs to both the system and the building. A program for monitoring the condition of the system and the operation of the auxiliary drains should be instituted. Auxiliary drains should be operated on a daily basis after a system operation until several days pass with no discharge of water from the drain valve. Thereafter, it might be possible to decrease the frequency to weekly or longer intervals depending on the volume of water discharged. Likewise, when preparing for cold weather, the auxiliary drains should be operated daily, with the frequency of operation decreasing depending on the discharge of accumulated water. In many cases, the frequency of the operation can decrease significantly if a system is shown to be dry.

A.13.4.5.2.1 High priming water levels can affect the operation of supervisory air or nitrogen pressure maintenance devices. Test the water level as follows:

(1) Open the priming level test valve.
(2) If water flows, drain it.
(3) Close the valve when water stops flowing and air discharges.
(4) If air discharges when the valve is opened, the priming water level could be too low. To add priming water, refer to the manufacturer's instructions.

△ **A.13.4.5.2.2** Dry pipe valves should be trip tested in the spring to allow time before the onset of cold weather for all water that has entered the system or condensation to drain to low points or back to the valve.

A.13.4.5.2.2.2 A full flow trip test generally requires at least two individuals, one of whom is situated at the dry pipe valve while the other is at the inspector's test. If possible, they should be in communication with each other. A full flow trip test is conducted as follows:

(1) The main drain valve is fully opened to clean any accumulated scale or foreign material from the supply water piping. The main drain valve then is closed.
(2) The system air or nitrogen pressure and the supply water pressure are recorded.
(3) The system air or nitrogen pressure is relieved by opening the inspector's test valve completely. Concurrent with opening the valve, both testers start their stopwatches. If two-way communication is not available, the tester at the dry valve is to react to the start of downward movement on the air pressure gauge.
(4) Testers at the dry pipe valve note the air pressure at which the valve trips and note the tripping time.
(5) Testers at the inspector's test note the time at which water flows steadily from the test connection. This time is noted for comparison purposes to previous tests and is not meant to be a specific pass/fail criterion. Note that NFPA 13 does not require water delivery in 60 seconds for all systems.
(6) When clean water flows, the test is terminated by closing the system control valve.
(7) The air or nitrogen pressure and the time elapsed are to be recorded as follows:

    (a) From the complete opening of the test valve to the tripping of the valve

    (b) From the complete opening of inspector's valve to the start of steady flow from the test connection

(8) All low-point drains are opened and then closed when water ceases to flow.
(9) The dry pipe valve and quick-opening device are reset, if installed, in accordance with the manufacturer's instructions, and the system is returned to service.

For dry pipe systems that were designed and installed using either a manual demonstration or a computer calculation to simulate multiple openings to predict water delivery time, a full flow trip test from a single inspector's test connection should have been conducted during the original system acceptance and a full flow trip test from the single inspector's test should continue to be conducted every 3 years. The system is not required to achieve water delivery to the inspector's test connection in 60 seconds, but comparison to the water delivery time during the original acceptance will determine if there is a problem with the system.

A.13.4.5.2.2.3 A partial flow trip test is conducted in the following manner:

(1) Fully open the main drain valve to clean any accumulated scale or foreign material from the supply water piping.
(2) Close the control valve to the point where additional closure cannot provide flow through the entire area of the drain outlet.
(3) Close the valve controlling flow to the device if a quick-opening device is installed.
(4) Record the system air or nitrogen pressure and the supply water pressure.
(5) Relieve system air or nitrogen pressure by opening the priming level test valve or the inspector's test valve.
(6) Note and record the air or nitrogen pressure, and supply water pressure when the dry pipe valve trips.
(7) Immediately close the system control valve, and open the main drain valve to minimize the amount of water entering the system piping.
(8) Trip test the quick-opening device, if installed, in accordance with the manufacturer's instructions.
(9) Open all low point drains, and close them when water ceases to flow.
(10) Reset the dry pipe valve and quick-opening device, if installed, in accordance with the manufacturer's instructions, and return the system to service.

CAUTION: A partial flow trip test does not provide a high enough rate of flow to latch the clappers of some dry pipe valve models in the open position. When resetting such valves, check that the latching equipment is operative.

△ **A.13.4.5.2.4** Except when a full flow trip test is conducted in accordance with A.13.4.5.2.2.2, a quick-opening device should be tested in the following manner:

(1) Close the system control valve
(2) Open the main drain valve, and keep it in the open position
(3) Verify that the quick-opening device control valve is open
(4) Open the inspector's test valve. (Note that a burst of air from the device indicates that it has tripped)
(5) Close the device's control valve
(6) Return the device to service in accordance with the manufacturer's instructions and return the system to service

A.13.4.5.3.2 Removing water from a dry system is an essential part of a good maintenance program. Failure to keep the dry system free of water can result in damage and expensive repairs to both the system and building. A program for monitoring the condition of the system and the operation of the auxiliary drains should be instituted. Auxiliary drains should be operated on a daily basis after a dry sprinkler system operation until several days pass with no discharge of water from the drain valve. Thereafter, it might be possible to decrease the frequency to weekly or longer intervals depending on the volume of water discharged. Likewise, when preparing for cold weather, the auxiliary drains should be operated daily with the frequency of operation decreasing depending on the discharge of accumulated water. In many cases, the frequency of the operation can decrease significantly if a system is shown to be dry. A quick-opening device, if installed, should be removed temporarily from service prior to draining low points.

A.13.5.2.2 PRV devices can be bench tested in accordance with the manufacturer's instructions or tested in place. To test in place, a gauge is connected on both the inlet side and the outlet side of the device, and flow readings are taken using a Pitot tube or a flowmeter. Water is discharged through a roof manifold, if available, or through hose to the exterior of the building. Another acceptable method for systems having at least two risers is to take one standpipe out of service and use it as a drain by removing PRV devices and attaching hoses at the outlets near the ground floor level. When testing in this manner, a flowmeter should be used and a hose line utilized to connect the riser being tested and the drain riser.

Readings are to be compared to the system's hydraulic demands at the test location. Field-adjustable valves are to be reset in accordance with manufacturer's instructions. Nonadjustable valves should be replaced. Extreme caution should be exercised because of the high pressure involved when testing.

A.13.5.4.1(1) Pressures downstream of the master PRV should not exceed the maximum pressure rating of the system components.

A.13.5.4.2 The partial flow test of the master PRV can be performed during the quarterly main drain test. *(See 13.2.3.2.)*

A.13.6.2.1 Hose valves can be tested without a full flow if the cap is left on the hose threads. The purpose of this requirement is to exercise the valve so it can be operated easily.

A.13.6.2.2 See A.13.6.2.1.

A.13.7.1.3 Where annual maintenance includes an internal inspection performed by a qualified person, this requirement is satisfied.

A.13.7.2.1 The full flow test of the backflow prevention valve can be performed with a test header or other connections downstream of the valve. A bypass around the check valve in the fire department connection line with a control valve in the normally closed position can be an acceptable arrangement. When flow to a visible drain cannot be accomplished, closed loop flow can be acceptable if a flowmeter or sight glass is incorporated into the system to ensure flow.

A.13.8.1(9) It is not the intent of this section for all fire department connection piping to be inspected for obstructions but only the interior of the connection itself.

A.13.10.3(2) Nitrogen generator might have to switch from maintain mode to fill mode to meet the restoration time.

A.13.11.3 Design review is outside the scope of this standard.

A.14.1 For obstruction investigation and prevention, see Annex D.

A.14.2.1 It is the intent of 14.2.1 to provide a reasonable assurance that corrosion and obstruction issues within fire protection systems are identified. It is not the intent to require verification that every piece of pipe in the system is free from corrosion and obstructions. An assessment of the internal condition of piping can be accomplished by several methods that meet the intent of this section. These methods include the following:

(1) Fire sprinkler systems, foam systems, and water mist systems as follows:

   (a) Opening a flushing connection at the end of one main and removing the end fitting or piece of branch line or a sprinkler for the purpose of inspecting for the presence of foreign organic and inorganic material, including the following:

      i. In dry pipe systems and preaction systems, the branch line inspected should be the most remote one from the source of water that is not equipped with the inspector's test valve.

      ii. When performing normal maintenance that involves draining down a system to modify a system such as for tenant fit out or building renovations, or when removing or replacing piping, this inspection can be performed as described and properly recorded at that time. The time interval would then start for the next assessment of that system at the frequency determined by 14.2.1.1 or 14.2.1.2.

      iii. When possible, investigative work should be focused at those areas most prone to experiencing accelerated corrosion rates. These areas include high points of wet systems where trapped air accumulates, low points of dry and preaction systems where water will be trapped, and any bulk piping that sees frequent high volume flow of fresh water (i.e., bulk supply piping near a fire pump).

      iv. If a sprinkler is removed to perform this inspection, 5.4.1.1 requires a new sprinkler matching the characteristics of the replaced sprinkler.

   (b) Utilizing alternative examination methods such as the following:

      i. Using video inspection equipment that is inserted into the system at strategic points to observe the internal condition of pipes. This equipment provides a visual exam of the pipes using a camera and lighting system on the end of a push cable. Video inspection equipment can be inserted in alarm, dry, and preaction valves for a look into risers, feed mains, some cross mains, and some branch lines, depending on the system configuration. The push cable can also be inserted in a check valve when performing the 5-year internal inspection required by 13.4.2.1 to view additional areas of a system, and in the fire department connection to perform the interior inspection required by 13.8.3.

ii. Ultrasonic or similar technology that allows the pipe wall to be tested to determine the extent of any deterioration due to microbiologically influenced corrosion (MIC) or other forms of corrosion. This method would not typically be used for the internal inspection of piping required by this section because it might not detect the presence of solid material in the piping, such as wood, plastic, or other foreign obstructions, that are not a by-product of corrosion, because only small representative sections of pipe are examined.

iii. A laboratory analysis of water samples obtained from the fire protection system, combined with collecting and inspecting solid material from fire protection system water discharged from a main drain, and an inspector's test connection, can provide an indication of the presence of corrosion, MIC, and/or foreign materials. If a high level of MIC is identified, or if a significant amount of foreign materials is found, further investigation might be warranted to verify the extent of corrosion, MIC, or other obstructions in the system. The solid materials should be collected with an appropriately sized strainer. If inspection of the solid materials identifies excessive rust, black water color, or sulfur (i.e., rotten egg) odors, an obstruction investigation as described in Section 14.3 is warranted.

iv. A laboratory analysis of a pipe sample taken from a system location most prone to experiencing accelerated corrosion rates can identify the root-cause of metal loss that has occurred and provide the building owner quantifiable data on the severity of the metal loss. This information would allow corrective action to be taken before the development of failures (i.e., leaks) in the system occur. Such locations include high points of wet systems where trapped air accumulates, low points of dry and preaction systems where water will be trapped, and any bulk piping that sees frequent high-volume flow of fresh water (i.e., bulk supply piping near a fire pump).

(2) Standpipe and hose systems as follows:

(a) Opening a flushing connection or fitting at the end of one main, removing a remote hose connection fitting, and removing the end fitting of horizontal branch line (if present) for the purpose of inspecting for the presence of foreign organic and inorganic material, including the following:

i. When performing normal maintenance that involves draining down a system to modify a system such as for tenant fit out or building renovations, or when removing or replacing piping, this inspection can be performed as described and properly recorded at that time. The time interval would then start for the next assessment of that system at the frequency determined by 14.2.1.1 or 14.2.1.2.

(b) Utilizing alternative examination methods such as the following:

i. Using video inspection equipment that is inserted into the system at strategic points to observe the internal condition of pipes. This equipment provides a visual exam of the pipes using a camera and lighting system on the end of a push cable. Video inspection equipment can be inserted in valves for a look into risers, feed mains, some cross mains, and some branch lines, depending on the system configuration. The push cable can also be inserted in a check valve when performing the 5-year internal inspection required by 13.4.2.1 to view additional areas of a system, and in the fire department connection to perform the interior inspection required by 13.8.3.

ii. Ultrasonic or similar technology that allows the pipe wall to be tested to determine the extent of any deterioration due to microbiologically influenced corrosion (MIC) or other forms of corrosion. This method would not typically be used for the internal inspection of piping required by this section because it might not detect the presence of solid material in the piping, such as wood, plastic, or other foreign obstructions, that are not a by-product of corrosion, because only small representative sections of pipe are examined.

iii. A laboratory analysis of water samples obtained from the fire protection system, combined with collecting and inspecting solid material from fire protection system water discharged from a main drain, and an inspector's test connection, can provide an indication of the presence of corrosion, MIC, and/or foreign materials. If a high level of MIC is identified, or if a significant amount of foreign materials is found, further investigation might be warranted to verify the extent of corrosion, MIC, or other obstructions in the system. The solid materials should be collected with an appropriately sized strainer. If inspection of the solid materials identifies excessive rust, black water color, or sulfur (i.e., rotten egg) odors, an obstruction investigation as described in Section 14.3 is warranted.

iv. A laboratory analysis of a pipe sample taken from a system location most prone to experiencing accelerated corrosion rates can identify the root-cause of metal loss that has occurred and provide the building owner quantifiable data on the severity of the metal loss. This information would allow corrective action to be taken before the development of failures (i.e., leaks) in the system occur.

(3) Private fire service mains, as follows:

(a) Opening an accessible point on one main for the purpose of inspecting for the presence of foreign organic and inorganic material, including the following:

i. When performing normal maintenance that involves draining down a system to modify a system such as for tenant fit out or building renovations, or when removing or replacing piping, this inspection can be performed as described and properly recorded at that time. The time interval would then start for the next assessment of that system at the frequency determined by 14.2.1.1 or 14.2.1.2

(b) Utilizing alternative examination methods such as the following:

i. Using video inspection equipment that is inserted into the system at strategic points to observe the internal condition of pipes. This equipment provides a visual exam of the pipes using a camera and lighting system on the end of a push cable. Video inspection equipment can be inserted in alarm, dry, and preaction valves for a look into the private main depending on the system configuration. The push cable can also be inserted in a check valve when performing the 5-year internal inspection required by 13.4.2.1 to view additional areas of a system, and in the fire department connection to perform the interior inspection required by 13.8.3.

ii. Ultrasonic or similar technology that allows the pipe wall to be tested to determine the extent of any deterioration due to microbiologically influenced corrosion (MIC) or other forms of corrosion. This method would not typically be used for the internal inspection of piping required by this section because it might not detect the presence of solid material in the piping, such as wood, plastic, or other foreign obstructions, that are not a byproduct of corrosion, because only small representative sections of pipe are examined.

iii. A laboratory analysis of water samples obtained from the fire protection system, combined with collecting and inspecting solid material from fire protection system water discharged from a main drain, and an inspector's test connection, can provide an indication of the presence of corrosion, MIC, and/or foreign materials. If a high level of MIC is identified, or if a significant amount of foreign materials is found, further investigation might be warranted to verify the extent of corrosion, MIC, or other obstructions in the system. The solid materials should be collected with an appropriately sized strainer. If inspection of the solid materials identifies excessive rust, black water color, or sulfur (i.e., rotten egg) odors, an obstruction investigation as described in Section 14.3 is warranted.

iv. A laboratory analysis of a pipe sample taken from a system location most prone to experiencing accelerated corrosion rates can identify the root-cause of metal loss that has occurred and provide the building owner quantifiable data on the severity of the metal loss. This information would allow corrective action to be taken before the development of failures (i.e., leaks) in the system occur.

A.14.2.1.2 The purpose of the assessment of the internal condition of piping is to identify whether foreign organic and inorganic material is present, since the presence of such material can potentially be detrimental to the performance of the sprinkler system. Corrosion, which includes general corrosion as well as microbiologically influenced corrosion (MIC), can be prevalent in sprinkler piping, but not necessarily in all systems, buildings, or geographic locations. Therefore, the risk analysis should be based upon evidence noted and/or data obtained from proximate sprinkler systems, known problems from the water supply, as well as other factors that could affect the integrity of the system piping such as the use of nitrogen generators on dry and preaction systems and nitrogen inerting with vents on wet systems. The decision of when, how often, and which method to use to conduct an assessment should also consider the risk of emptying and refilling the sprinkler system with water, which could adversely impact the sprinkler system by introducing foreign or inorganic material into the sprinkler system.

A.14.2.1.4 Most piping systems contain some foreign material or other evidence of corrosion but not sufficient to trigger an obstruction investigation. Furthermore, an internal inspection is primarily an inspection for determining corrosion of the pipe, but it can result in finding the presence of material that would be an obstruction to piping or sprinklers. If such is found, an obstruction investigation in Section 14.3 would be required.

A.14.2.2 In large warehouses, high-rise buildings, and other buildings having multiple systems, it is reasonable to perform the assessment on half of the systems, and conclude that these are representative of all systems in the building. The systems in the building not assessed during one frequency cycle should be assessed during the next one. As long as there is no evidence of any foreign organic and/or inorganic material found in any of the systems being assessed, every other system would be assessed once every frequency cycle. However, if foreign organic and/or inorganic material is found in any system in the building during the frequency cycle, all systems must would then be assessed during that frequency cycle.

A.14.3.1 Most piping systems contain some foreign material or other evidence of corrosion but not sufficient to trigger an obstruction investigation. Furthermore, an internal inspection is primarily an inspection for determining corrosion of the pipe, but it can result in finding the presence of material that would be an obstruction to piping or sprinklers. If such is found, an obstruction investigation in Section 14.3 would be required. For obstruction investigation procedures, see Section D.3. The type of obstruction investigation should be appropriately selected based on the observed condition. For instance, ordering an internal obstruction investigation would be inappropriate where the observed condition was broken public mains in the vicinity. On the other hand, such an investigation would be appropriate where foreign materials are observed in the dry pipe valve.

A.14.3.2 For obstruction prevention program recommendations, see Section D.4.

A.14.3.2.2 The indicated locations are presented as the minimum basis for determining the need for the initiation of a more extensive obstruction investigation effort. Additional points of examination can be appropriately dictated to assess the extent and severity of the obstructing material as determined by the observed conditions at these locations. See Section D.3 for further discussion.

△ A.14.3.2.3 Alternative examination methods can include the following:

(1) Using video inspection equipment that is inserted into the system at strategic points to observe the internal condition of pipes. This equipment provides a visual exam of the pipes using a camera and lighting system on the end of a push cable. Video inspection equipment can be inserted in alarm, dry, and preaction valves, in the risers, and into cross mains and branch lines, depending on the system configuration. This equipment can also be used to determine the results of any flushing that was performed.

(2) Ultrasonic or similar technology that allows the pipe wall to be externally tested to determine the extent of any deterioration due to MIC or other forms of corrosion. This method has advantages, including allowing the system to be left in service while performing the examination and pinpointing where pipes are about to fail before the actual failure occurs, allowing preventive action to be taken. This technology does have its limitations, and to be thorough all pipes would require access, even those in concealed spaces such as those above ceilings. This technology can detect the presence of a buildup of sludge, scale, or other by-products of corrosion, but cannot quantify the severity of the potential obstruction. It can detect existing air pockets in wet systems as well as trapped sections of pipe in dry systems that aren't adequately drained. This technology cannot determine the corrosion mechanisms responsible for pipe damage, but can determine the severity of the metal loss. In most cases this technology will not detect the presence of solid material in the piping such as wood, plastic, or other foreign obstructions that are not a by-product of corrosion, because only small representative sections of pipe are examined.

A.14.3.3 For obstruction investigation flushing procedures, see Section D.5.

A.15.3.1 A clearly visible tag alerts building occupants and the fire department that all or part of the water-based fire protection system is out of service. The tag should be weather resistant, plainly visible, and of sufficient size [typically 4 in. × 6 in. (100 mm × 150 mm)]. The tag should identify which system is impaired, the date and time impairment began, and the person responsible. Figure A.15.3.1 illustrates a typical impairment tag.

A.15.3.2 An impairment tag should be placed on the fire department connection to alert responding fire fighters of an abnormal condition. An impairment tag that is located on the system riser only could go unnoticed for an extended period if fire fighters encounter difficulty in gaining access to the building or sprinkler control room.

A.15.5 The need for temporary fire protection, termination of all hazardous operations, and frequency of inspections in the areas involved should be determined. All work possible should be done in advance to minimize the length of the impairment. Where possible, temporary feedlines should be used to maintain portions of systems while work is completed.

Water-based fire protection systems should not be removed from service when the building is not in use. Where a system that has been out of service for a prolonged period, such as in the case of idle or vacant properties, is returned to service,

FIGURE A.15.3.1　Sample Impairment Tag.

qualified personnel should be retained to inspect and test the systems.

A.15.5.2(4)(b) A fire watch should consist of trained personnel who continuously patrol the affected area. Ready access to fire extinguishers and the ability to promptly notify the fire department are important items to consider. During the patrol of the area, the person should not only be looking for fire, but making sure that the other fire protection features of the building such as egress routes and alarm systems are available and functioning properly.

A.15.5.2(4)(c) Temporary water supplies are possible from a number of sources, including use of a large-diameter hose from a fire hydrant to a fire department connection, use of a portable tank and a portable pump, or use of a standby fire department pumper and/or tanker.

A.15.5.2(4)(d) Depending on the use and occupancy of the building, it could be enough in some circumstances to stop certain processes in the building or to cut off the flow of fuel to some machines. It is also helpful to implement "No Smoking" and "No Hot Work" (cutting, grinding, or welding) policies while the system is out of service because these activities are responsible for many fire ignitions.

A.15.6 Emergency impairments include, but are not limited to, system leakage, interruption of water supply, frozen or ruptured piping, equipment failure, or other impairments found during inspection, testing, or maintenance activities.

Shaded text = Revisions.　△ = Text deletions and figure/table revisions.　• = Section deletions.　**N** = New material.

A.15.6.2 When one or more impairments are discovered during inspection, testing, and maintenance activities, the owner or owner's authorized representative should be notified in writing. See Figure A.15.6.2 for an example of written notification.

A.15.7 Occasionally, fire protection systems in idle or vacant buildings are shut off and drained. When the equipment is eventually restored to service after a long period of not being maintained, it is recommended that qualified personnel or a qualified contractor perform the work. The following is an example of a procedure:

(1) All piping should be traced from the extremities of the system to the main connections with a careful check for blank gaskets in flanges, closed valves, corroded or damaged sprinklers, nozzles, or piping, insecure or missing hangers, and insufficient support. Proper repairs or adjustments should be made, and needed extensions or alterations for the equipment should be completed.

(2) An air test at low pressure (40 psi) should be conducted prior to allowing water to fill the system. When the piping has been proven tight by passing the air test, water can be introduced slowly into the system, with proper precautions against damage by escape of water from previously undiscovered defects. When the system has been filled under normal service pressure, drain valve tests should be made to detect any closed valve that possibly could have

been overlooked. All available pipes should be flushed, and an obstruction investigation completed to make sure that the system is clear of debris.

(3) Where the system was known to have been damaged by freezing or where other extensive damage might have occurred, a full hydrostatic test can be performed in accordance with NFPA 13 to determine whether the system integrity has been maintained.

(4) Dry pipe valves, quick-opening devices, alarm valves, and all alarm connections should be examined, put in proper condition, and tested.

(5) Fire pumps, pressure and gravity tanks, reservoirs, and other water supply equipment should receive proper attention before being placed in service. Each supply should be tested separately and then together if they are designed to work together.

(6) All control valves should be operated from the closed to fully open position and should be left sealed, locked, or equipped with a tamper switch.

A.16.1.1.1 There are numerous NFPA documents that have special requirements for the inspection, testing, and maintenance of water-based fire protection systems that are different from those in NFPA 25. In many cases those documents reference NFPA 25 and could have either more stringent or even less stringent requirements than those in NFPA 25.

A.16.1.1.2 These requirements are not written by or able to be amended by the technical committee of this standard, and therefore the text is an extract from the document that has the requirements.

Annex B   Forms and Reports for Inspection, Testing, and Maintenance

This annex is not a part of the requirements of this NFPA document but is included for informational purposes only.

B.1 General. Forms need to be complete with respect to the requirements of NFPA 25 for the system being inspected, tested, or maintained, or any combination thereof. Because water-based fire protection systems comprise many components, it could be necessary to complete more than one form for each system. Reports translate the results of the inspection, testing, and maintenance process to the building owner and the authority having jurisdiction where applicable. The inspection form could also serve as the inspection report if the form contains the information suggested by the report guidance in Section B.4.

Authorities having jurisdiction are legitimately concerned that the forms used are comprehensive. Therefore, they could develop their own forms or utilize those already developed and reviewed by their jurisdiction.

B.2 Inspection, Testing, and Maintenance Forms. At least five formats can be used and are described as follows:

(1) One form in which all requirements for NFPA 25 are specified and large sections of information do not apply to most systems

(2) Individual forms that provide requirements corresponding to each chapter of NFPA 25 and address the following:

(a) Sprinkler systems

(b) Standpipe systems

(c) Private fire service mains

IMPAIRMENT NOTICE

DURING A RECENT INSPECTION OF YOUR FIRE PROTECTION SYSTEM(S), AN **EMERGENCY IMPAIRMENT** WAS DISCOVERED AND INDICATED ON THE INSPECTION REPORT. AS DEFINED BY NFPA 25, AN **EMERGENCY IMPAIRMENT** IS "A CONDITION WHERE A WATER-BASED FIRE PROTECTION SYSTEM OR PORTION THEREOF IS OUT OF ORDER DUE TO AN UNEXPECTED OCCURRENCE, SUCH AS A RUPTURED PIPE, OPERATED SPRINKLER, OR AN INTERRUPTION OF WATER SUPPLY TO THE SYSTEM." NFPA 25 FURTHER STATES, "EMERGENCY IMPAIRMENTS INCLUDE BUT ARE NOT LIMITED TO SYSTEM LEAKAGE, INTERRUPTION OF WATER SUPPLY, FROZEN OR RUPTURED PIPING, AND EQUIPMENT FAILURE."

WE RECOMMEND THAT IMMEDIATE STEPS BE TAKEN, AS DESCRIBED IN THE ATTACHED COPY OF CHAPTER 15 OF NFPA 25, TO CORRECT THE FOLLOWING IMPAIRMENT(S) TO YOUR FIRE PROTECTION SYSTEM(S):

❏ CONTROL VALVE SHUT. SYSTEM OUT OF SERVICE.
❏ LOW WATER PRESSURE DURING FLOW TEST. POSSIBLE OBSTRUCTION IN WATER SUPPLY OR PARTIALLY SHUT VALVE.
❏ PIPE(S) FROZEN.
❏ PIPE(S) LEAKING.
❏ PIPE(S) ARE OBSTRUCTED.
❏ SYSTEM PIPING OR PORTIONS OF SYSTEM PIPING ARE DISCONNECTED.
❏ FIRE DEPT. CONNECTION MISSING OR DAMAGED OR OBSTRUCTED.
❏ DRY PIPE VALVE CANNOT BE RESET.
❏ DRY PIPE SYSTEM QUICK-OPENING DEVICE IS OUT OF SERVICE.
❏ SPRINKLERS ARE PAINTED, CORRODED, DAMAGED, OR LOADED.
❏ FIRE PUMP IS OUT OF SERVICE.
❏ DETECTION/ACTUATION SYSTEM IS OUT OF SERVICE.
❏ OTHER:_____

FIGURE A.15.6.2   Sample Impairment Notice.

(d) Fire pumps
(e) Storage tanks
(f) Water spray systems
(g) Foam-water sprinkler systems

(3) Forms that include information from the specific system chapter: Chapter 1, Chapter 13, and Chapter 14

(4) A series of forms similar to option (2) but with a more detailed breakdown of system types. For example, fire sprinkler systems are divided into the following five forms:

(a) Wet pipe fire sprinkler systems
(b) Dry pipe fire sprinkler systems
(c) Preaction fire sprinkler systems
(d) Deluge fire sprinkler systems
(e) Foam-water sprinkler systems

(5) Separate forms for each individual component of each fire protection system

B.3 Sample Forms. Sample forms are available for downloading at www.nfpa.org, www.nfsa.org, and www.firesprinkler.org. Additional forms might be available through commercial insurance carriers.

B.4 Recommendations for Inspection, Testing, and Maintenance Reports. Where reports are generated from the inspection, testing, and maintenance requirements of NFPA 25, consistent information should be included in the report. All inspection, testing, and maintenance reports developed for building owners and authorities having jurisdiction where applicable should include, at a minimum, the following information:

(1) Administrative information

(a) Name of property (if applicable)

i. Address, including city, state and zip code
ii. Name of property owner or designated representative
iii. Job title
iv. Voice phone
v. Fax
vi. Email address

(b) Inspection and testing organization/office locator

i. Address, including city, state and zip code
ii. Voice phone
iii. Fax

(c) Name of lead inspector performing inspection/testing
(d) Applicable licenses and certifications
(e) Start date of inspection/testing
(f) Completion date of inspection/testing
(g) Report issuance date

(2) Frequency of activity and summary of fire protection systems

(a) As defined in Section 3.6, the type of each water-based fire protection system being inspected, tested, or maintained should be recorded.
(b) For each system being inspected, tested, or maintained, the frequency of inspection, testing, and maintenance applicable for the inspection should be recorded consistent with Section 3.7.

(c) Where a premise being inspected, tested, or maintained has more than one type or multiples of one type of system, the number of each system inspected should also be recorded.

(3) Notifications for testing or maintenance

(a) If multiple notifications are required (e.g., to the fire department, authority having jurisdiction, and the alarm receiving facility), each notification should be recorded.
(b) The name of the property owner or designated representative who made the notification before testing or maintenance, the time notification was made, and to whom the notification was made should be recorded.
(c) The name of the property owner or designated representative who made the notification after testing or maintenance was completed, the time notification was made, and to whom the notification was made should be recorded.

(4) Impairments and deficiencies

(a) Forms and reports that are used for recording the activities and results of inspections, testing, and maintenance, should contain a section that specifically identifies any deficiencies and impairments that were observed. It is recommended that the section be clearly marked and formatted in a way that is easy for the property owner or the designated representative to identify each impairment and deficiency, and, if applicable, where the deficiencies and impairments are located. If required by the jurisdiction, impairments and deficiencies should be organized by classification, that is, critical, noncritical, or impairment.
(b) Where the authority having jurisdiction has mandated specific requirements regarding timelines for addressing deficiencies, it is helpful to include these in the reporting format. For many deficiencies, it is beneficial to attach a photograph or digital image of the deficiency, particularly where the property owner or the designated representative is not familiar with the water-based fire protection system.
(c) Where an impairment is found while performing inspection, testing, and maintenance, the property owner or designated representative should be notified in writing. *(See A.15.6.2.)*

(5) Signatures section

(a) Signature of property owner or designated representative
(b) Signature of lead inspector

i. It is recommended that signatures for the lead inspector and property owner, or their designated representatives, be placed at the end of the report. Placing signatures at the end of the report indicates that all activities in the preceding sections of the report have been performed and their completion has been verified by the property owner or designated representative.

Annex C   Possible Causes of Pump Troubles

This annex is not a part of the requirements of this NFPA document but is included for informational purposes only.

This annex is extracted from NFPA 20.

C.1 Causes of Pump Troubles. This annex contains a partial guide for locating pump troubles and their possible causes *(see Figure C.1)*. It also contains a partial list of suggested remedies. *(For other information on this subject, see Hydraulic Institute Standards for Centrifugal, Rotary and Reciprocating Pumps.)* The causes listed here are in addition to possible mechanical breakage that would be obvious on visual inspection. In case of trouble, it is suggested that those troubles that can be inspected easily should be corrected first or eliminated as possibilities.

C.1.1 Air Drawn into Suction Connection Through Leak(s). Air drawn into suction line through leaks causes a pump to lose suction or fail to maintain its discharge pressure. Uncover suction pipe and locate and repair leak(s).

C.1.2 Suction Connection Obstructed. Examine suction intake, screen, and suction pipe and remove obstruction. Repair or provide screens to prevent recurrence.

C.1.3 Air Pocket in Suction Pipe. Air pockets cause a reduction in delivery and pressure similar to an obstructed pipe. Uncover suction pipe and rearrange to eliminate pocket.

C.1.4 Well Collapsed or Serious Misalignment. Consult a reliable well drilling company and the pump manufacturer regarding recommended repairs.

Column legend for Figure C.1:

Suction
1. Air drawn into suction connection through leak(s)
2. Suction connection obstructed
3. Air pocket in suction pipe
4. Well collapsed or serious misalignment

Pump
5. Stuffing box too tight or packing improperly installed, worn, defective, too tight, or incorrect type
6. Water seal or pipe to seal obstructed
7. Air leak into pump through stuffing boxes
8. Impeller obstructed
9. Wearing rings worn
10. Impeller damaged
11. Wrong diameter impeller
12. Actual net head lower than rated
13. Casing gasket defective, permitting internal leakage (single-stage and multistage pumps)
14. Pressure gauge is on top of pump casing
15. Incorrect impeller adjustment (vertical shaft turbine-type pump only)
16. Impellers locked
17. Pump is frozen
18. Pump shaft or shaft sleeve scored, bent, or worn
19. Pump not primed
20. Seal ring improperly located in stuffing box, preventing water from entering space to form seal

Driver and/or Pump
21. Excess bearing friction due to lack of lubrication, wear, dirt, rusting, failure, or improper installation
22. Rotating element binds against stationary element
23. Pump and driver misaligned
24. Foundation not rigid
25. Engine-cooling system obstructed

Driver
26. Faulty driver
27. Lack of lubrication
28. Speed too low
29. Wrong direction of rotation
30. Speed too high
31. Rated motor voltage different from line voltage
32. Faulty electrical circuit, obstructed fuel system obstructed steam pipe, or dead battery

Fire pump troubles	1	2	3	4	5	6	7	8	9	10	11	12	13	14	15	16	17	18	19	20	21	22	23	24	25	26	27	28	29	30	31	32
Excessive leakage at stuffing box					X													X					X									
Pump or driver overheats			X		X	X		X			X				X			X	X	X	X	X	X	X	X		X		X	X	X	
Pump unit will not start			X		X										X	X	X				X					X	X					X
No water discharge	X	X	X					X											X													
Pump is noisy or vibrates			X		X			X		X								X			X	X	X	X			X					
Too much power required			X		X			X	X		X		X		X			X			X	X	X	X			X		X	X	X	
Discharge pressure not constant for same gpm	X				X	X	X																									
Pump loses suction after starting	X	X	X			X	X															X										
Insufficient water discharge	X	X	X		X			X	X	X	X	X	X		X													X	X		X	
Discharge pressure too low for gpm discharge	X	X	X		X			X	X	X	X	X	X	X														X	X		X	

FIGURE C.1   Possible Causes of Fire Pump Troubles.

C.1.5 Stuffing Box Too Tight or Packing Improperly Installed, Worn, Defective, Too Tight, or of Incorrect Type. Loosen gland swing bolts and remove stuffing box gland halves. Replace packing.

C.1.6 Water Seal or Pipe to Seal Obstructed. Loosen gland swing bolt and remove stuffing box gland halves along with the water seal ring and packing. Clean the water passage to and in the water seal ring. Replace water seal ring, packing gland, and packing in accordance with manufacturer's instructions.

C.1.7 Air Leak into Pump Through Stuffing Boxes. Same as possible cause in C.1.6.

C.1.8 Impeller Obstructed. Does not show on any one instrument, but pressures fall off rapidly when an attempt is made to draw a large amount of water.

For horizontal split-case pumps, remove upper case of pump and remove obstruction from impeller. Repair or provide screens on suction intake to prevent recurrence.

For vertical shaft turbine-type pumps, lift out column pipe and pump bowls from wet pit or well and disassemble pump bowl to remove obstruction from impeller.

For close-coupled, vertical in-line pumps, lift motor on top pull-out design and remove obstruction from impeller.

C.1.9 Wearing Rings Worn. Remove upper case and insert feeler gauge between case wearing ring and impeller wearing ring. Clearance when new is 0.0075 in. (0.19 mm). Clearances of more than 0.015 in. (0.38 mm) are excessive.

C.1.10 Impeller Damaged. Make minor repairs or return to manufacturer for replacement. If defect is not too serious, order new impeller and use damaged one until replacement arrives.

C.1.11 Wrong Diameter Impeller. Replace with impeller of proper diameter.

C.1.12 Actual Net Head Lower than Rated. Check impeller diameter and number and pump model number to make sure correct head curve is being used.

C.1.13 Casing Gasket Defective, Permitting Internal Leakage (Single-Stage and Multistage Pumps). Replace defective gasket. Check manufacturer's drawing to see whether gasket is required.

C.1.14 Pressure Gauge Is on Top of Pump Casing. Place gauges in correct location.

C.1.15 Incorrect Impeller Adjustment (Vertical Shaft Turbine-Type Pump Only). Adjust impellers according to manufacturer's instructions.

C.1.16 Impellers Locked. For vertical shaft turbine-type pumps, raise and lower impellers by the top shaft adjusting nut. If this adjustment is not successful, follow the manufacturer's instructions.

For horizontal split-case pumps, remove upper case and locate and eliminate obstruction.

C.1.17 Pump Is Frozen. Provide heat in the pump room. Disassemble pump and remove ice as necessary. Examine parts carefully for damage.

C.1.18 Pump Shaft or Shaft Sleeve Scored, Bent, or Worn. Replace shaft or shaft sleeve.

C.1.19 Pump Not Primed. If a pump is operated without water in its casing, the wearing rings are likely to seize. The first warning is a change in pitch of the sound of the driver. Shut down the pump.

For vertical shaft turbine-type pumps, check water level to determine whether pump bowls have proper submergence.

C.1.20 Seal Ring Improperly Located in Stuffing Box, Preventing Water from Entering Space to Form Seal. Loosen gland swing bolt and remove stuffing box gland halves along with the water-seal ring and packing. Replace, putting seal ring in proper location.

C.1.21 Excess Bearing Friction Due to Lack of Lubrication, Wear, Dirt, Rusting, Failure, or Improper Installation. Remove bearings and clean, lubricate, or replace as necessary.

C.1.22 Rotating Element Binds Against Stationary Element. Inspect clearances and lubrication and replace or repair the defective part.

C.1.23 Pump and Driver Misaligned. Shaft running off center because of worn bearings or misalignment. Align pump and driver according to manufacturer's instructions. Replace bearings according to manufacturer's instructions.

C.1.24 Foundation Not Rigid. Tighten foundation bolts or replace foundation if necessary.

C.1.25 Engine-Cooling System Obstructed. Heat exchanger or cooling water systems too small. Cooling pump faulty. Remove thermostats. Open bypass around regulator valve and strainer. Inspect regulator valve operation. Inspect strainer. Clean and repair if necessary. Disconnect sections of cooling system to locate and remove possible obstruction. Adjust engine-cooling water-circulating pump belt to obtain proper speed without binding. Lubricate bearings of this pump.

If overheating still occurs at loads up to 150 percent of rated capacity, contact pump or engine manufacturer so that necessary steps can be taken to eliminate overheating.

C.1.26 Faulty Driver. Inspect electric motor, internal combustion engine, or steam turbine, in accordance with manufacturer's instructions, to locate reason for failure to start.

C.1.27 Lack of Lubrication. If parts have seized, replace damaged parts and provide proper lubrication. If not, stop pump and provide proper lubrication.

C.1.28 Speed Too Low. For electric motor drive, confirm that rated motor speed corresponds to rated speed of pump, voltage is correct, and starting equipment is operating properly.

Low frequency and low voltage in the electric power supply prevent a motor from running at rated speed. Low voltage can be due to excessive loads and inadequate feeder capacity or (with private generating plants) low generator voltage. The generator voltage of private generating plants can be corrected by changing the field excitation. When low voltage is from the other causes mentioned, it can be necessary to replace transformer taps or increase feeder capacity.

Low frequency usually occurs with a private generating plant and should be corrected at the source. Low speed can result in older type squirrel-cage-type motors if fastenings of copper bars to end rings become loose. The remedy is to weld or braze these joints.

For steam turbine drive, confirm that valves in steam supply pipe are wide open; boiler steam pressure is adequate; steam pressure is adequate at the turbine; strainer in the steam supply pipe is not plugged; steam supply pipe is of adequate size; condensate is removed from steam supply pipe, trap, and turbine; turbine nozzles are not plugged; and setting of speed and emergency governor is correct.

For internal combustion engine drive, confirm that setting of speed governor is correct; hand throttle is opened wide; and there are no mechanical defects such as sticking valves, timing off, or spark plugs fouled, and so forth. The latter can require the services of a trained mechanic.

C.1.29 Wrong Direction of Rotation. Instances of an impeller turning backward are rare but are clearly recognizable by the extreme deficiency of pump delivery. Wrong direction of rotation can be determined by comparing the direction in which the flexible coupling is turning with the directional arrow on the pump casing.

With polyphase electric motor drive, two wires must be reversed; with dc driver, the armature connections must be reversed with respect to the field connections. Where two sources of electrical current are available, the direction of rotation produced by each should be inspected.

C.1.30 Speed Too High. See that pump- and driver-rated speed correspond. Replace electric motor with one of correct rated speed. Set governors of variable-speed drivers for correct speed. Frequency at private generating stations can be too high.

C.1.31 Rated Motor Voltage Different from Line Voltage. For example, a 220 or 440 V motor on 208 or 416 V line. Obtain motor of correct rated voltage or a larger size motor.

C.1.32 Faulty Electric Circuit, Obstructed Fuel System, Obstructed Steam Pipe, or Dead Battery. Inspect for break in wiring open switch, open circuit breaker, or dead battery. If circuit breaker in controller trips for no apparent reason, make sure oil is in dash pots in accordance with manufacturer's specifications. Make sure fuel pipe is clear, strainers are clean, and control valves open in fuel system to internal combustion engine. Make sure all valves are open and strainer is clean in steam line to turbine.

C.2 Warning. Chapters 6 and 7 of NFPA 20 include electrical requirements that discourage the installation of disconnect means in the power supply to electric motor–driven fire pumps. This requirement is intended to ensure the availability of power to the fire pumps. When equipment connected to those circuits is serviced or maintained, the employee can have unusual exposure to electrical and other hazards. It can be necessary to require special safe work practices and special safeguards, personal protective clothing, or both.

C.3 Maintenance of Fire Pump Controllers After Fault Condition.

C.3.1 Introduction. In a fire pump motor circuit that has been properly installed, coordinated, and in service prior to the fault, tripping of the circuit breaker or the isolating switch indicates a fault condition in excess of operating overload.

It is recommended that the following general procedures be observed by qualified personnel in the inspection and repair of the controller involved in the fault. These procedures are not intended to cover other elements of the circuit, such as wiring and motor, which can also require attention.

C.3.2 Caution. All inspections and tests are to be made on controllers that are de-energized at the line terminal, disconnected, locked out, and tagged so that accidental contact cannot be made with live parts and so that all plant safety procedures will be observed.

C.3.2.1 Enclosure. Where substantial damage to the enclosure, such as deformation, displacement of parts, or burning has occurred, replace the entire controller.

C.3.2.2 Circuit Breaker and Isolating Switch. Examine the enclosure interior, circuit breaker, and isolating switch for evidence of possible damage. If evidence of damage is not apparent, the circuit breaker and isolating switch can continue to be used after the door is closed.

If there is any indication that the circuit breaker has opened several short-circuit faults, or if signs of possible deterioration appear within either the enclosure, circuit breaker, or isolating switch (e.g., deposits on surface, surface discoloration, insulation cracking, or unusual toggle operation), replace the components. Verify that the external operating handle is capable of opening and closing the circuit breaker and isolating switch. If the handle fails to operate the device, this would also indicate the need for adjustment or replacement.

C.3.2.3 Terminals and Internal Conductors. Where there are indications of arcing damage, overheating, or both, such as discoloration and melting of insulation, replace the damaged parts.

C.3.2.4 Contactor. Replace contacts showing heat damage, displacement of metal, or loss of adequate wear allowance of the contacts. Replace the contact springs where applicable. If deterioration extends beyond the contacts, such as binding in the guides or evidence of insulation damage, replace the damaged parts or the entire contactor.

C.3.2.5 Return to Service. Before returning the controller to service, inspect for the tightness of electrical connections and for the absence of short circuits, ground faults, and leakage current.

Close and secure the enclosure before the controller circuit breaker and isolating switch are energized. Follow operating procedures on the controller to bring it into standby condition.

Annex D Obstruction Investigation

This annex is not a part of the requirements of this NFPA document but is included for informational purposes only.

D.1 General. For effective control and extinguishment of fire, automatic sprinklers should receive an unobstructed flow of water. Although the overall performance record of automatic sprinklers has been very satisfactory, there have been numerous instances of impaired efficiency because sprinkler piping or sprinklers were plugged with pipe scale, corrosion products, including those produced by microbiologically influenced corrosion, mud, stones, or other foreign material. If the first sprinklers to open in a fire are plugged, the fire in that area cannot be extinguished or controlled by prewetting of adjacent combustibles. In such a situation, the fire can grow to an uncontrollable size, resulting in greater fire damage and excessive sprinkler operation and even threatening the structural integrity of the building, depending on the number of plugged sprinklers and fire severity.

Keeping the inside of sprinkler system piping free of scale, silt, or other obstructing material is an integral part of an effective loss prevention program.

D.1.1 While this chapter provides minimum requirements for the investigation and prevention of obstructions, authorities having jurisdiction must also consider regional, local, and project-specific propensities and histories to determine reasonable testing and obstruction mitigation measures.

D.2 Obstruction Sources.

D.2.1 Pipe Scale. Loss studies have shown that dry pipe sprinkler systems are involved in the majority of obstructed sprinkler fire losses. Pipe scale was found to be the most frequent obstructing material (it is likely that some of the scale was composed of corrosion products, including those produced by microbiologically influenced corrosion). Dry pipe systems that have been maintained wet and then dry alternately over a period of years are particularly susceptible to the accumulation of scale. Also, in systems that are continuously dry, condensation of moisture in the air supply can result in the formation of a hard scale, microbiological materials, and corrosion products along the bottom of the piping. When sprinklers open, the scale is broken loose and carried along the pipe, plugging some of the sprinklers or forming obstructions at the fittings.

D.2.2 Careless Installation or Repair. Many obstructions are caused by careless workers during installation or repair of yard or public mains and sprinkler systems. Wood, paint brushes, buckets, gravel, sand, and gloves have been found as obstructions. In some instances, with welded sprinkler systems and systems with holes for quick-connect fittings, the cutout discs or coupons have been left within the piping, obstructing flow to sprinklers.

D.2.3 Raw Water Sources. Materials can be sucked up from the bottoms of rivers, ponds, or open reservoirs by fire pumps with poorly arranged or inadequately screened intakes and then forced into the system. Sometimes floods damage intakes. Obstructions include fine, compacted materials such as rust, mud, and sand. Coarse materials, such as stones, cinders, cast-iron tubercles, chips of wood, and sticks, also are common.

D.2.4 Biological Growth. Biological growth has been known to cause obstructions in sprinkler piping. The Asiatic clam has been found in fire protection systems supplied by raw river or lake water. With an available food supply and sunlight, these clams grow to approximately $\frac{3}{8}$ in. to $\frac{7}{16}$ in. (9 mm to 11 mm) across the shell in 1 year and up to $2\frac{1}{8}$ in. (54 mm) and larger by the sixth year. However, once in fire mains and sprinkler piping, the growth rate is much slower. The clams get into the fire protection systems in the larval stage or while still small clams. They then attach themselves to the pipe and feed on bacteria or algae that pass through.

Originally brought to Washington state from Asia in the 1930s, the clams have spread throughout at least 33 states and possibly are present in every state. River areas reported to be highly infested include the Ohio River, Tennessee River Valley, Savannah River (South Carolina), Altamaha River (Georgia), Columbia River (Washington), and Delta-Mendota Canal (California).

D.2.5 Sprinkler Calcium Carbonate Deposits. Natural freshwaters contain dissolved calcium and magnesium salts in varying concentrations, depending on the sources and location of the water. If the concentration of these salts is high, the water is considered hard. A thin film composed largely of calcium carbonate, $CaCO_3$, affords some protection against corrosion where hard water flows through the pipes. However, hardness is not the only factor to determine whether a film forms. The ability of $CaCO_3$ to precipitate on the metal pipe surface also depends on the water's total acidity or alkalinity, the concentration of dissolved solids in the water, and its pH. In soft water, no such film can form.

In automatic sprinkler systems, the calcium carbonate scale formation tends to occur on the more noble metal in the electrochemical series, which is copper, just as corrosion affects the less noble metal, iron. Consequently, scale formation naturally forms on sprinklers, often plugging the orifice. The piping itself could be relatively clear. This type of sprinkler obstruction cannot be detected or corrected by normal flushing procedures. It can be found only by inspection of sprinklers in suspected areas and then removed.

Most public water utilities in very hard water areas soften their water to reduce consumer complaints of scale buildup in water heaters. Thus, the most likely locations for deposits in sprinkler systems are where sprinklers are not connected to public water but supplied without treatment directly from wells or surface water in areas that have very hard water. These areas generally include the Mississippi basin west of the Mississippi River and north of the Ohio River, the rivers of Texas and the Colorado basin, and other white areas in Figure D.2.5(a). (The water of the Great Lakes is only moderately hard.)

Within individual plants, the sprinklers most likely to have deposits are located as follows:

(1) In wet systems only.
(2) In high temperature areas, except where water has unusually high pH *[see Figure D.2.5(b)]*. High temperature areas include those near dryers, ovens, and skylights or at roof peaks.
(3) In old sprinkler systems that are frequently drained and refilled.
(4) In pendent sprinklers that are located away from air pockets and near convection currents.

Degree of tuberculation of water supplies

☐ None to slight   ▨ Slight to moderate   ▨ Moderate to severe

FIGURE D.2.5(a)   Map of Hard Water Areas. *(Provided by Cast Iron Pipe Research Association. Used with permission.)*

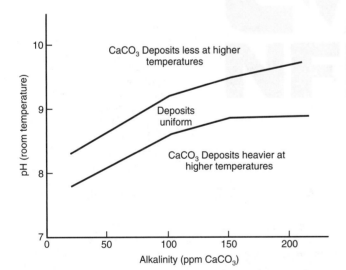

FIGURE D.2.5(b)   Scale Deposition as Function of Alkalinity/pH Ratio.

D.2.6 Forms of Corrosion. Corrosion is defined as the deterioration of a material, usually a metal, resulting from a chemical or electrochemical reaction. The eight main forms of corrosion include (1) uniform corrosion, (2) pitting, (3) galvanic corrosion, (4) crevice corrosion, (5) selective leaching (parting), (6) erosion corrosion, (7) environmental cracking, and (8) intergranular corrosion. Microbiologically influenced corrosion (MIC) is included herein as a ninth form of corrosion, although it is usually a secondary factor that accelerates or exacerbates the rate of another form of corrosion. Definitions of the different forms of corrosion are discussed next.

(1) *Uniform (or general) corrosion:* A regular loss of a small quantity of metal over the entire area or over a large section of the total area, which is evenly distributed within a pipe(s).

(2) *Pitting:* A localized form of corrosion that results in holes or cavities in the metal. Pitting is considered to be one of the more destructive forms of corrosion and is often difficult to detect. Pits can be covered or open and normally grow in the direction of gravity — for example, at the bottom of a horizontal surface.

(3) *Galvanic corrosion:* An electric potential exists between dissimilar metals in a conductive (corrosive) solution. The contact between the two materials allows electrons to transfer from one metal to the other. One metal acts as a cathode and the other as an anode. Corrosion usually occurs at anodic metal only.

(4) *Crevice corrosion:* A localized form of corrosion that occurs within crevices and other shielded areas on metal surfaces exposed to a stagnant corrosive solution. This form of corrosion usually occurs beneath gaskets, in holes, surface deposits, in thread and groove joints. Crevice corrosion is also referred to as gasket corrosion, deposit corrosion, and under-deposit corrosion.

(5) *Selective leaching:* The selective removal of one element from an alloy by corrosion. A common example is dezincification (selective removal of zinc) of unstabilized brass, resulting in a porous copper structure.

(6) *Erosion corrosion:* Corrosion resulting from the cumulative damage of electrochemical reactions and mechanical effects. Erosion corrosion is the acceleration or increase in the rate of corrosion created by the relative movement of a corrosive fluid and a metal surface. Erosion corrosion is observed as grooves, gullies, waves, rounded holes, or valleys in a metal surface.

(7) *Environmental cracking:* An acute form of localized corrosion caused by mechanical stresses, embrittlement, or fatigue.

(8) *Integranular corrosion:* Corrosion caused by impurities at grain boundaries, enrichment of one alloying element, or depletion of one of the elements in the grain boundary areas.

(9) *Microbiologically influenced corrosion (MIC):* Corrosion initiated or accelerated by the presence and activities of microorganisms, including bacteria and fungi. Colonies (also called bio-films and slimes) are formed in the surface of pipes among a variety of types of microbes. Microbes deposit iron, manganese, and various salts into the pipe surfaces, forming nodules, tubercles, and carbuncles. The formation of these deposits can cause obstruction to flow and dislodge, causing blockage (plugging) of system piping, valves, and sprinklers.

△ **D.2.7 Microbiologically Influenced Corrosion (MIC).** The most common biological growths in sprinkler system piping are those formed by microorganisms, including bacteria and fungi. These microbes produce colonies (also called bio-films, slimes) containing a variety of types of microbes. Colonies form on the surface of wetted pipe in both wet and dry systems. Microbes also deposit iron, manganese, and various salts onto the pipe surface, forming discrete deposits (also termed nodules, tubercles, and carbuncles). These deposits can cause obstruction to flow and dislodge, causing plugging of fire sprinkler components. Subsequent under-deposit pitting can also result in pinhole leaks.

Microbiologically influenced corrosion (MIC) is corrosion influenced by the presence and activities of microorganisms. MIC is almost always a secondary form of corrosion driven by oxygen corrosion activity. MIC starts as microbial communities (also called bio-films, slimes) growing on the interior surface of the wetted sprinkler piping components in both wet and dry systems. The microbial communities contain many types of microbes, including slime formers, acid-producing bacteria, iron-depositing bacteria, and sulfate-reducing bacteria. The microbes deposit iron, manganese, and various salts onto the pipe surface, forming discrete deposits (also termed nodules, tubercles, and carbuncles). These deposits can cause obstruction to flow and dislodge, causing plugging of fire sprinkler components.

MIC of copper and copper alloys occurs as discrete deposits of smaller size, which are green to blue in color. Blue slimes can also be produced in copper piping or copper components (e.g., brass heads).

MIC is often first noticed as a result of pinhole leaks after only months to a few years of service. Confirmation of MIC can be made by examination of interior of pipes for deposits and under-deposit corrosion with pit morphology consistent with MIC (cup-like pits within pits and striations).

The occurrence and severity of MIC is enhanced by the following:

(1) Using untreated water to test and fill sprinkler piping. This is made worse by leaving the water in the system for long periods of time.
(2) Introduction of new and untreated water containing oxygen, microbes, salts, and nutrients into the system on a frequent basis (during repair, renovation, and/or frequent flow tests).
(3) Leaving dirt, debris, and especially oils, pipe joint compound, and so forth in the piping. These provide nutrients and protection for the microbes, often preventing biocides and corrosion inhibitors from reaching the microbes and corrosion sites.

Once the presence of MIC has been confirmed, the system should be assessed to determine the extent and severity of MIC. Severely affected portions should be replaced or cleaned to remove obstructions and pipe not meeting minimal mechanical specifications.

D.3 Investigation Procedures. If unsatisfactory conditions are observed as outlined in Section 14.3, investigations should be made to determine the extent and severity of the obstructing material. From the fire protection system plan, determine the water supply sources, age of underground mains and sprinkler systems, types of systems, and general piping arrangement. Consider the possible sources of obstruction material.

Examine the fire pump suction supply and screening arrangements. If necessary, have the suction cleaned before using the pump in tests and flushing operations. Gravity tanks should be inspected internally, with the exception of steel tanks that have been recently cleaned and painted. If possible, have the tank drained and determine whether loose scale is on the shell or if sludge or other obstructions are on the tank bottom. Cleaning and repainting could be in order, particularly if it has not been done within the previous 5 years.

Investigate yard mains first, then sprinkler systems.

Where fire protection control valves are closed during investigation procedures, the fire protection impairment precautions outlined in Chapter 15 should be followed.

Large quantities of water are needed for investigation and for flushing. It is important to plan the safest means of disposal in advance. Cover stock and machinery susceptible to water damage, and keep equipment on hand for mopping up any accidental discharge of water.

D.3.1 Investigating Yard Mains. Flow water through yard hydrants, preferably near the extremes of selected mains, to determine whether mains contain obstructive material. It is preferable to connect two lengths of 2½ in. (65 mm) hose to the hydrant. Attach burlap bags to the free ends of the hose from which the nozzles have been removed to collect any material flushed out, and flow water long enough to determine the condition of the main being investigated. If there are several water supply sources, investigate each independently, avoiding any unnecessary interruptions to sprinkler protection. In extensive yard layouts, repeat the tests at several locations, if necessary, to determine general conditions.

If obstructive material is found, all mains should be flushed thoroughly before investigating the sprinkler systems. *(See Section D.5.)*

D.3.2 Investigating Sprinkler Systems. Investigate dry systems first. Tests on several carefully selected, representative systems usually are sufficient to indicate general conditions throughout the plant. If, however, preliminary investigations indicate the presence of obstructing material, this justifies investigating all systems (both wet and dry) before outlining needed flushing operations. Generally, the system can be considered reasonably free of obstructing material, provided the following conditions apply:

(1) Less than ½ cup of scale is washed from the cross mains.
(2) Scale fragments are not large enough to plug a sprinkler orifice.
(3) A full, unobstructed flow is obtained from each branch line inspected.

Where other types of foreign material are found, judgment should be used before considering the system unobstructed. Obstruction potential is based on the physical characteristics and source of the foreign material.

In selecting specific systems or branch lines for investigation, the following should be considered:

(1) Lines found obstructed during a fire or during maintenance work
(2) Systems adjacent to points of recent repair to yard mains, particularly if hydrant flow shows material in the main

Tests should include flows through 2½ in. (65 mm) fire hose directly from cross mains *[see Figure D.3.2(a) and Figure D.3.2(b)]* and flows through 1½ in. (40 mm) hose from representative branch lines. Two or three branch lines per system is a representative number of branch lines where investigating for scale accumulation. If significant scale is found, investigation of additional branch lines is warranted. Where investigating for foreign material (other than scale), the number of branch lines needed for representative sampling is dependent on the source and characteristic of the foreign material.

If provided, fire pumps should be operated for the large line flows, since maximum flow is desirable. Burlap bags should be used to collect dislodged material as is done in the investigation of yard mains. Each flow should be continued until the water clears (i.e., a minimum of 2 to 3 minutes at full flow for sprinkler mains). This is likely to be sufficient to indicate the condition of the piping interior.

D.3.3 Investigating Dry Pipe Systems. Flood dry pipe systems one or two days before obstruction investigations to soften pipe scale and deposits. After selecting the test points of a dry pipe system, close the main control valve and drain the system. Check the piping visually with a flashlight while it is being dismantled. Attach hose valves and 1½ in. (40 mm) hose to the

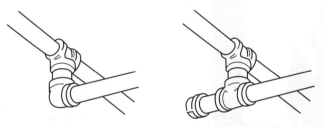

△ **FIGURE D.3.2(a)   Replacement of Elbow at End of Cross Main with Flushing Connection Consisting of 2 in. (50 mm) Nipple and Cap.**

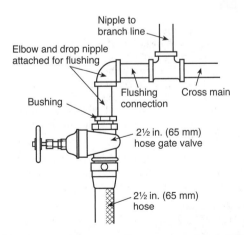

△ **FIGURE D.3.2(b)   Connection of 2½ in. (65 mm) Hose Gate Valve with 2 in. (50 mm) Bushing and Nipple and Elbow to 2 in. (50 mm) Cross Main.**

ends of the lines to be tested, shut the valves, have air pressure restored on the system, and reopen the control valve. Open the hose valve on the end branch line, allowing the system to trip in simulation of normal action. Any obstructions should be cleared from the branch line before proceeding with further tests.

After flowing the small end line, shut its hose valve and test the feed or cross main by discharging water through a 2½ in. (65 mm) fire hose, collecting any foreign material in a burlap bag.

After the test, the dry pipe valve should be cleaned internally and reset. Its control valve should be locked open and a drain test performed.

D.3.4 Investigating Wet Pipe Systems. Testing of wet systems is similar to that of dry systems, except that the system should be drained after closing the control valve to permit installation of hose valves for the test. Slowly reopen the control valve and make a small hose flow as specified for the branch line, followed by the 2½ in. (65 mm) hose flow for the cross main.

In any case, if lines become plugged during the tests, piping should be dismantled and cleaned, the extent of plugging noted, and a clear flow obtained from the branch line before proceeding further.

Perform similar tests on representative systems to indicate the general condition of the wet systems throughout the plant, keeping a detailed record of the procedures performed.

D.3.5 Other Obstruction Investigation Methods. Other obstruction investigation methods, such as technically proven ultrasonic and x-ray examination, have been evaluated and if applied correctly, are successful at detecting obstructions.

The sources of the obstructing material should be determined and steps taken to prevent further entrance of such material. This entails work such as inspection and cleaning of pump suction screening facilities or cleaning of private reservoirs. If recently laid public mains appear to be the source of the obstructing material, waterworks authorities should be requested to flush their system.

D.4 Obstruction Prevention Program.

D.4.1 Dry Pipe and Preaction Systems — Scale.

(1) Dry pipe and preaction systems using noncoated ferrous piping should be thoroughly investigated for obstruction from corrosion after they have been in service for 15 years, for 25 years, and every 5 years thereafter.

(2) Dry pipe systems with noncoated ferrous piping should be kept on air year-round, rather than on air and water alternately, to inhibit formation of rust and scale.

D.4.2 Flushing Connections. Sprinkler systems installed in accordance with recent editions of NFPA 13 should have provisions for flushing each cross main. Similarly, branch lines on gridded systems should be capable of being readily "broken" at a simple union or flexible joint. Property owners of systems installed without these provisions should be encouraged to provide them when replacement or repair work is being done.

D.4.3 Suction Supplies.

(1) Screen pump suction supplies and screens should be maintained. Connections from penstocks should be equipped with strainers or grids, unless the penstock inlets themselves are so equipped. Pump suction screens of copper or brass wire tend to promote less aquatic growth.

(2) Extreme care should be used to prevent material from entering the suction piping when cleaning tanks and open reservoirs. Materials removed from the interior of gravity tanks during cleaning should not be allowed to enter the discharge pipe.

(3) Small mill ponds could need periodic dredging where weeds and other aquatic growth are inherent.

D.4.4 Asian Clams. Effective screening of larvae and small-size, juvenile Asian clams from fire protection systems is very difficult. To date, no effective method of total control has been found. Such controls can be difficult to achieve in fire protection systems.

D.4.5 Calcium Carbonate. For localities suspected of having hard water, sample sprinklers should be removed and inspected yearly. Subsection D.2.5 outlines sprinkler locations prone to the accumulation of deposits where hard water is a problem. Sprinklers found with deposits should be replaced, and adjacent sprinklers should be inspected.

D.4.6 Zebra Mussels. Several means of controlling the zebra mussel are being studied, including molluscicides, chlorines, ozone, shell strainers, manual removal, robotic cleaning, water jetting, line pigging, sonic pulses, high-voltage electrical fields, and thermal backwashing. It is believed that these controls might need to be applied only during spawning periods when water temperatures are 57°F to 61°F (14°C to 16°C) and veligers are present. Several silicon grease-based coatings also are being investigated for use within piping systems.

While it appears that the use of molluscicides could provide the most effective means of controlling the mussel, these chemicals are costly. It is believed that chlorination is the best available short-term treatment, but there are problems associated with the use of chlorine, including strict Environmental Protection Agency regulations on the release of chlorine into lakes and streams. The use of nonselective poison, such as chlorine, in the amounts necessary to kill the mussels in large bodies of water could be devastating to entire ecosystems.

To provide an effective means of control against zebra mussels in fire protection systems, control measures should be applied at the water source, instead of within the piping system. Effective controls for growth of the zebra mussel within fire protection systems include the following:

(1) Selecting a water source that is not subject to infestation. This could include well water or potable or pretreated water.

(2) Implementing a water treatment program that includes biocides or elevated pH, or both.

(3) Implementing a water treatment program to remove oxygen, to ensure control of biological growth within piping.

(4) Relying on a tight system approach to deny oxygen and nutrients that are necessary to support growth.

D.5 Flushing Procedures.

D.5.1 Yard Mains. Yard mains should be flushed thoroughly before flushing any interior piping. Flush yard piping through hydrants at dead ends of the system or through blowoff valves, allowing the water to run until clear. If the water is supplied from more than one direction or from a looped system, close divisional valves to produce a high-velocity flow through each single line. A velocity of at least 10 ft/sec (3 m/sec) is necessary for scouring the pipe and for lifting foreign material to an aboveground flushing outlet. Use the flow specified in Table D.5.1 or the maximum flow available for the size of the yard main being flushed.

Connections from the yard piping to the sprinkler riser should be flushed. These are usually 6 in. (150 mm) mains. Although flow through a short, open-ended 2 in. (50 mm) drain can create sufficient velocity in a 6 in. (150 mm) main to move small obstructing material, the restricted waterway of the globe valve usually found on a sprinkler drain might not allow stones and other large objects to pass. If the presence of large size material is suspected, a larger outlet is needed to pass such material and to create the flow necessary to move it. Fire department connections on sprinkler risers can be used as flushing outlets by removing the clappers. Yard mains also can be flushed through a temporary Siamese fitting attached to the riser connection before the sprinkler system is installed. *[See Figure D.5.1.]*

D.5.2 Sprinkler Piping. Two methods commonly are used for flushing sprinkler piping:

(1) The hydraulic method
(2) The hydropneumatic method

The hydraulic method consists of flowing water from the yard mains, sprinkler risers, feed mains, cross mains, and branch lines, respectively, in the same direction in which water would flow during a fire.

The hydropneumatic method uses special equipment and compressed air to blow a charge of about 30 gal (114 dm³) of water from the ends of branch lines back into feed mains and down the riser, washing the foreign material out of an opening at the base of the riser.

The choice of method depends on conditions at the individual plant and the type of material installed. If examination indicates the presence of loose sand, mud, or moderate amounts of pipe scale, the piping generally can be flushed satisfactorily by the hydraulic method. Where the material is more difficult to remove and available water pressures are too low for effective scouring action, the hydropneumatic method generally is more satisfactory. The hydropneumatic method should not be used with listed CPVC sprinkler piping.

In some cases, where obstructive material is solidly packed or adheres tightly to the walls of the piping, the pipe needs to be dismantled and cleaned by rodding or other means.

Dry pipe systems should be flooded one or two days before flushing to soften pipe scale and deposits.

Successful flushing by either the hydraulic or hydropneumatic method is dependent on establishing sufficient velocity of flow in the pipes to remove silt, scale, and other obstructive material. With the hydraulic method, water should be moved through the pipe at least at the rate of flow indicated in Table D.5.1.

Where flushing a branch line through the end pipe, sufficient water should be discharged to scour the largest pipe in the branch line. Lower rates of flow can reduce the efficiency of the flushing operation. To establish the recommended flow, remove the small end piping and connect the hose to a larger section, if necessary.

Where pipe conditions indicate internal or external corrosion, a section of the pipe affected should be cleaned thoroughly to determine whether the walls of the pipe have seriously weakened. Hydrostatic testing should be performed as outlined in NFPA 13.

Pendent sprinklers should be removed and inspected until it is reasonably certain that all are free of obstruction material.

Painting the ends of branch lines and cross mains is a convenient method for keeping a record of those pipes that have been flushed.

D.5.3 Hydraulic Method. After the yard mains have been thoroughly cleaned, flush risers, feed mains, cross mains, and finally the branch lines. In multistory buildings, systems should be flushed by starting at the lowest story and working up. Branch line flushing in any story can immediately follow the flushing of feed and cross mains in that story, allowing one story to be completed at a time. Following this sequence prevents drawing obstructing material into the interior piping.

To flush risers, feed mains, and cross mains, attach 2½ in. (65 mm) hose gate valves to the extreme ends of these lines [see Figure D.5.3]. Such valves usually can be procured from the manifold of fire pumps or hose standpipes. As an alternative, an adapter with 2½ in. (65 mm) hose thread and standard pipe thread can be used with a regular gate valve. A length of fire hose without a nozzle should be attached to the flushing connection. To prevent kinking of the hose and to obtain maximum flow, an elbow usually should be installed between the end of the sprinkler pipe and the hose gate valve. Attach the valve and hose so that no excessive strain will be placed on the threaded pipe and fittings. Support hose lines properly.

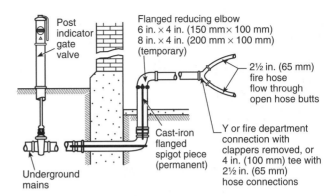

FIGURE D.5.1 Arrangement for Flushing Branches from Underground Mains to Sprinkler Risers.

Where feed and cross mains and risers contain pipe 4 in., 5 in., and 6 in. (100 mm, 125 mm, and 150 mm) in diameter, it could be necessary to use a Siamese with two hose connections to obtain sufficient flow to scour this larger pipe.

Flush branch lines after feed and cross mains have been thoroughly cleared. Equip the ends of several branch lines with gate valves, and flush individual lines of the group consecutively. This eliminates the need for shutting off and draining the sprinkler system to replace a single hose line. The hose should be 1½ in. (40 mm) in diameter and as short as practicable. Branch lines can be permitted to be flushed in any order that expedites the work.

Branch lines also can be permitted to be flushed through pipe 1½ in. (40 mm) in diameter or larger while extended through a convenient window. If pipe is used, 45 degree fittings should be provided at the ends of branch lines. Where flushing branch lines, hammering the pipes is an effective method of moving obstructions.

△ **Table D.5.1 Flushing Rates to Accomplish Flow of 10 ft/sec (3 m/sec)**

Pipe Size (in.)	Steel			Copper			CPVC (gpm)	Polybutylene	
	SCH 10 (gpm)	SCH 40 (gpm)	XL (gpm)	K (gpm)	L (gpm)	M (gpm)		CTS (gpm)	IPS (gpm)
¾	—	—	—	14	15	16	19	12	17
1	29	24	30	24	26	27	30	20	27
1¼	51	47	52	38	39	41	48	30	43
1½	69	63	70	54	55	57	63	42	57
2	114	105	114	94	96	99	98	72	90
2½	170	149	163	145	149	152	144	—	—
3	260	230	251	207	212	217	213	—	—
4	449	396	—	364	373	379	—	—	—
5	686	623	—	565	582	589	—	—	—
6	989	880	—	807	836	846	—	—	—
8	1665	1560	—	1407	1460	1483	—	—	—
10	2632	2440	—	2185	2267	2303	—	—	—
12	—	3520	—	—	—	—	—	—	—

For SI units, 1 gpm = 3.785 L/min.

Shaded text = Revisions.   △ = Text deletions and figure/table revisions.   • = Section deletions.   *N* = New material.

Figure D.5.3 shows a typical gridded piping arrangement prior to flushing. The flushing procedure is as follows:

(1) Disconnect all branch lines and cap all open ends.
(2) Remove the cap from the east end of the south cross main, flush the main, and replace the cap.
(3) Remove the cap from branch line 1, flush the line, and replace the cap.
(4) Repeat step (3) for the remaining branch lines.
(5) Reconnect enough branch lines at the west end of the system so that the aggregate cross-sectional area of the branch lines approximately equals the area of the north cross main. For example, three 1¼ in. (32 mm) branch lines approximately equal a 2½ in. (65 mm) cross main. Remove the cap from the east end of the north cross main, flush the main, and replace the cap.
(6) Disconnect and recap the branch lines. Repeat step (5), but reconnect branch lines at the east end of the system and flush the north cross main through its west end.
(7) Reconnect all branch lines and recap the cross main. Verify that the sprinkler control valve is left in the open and locked position.

D.5.4 Hydropneumatic Method. The apparatus used for hydropneumatic flushing consists of a hydropneumatic machine, a source of water, a source of compressed air, 1 in. (25 mm) rubber hose for connecting to branch lines, and 2½ in. (65 mm) hose for connecting to cross mains.

The hydropneumatic machine [see Figure D.5.4(a)] consists of a 30 gal (114 dm³) (4 ft³) water tank mounted over a 185 gal (700 dm³) (25 ft³) compressed air tank. The compressed air tank is connected to the top of the water tank through a 2 in. (50 mm) lubricated plug cock. The bottom of the water tank is connected through hose to a suitable water supply. The compressed air tank is connected through suitable air hose to either the plant air system or a separate air compressor.

To flush the sprinkler piping, the water tank is filled with water, the pressure is raised to 100 psi (6.9 bar) in the compressed air tank, and the plug cock between tanks is opened to put air pressure on the water. The water tank is connected by hose to the sprinkler pipe to be flushed. The lubricated plug cock on the discharge outlet at the bottom of the water tank then is snapped open, allowing the water to be "blown" through the hose and sprinkler pipe by the compressed air. The water tank and air tank should be recharged after each blow.

Outlets for discharging water and obstructing material from the sprinkler system should be arranged. With the clappers of dry pipe valves and alarm check valves on their seats and cover plates removed, sheet metal fittings can be used for connection to 2½ in. (65 mm) hose lines or for discharge into a drum [maximum capacity per blow is approximately 30 gal (114 dm³)]. If the 2 in. (50 mm) riser drain is to be used, the drain valve should be removed and a direct hose connection made. For wet pipe systems with no alarm check valves, the riser should be taken apart just below the drain opening and a plate inserted to prevent foreign material from dropping to the base of the riser. Where dismantling of a section of the riser for this purpose is impractical, the hydropneumatic method should not be used.

Before starting a flushing job, each sprinkler system to be cleaned should be studied and a schematic plan prepared showing the order of the blows.

To determine that the piping is clear after it has been flushed, representative branch lines and cross mains should be investigated, using both visual examination and sample flushings.

(1) *Branch Lines.* With the yard mains already flushed or known to be clear, the sprinkler branch lines should be flushed next. The order of cleaning individual branch lines should be laid out carefully if an effective job is to be done. In general, the branch lines should be flushed, starting with the branch closest to the riser and working toward the dead end of the cross main. [See Figure D.5.4(b).] The order for flushing the branch lines is shown by the circled numerals. In this example, the southeast quadrant is flushed first, then the southwest, followed by the northeast, and, finally, the northwest. Air hose 1 in. (25 mm) in diameter is used to connect the machine with the end of the branch line being flushed. This hose air pressure should be allowed to drop to 85 psi (5.9 bar) before the valve is closed. The resulting short slug of water experiences less friction loss and a higher velocity and, therefore, cleans more effectively than if the full 30 gal (114 dm³) of water were to be used. One blow is made for each branch line.

(2) *Large Piping.* Where flushing cross mains, fill the water tank completely and raise the pressure in the air receiver to 100 psi (6.9 bar) (690 kPa). Connect the machine to the end of the cross main to be flushed with no more than 50 ft (15.2 m) of 2½ in. (65 mm) hose. After opening the valve, allow air pressure in the machine to drop to zero (0). Two to six blows are necessary at each location, depending on the size and length of the main. In Figure D.5.4(b), the numerals in squares indicate the location and order of the cross main blows. Because the last branch line blows performed were located west of the riser, clean the cross main located east of the riser first. Where large cross mains are to be cleaned, it is best, if practical, to make one blow at 38, one at 39, the next again at 38, then again at 39, alternating in this manner until the required number of blows has been made at each location.

(3) Where flushing cross mains and feed mains, arrange the work so that the water passes through a minimum of right-angle bends. In Figure D.5.4(b), blows at 38 should

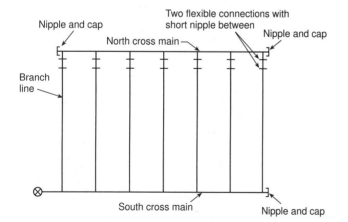

FIGURE D.5.3   Gridded Sprinkler System Piping.

Shaded text = Revisions.   Δ = Text deletions and figure/table revisions.   • = Section deletions.   *N* = New material.

be adequate to flush the cross mains back to the riser. Do not attempt to clean the cross main from location A to the riser by backing out branch line 16 and connecting the hose to the open side of the tee. If this were to be done, a considerable portion of the blow would pass northward up the 3 in. (76 mm) line supplying branches 34 to 37, and the portion passing eastward to the riser could be ineffective. Where the size, length, and condition of cross mains necessitate blowing from a location corresponding to location A, the connection should be made directly to the cross main corresponding to the 3½ in. (90 mm) pipe so that the entire flow travels to the riser. Where flushing through a tee, always flush the run of the tee after flushing the branch. Note the location of blows 35, 36, and 37 in Figure D.5.4(b). Gridded systems can be flushed in a similar fashion. With branch lines disconnected and capped, begin flushing the branch line closest to the riser (branch line 1 in Figure D.5.3), working toward the most remote line. Then flush the south cross main in Figure D.5.3 by connecting the hose to the east end. Flushing the north cross main involves connecting the hose to one end while discharging to a safe location from the other end.

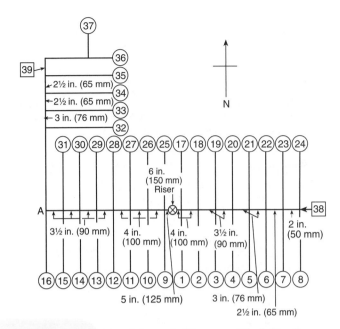

FIGURE D.5.4(b)   Schematic Diagram of Sprinkler System Showing Sequence To Be Followed Where Hydropneumatic Method Is To Be Utilized.

Annex E   Hazard Evaluation Form

This annex is not a part of the requirements of this NFPA document but is included for informational purposes only.

△ **E.1 Conducting Hazard Evaluations.** This annex provides one example of a hazard evaluation form. A hazard evaluation is not part of a system inspection. *(See Figure E.1.)*

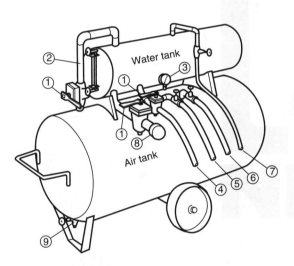

1 Lubricated plug cocks
2 Pipe connection between air and water tanks (This connection is open when flushing sprinkler system.)
3 Air pressure gauge
4 1 in. (25 mm) rubber hose (air type) (Used to flush sprinkler branch lines.)
5 Hose connected to source of water (Used to fill water tank.)
6 Hose connected to ample source of compressed air (Used to supply air tank.)
7 Water tank overflow hose
8 2½ in. (65 mm) pipe connection [Where flushing large interior piping, connect woven jacket fire hose here and close 1 in. (25 mm) plug cock hose connection (4) used for flushing sprinkler branch lines.]
9 Air tank drain valve

FIGURE D.5.4(a)   Hydropneumatic Machine.

FIRE SPRINKLER SYSTEM HAZARD EVALUATION

Changes in building occupancy, use, or process, or material used or stored, create the need for evaluation of the installed fire protection systems. This form is intended to identify and evaluate such changes and should be completed only by an individual properly qualified in the area of system design.

Owner: _____ Owner's address: _____

Property being evaluated: _____

Property address: _____

Date of work: _____

(All responses refer to the current hazard evaluation performed on this date.)

Section 1. Identification of Sprinklered Occupancy and Storage Hazards

(Use additional pages as needed.)

Area of Property (List nonsprinklered areas separately in Section 3.)	Type of System and Sprinklers	Design Capability of System	Hazard Protected (Uses or storage arrangements, including commodity)	Improvements Needed to Address Hazard
1.				
2.				
3.				
4.				
5.				

© 2019 National Fire Protection Association NFPA 25 (p. 1 of 4)

Δ **FIGURE E.1** **Sample of Fire Sprinkler Hazard Evaluation.**

Shaded text = Revisions. Δ = Text deletions and figure/table revisions. • = Section deletions. *N* = New material.

FIRE SPRINKLER SYSTEM HAZARD EVALUATION *(continued)*

Section 2. Evaluation of Protection

For each area of the property evaluated in Section 1, please answer the following questions with a "yes," "no," "N/A," or "?," and explain all "no" and "?" responses below by row and column identification:

Answer the following for each identified property area:	1	2	3	4	5
a. Are all sprinklers the correct type for their application?					
b. Are the obstructions to sprinklers in all areas within acceptable limits for the specific types of sprinklers used?					
c. Are hazards associated with all occupancy areas consistent with hazards typical for that occupancy hazard classification?					
d. Are stockpiles of combustibles located within occupancy areas limited to appropriate heights?					
e. Are miscellaneous and dedicated storage areas properly identified and managed?					
f. Are all dedicated storage areas protected in accordance with the proper storage configuration and commodity classification?					
g. Is the storage or use of flammable liquids, combustible liquids, or aerosol products in any area properly addressed?					
h. Is all idle pallet storage properly protected?					
i. Is there any presence of nitrate film, pyroxylin plastic, compressed or liquefied gas cylinders, liquid or solid oxidizers, or organic peroxide formulations except where specifically addressed by appropriate protection measures?					
j. Are all sprinklers spaced appropriately for the hazard and the type of sprinkler?					
k. Do the available sources of heat and cooling appear adequate for the type of system and temperature rating of sprinklers?					

Explanation of "no" and "?" answers:

Examples:

b2 – no – Obstructions to ESFR sprinklers exceed currently accepted standards

e3 – ? – Owner must provide information on type of plastic involved in product before evaluation can be finalized.

_____

_____

_____

_____

_____

_____

_____

© 2019 National Fire Protection Association   NFPA 25 (p. 2 of 4)

Δ **FIGURE E.1**   *Continued*

FIRE SPRINKLER SYSTEM HAZARD EVALUATION *(continued)*

Section 3. Evaluation of Unsprinklered Areas

Area of Property for Which Protection Is Not Provided	Basis of Lack of Protection (if known)	Basis for Omission Under Current Codes/Standards
1.		
2.		
3.		
4.		
5.		

Section 4. Water Supply Evaluation

If this hazard evaluation is the result of a reduction in the residual pressure during routine inspections, explain the results of the investigation made to determine the reasons for this change:

_____

_____

_____

Explain the basis of continued acceptability of the water supply or proposed improvements:

_____

_____

_____

_____

_____

_____

_____

_____

_____

© 2019 National Fire Protection Association

NFPA 25 (p. 3 of 4)

Δ **FIGURE E.1** *Continued*

Shaded text = Revisions.   Δ = Text deletions and figure/table revisions.   • = Section deletions.   *N* = New material.

FIRE SPRINKLER SYSTEM HAZARD EVALUATION *(continued)*

Section 5. Hazard Evaluator's Information and Certification

Evaluator: _____

Company: _____

Company address: _____

I state that the information on this form is correct at the time and place of my review of my evaluation.

Is this hazard evaluation completed? (Note: All "?" must be resolved.)   ❑ Yes   ❑ No

Explain if answer is not "yes":

_____

_____

Have deficiencies in protection been identified that should be improved or corrected?   ❑ Yes   ❑ No

Summarize improvements of corrections needed:

_____

_____

_____

_____

Signature of Evaluator: _____   Date: _____

License or Certification Number (if applicable): _____

© 2019 National Fire Protection Association   NFPA 25 (p. 4 of 4)

△ **FIGURE E.1**   *Continued*

Annex F   Connectivity and Data Collection

This annex is not a part of the requirements of this NFPA document but is included for informational purposes only.

F.1 Scope.

F.1.1 This annex covers considerations relating to the collection of inspection, test, maintenance, and monitoring data.

F.1.2 Potential use of accessible information includes remote supervision, remote monitoring that may include specific components for failure forecasting/component replacement, reliability analysis for owner, manufacturer, and NFPA or similar group for obtaining information only. No remote operation nor remote changing of any controller settings should be permitted.

F.1.3 Connectivity is for remote monitoring and data gathering. It does not replace any of the alarm and signaling requirements of this or other standards.

F.1.4 This annex is intended to be complementary to Annex D in NFPA 20 and relies on that annex for common concerns and elements.

F.1.5 Although none of the clauses in this annex are enforceable, future editions of this standard might incorporate requirements for connectivity and data collection into the enforceable portion of this standard. Public review and comment are encouraged.

F.2 Internet Protocol (IP).   See Annex D of NFPA 20.

F.3 Possible Configurations.

F.3.1 Standalone Laptop Computers, Tablets, Smart Cell Phones.

F.3.1.1 The devices could be provided with software or connected to a control panel for downloading data, plugged into data recording equipment, or used for manual data entry.

F.3.2 Control Panels.

F.3.2.1 These devices could have direct access to a network — the network could be local WAN or Internet.

F.3.2.2 These devices could be standalone devices and require a direct connection to download data.

F.3.2.3 Data collection capability is almost universal in modern fire pump controllers. Manual (user) intervention is required to access (read or download).

F.3.3 User Connection.   See Annex D of NFPA 20.

F.4 Security Concerns.   See Annex D of NFPA 20.

F.5 Recommended Requirements.

F.5.1 Separate access protocols should be used for different access levels.

F.5.1.1 Level 1 allows read-only access to performance information for user benefit.

F.5.1.2 Level 2a allows access for statistical analysis by an independent body. Information that identifies the user should be transformed to conceal the user's identity and should provide a GPS location that identifies latitude and longitude within 100 miles.

F.5.1.3 Level 1 allows access for manufacturer analysis with the owner's permission.

F.5.1.4 Level 2b allows access for manufacturer analysis without the owner's permission. Information that identifies the user should be transformed to conceal the user's identity and should provide a GPS location that identifies state and latitude and longitude within 100 miles.

F.5.1.5 Level 2c allows access for manufacturer analysis of the control panel.

F.5.1.6 Level 2d allows access for remote testing, with an alarm to be triggered if the control panel is not restored to automatic mode within eight hours.

F.5.2 Information Recorded for External Access.

F.5.2.1 The data formats shown in Table F.5.2.1 are used in Table F.5.2(a), Table F.5.2(b), Table F.5.2(c), and Table F.5.2(d).

F.5.2.2 All inspection, test, and maintenance data should be recorded in the format provided in Table F.5.2(a). All repair data should be recorded in the format provided in Table F.5.2(b).

F.5.2.3 All recorded information should be protected in accordance with F.5.1 and/or other appropriate security to limit access to appropriate entities.

Table F.5.2(a) Inspection, Test, Maintenance, and Repair Record Layout

Category	Item Format	Format	Possible Values
Basic information	Type of record	String (48)	Inspection, test, and maintenance
	Facility name	String (96)	Alphanumeric
	Location — GPS coordinates (longitude)	Number	−183333330° to +180°
	Location — GPS coordinates (latitude)	Number	−90° to +90°
	Location — GPS coordinates (elevation)	Number	Feet or meters
	Location adjusted for privacy — GPS coordinates (longitude)	Number	−180° to +180°
	Location adjusted for privacy — GPS coordinates (latitude)	Number	−90° to +90°
	Location adjusted for privacy — GPS coordinates (elevation)	Number	Feet or meters
	Reporting units pressure	Character	(1) psi (2) bar (3) Pascals (4) other
	Reporting units flow	Character	(1) gpm (2) L/min (3) L/sec (4) m^3/min (5) ft^3/min (6) Other
	Type of inspection or test	Character	(I) Inspection (T) Test (M) Maintenance (R) Repair
Item inspected, tested, maintained, or repaired — repeat for each item	Start of record marker for item	String (16)	Record start
	Unit type identifier (develop list)	String (48)	Alphanumeric
	Passed; failed; passed, but needs attention	Character	(P) Passed (F) Failed (A) Passed, but needs attention
	See Table F.2.5(d).		See Table F.2.5(d).
	Passed visual inspection	Character	(Y) Yes (N) No (A) Not Applicable
	Maintenance required	Number	≥ 0
	Maintenance done	Character	(1) Not applicable (2) Completed (3) Ordered but not completed (4) Not ordered
	End of item record marker	String (16)	Record end
End of ITC record	End of ITC (all components reported)	String (48)	End of inspection, test, and maintenance report

Table F.5.2(b) Equipment Repair Data Record Layout

Equipment repair data	Type of record	String (48)	Repair
	Facility name	String (96)	Alphanumeric
	Location — GPS coordinates (longitude)	Number	−180° to +180°
	Location — GPS coordinates (latitude)	Number	−90° to +90°
	Location — GPS coordinates (elevation)	Number	Feet or meters
	Location adjusted for privacy — GPS coordinates (longitude)	Number	−180° to +180°
	Location adjusted for privacy — GPS coordinates (latitude)	Number	−90° to +90°
	Location adjusted for privacy — GPS coordinates (elevation)	Number	Feet or meters
	Repair date	Date	Year/month/day
	Common data		See Table F.5.2(c).
	Repair preventative or result of failure	Character	(P) Preventative (F) Failure
	Failure mode (develop list)	5 Characters	Correspond to list
	Failure impaired fire protection system	Character	(I) Impaired (P) Partially functional (N) Not impaired
	Repair code (develop list)	5 Characters	Correspond to list
	Component replaced (develop list)	5 Characters	Correspond to list
	Repair description	String (96)	Alphanumeric
	Component replacement date	Date	Year/month/day
	End of repair record	String (48)	End of repair

Table F.5.2(c) Common Equipment Data

Category	Item	Format	Possible Values
	Manufacturer (develop list)	String (48)	Alphanumeric
	Model number	String (48)	Alphanumeric
	Size	String (48)	Alphanumeric
	Serial number	String (48)	Alphanumeric
	Year manufactured	4 Characters	xxxx (year)
	Device/component identifier tag	String (48)	Alphanumeric

Shaded text = Revisions.   Δ = Text deletions and figure/table revisions.   • = Section deletions.   N = New material.

△ Table F.5.2(d) Item Information

Item	Item Component	Format	Possible Values
Air compressor	Common data		See Table F.5.2(c).
	Type of system served	Character	(1) Dry (2) Non-interlock preaction (3) Single interlock preaction (4) Double interlock preaction (5) Other
	Filled system in 30 minutes or less	Character	(Y) Yes (N) No (3) N/A
Alarm check valve	Common data		See Table F.5.2(c).
	Operated satisfactorily	Character	(Y) Yes (N) No (3) N/A
Alarm device	Common data		See Table F.5.2(c).
	Operated satisfactorily	Character	(Y) Yes (N) No (3) N/A
Alarm valves	Common data		See Table F.5.2(c).
	Operated satisfactorily	Character	(Y) Yes (N) No (3) N/A
Antifreeze solution	Unit type identifier	String (48)	
	Type of antifreeze	Character	(1) Glycerin (2) Ethylene glycol (3) Other
	Tested satisfactorily	Character	(Y) Yes (1) Concentration too low/high (2) Antifreeze dirty (3) Other
Auxiliary drains	Operated satisfactorily	Character	(Y) Yes (N) No (3) N/A
Backflow preventer	Common data		See Table F.5.2(c).
	Type		(1) DC (2) DDC (3) RPZ (4) RPZDC (5) Air gap (6) Check valve (7) Single-check DC (8) Other
	Nonflow upstream pressure	Number	Two decimal places
	Nonflow intermediate chamber pressure	Number	Two decimal places
	Nonflow downstream pressure	Number	Two decimal places
	ITC flow upstream pressure	Number	Two decimal places
	ITC flow intermediate chamber pressure	Number	Two decimal places
	ITC flow downstream pressure	Number	Two decimal places
	Demand test flow rate	Number	Two decimal places
	Demand flow upstream pressure	Number	Two decimal places

(continues)

Δ **Table F.5.2(d)**   *Continued*

Item	Item Component	Format	Possible Values
	Demand flow intermediate chamber pressure	Number	Two decimal places
	Demand flow downstream pressure	Number	Two decimal places
Balancing valve diaphragm	Common data		See Table F.5.2(c).
	Operated satisfactorily	Character	(Y) Yes (N) No (3) N/A
Ball drip (automatic type) drain valves	Common data		See Table F.5.2(c).
	Operated satisfactorily	Character	(Y) Yes (N) No (3) N/A
Bladder tank	Common data		See Table F.5.2(c).
	Fill level OK	Character	(Y) Yes (N) No (3) N/A
	Operated satisfactorily	Character	(Y) Yes (N) No (3) N/A
	Comment if needed	String (80)	Alphanumeric
Spare head cabinet	Unit type identifier	String (48)	Alphanumeric
	Adequate stock of spare sprinklers	Character	(Y) Yes (N) No (3) N/A
	Comment if needed	String (80)	Alphanumeric
Check valve(s)	Common data		See Table F.5.2(c).
	Type	Character	(1) Flanged swing (2) Grooved swing (3) Sprinkler-loaded flanged swing (4) Spring-loaded grooved swing (5) Spring-loaded duo-wafer (6) Spring-loaded duo-grooved (7) Spring-loaded duo-flanged (8) Other
	Prevents backflow	Character	(Y) Yes (N) No (3) N/A
	Nonflow upstream pressure	Number	≥0
	Nonflow downstream pressure	Number	≥0
	Demand test flow rate	Number	≥0
	Demand flow upstream pressure	Number	≥0
	Demand flow downstream pressure	Number	≥0
	Unit type identifier	String (48)	Alphanumeric
	Where installed	Character	(1) On fire pump discharge (2) Loop piped back to suction
	Operated satisfactorily	Character	(Y) Yes (N) No (3) N/A

(continues)

Shaded text = Revisions.   Δ = Text deletions and figure/table revisions.   • = Section deletions.   *N* = New material.

Δ **Table F.5.2(d)**   *Continued*

Item	Item Component	Format	Possible Values
Control valve(s)	Common data		See Table F.5.2(c).
	Type of valve	Character	(1) OS&Y (2) Butterfly (3) Ball (4) NRS gate (5) Post indicator gate (6) Post indicator butterfly (7) Wall indicator gate (8) Wall indicator butterfly (9) Other
	Nominal valve size [in. (mm)]	Number	≥0
	Original position of valve	Character	(1) Normally open valve, open (N) Normally open valve, closed (3) Normally closed valve, closed (4) Normally closed valve, open (5) Valve partially closed
	Stops flow of water when closed	Character	(Y) Yes (2) Minor leakage (3) No (4) Not tested for flow
	Obstructs flow of water when open	Character	(Y) Yes (N) No (3) Not tested for flow
	Operated satisfactorily	Character	(Y) Yes (N) No (3) N/A
Deluge/preaction valve	Common data		See Table F.5.2(c).
	Type of system	Character	(1) Deluge (2) Non-interlock preaction (3) Single interlock preaction (4) Double interlock preaction (5) Other
	Activation mechanism	Character	(1) Pilot line (2) Heat detection (3) Smoke detection (4) Manual (5) Other
	Automatic actuation OK	Character	(Y) Yes (N) No (3) Not tested (4) N/A
	Manual actuation OK	Character	(Y) Yes (N) No (3) Not tested (4) N/A
	Operated satisfactorily	Character	(Y) Yes (N) No (3) N/A
	See Backflow Prevention Devices.		
Detector check valve	Common data		See Table F.5.2(c).
	Nozzle size [in. (mm)]	Number	≥0
	Flowed without obstruction	Character	(Y) Yes

(continues)

△ **Table F.5.2(d)**   *Continued*

Item	Item Component	Format	Possible Values
			(2) Minor obstructed nozzles (3) Significant obstructions
	Flowed at or above system design	Character	(Y) Yes (N) No (3) Not determined
	Concentrate percentage correct	Character	(Y) Yes (N) No
Drain riser	Operated satisfactorily	Character	(Y) Yes (N) No (3) N/A
Dry pipe valve	Common data		See Table F.5.2(c).
	Accelerator	Character	(Y) Yes (N) No
	Time to trip with accelerator (sec)	Number	≥0
	Water delivery time with accelerator (sec)	Number	≥0
	Time to trip without accelerator (sec)	Number	≥0
	Water delivery time without accelerator (sec)	Number	≥0
	System passed	Character	(Y) Yes (N) No
Accelerator	Common data		See Table F.5.2(c).
	Time to trip with accelerator (sec)	Number	≥0
	System passed	Character	(Y) Yes (N) No
Enclosure (during cold weather)	Adequate heat	Character	(Y) Yes (N) No
Fire department connection	Connection supplies	Character	(1) Sprinkler (2) Standpipe (3) Standpipe and sprinkler (4) Other
	Connection flushed	Character	(Y) Yes (N) No
	Connection tested	Character	(Y) Yes (N) No
	System passed	Character	(Y) Yes (N) No
Fire hose	Hydrostatically tested within last 5 years	Character	(Y) Yes (N) No
Fire pumps	See NFPA 20 and Table F.5.2(e).		
Fittings — except those with rubber gaskets	Indication of leakage present	Character	(1) No (2) Minor (3) Significant
Fittings — those with rubber gaskets	Indication of leakage present	Character	(1) No (2) Minor (3) Significant
Foam concentrate	Manufacturer	String (48)	Alphanumeric
	Type	String (48)	Alphanumeric
	Adequate quantity	Character	(Y) Yes (N) No

(continues)

    Shaded text = Revisions.   △ = Text deletions and figure/table revisions.   • = Section deletions.   *N* = New material.

Δ Table F.5.2(d)   *Continued*

Item	Item Component	Format	Possible Values
	Samples submitted for testing	Character	(Y) Yes (N) No
	Samples tested satisfactory	Character	(Y) Yes (N) No
Foam concentrate strainer(s)	Strainer clear initial	Character	(Y) Yes (N) No
Foam concentrate tank	Tank full	Character	(Y) Yes (N) No
	Protective coating (mineral oil) on top of foam concentrate OK	Character	(Y) Yes (N) No
Foam-water solution	Foam percentage	Number	≥0
	Solution passed	Character	(Y) Yes (N) No
Gauges	Gauge on	Character	(1) System side, wet pipe system (2) Supply side, wet pipe system (3) Air side, dry pipe system (4) Supply side, dry pipe system (5) Air side, preaction system (6) Supply side, preaction system (7) Fire pump suction (8) Fire pump discharge (9) Water mist system (10) Pressure tank (11) Water storage tank (12) Other
	Gauges reading correctly	Character	(Y) Yes (N) No
General information sign	Required signs provided	Character	(Y) Yes (N) No
	Signs readable and correct	Character	(Y) Yes (N) No
Gravity tanks	Water level OK	Character	(Y) Yes (N) No
	Adequate heat provided	Character	(Y) Yes (N) No
Hanger/pipe supports	Passed visual inspection	Character	(Y) Yes (N) No
High and low air pressure switch	Common data		See Table F.5.2(c).
	Sends low air signal at the appropriate pressure setting	Character	(Y) Yes (N) No
	Sends high air signal at the appropriate pressure setting	Character	(Y) Yes (N) No
Hose houses	Properly equipped and maintained	Character	(Y) Yes (N) No
Hose nozzle	Type of nozzle	Character	(1) Straight stream (2) Fog (3) Other
	Properly maintained	Character	(Y) Yes (N) No
Hose racks	Properly maintained	Character	(Y) Yes

(continues)

Shaded text = Revisions.   Δ = Text deletions and figure/table revisions.   • = Section deletions.   *N* = New material.

2020 Edition

Δ **Table F.5.2(d)**   *Continued*

Item	Item Component	Format	Possible Values
			(N) No
Hose storage device	Properly maintained	Character	(Y) Yes (N) No
Hose valve (non–pressure-regulating)	Properly maintained	Character	(Y) Yes (N) No
Hose valve pressure-regulating devices	Common data		See Table F.5.2(c).
	Inlet pressure while flowing	Character	(Y) Yes (N) No
	Outlet pressure while flowing	Character	(Y) Yes (N) No
	Test flow rate	Number	≥0
	Passed test	Character	(Y) Yes (N) No
Hydrants (dry barrel and wall)	Common data		See Table F.5.2(c).
	Hydrant opened and closed	Character	(Y) Yes (N) No
	Hydrant barrel drained	Character	(Y) Yes (N) No
	Hydrant shows need of maintenance	Character	(Y) Yes (N) No
Hydrants (wet barrel)	Common data		See Table F.5.2(c).
	Hydrant opened and closed	Character	(Y) Yes (N) No
	Hydrant shows need of maintenance	Character	(Y) Yes (N) No
Hydraulic design, information sign, and hydraulic placards	Required signs/placards provided	Character	(Y) Yes (N) No
	Signs readable and correct	Character	(Y) Yes (N) No
Identification signs	Required signs/placards provided	Character	(Y) Yes (N) No
	Signs readable and correct	Character	(Y) Yes (N) No
Information sign	Required signs/placards provided	Character	(Y) Yes (N) No
	Signs readable and correct	Character	(Y) Yes (N) No
Inspector's test connection	Flowed without obstruction	Character	(Y) Yes (N) No
	Activated alarm	Character	(Y) Yes (N) No
Low-point drains (dry pipe system)	Drained without obstruction	Character	(Y) Yes (N) No
	Passed visual inspection	Character	(Y) Yes (N) No
	Excessive water at drain	Character	(Y) Yes (N) No

(continues)

Shaded text = Revisions.   Δ = Text deletions and figure/table revisions.   • = Section deletions.   *N* = New material.

△ **Table F.5.2(d)**   *Continued*

Item	Item Component	Format	Possible Values
Main drain	Static pressure	Number	≥0
	Residual pressure	Number	≥0
Main drain valves	Free of corrosion and damage	Character	(Y) Yes (N) No
Mainline strainers	Strainer without excessive debris and damage	Character	(Y) Yes (N) No
Manual actuation device(s)	Passed test	Character	(Y) Yes (N) No
Mist system compressed gas cylinder	Cylinders full	Character	(Y) Yes (N) No
Mist system control equipment	Passed test	Character	(Y) Yes (N) No
Mist system plant air, compressors, and receivers	Operated satisfactorily	Character	(Y) Yes (N) No
Mist system pneumatic valves, cylinder valves, and master release valves	Passed test	Character	(Y) Yes (N) No
Mist system standby pump	Passed test	Character	(Y) Yes (N) No
Mist system water storage cylinder (additive storage cylinder)	Passed test	Character	(Y) Yes (N) No
Mist system water storage cylinder (high pressure)	Passed test	Character	(Y) Yes (N) No
Mist system water storage cylinder (high pressure), filters on refill connection	Passed test	Character	(Y) Yes (N) No
Mist system water storage cylinder (high pressure), support frame/restraints	Passed visual inspection	Character	(Y) Yes (N) No
Mist system water storage cylinder (high pressure), vent plugs at refilling	Operated satisfactorily	Character	(Y) Yes (N) No
Mist system water storage cylinder (high pressure), water level (load cells)	Passed test	Character	(Y) Yes (N) No
Mist system water storage tank	Tank full without leaks	Character	(Y) Yes (N) No
Mist system water storage tank, all valves and appurtenances	Passed test	Character	(Y) Yes (N) No
Mist system water storage tank, sight glass valves (confirm open)	Operated satisfactorily	Character	(Y) Yes (N) No
Mist system water storage tank, water level (supervised)	Passed test	Character	(Y) Yes (N) No
Monitor nozzles	Passed test	Character	(Y) Yes (N) No
Pipes (above ground)	Type of system	Character	(1) Wet pipe sprinkler (2) Dry pipe sprinkler (3) Preaction (4) Deluge (5) Water mist (6) Other

(continues)

Shaded text = Revisions.   △ = Text deletions and figure/table revisions.   • = Section deletions.   *N* = New material.

△ **Table F.5.2(d)**   *Continued*

Item	Item Component	Format	Possible Values
	Environment	Character	(1) Indoors, heated (2) Indoors, unheated (3) Covered, exposed to exterior atmosphere (4) Covered, exposed to exterior, salt air (5) Exposed, exterior (6) Exposed, exterior, salt air (7) Hostile chemical (8) Other
	Free of leads and excessive corrosion	Character	(Y) Yes (N) No
Fittings (above ground)	Type of system	Character	(1) Wet pipe sprinkler (2) Dry pipe sprinkler (3) Preaction (4) Deluge (5) Water mist (6) Other
	Environment	Character	(1) Indoors, heated (2) Indoors, unheated (3) Covered, exposed to exterior atmosphere (4) Covered, exposed to exterior, salt air (5) Exposed, exterior (6) Exposed, exterior, salt air (7) Hostile chemical (8) Other
	Free of leaks and excessive corrosion	Character	(Y) Yes (N) No
Pipes and fittings (underground)	Environment	Character	(1) Sandy soil (2) Clay soil (3) Corrosive soil (4) Other
	Unit type identifier	String (48)	Alphanumeric
	Type of pipe	Character	(1) Ductile iron (2) Steel (3) CPVC (4) Polyethylene (5) Other
	Pipe encasement	Character	(1) Polyethylene wrap (2) Culvert (3) None
	Water supply source	Character	(1) From municipal system (2) From water storage tank (3) From pond, lake, river, etc. (4) Other
	Free of excessive leakage	Character	(Y) Yes (N) No
	Excessive friction loss	Character	(Y) Yes (N) No
Pipe stands	Passed visual inspection	Character	(Y) Yes (N) No

(continues)

△ **Table F.5.2(d)** *Continued*

Item	Item Component	Format	Possible Values
Post indicator and wall indicator valves	Opened and closed	Character	(Y) Yes (N) No
	Stopped flow of water when closed	Character	(Y) Yes (N) No (3) Not verified
Low flow pressure relief valves (e.g., sprinkler system)	Relief pressure	Number	≥0
	Functioning properly	Character	(Y) Yes (N) No
High flow pressure relief valves (e.g., fire pump)	Common data		See Table F.5.2(c).
	Type	Character	(1) Pilot-operated (2) Spring-loaded (3) Other
	Discharge to…	Character	(1) Atmosphere (2) Tank (3) Fire pump suction (4) Other
	Relief pressure	Number	≥0
	Shutoff pressure	Number	≥0
	Functioning properly	Character	(Y) Yes (N) No
Pressure reducing valves	Common data		See Table F.5.2(c).
	Type	Character	(1) Pilot-operated (2) Spring-loaded (3) Other
	Installation with other pressure reducing valves	Character	(1) Standalone (2) Series upstream (3) Series downstream (4) Parallel, with smaller (5) Parallel, with larger (6) Parallel, same size (7) Combination series and parallel (8) Other
	Static inlet pressure	Number	≥0
	Static outlet pressure	Number	≥0
	Residual low flow inlet pressure	Number	≥0
	Residual low flow outlet pressure	Number	≥0
	Residual low flow inlet pressure	Number	≥0
	Residual low flow outlet pressure	Number	≥0
	Functioning properly	Character	(Y) Yes (N) No
Pump suction control valves	Common data		See Table F.5.2(c).
	Type	Character	(1) Pilot-operated (2) Spring-loaded (3) Other
	Set suction pressure	Number	≥0

(continues)

Shaded text = Revisions.   △ = Text deletions and figure/table revisions.   • = Section deletions.   *N* = New material.

2020 Edition

△ **Table F.5.2(d)** *Continued*

Item	Item Component	Format	Possible Values
	Static inlet pressure	Number	≥0
	Static outlet pressure	Number	≥0
	Inlet pressure at 100 percent rated pump capacity	Number	≥0
	Outlet pressure at 100 percent rated pump capacity	Number	≥0
	Inlet pressure at 150 percent rated pump capacity	Number	≥0
	Outlet pressure at 150 percent rated pump capacity	Number	≥0
	Functioning properly	Character	(Y) Yes (N) No
Pressure tanks	Air pressure (supervised)	Character	(Y) Yes (N) No
	Air pressure	Number	≥0
	Water level OK	Character	(Y) Yes (N) No
	Air pressure water level normal	Character	(Y) Yes (N) No
Pressure vacuum vents	Functioning correctly	Character	(Y) Yes (N) No (3) Not verified
Proportioning system(s)	Common data		See Table F.5.2(c).
	Functioning properly	Character	(Y) Yes (N) No
Reduced-pressure detectors	Common data		See Table F.5.2(c).
	Functioning properly	Character	(Y) Yes (N) No
Retainer glands	No visible leakage or damage	Character	(Y) Yes (N) No
Sight glass	No visible leakage or damage	Character	(Y) Yes (N) No
Spare sprinklers	Adequate number of each type	Character	(Y) Yes (N) No
	Visible leakage or damage	Character	(Y) Yes (N) No
Sprinkler systems	Visible leakage or significant corrosion or damage	Character	(Y) Yes (N) No
Sprinklers	Manufacturer	String (48)	Alphanumeric
	SIN	String (48)	Alphanumeric
	Quick response	Character	(Y) Yes (N) No
	Year manufactured	4 Characters	xxxx (year)
	Approximate number of sprinkler	Number	≥0
	Visible leakage or significant corrosion or damage	Character	(Y) Yes (N) No
	Approximate percent substandard	Number	0–100
Sprinklers (dry)	Manufacturer	String (48)	Alphanumeric

(continues)

Shaded text = Revisions.   △ = Text deletions and figure/table revisions.   • = Section deletions.   *N* = New material.

Δ **Table F.5.2(d)** *Continued*

Item	Item Component	Format	Possible Values
	SIN	String (48)	Alphanumeric
	Quick response	Character	(Y) Yes (N) No
	Year manufactured	4 Characters	xxxx (year)
	Approximate number of sprinkler Visible leakage or significant corrosion or damage	Number Character	≥0 (Y) Yes (N) No
	Approximate percent substandard	Number	0–100
Sprinklers (extra-high or greater temperature solder type)	Manufacturer	String (48)	Alphanumeric
	SIN	String (48)	Alphanumeric
	Quick response	Character	(Y) Yes (N) No
	Year manufactured	4 Characters	xxxx (year)
	Approximate number of sprinkler	Number	≥0
	Visible leakage or significant corrosion or damage	Character	(Y) Yes (N) No
	Approximate percent substandard	Number	0–100
	Approximate percent substandard	Number	0–100
Sprinklers (in harsh environments)	Manufacturer	String (48)	Alphanumeric
	SIN	String (48)	Alphanumeric
	Quick response	Character	(Y) Yes (N) No
	Year manufactured	4 Characters	xxxx (year)
	Approximate number of sprinkler	Number	≥0
	Visible leakage or significant corrosion or damage	Character	(Y) Yes (N) No
	Approximate percent substandard	Number	0–100
	Approximate percent substandard	Number	0–100
Sprinklers and automatic spray nozzles protecting commercial cooking equipment and ventilation systems	Manufacturer	String (48)	Alphanumeric
	SIN	String (48)	Alphanumeric
	Quick response	Character	(Y) Yes (N) No
	Year manufactured	4 characters	xxxx (year)
	Approximate number of sprinkler	Number	≥0
	Visible·leakage or significant corrosion or damage	Character	(Y) Yes (N) No
	Approximate percent substandard	Number	0 –100
	Approximate percent substandard	Number	0 –100
Suction tanks	Tank full	Character	(Y) Yes (N) No
Supervisory device	Functioned correctly	Character	(Y) Yes

(continues)

Shaded text = Revisions.   Δ = Text deletions and figure/table revisions.   • = Section deletions.   *N* = New material.   2020 Edition

△ **Table F.5.2(d)**   *Continued*

Item	Item Component	Format	Possible Values
			(N) No
Supports	Correctly installed	Character	(Y) Yes (N) No
System pressure-regulating devices	Functioned correctly	Character	(Y) Yes (N) No
Tank alarm and supervisory component, enclosure temperature	Connected to constantly monitored location	Character	(Y) Yes (N) No
	Functioned correctly	Character	(Y) Yes (N) No
Tank alarm and supervisory component, high and low water level	Connected to constantly monitored location	Character	(Y) Yes (N) No
	Functioned correctly	Character	(Y) Yes (N) No
Tank alarm and supervisory component, low water temperature alarms	Connected to constantly monitored location	Character	(Y) Yes (N) No
	Functioned correctly	Character	(Y) Yes (N) No
Tank alarm and supervisory component, temperature alarms	Connected to constantly monitored location	Character	(Y) Yes (N) No
	Functioned correctly	Character	(Y) Yes (N) No
Tank alarm and supervisory component, valve supervision	Connected to constantly monitored location	Character	(Y) Yes (N) No
	Functioned correctly	Character	(Y) Yes (N) No
Tank alarm and supervisory component, water level alarms	Connected to constantly monitored location	Character	(Y) Yes (N) No
	Functioned correctly	Character	(Y) Yes (N) No
Tank alarm and supervisory component, water temperature	Connected to constantly monitored location	Character	(Y) Yes (N) No
	Functioned correctly	Character	(Y) Yes (N) No
Tank catwalks and ladders	Passed visual inspection	Character	(Y) Yes (N) No
Tank check valves	Functioned correctly	Character	(Y) Yes (N) No (3) Not verified

Shaded text = Revisions.   △ = Text deletions and figure/table revisions.   • = Section deletions.   *N* = New material.

Table F.5.2(e) Fire Pump Information and Testing

Item	Item Component	Item	Item
Basic information (should be supplied by the fire pump package integrator)	Common equipment data		See Table F.5.2(c).
	Fire pump type	String (40)	P
	Rated flow	Number	>0
	Rated pressure	Number	>0
	Rated speed	Number	>0
	Rated horsepower	Number	>0
	Factory test pressure	Number	>0
	Design net churn pressure	Number	>0
	Design net 150 percent pressure	Number	>0
Basic information	Pump start pressure	Number	>0
	Pump reset pressure	Number	>0
	Design suction pressure	Number	>0
	Design discharge pressure	Number	>0
	Electric motor manufacturer	String (40)	Alphanumeric
	Electric motor type	String (40)	Alphanumeric
	Electric motor serial number	String (40)	Alphanumeric
	Electric motor model number	String (40)	Alphanumeric
	Electric motor date in service	Date	Year/month/day
	Nominal system voltage	Number	>0
	Electric motor rated horsepower	Number	>0
	Electric motor rated speed	Number	>0
	Motor rated FLA at the system nominal voltage	Number	>0
	Motor service factor	Number	>0
	Motor starting code	ASCII	A–H
	Nameplate full load amps	Number	>0
	Diesel engine manufacturer	String (40)	Alphanumeric
	Diesel engine serial number	String (40)	Alphanumeric
	Diesel engine model number	String (40)	Alphanumeric
	Diesel engine date in service	Date	Year/month/day
	Diesel engine rated horsepower	Number	>0
	Diesel engine rated speed	Number	>0
	Controller manufacturer	String (40)	Alphanumeric
	Controller type	String (40)	Alphanumeric
	Controller serial number	String (40)	Alphanumeric
	Controller model number	String (40)	Alphanumeric
	Controller date in service	Date	Year/month/day
	Jockey pump manufacturer	String (40)	Alphanumeric
	Jockey pump type	String (40)	Alphanumeric
	Jockey pump serial number	String (40)	Alphanumeric
	Jockey pump model number	String (40)	Alphanumeric
	Jockey pump date in service	Date	Year/month/day
	Jockey pump horsepower	Number	>0
	Jockey pump start pressure	Number	>0
	Jockey pump reset pressure	Number	>0
	Jockey pump controller manufacturer	String (40)	Alphanumeric
	Jockey pump controller type	String (40)	Alphanumeric
	Jockey pump controller serial number	String (40)	Alphanumeric
	Jockey pump controller model number	String (40)	Alphanumeric
	Jockey pump controller date in service	Date	Year/month/day
	Maximum system flow demand (at pump discharge flange)	Number	>0
	Maximum system pressure demand (at pump discharge flange)	Number	>0
Continuously monitored data	Fire pump power status	Number	(0) Off (1) On
	Fire pump running status		(0) Off (1) Running
	Fire pump test running		(0) No (1) Yes
	Suction pressure [psi (bar)]	Number	>0

(continues)

Table F.5.2(e)   *Continued*

Item	Item Component	Item	Item
	System pressure [psi (bar)]	Number	>0
	Pump discharge pressure [psi (bar)]	Number	>0
	Water temperature in pump casing	Number	>0
	Room temperature	Number	>0
	Last pump start date	Date	Year/month/day
	Last pump start time	Time	Hour(n)/min(n)/sec(n)
	Pressure at pump start	Number	>0
	Type of start		(1) Automatic demand (2) Automatic test (3) Manual
	Last pump shutdown date	Date	Year/month/day
	Last pump shutdown time	Time	Hour(n)/min(n)/sec(n)
	System pressure at pump shutdown	Number	>0
	Type of shutdown	Number	(1) Automatic demand (2) Automatic test (3) Manual (4) Overspeed (5) Other trouble
	Loss of power	Number	(1) Power on (2) Power off
	Transfer of power	Number	(1) Normal power (2) Standby power
	Fuel tank level (0-Above 2/3, 1-below 2/3)	Number	>0
	Fuel tank level (percentage full)	Number	>0
	Fuel maintenance system status	Number	(1) On (2) Off (3) Needs maintenance
Nonflow test data sets — 10 sets maintained in local equipment	Last nonflow monitoring reset date	Date	Year/month/day
	Last nonflow monitoring reset time	Time	Hour(n)/min(n)/sec(n)
	Total number of nonflow tests during monitored period	Number	>0
	Total pump test run time during monitored period (minutes)	Number	>0
	Nonflow test date start	Date	Year/month/day
	Nonflow test time start		Hour(n)/min(n)/sec(n)
	Nonflow test date end	Date	Year/month/day
	Nonflow test time end		Hour(n)/min(n)/sec(n)
	Nonflow test reference identifier	Number	>0
	Nonflow test data set reference identifier	Number	>0
	Nonflow test suction pressure [psi (bar)]	Number	>0
	Nonflow test system pressure [psi (bar)]	Number	>0
	Nonflow test pump discharge pressure [psi (bar)]	Number	>0
	Nonflow test net pressure [psi (bar)]	Number	>0
	Nonflow test water temperature in pump casing	Number	>0
	Nonflow test room temperature	Number	>0
	Nonflow test pump start date	Date	Year/month/day
	Nonflow test pump start time	Time	Hour(n)/min(n)/sec(n)
	Nonflow test pressure at pump start	Number	>0
	Nonflow test minimum transducer pressure	Number	>0
	Nonflow test type of start (1-automatic demand, 2-automatic test, 3-manual)	Number	>0
	Nonflow test pump shutdown time	Number	>0
	Nonflow test system pressure at pump shutdown	Number	>0
	Nonflow test type of shutdown	Number	(1) Automatic demand (2) Automatic test (3) Manual (4) Overspeed (5) Other trouble
	Nonflow test RPM	Number	>0

(continues)

Table F.5.2(e)　*Continued*

Item	Item Component	Item	Item
	Nonflow test voltage, Phase A–B	Analog signal converted to number	>0
	Nonflow test voltage, Phase B–C	Analog signal converted to number	>0
	Nonflow test voltage, Phase C–A	Analog signal converted to number	>0
	Nonflow test amperage, Phase 1	Analog signal converted to number	>0
	Nonflow test amperage, Phase 2	Analog signal converted to number	>0
	Nonflow test amperage, Phase 3	Analog signal converted to number	>0
Acceptance test data set (percentage) — permanent — 0, 25, 50, 75, 100, 125, and 150	Test date acceptance test	Date	Year/month/day
	Test reference identifier acceptance test	Number	>0
	Data set reference identifier acceptance test	Number	>0
	Suction pressure acceptance test	Number	>0
	System pressure acceptance test	Number	>0
	Discharge pressure acceptance test	Number	>0
	Net pressure	Number	>0
	Water temperature in pump casing acceptance test	Number	>0
	Room temperature — acceptance test	Number	>0
	Initial pump start date — acceptance test	Date	Year/month/day
	Initial pump start time — acceptance test	Time	Hour(n)/min(n)/sec(n)
	Final pump stop date — acceptance test	Date	Year/month/day
	Final pump stop time — acceptance test	Time	Hour(n)/min(n)/sec(n)
	Pump start dates — acceptance test (record up to 10)	Date	Year/month/day
	Pump start times — acceptance test (record up to 10)	Date	Year/month/day
	Pump stop dates — acceptance test (record up to 10)	Date	Year/month/day
	Pump Stop Times — acceptance test (record up to 10)	Number	>0
	Pressure at pump start acceptance test	Number	>0
	Type of start acceptance test	Number	(1) Automatic demand (2) Automatic test (3) Manual
	Minimum transducer pressure at startup acceptance test	Number	>0
	Number of starts and stops during acceptance test	Number	>0
	Final pump shutdown time acceptance test	Number	>0
	System pressure at final pump shutdown	Number	>0
	Type of shutdown		(1) Automatic demand (2) Automatic test (3) Manual (4) Overspeed (5) Other trouble
	Loss of power (for transfer) date	Date	Year/month/day
	Loss of power (for transfer) time	Time	Hour(n)/min(n)/sec(n)
	Transfer of power date	Date	Year/month/day
	Transfer of power time	Time	Hour(n)/min(n)/sec(n)
	Day power restored to normal	Date	Year/month/day
	Time power restored to normal	Time	Hour(n)/min(n)/sec(n)

(continues)

Shaded text = Revisions.　Δ = Text deletions and figure/table revisions.　• = Section deletions.　*N* = New material.

2020 Edition

Table F.5.2(e) *Continued*

Item	Item Component	Item	Item
	Date readings recorded	Date	Year/month/day
	Time readings recorded	Time	Hour(n)/min(n)/sec(n)
	RPM	Number	>0
	Voltage Phase A–B acceptance test	Analog signal converted to number	>0
	Voltage Phase B–C acceptance test	Analog signal converted to number	>0
	Voltage Phase C–A acceptance test	Analog signal converted to number	>0
	Amperage Phase 1 acceptance test	Analog signal converted to number	>0
	Amperage Phase 2 acceptance test	Analog signal converted to number	>0
	Amperage Phase 3 acceptance test	Analog signal converted to number	>0
	Nozzle coefficient acceptance test, up to 20 per test	Number	>0
	Nozzle size acceptance test, up to 20 per test [in. (mm)]	Number	>0
	Nozzle pitot pressure acceptance test, up to 20 per test	Number	>0
	Fuel tank level acceptance test (0-Above 2/3, 1-below 2/3)	Number	>0
	Fuel tank level acceptance test (percentage full)	Number	>0
	Flow through pump acceptance test	Number	>0
	RPM adjusted net pressure acceptance test	Number	>0
	RPM adjusted flow acceptance test [gpm (L/min)]	Number	>0
	Percentage of factory-certified curve acceptance test	Number	>0
	Hours on diesel engine or electric motor at start of acceptance test	Number	>0
	Hours on diesel engine or electric motor at conclusion of acceptance test	Number	>0
	Pump passed initial acceptance test	Character	(Y) Yes (N) No
	Pump could supply maximum system demand acceptance test	Number	(1) Yes (2) No (3) Demand not known
	Pump was significantly impaired acceptance test	Character	(Y) Yes (N) No
	Pump was partially impaired acceptance test	Character	(Y) Yes (N) No
	Pump passed after adjustments acceptance test	Character	(Y) Yes (N) No
	Failure mode acceptance test (See Standardized List.)	Number	>0
	Explanation of failure acceptance test	String (80)	Alphanumeric

(continues)

Shaded text = Revisions.   Δ = Text deletions and figure/table revisions.   • = Section deletions.   *N* = New material.

Table F.5.2(e)   *Continued*

Item	Item Component	Item	Item
Current performance test data set (percentage) — permanent — 0, 25, 50, 75, 100, 125, and 150	Test date — current performance test	Date	Year/month/day
	Test reference identifier — current performance test	Number	>0
	Data set reference identifier — current performance test	Number	>0
	Suction pressure — current performance test	Number	>0
	System pressure — current performance test	Number	>0
	Discharge pressure — current performance test	Number	>0
	Net pressure	Number	>0
	Water temperature in pump casing — current performance test	Number	>0
	Room temperature — current performance test	Number	>0
	Initial pump start date — current performance test	Date	Year/month/day
	Initial pump start time — current performance test	Time	Hour(n)/min(n)/sec(n)
	Final pump stop date — current performance test	Date	Year/month/day
	Final pump stop time — current performance test	Time	Hour(n)/min(n)/sec(n)
	Pump start dates — current performance test (record up to 10)	Date	Year/month/day
	Pump start times — current performance test (record up to 10)	Time	Hour(n)/min(n)/sec(n)
	Pump stop dates — current performance test (record up to 10)	Date	Year/month/day
	Pump stop times — current performance test (record up to 10)	Time	Hour(n)/min(n)/sec(n)
	Pressure at pump start — current performance test	Number	>0
	Type of start — current performance test	Number	(1) Automatic demand (2) Automatic test (3) Manual
	Minimum transducer pressure at startup — current performance test	Number	>0
	Number of starts and stops during — current performance test	Number	>0
		Number	>0
	System pressure at final pump shutdown	Number	>0
	Type of shutdown	Number	(1) Automatic demand (2) Automatic test (3) Manual (4) Overspeed (5) Other trouble
	Loss of power (for transfer) date	Date	Year/month/day
	Loss of power (for transfer) time	Time	Hour(n)/min(n)/sec(n)
	Transfer of power date	Date	Year/month/day
	Transfer of power time	Time	Hour(n)/min(n)/sec(n)
	Day power restored to normal	Date	Year/month/day
	Time power restored to normal	Time	Hour(n)/min(n)/sec(n)
	Date readings recorded	Date	Year/month/day
	Time readings recorded	Time	Hour(n)/min(n)/sec(n)
	RPM	Number	>0
	Voltage Phase A–B current performance test	Analog signal converted to number	>0
	Voltage Phase B–C current performance test	Analog signal converted to number	>0

(continues)

Shaded text = Revisions.   Δ = Text deletions and figure/table revisions.   • = Section deletions.   *N* = New material.

2020 Edition

Table F.5.2(e) *Continued*

Item	Item Component	Item	Item
	Voltage Phase C–A current performance test	Analog signal converted to number	>0
	Amperage Phase 1 current performance test	Analog signal converted to number	>0
	Amperage Phase 2 current performance test	Analog signal converted to number	>0
	Amperage Phase 3 current performance test	Analog signal converted to number	>0
	Nozzle coefficient — current performance test, up to 20 per test	Number	>0
	Nozzle size — current performance test, up to 20 per test [in. (mm)]	Number	>0
	Nozzle pitot pressure — current performance test, up to 20 per test	Number	>0
	Fuel tank level — current performance test (0-Above 2/3, 1-below 2/3)	Number	>0
	Fuel tank level — current performance test (percentage full)	Number	>0
	Flow through pump — current performance test	Number	>0
	RPM adjusted net pressure — current performance test	Number	>0
	RPM adjusted flow — current performance test [gpm (L/min)]	Number	>0
	Percentage of factory-certified curve — current performance test	Number	>0
	Hours on diesel engine or electric motor at start of current performance test	Number	>0
	Hours on diesel engine or electric motor at conclusion of current performance test	Number	>0
	Pump passed initial — current performance test	Character	Y/N
	Pump could supply maximum system demand — current performance test	Number	(1) Yes (2) No (3) Demand not known
	Pump was significantly impaired — current performance test	Character	Y/N
	Pump was partially impaired — current performance test	Character	Y/N
	Pump passed after adjustments — current performance test	Character	Y/N
	Failure mode — current performance test	Number	See Standardized List.
	Explanation of failure — current performance test	String (80)	Alphanumeric
Previous performance test data set (percentage) — static — 0, 25, 50, 75, 100, 125, and 150	Test date — previous performance test	Date	Year/month/day
	Test reference identifier — previous performance test	Time	Hour(n)/min(n)/sec(n)
	Data set reference identifier — previous performance test	Number	>0
	Suction pressure — previous performance test	Number	>0
	System pressure — previous performance test	Number	>0
	Discharge pressure — previous performance test	Number	>0
	Net pressure	Number	>0
	Water temperature in pump casing — previous performance test	Number	>0

(continues)

Shaded text = Revisions.   Δ = Text deletions and figure/table revisions.   • = Section deletions.   *N* = New material.

Table F.5.2(e) *Continued*

Item	Item Component	Item	Item
	Room temperature — previous performance test	Number	>0
	Initial pump start date — previous performance test	Date	Year/month/day
	Initial pump start time — previous performance test	Time	Hour(n)/min(n)/sec(n)
	Final pump stop date — previous performance Test	Date	Year/month/day
	Final pump stop time — previous performance test	Time	Hour(n)/min(n)/sec(n)
	Pump start dates — previous performance test (record up to 10)	Date	Year/month/day
	Pump start times — previous performance test (record up to 10)	Time	Hour(n)/min(n)/sec(n)
	Pump stop dates — previous performance test (record up to 10)	Date	Year/month/day
	Pump stop times — previous performance test (record up to 10)	Time	Hour(n)/min(n)/sec(n)
	Pressure at pump start — previous performance test	Number	>0
	Type of start — previous performance test (1-automatic demand, 2-automatic test, 3-manual)	Number	>0
	Minimum transducer pressure at startup — previous performance test	Number	>0
	Number of starts and stops —previous performance test	Number	>0
	Final pump shutdown time — previous performance test	Number	>0
	System pressure at final pump shutdown	Number	>0
	Type of shutdown	Number	(1) Automatic demand (2) Automatic test (3) Manual (4) Overspeed (5) Other trouble
	Loss of power (for transfer) date	Date	Year/month/day
	Loss of power (for transfer) time	Time	Hour(n)/min(n)/sec(n)
	Transfer of power date	Date	Year/month/day
	Transfer of power time	Time	Hour(n)/min(n)/sec(n)
	Day power restored to normal	Date	Year/month/day
	Time power restored to normal	Time	Hour(n)/min(n)/sec(n)
	Date readings recorded	Date	Year/month/day
	Time readings recorded	Time	Hour(n)/min(n)/sec(n)
	RPM		>0
	Voltage Phase A–B previous performance test	Analog signal converted to number	>0
	Voltage Phase B–C previous performance test	Analog signal converted to number	>0
	Voltage Phase C–A previous performance test	Analog signal converted to number	>0
	Amperage Phase 1 previous performance test	Analog signal converted to number	>0
	Amperage Phase 2 previous performance test	Analog signal converted to number	>0

(continues)

Shaded text = Revisions. Δ = Text deletions and figure/table revisions.   • = Section deletions.   *N* = New material.

Table F.5.2(e) *Continued*

Item	Item Component	Item	Item
	Amperage Phase 3 previous performance test	Analog signal converted to number	>0
	Nozzle coefficient — previous performance test, up to 20 per test	Number	>0
	Nozzle size — previous performance test, up to 20 per test [in. (mm)]	Number	>0
	Nozzle pitot pressure — previous performance test, up to 20 per test	Number	>0
	Fuel tank level previous performance test (0-Above 2/3, 1-below 2/3)	Number	>0
	Fuel tank level — previous performance test (percentage full)	Number	>0
	Flow through pump — previous performance test	Number	>0
	RPM adjusted net pressure — previous performance test	Number	>0
	RPM adjusted flow — previous performance test [gpm (L/min)]	Number	>0
	Percentage of factory-certified curve — previous performance test	Number	>0
	Hours on diesel engine or electric motor at start of previous performance test	Number	>0
	Hours on diesel engine or electric motor at conclusion of previous performance test	Number	>0
	Pump passed initial — previous performance test	Character	Y/N
	Pump could supply maximum system demand — previous performance test	Number	(1) Yes (2) No (3) Demand not known
	Pump was significantly impaired — previous performance test	Character	Y/N
	Pump was partially impaired — previous performance test	Character	Y/N
	Pump passed after adjustments — previous performance test	Character	Y/N
	Failure mode — previous performance test	Number	See Standardized List.
	Explanation of failure — previous performance test	String (80)	Alphanumeric
Repair maintenance data (20 sets)	Date of maintenance/repair	Date	Year/month/day
	Maintenance/repair identifier	Number	>0
	Routine maintenance/repair	Character	Y/N
	Pump out of service during maintenance/repair	Character	Y/N
	Date pump out of service	Date	Year/month/day
	Time pump out of service	Time	Hour(n)/min(n)/sec(n)
	Date pump restored to service	Date	Year/month/day
	Time pump restored to service	Time	Hour(n)/min(n)/sec(n)
	Date pump maintenance/repair completed	Date	Year/month/day
	Part replaced (1)	String (40)	Alphanumeric
	Description of maintenance, repair, and/or Part 1 replacement	String (80)	Alphanumeric
	Part replaced (2)	String (40)	Alphanumeric
	Description of maintenance, repair, and/or Part 2 replacement	String (80)	Alphanumeric
	Part replaced (3)	String (40)	Alphanumeric
	Description of maintenance, repair, and/or Part 3 replacement	String (80)	Alphanumeric
	Part replaced (4)	String (40)	Alphanumeric

(continues)

Shaded text = Revisions.   Δ = Text deletions and figure/table revisions.   • = Section deletions.   *N* = New material.

Table F.5.2(e) *Continued*

Item	Item Component	Item	Item
	Description of maintenance, repair, and/or Part 4 replacement	String (80)	Alphanumeric
	Routine maintenance or repair	String (40)	Alphanumeric
	Date repair completed	Date	Year/month/day
	Fuel tank level — current performance test	Number	(0) Above 2/3 (1) Below 2/3
	Fuel tank level — current performance test (percentage full)	Number	>0
	Fuel maintenance system status	Number	(1) In service (2) Out of service (3) Needs maintenance
	19 additional repair maintenance data sets		S
Jockey pump operation	Last jockey pump monitoring reset date	Date	Year/month/day
	Last jockey pump monitoring reset time	Time	Hour(n)/min(n)/sec(n)
	Total number of starts (since reset)	Number	>0
	Total jockey pump run time (minutes since last reset)	Number	>0
	Jockey Pump start pressure (most recent)	Number	>0
	Jockey pump stop pressure	Number	>0
	Most recent run time (seconds)	Number	>0
Fire pump operation	Last fire pump monitoring reset date	Date	Year/month/day
	Last fire pump monitoring reset time	Time	Hour(n)/min(n)/sec(n)
	Fire pump start date and time (last 10 times)	Date	Year/month/day
	Fire pump stop date and time (last 10 times)	Time	Hour(n)/min(n)/sec(n)
	Fire pump start pressure (most recent)	Number	>0
	Fire pump stop pressure (most recent)	Number	>0
	Stop automatic or manual (most recent)	Number	>0
	Total number of starts since reset	Number	>0
	Total run time since reset (minutes)	Number	>0
	Date loss of electrical power with switch in "on" position since last reset (50 sets)	Number	>0
	Time loss of electrical power with switch in "on" position since last reset (50 sets)	Number	>0
	Date power restored after loss of power with switch in "on" position since last reset (50 sets)	Date	Year/month/day
	Time power restored after loss of power with switch in "on" position since last reset (50 sets)	Time	Hour(n)/min(n)/sec(n)
	Date power switch turned off (50 sets)	Date	Year/month/day
	Time power switch turned off (50 sets)	Time	Hour(n)/min(n)/sec(n)
	Date power switch turned back on (50 sets)	Date	Year/month/day
	Time power switch turned back on (50 sets)	Time	Hour(n)/min(n)/sec(n)

Shaded text = Revisions.   Δ = Text deletions and figure/table revisions.   • = Section deletions.   *N* = New material.

2020 Edition

Table F.5.2.1 Data Formats

Reference Name	Format	Possible Values			
Bit		0 or 1			
Byte	8 bits	0–256			
Character	1 byte	0–256 (These can be interpreted as letters, numbers, or symbols using ASCII convention.)			
Integer	2 bytes	0–65,534 (During interpretation, a decimal place may be assumed. When using an assumed decimal place for a number in which the first digit might exceed 5, the number is limited to four digits.)			
Number	5 bytes	Byte	Value	Number	Power of 10
		1st byte	0	Positive	Positive
			1	Positive	Negative
			2	Negative	Positive
			3	Negative	Negative
		2nd–4th bytes	0–16,777,216		
		5th byte	0–255 (10^n)		
String	Multibytes as specified [e.g., String (80) is 80 bytes]	Any letters, numbers, or symbols represented in the ASCII convention			
Date	8 characters	xxxx (year) xx (month) xx (day)			
Time	3 bytes	n (hours, 0–24) n (minutes, 0–60) n (seconds, 0–60)			

Annex G   Color-Coded Tagging Program

This annex is not a part of the requirements of this NFPA document but is included for informational purposes only.

G.1 Tagging Program. To assist with the enforcement and application of NFPA 25, some authorities having jurisdiction (AHJs) adopt color-coded system status tagging programs. The purpose of these programs varies, but the typical goal is to promote the timely determination of the following:

(1) Have the inspections and tests required by this standard been completed at their designated frequencies?

(2) Were the systems inspected and/or tested in compliance with this standard at the time of the inspections and tests?

While NFPA 25 does not mandate system status tagging, it is desirable that a certain level of consistency exist between programs. With that in mind, AHJs using a color-coded system status tagging program are urged to consider the following:

(1) *Overall Goal of the Program.* Once that is determined, questions to ask about the program might include the following:

   (a) Does the presence of a particular color tag indicate that all tasks are completed at the required frequency, and, if so, how often are the tags placed? For example, if a green tag is meant to signify compliance with NFPA 25, which frequency does that compliance correspond to? (NFPA 25 establishes frequencies from daily through 5 years and beyond.) Additionally, what should happen when a more frequent inspection (daily/weekly/monthly/ quarterly/etc.) reveals no deficiencies, but later, during the annual frequency inspection, deficiencies are found?

   (b) Is the goal to inform fire department inspectors, emergency responders, and others?

(2) *Benefits and Pitfalls of a Color-Coded Tagging Program.* These might include the following:

   (a) Benefit: Quicker recognition of a system with deficiencies would promote a quicker response to system deficiencies by the owner and trigger a more in-depth review of ITM records.

   (b) Pitfalls: The presence of a tag indicating compliance with the standard might give a false sense of security if question (1)(a) is not addressed adequately, or it might create confusion between the owner and sprinkler contractor(s) if repair work is not done thoroughly; tags are not filled out completely, accurately, and consistently; or multiple contractors are employed for corrections/repairs on a single tag.

(3) *The Type and Amount of Information Contained on the Tag.* ITM records are comprehensive and contain much more information than could be condensed onto a tag. With that in mind, information required to be written on a tag should include the following as a minimum:

   (a) Identification of the system that the information on the tag represents

   (b) Employer of the technician who performed inspections, tests, or maintenance and any license or certification information required by the AHJ.

Shaded text = Revisions.   **Δ** = Text deletions and figure/table revisions.   • = Section deletions.   *N* = New material.

(c) Date inspections, tests, or maintenance was performed

(d) Type and frequency of inspections, tests, or maintenance

(4) *The Four Conditions.* This standard identifies four conditions as follows:

(a) No deficiencies or impairments

(b) Noncritical deficiencies

(c) Critical deficiencies

(d) Impairments

(5) *The Tag Colors and What the Colors Represent.* A color-coded tagging system that mirrors the standard would include the following tags:

(a) Green tag — No deficiencies or impairments found when inspections and tests performed at the required frequency were completed as indicated on the ITM report provided to the owner

(b) Yellow tag — Noncritical deficiencies found and recorded on the ITM report

(c) Orange tag — Critical deficiencies found and recorded on the ITM report

(d) Red tag — Impairments found and recorded on the ITM report (The color-coded tagging program should be kept separate from the impairment tag and other requirements outlined in Chapter 15.)

(e) White tag — Correction/repair tag (placed along with color-coded tag after work to correct/repair deficiencies or impairments has been completed) indicating specifically which corrections or repairs were made.

(6) *How to Address Corrections or Repairs.* A tag that indicates deficiencies or impairments were corrected and when and by who is important. A green tag should only be placed on a system when inspections and tests at the required frequency have been performed and no deficiencies have been found. Many times this is not part of the work done following corrections and repairs. Following completion of corrections or repairs, a white tag should be placed, along with the yellow, orange, or red tag, briefly describing what was done to correct or repair the deficiencies or impairments. Also, all corrections and repairs should include the appropriate inspections and tests as outlined in Tables 5.5.1, 6.5.1, 7.5.1, 8.6.1, 9.6.1, 10.5.1, and 11.5.1 before they are tagged as completed.

(7) *How Long Tags Should Remain.* Subsection 4.3.5 outlines a timeline for record retention. Consideration should be given to coordinating those requirements with tagging programs.

(8) *Who Can Place or Remove Tags.* The standard requires that persons who perform ITM work must be qualified. Consideration should be given to only permitting those who are qualified to place or remove tags.

All tags should be made of durable, weatherproof, colorfast materials and should be securely affixed to the main control valve of each system. If the main control valve is not accessible, as with underground piping, the tag should be attached at a point as close as possible to the main control valve, but still visible and accessible, as on a system pressure gauge or for an underground system on a hydrant.

These are just a few of the most common points for an AHJ to consider, but this is certainly not a complete list. A well-thought-out program will be more likely to succeed than one that leaves questions unanswered.

G.2 Sample Tags. Figure G.2(a), Figure G.2(b), Figure G.2(c), Figure G.2(d), and Figure G.2(e) illustrate typical color-coded tags.

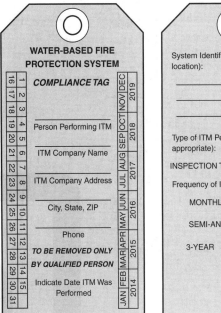
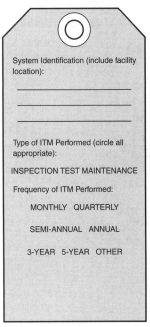

FIGURE G.2(a)   Sample Compliance Tag (Green Tag).

FIGURE G.2(b)   Sample Noncritical Deficiency Tag (Yellow Tag).

Shaded text = Revisions.   Δ = Text deletions and figure/table revisions.   • = Section deletions.   *N* = New material.

2020 Edition

FIGURE G.2(c)   **Sample Critical Deficiency Tag (Orange Tag).**

FIGURE G.2(e)   **Sample Correction/Repair Tag (White Tag).**

FIGURE G.2(d)   **Sample Impairment Tag (Red Tag).**

Annex H   Informational References

H.1 Referenced Publications. The documents or portions thereof listed in this annex are referenced within the informational sections of this standard and are not part of the requirements of this document unless also listed in Chapter 2 for other reasons.

△ **H.1.1 NFPA Publications.** National Fire Protection Association, 1 Batterymarch Park, Quincy, MA 02169-7471.

NFPA 13, *Standard for the Installation of Sprinkler Systems*, 2019 edition.

NFPA 13R, *Standard for the Installation of Sprinkler Systems in Low-Rise Residential Occupancies*, 2019 edition.

NFPA 14, *Standard for the Installation of Standpipe and Hose Systems*, 2019 edition.

NFPA 15, *Standard for Water Spray Fixed Systems for Fire Protection*, 2017 edition.

NFPA 16, *Standard for the Installation of Foam-Water Sprinkler and Foam-Water Spray Systems*, 2019 edition.

NFPA 20, *Standard for the Installation of Stationary Pumps for Fire Protection*, 2019 edition.

NFPA 22, *Standard for Water Tanks for Private Fire Protection*, 2018 edition.

NFPA 24, *Standard for the Installation of Private Fire Service Mains and Their Appurtenances*, 2019 edition.

NFPA 70E®, *Standard for Electrical Safety in the Workplace*®, 2018 edition.

NFPA 72 ®, *National Fire Alarm and Signaling Code*®, 2019 edition.

NFPA 110, *Standard for Emergency and Standby Power Systems,* 2019 edition

NFPA 291, *Recommended Practice for Fire Flow Testing and Marking of Hydrants,* 2019 edition.

NFPA 551, *Guide for the Evaluation of Fire Risk Assessments,* 2019 edition.

NFPA 750, *Standard on Water Mist Fire Protection Systems,* 2019 edition.

NFPA 780, *Standard for the Installation of Lightning Protection Systems,* 2020 edition.

NFPA 1962, *Standard for the Care, Use, Inspection, Service Testing, and Replacement of Fire Hose, Couplings, Nozzles, and Fire Hose Appliances,* 2018 edition.

Antifreeze Systems in Home Fire Sprinkler Systems — Literature Review and Research Plan, Fire Protection Research Foundation, June 2010.

Antifreeze Systems in Home Fire Sprinkler Systems — Phase II Final Report, Fire Protection Research Foundation, December 2010.

Antifreeze Solutions Supplied through Spray Sprinklers — Interim Report, Fire Protection Research Foundation, February 2012.

"Fire Pump Field Data Collection and Analysis Report," available for download at www.nfpa.org/Foundation, 2011.

NFPA's Future in Performance Based Codes and Standards, July 1995.

NFPA Performance Based Codes and Standards Primer, December 1999.

H.1.2 Other Publications.

H.1.2.1 ASTM Publications. ASTM International, 100 Barr Harbor Drive, P.O. Box C700, West Conshohocken, PA 19428-2959.

IEEE/ASTM-SI-10, *American National Standard for Metric Practice,* 2016.

H.1.2.2 AWWA Publications. American Water Works Association, 6666 West Quincy Avenue, Denver, CO 80235.

AWWA *Manual of Water Supply Practices — M42 Steel Water Storage Tanks,* 2013.

N H.1.2.3 BSI Publications. British Standards Institution, 389 Chiswick High Road, London, W4 4AL, United Kingdom.

EN 12259-1, *Fixed firefighting systems – Components for sprinkler and water spray systems – Part 1: Sprinklers,* 1999 edition.

N H.1.2.4 FM Publications. FM Approvals LLC, 1151 Boston-Providence Turnpike, P.O. Box 9102, Norwood, MA 02062.

FM Approvals Standard 5560, *Water Mist Systems,* 2012 edition.

N H.1.2.5 CGA Publications. CGA Publications. Compressed Gas Association, 14501 George Carter Way, Suite 103, Chantilly, VA 20151.

CGA C-6, *Standard for Visual Inspection of Steel Compressed Gas Cylinders,* 2013.

H.1.2.6 Hydraulic Institute Publications. Hydraulic Institute, 9 Sylvan Way, Parsippany, NJ 07054.

Hydraulic Institute Standards for Centrifugal, Rotary and Reciprocating Pumps, 14th edition, 1983.

N H.1.2.7 UL Publications. Underwriters Laboratories Inc., 333 Pfingsten Road, Northbrook, IL 60062-2096.

UL 2167, *Standard for Water Mist Nozzles for Fire Protection Service,* 2017.

N H.1.2.8 IMO Publications. International Maritime Organization, 4 Albert Embankment, London SE1 7SR.

MSC.1/Circular 1432, *Guidelines for the Maintenance and Inspection of Fire Protection Systems and Appliances,* 2012.

H.1.2.9 SFPE Publications. Society of Fire Protection Engineers, 9711 Washington Blvd., Suite 380 W, Gaithersburg, MD 20878.

SFPE *Engineering Guide: Fire Risk Assessment,* 2006.

SFPE *Engineering Guide to Performance-Based Fire Protection,* 2nd edition, 2007.

SFPE *Handbook of Fire Protection Engineering,* 5th edition, 2016.

N H.1.2.10 U.S. Government Publications. U.S. Government Publishing Office, 732 North Capitol Street, NW, Washington, DC 20401-0001.

Department of Defense Handbook MIL-HDBK-695D, *Rubber Products: Recommended Shelf Life,* 23 May 2005.

Title 49, Code of Federal Regulations.

H.1.2.11 Other Publications.

Edward K. Budnick, P.E., "Automatic Sprinkler System Reliability," *Fire Protection Engineering,* SFPE, Winter 2001.

Fire Protection Equipment Surveillance Optimization and Maintenance Guide, Electric Power Research Institute, July 2003.

Kenneth W. Dungan, P.E., "Performance-Based Inspection, Testing, and Maintenance," *Fire Protection Engineering,* SFPE, Quarter 4, 2016.

William E. Koffel, P.E., *Reliability of Automatic Sprinkler Systems,* Alliance for Fire Safety.

H.2 Informational References. The following documents or portions thereof are listed here as informational resources only. They are not a part of the requirements of this document.

H.2.1 NFPA Publications. National Fire Protection Association, 1 Batterymarch Park, Quincy, MA 02169-7471.

NFPA 1, *Fire Code,* 2018 edition.

Water-Based Fire Protection Systems Handbook, 2020 edition.

H.2.2 Other Publications.

H.2.2.1 AWWA Publications. American Water Works Association, 6666 West Quincy Avenue, Denver, CO 80235.

AWWA D101, *Inspecting and Repairing Steel Water Tanks, Standpipes, Reservoirs, and Elevated Tanks, for Water Storage,* 1986.

Δ **H.2.2.2 SSPC Publications.** Society for Protective Coatings, 800 Trumbull Drive, Pittsburgh, PA 15205.

SSPC Chapter 3, "Special Pre-Paint Treatments," 1993.

SSPC-PA 1, *Shop, Field, and Maintenance Coating of Metals,* 2016.

SSPC PA 9, *White (or Colored) Vinyl Paint,* 2015.

SSPC-SP 6, *Commercial Blast Cleaning,* 2007.

SSPC-SP 8, *Pickling,* 2004.

SSPC-SP 10, *Near-White Blast Cleaning,* 2007.

H.2.2.3 U.S. Government Publications. U.S. Government Publishing Office, Washington, DC 20402.

Bureau of Reclamation Specification VR-3.

Federal Specification TT-P-86, *Specifications for Vinyl Resin Paint,* M-54, 1995.

H.3 References for Extracts in Informational Sections.

NFPA 13, *Standard for the Installation of Sprinkler Systems,* 2019 edition.

NFPA 14, *Standard for the Installation of Standpipe and Hose Systems,* 2019 edition.

NFPA 15, *Standard for Water Spray Fixed Systems for Fire Protection,* 2017 edition.

NFPA 20, *Standard for the Installation of Stationary Pumps for Fire Protection,* 2019 edition.

NFPA 24, *Standard for the Installation of Private Fire Service Mains and Their Appurtenances,* 2019 edition.

NFPA 1142, *Standard on Water Supplies for Suburban and Rural Fire Fighting,* 2017 edition.

Index

Copyright © 2019 National Fire Protection Association. All Rights Reserved.

The copyright in this index is separate and distinct from the copyright in the document that it indexes. The licensing provisions set forth for the document are not applicable to this index. This index may not be reproduced in whole or in part by any means without the express written permission of NFPA.

Sequence of Events for the Standards Development Process

Once the current edition is published, a Standard is opened for Public Input.

Step 1 – Input Stage

- Input accepted from the public or other committees for consideration to develop the First Draft
- Technical Committee holds First Draft Meeting to revise Standard (23 weeks); Technical Committee(s) with Correlating Committee (10 weeks)
- Technical Committee ballots on First Draft (12 weeks); Technical Committee(s) with Correlating Committee (11 weeks)
- Correlating Committee First Draft Meeting (9 weeks)
- Correlating Committee ballots on First Draft (5 weeks)
- First Draft Report posted on the document information page

Step 2 – Comment Stage

- Public Comments accepted on First Draft (10 weeks) following posting of First Draft Report
- If Standard does not receive Public Comments and the Technical Committee chooses not to hold a Second Draft meeting, the Standard becomes a Consent Standard and is sent directly to the Standards Council for issuance (see Step 4) or
- Technical Committee holds Second Draft Meeting (21 weeks); Technical Committee(s) with Correlating Committee (7 weeks)
- Technical Committee ballots on Second Draft (11 weeks); Technical Committee(s) with Correlating Committee (10 weeks)
- Correlating Committee Second Draft Meeting (9 weeks)
- Correlating Committee ballots on Second Draft (8 weeks)
- Second Draft Report posted on the document information page

Step 3 – NFPA Technical Meeting

- Notice of Intent to Make a Motion (NITMAM) accepted (5 weeks) following the posting of Second Draft Report
- NITMAMs are reviewed and valid motions are certified by the Motions Committee for presentation at the NFPA Technical Meeting
- NFPA membership meets each June at the NFPA Technical Meeting to act on Standards with "Certified Amending Motions" (certified NITMAMs)
- Committee(s) vote on any successful amendments to the Technical Committee Reports made by the NFPA membership at the NFPA Technical Meeting

Step 4 – Council Appeals and Issuance of Standard

- Notification of intent to file an appeal to the Standards Council on Technical Meeting action must be filed within 20 days of the NFPA Technical Meeting
- Standards Council decides, based on all evidence, whether to issue the standard or to take other action

Notes:

1. Time periods are approximate; refer to published schedules for actual dates.
2. Annual revision cycle documents with certified amending motions take approximately 101 weeks to complete.
3. Fall revision cycle documents receiving certified amending motions take approximately 141 weeks to complete.

Committee Membership Classifications[1,2,3,4]

The following classifications apply to Committee members and represent their principal interest in the activity of the Committee.

1. M *Manufacturer:* A representative of a maker or marketer of a product, assembly, or system, or portion thereof, that is affected by the standard.
2. U *User:* A representative of an entity that is subject to the provisions of the standard or that voluntarily uses the standard.
3. IM *Installer/Maintainer:* A representative of an entity that is in the business of installing or maintaining a product, assembly, or system affected by the standard.
4. L *Labor:* A labor representative or employee concerned with safety in the workplace.
5. RT *Applied Research/Testing Laboratory:* A representative of an independent testing laboratory or independent applied research organization that promulgates and/or enforces standards.
6. E *Enforcing Authority:* A representative of an agency or an organization that promulgates or enforces standards.
7. I *Insurance:* A representative of an insurance company, broker, agent, bureau, or inspection agency.
8. C *Consumer:* A person who is or represents the ultimate purchaser of a product, system, or service affected by the standard, but who is not included in (2).
9. SE *Special Expert:* A person not representing (1) through (8) and who has special expertise in the scope of the standard or portion thereof.

NOTE 1: "Standard" connotes code, standard, recommended practice, or guide.

NOTE 2: A representative includes an employee.

NOTE 3: While these classifications will be used by the Standards Council to achieve a balance for Technical Committees, the Standards Council may determine that new classifications of member or unique interests need representation in order to foster the best possible Committee deliberations on any project. In this connection, the Standards Council may make such appointments as it deems appropriate in the public interest, such as the classification of "Utilities" in the National Electrical Code Committee.

NOTE 4: Representatives of subsidiaries of any group are generally considered to have the same classification as the parent organization.

Submitting Public Input / Public Comment Through the Online Submission System

Following publication of the current edition of an NFPA standard, the development of the next edition begins and the standard is open for Public Input.

Submit a Public Input

NFPA accepts Public Input on documents through our online submission system at www.nfpa.org. To use the online submission system:

- Choose a document from the List of NFPA codes & standards or filter by Development Stage for "codes accepting public input."
- Once you are on the document page, select the "Next Edition" tab.
- Choose the link "The next edition of this standard is now open for Public Input." You will be asked to sign in or create a free online account with NFPA before using this system.
- Follow the online instructions to submit your Public Input (see www.nfpa.org/publicinput for detailed instructions).
- Once a Public Input is saved or submitted in the system, it can be located on the "My Profile" page by selecting the "My Public Inputs/Comments/NITMAMs" section.

Submit a Public Comment

Once the First Draft Report becomes available there is a Public Comment period. Any objections or further related changes to the content of the First Draft must be submitted at the Comment Stage. To submit a Public Comment follow the same steps as previously explained for the submission of Public Input.

Other Resources Available on the Document Information Pages

Header: View document title and scope, access to our codes and standards or NFCSS subscription, and sign up to receive email alerts.

Current & Prior Editions	Research current and previous edition information.
Next Edition	Follow the committee's progress in the processing of a standard in its next revision cycle.
Technical Committee	View current committee rosters or apply to a committee.
Ask a Technical Question	For members, officials, and AHJs to submit standards questions to NFPA staff. Our Technical Questions Service provides a convenient way to receive timely and consistent technical assistance when you need to know more about NFPA standards relevant to your work.
News	Provides links to available articles and research and statistical reports related to our standards.
Purchase Products & Training	Discover and purchase the latest products and training.
Related Products	View related publications, training, and other resources available for purchase.

Information on the NFPA Standards Development Process

I. Applicable Regulations. The primary rules governing the processing of NFPA standards (codes, standards, recommended practices, and guides) are the NFPA *Regulations Governing the Development of NFPA Standards (Regs)*. Other applicable rules include NFPA *Bylaws*, NFPA *Technical Meeting Convention Rules*, NFPA *Guide for the Conduct of Participants in the NFPA Standards Development Process*, and the NFPA *Regulations Governing Petitions to the Board of Directors from Decisions of the Standards Council*. Most of these rules and regulations are contained in the *NFPA Standards Directory*. For copies of the *Directory*, contact Codes and Standards Administration at NFPA headquarters; all these documents are also available on the NFPA website at "www.nfpa.org/regs."

The following is general information on the NFPA process. All participants, however, should refer to the actual rules and regulations for a full understanding of this process and for the criteria that govern participation.

II. Technical Committee Report. The Technical Committee Report is defined as "the Report of the responsible Committee(s), in accordance with the Regulations, in preparation of a new or revised NFPA Standard." The Technical Committee Report is in two parts and consists of the First Draft Report and the Second Draft Report. (See *Regs* at Section 1.4.)

III. Step 1: First Draft Report. The First Draft Report is defined as "Part one of the Technical Committee Report, which documents the Input Stage." The First Draft Report consists of the First Draft, Public Input, Committee Input, Committee and Correlating Committee Statements, Correlating Notes, and Ballot Statements. (See *Regs* at 4.2.5.2 and Section 4.3.) Any objection to an action in the First Draft Report must be raised through the filing of an appropriate Comment for consideration in the Second Draft Report or the objection will be considered resolved. [See *Regs* at 4.3.1(b).]

IV. Step 2: Second Draft Report. The Second Draft Report is defined as "Part two of the Technical Committee Report, which documents the Comment Stage." The Second Draft Report consists of the Second Draft, Public Comments with corresponding Committee Actions and Committee Statements, Correlating Notes and their respective Committee Statements, Committee Comments, Correlating Revisions, and Ballot Statements. (See *Regs* at 4.2.5.2 and Section 4.4.) The First Draft Report and the Second Draft Report together constitute the Technical Committee Report. Any outstanding objection following the Second Draft Report must be raised through an appropriate Amending Motion at the NFPA Technical Meeting or the objection will be considered resolved. [See *Regs* at 4.4.1(b).]

V. Step 3a: Action at NFPA Technical Meeting. Following the publication of the Second Draft Report, there is a period during which those wishing to make proper Amending Motions on the Technical Committee Reports must signal their intention by submitting a Notice of Intent to Make a Motion (NITMAM). (See *Regs* at 4.5.2.) Standards that receive notice of proper Amending Motions (Certified Amending Motions) will be presented for action at the annual June NFPA Technical Meeting. At the meeting, the NFPA membership can consider and act on these Certified Amending Motions as well as Follow-up Amending Motions, that is, motions that become necessary as a result of a previous successful Amending Motion. (See 4.5.3.2 through 4.5.3.6 and Table 1, Columns 1-3 of *Regs* for a summary of the available Amending Motions and who may make them.) Any outstanding objection following action at an NFPA Technical Meeting (and any further Technical Committee consideration following successful Amending Motions, see *Regs* at 4.5.3.7 through 4.6.5) must be raised through an appeal to the Standards Council or it will be considered to be resolved.

VI. Step 3b: Documents Forwarded Directly to the Council. Where no NITMAM is received and certified in accordance with the *Technical Meeting Convention Rules*, the standard is forwarded directly to the Standards Council for action on issuance. Objections are deemed to be resolved for these documents. (See *Regs* at 4.5.2.5.)

VII. Step 4a: Council Appeals. Anyone can appeal to the Standards Council concerning procedural or substantive matters related to the development, content, or issuance of any document of the NFPA or on matters within the purview of the authority of the Council, as established by the *Bylaws* and as determined by the Board of Directors. Such appeals must be in written form and filed with the Secretary of the Standards Council (see *Regs* at Section 1.6). Time constraints for filing an appeal must be in accordance with 1.6.2 of the *Regs*. Objections are deemed to be resolved if not pursued at this level.

VIII. Step 4b: Document Issuance. The Standards Council is the issuer of all documents (see Article 8 of *Bylaws*). The Council acts on the issuance of a document presented for action at an NFPA Technical Meeting within 75 days from the date of the recommendation from the NFPA Technical Meeting, unless this period is extended by the Council (see *Regs* at 4.7.2). For documents forwarded directly to the Standards Council, the Council acts on the issuance of the document at its next scheduled meeting, or at such other meeting as the Council may determine (see *Regs* at 4.5.2.5 and 4.7.4).

IX. Petitions to the Board of Directors. The Standards Council has been delegated the responsibility for the administration of the codes and standards development process and the issuance of documents. However, where extraordinary circumstances requiring the intervention of the Board of Directors exist, the Board of Directors may take any action necessary to fulfill its obligations to preserve the integrity of the codes and standards development process and to protect the interests of the NFPA. The rules for petitioning the Board of Directors can be found in the *Regulations Governing Petitions to the Board of Directors from Decisions of the Standards Council* and in Section 1.7 of the *Regs*.

X. For More Information. The program for the NFPA Technical Meeting (as well as the NFPA website as information becomes available) should be consulted for the date on which each report scheduled for consideration at the meeting will be presented. To view the First Draft Report and Second Draft Report as well as information on NFPA rules and for up-to-date information on schedules and deadlines for processing NFPA documents, check the NFPA website (www.nfpa.org/docinfo) or contact NFPA Codes & Standards Administration at (617) 984-7246.

DIGITAL ACCESS TO NFPA CODES AND STANDARDS.
AT WORK. AND AT YOUR FINGERTIPS.

SUBSCRIPTIONS STARTING AS LOW AS $9.99/MONTH.

Presenting NFPA LiNK.™ NFPA LiNK™ provides digital access to codes and standards. Find, bookmark, organize, and share knowledge anytime and anywhere. Transform the speed, accuracy, and efficiency of your work.

Learn more at NFPA.org/LiNK

NFPA LiNK™

ADDITIONAL IMPORTANT NOTICES AND DISCLAIMERS CONCERNING NFPA® STANDARDS

Updating of NFPA Standards

Users of NFPA codes, standards, recommended practices, and guides ("NFPA Standards") should be aware that these documents may be superseded at any time by the issuance of a new edition, may be amended with the issuance of Tentative Interim Amendments (TIAs), or be corrected by Errata. It is intended that through regular revisions and amendments, participants in the NFPA standards development process consider the then-current and available information on incidents, materials, technologies, innovations, and methods as these develop over time and that NFPA Standards reflect this consideration. Therefore, any previous edition of this document no longer represents the current NFPA Standard on the subject matter addressed. NFPA encourages the use of the most current edition of any NFPA Standard [as it may be amended by TIA(s) or Errata] to take advantage of current experience and understanding. An official NFPA Standard at any point in time consists of the current edition of the document, including any issued TIAs and Errata then in effect.

To determine whether an NFPA Standard has been amended through the issuance of TIAs or corrected by Errata, visit the "Codes & Standards" section at www.nfpa.org.

Interpretations of NFPA Standards

A statement, written or oral, that is not processed in accordance with Section 6 of the Regulations Governing the Development of NFPA Standards shall not be considered the official position of NFPA or any of its Committees and shall not be considered to be, nor be relied upon as, a Formal Interpretation.

Patents

The NFPA does not take any position with respect to the validity of any patent rights referenced in, related to, or asserted in connection with an NFPA Standard. The users of NFPA Standards bear the sole responsibility for determining the validity of any such patent rights, as well as the risk of infringement of such rights, and the NFPA disclaims liability for the infringement of any patent resulting from the use of or reliance on NFPA Standards.

NFPA adheres to the policy of the American National Standards Institute (ANSI) regarding the inclusion of patents in American National Standards ("the ANSI Patent Policy"), and hereby gives the following notice pursuant to that policy:

NOTICE: The user's attention is called to the possibility that compliance with an NFPA Standard may require use of an invention covered by patent rights. NFPA takes no position as to the validity of any such patent rights or as to whether such patent rights constitute or include essential patent claims under the ANSI Patent Policy. If, in connection with the ANSI Patent Policy, a patent holder has filed a statement of willingness to grant licenses under these rights on reasonable and nondiscriminatory terms and conditions to applicants desiring to obtain such a license, copies of such filed statements can be obtained, on request, from NFPA. For further information, contact the NFPA at the address listed below.

Law and Regulations

Users of NFPA Standards should consult applicable federal, state, and local laws and regulations. NFPA does not, by the publication of its codes, standards, recommended practices, and guides, intend to urge action that is not in compliance with applicable laws, and these documents may not be construed as doing so.

Copyrights

NFPA Standards are copyrighted. They are made available for a wide variety of both public and private uses. These include both use, by reference, in laws and regulations, and use in private self-regulation, standardization, and the promotion of safe practices and methods. By making these documents available for use and adoption by public authorities and private users, the NFPA does not waive any rights in copyright to these documents.

Use of NFPA Standards for regulatory purposes should be accomplished through adoption by reference. The term "adoption by reference" means the citing of title, edition, and publishing information only. Any deletions, additions, and changes desired by the adopting authority should be noted separately in the adopting instrument. In order to assist NFPA in following the uses made of its documents, adopting authorities are requested to notify the NFPA (Attention: Secretary, Standards Council) in writing of such use. For technical assistance and questions concerning adoption of NFPA Standards, contact NFPA at the address below.

For Further Information

All questions or other communications relating to NFPA Standards and all requests for information on NFPA procedures governing its codes and standards development process, including information on the procedures for requesting Formal Interpretations, for proposing Tentative Interim Amendments, and for proposing revisions to NFPA standards during regular revision cycles, should be sent to NFPA headquarters, addressed to the attention of the Secretary, Standards Council, NFPA, 1 Batterymarch Park, P.O. Box 9101, Quincy, MA 02269-9101; email: stds_admin@nfpa.org.

For more information about NFPA, visit the NFPA website at www.nfpa.org. All NFPA codes and standards can be viewed at no cost at www.nfpa.org/docinfo.

ORDER TODAY!

 Phone
1.800.344.3555

Online
catalog.nfpa.org

ISBN 978-1-4559-2390-8

9 781455 923908